Comparative Criminal Justice

Comparative Criminal Justice

International Trends and Practices

Edited by Jospeter M. Mbuba

ROWMAN & LITTLEFIELD
Lanham • Boulder • New York • London

Published by Rowman & Littlefield
An imprint of The Rowman & Littlefield Publishing Group, Inc.
4501 Forbes Boulevard, Suite 200, Lanham, Maryland 20706
www.rowman.com

86-90 Paul Street, London EC2A 4NE

British Library Cataloguing in Publication Information Available

Library of Congress Cataloging-in-Publication Data
Names: Mbuba, Jospeter M., editor.
Title: Comparative criminal justice : international trends and practices / edited by Jospeter M. Mbuba.
Description: Lanham : Rowman & Littlefield, [2023] | Includes bibliographical references and index.
Identifiers: LCCN 2022049241 (print) | LCCN 2022049242 (ebook) | ISBN 9781538173145 (cloth) | ISBN 9781538173152 (ebook)
Subjects: LCSH: Criminal justice, Administration of—Cross-cultural studies.
Classification: LCC HV7419 .C66 2023 (print) | LCC HV7419 (ebook) | DDC 364.068—dc23/eng/20230210
LC record available at https://lccn.loc.gov/2022049241
LC ebook record available at https://lccn.loc.gov/2022049242

This book is dedicated to my elder brother, the late Ephanuel Gitonga Mbuba,
for the values I learned from him during my early years.

Contents

Acknowledgments

I am grateful to my global collaborators who shared their expertise to make this book a reality. I am also grateful to Purdue University Fort Wayne for providing the support necessary for a project of this magnitude. I express my gratitude to the Carnegie African Diaspora Fellowship Program and the Council for the Development of Social Science Research in Africa for awarding me the international fellowships, which were instrumental for data collection and for expanding my professional network. Additionally, I express appreciation to Dr. Erin Williams-Maxwell Meyer of Laughing Saint Editorial for leading the copyediting efforts for this book. To my family, from whom I draw my inspiration, I say thank you for your resolute support. Finally, I thank the staff of Rowman & Littlefield for the editorial work that goes into book publishing.

Introduction

Jospeter M. Mbuba

As the world becomes increasingly globalized, a shared understanding of the various aspects of the criminal justice system becomes imperative. Globalization lends credence to the necessity of expanding the knowledge of criminal justice among the citizens of the globalized world, of helping future professionals in criminal justice appreciate varied approaches to the universal problem of crime, and of developing sound strategies for confronting that problem. Because crime is one of the most pervasive social problems of our time, different methods of tackling the problem have been tried and adopted throughout human history. Although some of those methods have been discarded, others have endured across historic epochs. The common denominator in handling the problem of crime begins with the enforcement of societal norms, especially those of the codified variety, which are referred to as "law." Enforcement is conducted by law enforcement personnel, represented by the police. Policing serves to prevent crime and to apprehend law violators. Individuals who do not abide by existing laws are arraigned before impartial arbiters who, in most parts of the world, comprise judges, magistrates, juries, and other actors of the judiciary. The judiciary adjudicates between law violators and the government, in criminal proceedings, and between private parties in civil proceedings, although the nature of adjudication may take different forms in different societies. Persons who do not abide by the law and are found to be liable are subject to one or more of the several available sanctions or correctional methods.

Scholars and policymakers refer to the entire process of handling law violators as the criminal justice system. The criminal justice system comprises three key components, namely, policing or law enforcement, courts or the judiciary, and corrections or the penal system. Policing and law enforcement practices vary widely across societies. As a government agency, the police force in most countries falls under the purview of the Ministry of the Interior or the State Department in charge of home or domestic affairs. Law enforcement agencies in some countries may appear to be somewhat independent, whereas other countries may utilize their police departments as a tool for fostering the implementation of the agenda and interests of the government of the day. Transitional societies are replete with examples in which policing has been used to repress voices that are discordant with the whims of the government. Yet in other societies, law enforcement is organized along religious lines, with sections of the police force dedicated to enforcing religious laws and others meant for the secular realms of policing.

Some countries have centralized police agencies, in which all police officers answer to one national central command; others have decentralized policing, in which different jurisdictions have their own police agencies, each with its own center of power. However, regardless of whether policing is centralized or decentralized, most societies organize their police agencies in a similar chain of command that begins with constables at the entry level and progresses through various ranks to the top. Common police ranks include constable, corporal sergeant, inspector, major, lieutenant, superintendent, captain, commissioner, and chief of police.

The main function of police agencies is to enforce the law and to apprehend lawbreakers. To do so, police personnel conduct patrols that vary from one society to another, depending on such factors as the risk posed and the type of laws to be enforced, such as traffic law, customary law in transitional societies, and religious law in the Islamic world. Low-risk places may be patrolled on foot, climatic and geographic conditions permitting, whereas other places may be patrolled only by motorized, aerial, or naval means. Moreover, although armed patrols are the dominant style, there are societies, mostly in Scandinavia, in which local police officers conduct patrols without carrying firearms.[1] Among the main issues that face policing globally are citizens' complaints about police brutality, that is, the use of excessive force in confronting criminal suspects; misuse of police discretion or the authority they are entrusted to by the law; unethical practices, such as selective enforcement of the law; and racial discrimination, especially in societies that are characterized by multiracial populations.

Courts, which constitute the judiciary in the criminal justice system, are almost universally structured in terms of the powers they yield, their jurisdiction over the various types of crime, and the geographic territories of their influence. Most countries have similarly organized courts. Courts with limited jurisdiction have authority over specific cases. For example, drug courts have authority that is limited to cases involving violations of drug law. General trial courts hear most common cases, such as those involving assault, theft, or arson. Courts of appeals review the outcomes of cases from lower courts. Supreme courts in most cases are the apex courts, beyond which there are no appeals. Supreme courts are often the courts of last resort, but this is not always the case. In some countries, such as Afghanistan, where the rule of law, human rights, and impunity form a complex matrix,[2] court decisions can be reversed if they contradict the provisions of the Quran, which is the central text of the country's main religion, Islam.

In terms of process, criminal procedures vary vastly across the globe. Criminal procedure refers to the way in which criminal trials are conducted. The overall function of courts is to determine guilt or innocence of a criminal suspect following an arrest by law enforcement. Courts make this determination by conducting trials. Court trials take on different forms, the main ones being adversarial and inquisitorial.[3] The adversarial system finds facts by pitting the prosecution and defense against each other. Both sides assemble witnesses and evidence to prove their case while weakening the opponent's. The judge or jury decides on the guilt or innocence of the accused person based on the adduced evidence. The court, in such a system, assumes an impartial position throughout the trial process. However, in inquisitorial systems, such as in Iran and Egypt, the court or judges are actively involved in interrogating the evidence and investigating the matter at hand rather than remaining impartial arbiters.

The penal agency in the criminal justice system is commonly referred to as "corrections," which euphemistically deflects the view of an inherent punishment and implies behavior modification.[4] The correctional phase follows a guilt finding by a competent court or by other systems that declare the accused person to be guilty of law violation. The commonly used methods of punishing criminal offenders include the imposition of fines for minor infractions, community service for offenders who pose no danger to society, imprisonment for dangerous offenders who must be removed from society to prevent further harm, and execution for offenders deemed to have caused the most serious harm to society or its members. Execution or capital punishment, in societies where it is an option, is usually reserved for crimes such as premeditated murder, terrorism, espionage, or engaging in activities that undermine lawfully constituted governments. There are other less commonly used methods of sanctioning crime, such as public shaming and corporal punishment. The latter, which is used mostly in Islamic countries, may include flogging and even amputation of limbs.

Punishment for law violation is grounded in certain ideals. Each method of punishment is based on specific aims and intended to produce particular outcomes, although the aims and outcomes may overlap across the various methods. Scholars identify the main aims of punishment to be deterrence, rehabilitation, retribution, restitution, and incapacitation:

- Deterrence aims to discourage an offender from committing further offenses while also sending a strong message to potential offenders against criminal behavior.
- Rehabilitation as an aim of punishment is achieved through the reformation that the offender experiences, especially by participating in life-transforming programs in or out of prison environments.
- Retribution, which is based on the medieval doctrine of lex talionis, or desire for revenge, is based on the notion that the severity of punishment must be reflective of the seriousness of the crime. This doctrine is akin to the principles of Hammurabi, king of Babylon in the years 1792–1750 BC, who is credited with the law of "an eye for an eye and a tooth for a tooth."[5]
- Restitution aims to restore the community back to the state it was in before the crime occurred. It involves paying or compensating the crime victims for losses incurred and anguish endured.
- Incapacitation is intended to render the offender incapable of committing more offenses, typically described by scholars as "removing the offender from the society"[6] or as "time out."[7] Incapacitation works either through incarcerating offenders and thereby restraining them from continuing with criminal activities or executing them so that they will never have another chance to commit crime.

Most modern societies distinguish minors from adults when considering criminal culpability. The term used to describe the process of dealing with young offenders in the criminal justice system is "juvenile justice." Indeed, most countries have clearly distinguishable procedures of seizing and processing minors. Although age eighteen is commonly the magical milestone for a person to enter adulthood, there are several other factors that are considered before a person can be processed for allegations of law violations as an adult. Intelligence or ability to execute a criminal act, whether the alleged minor was accompanied by an adult in committing the alleged act, and the type of offense have all been used to determine how a juvenile offender is processed in various societies.

The variability in delineating the age limits for juveniles is wide. This delineation becomes even more complex when different jurisdictions within the same country use different upper and lower limits in deciding whether a criminal suspect will be processed as a juvenile or as an adult. In the United States, for example, the maximum age of juvenile court jurisdiction in forty-six states is seventeen years of age, yet three states—Georgia, Texas, and Wisconsin—use age sixteen as the age of majority. In Vermont, people are not considered to be adults for the purpose of adult legal trial until they reach the age of eighteen.[8] The lower limit of criminal culpability is far more fluid, with some states maintaining it at seven years old (Oklahoma) and others going as high as fourteen (Idaho) and still others leaving it unspecified to let the courts decide on a case-by-case basis.

The same variability exists across the globe, with some countries maintaining the age of adulthood for purposes of criminal responsibility as fourteen to eighteen years old (Serbia) and others having different ages for boys and girls, such as in Iran, where attaining puberty is used as the lower limit for criminal responsibility, with girls attaining puberty at age nine and boys at fifteen. Other countries, such as Kenya, define "children" as "any human being under the age of eighteen years."[9]

Synopsis

This book draws together the experiences of nineteen countries that represent most major regions of the world. The countries were purposefully selected to ensure not only broad geographic distribution but also cultural and religious diversity, political differentiation, and historical experiences. Although each chapter represents a different country, all chapters have similar thematic sections. It was not the aim of the book to compare the same details of the criminal justice systems of the included countries. Rather, the aim was to provide summaries of the wide array of policing practices, to explore the different types of criminal procedure used across the world, and to discover the many methods that different societies use to sanction criminal behavior among their citizens. As such, there are occasions in which the chapters vary considerably with respect to section content, partly because of the diversity of the parameters set forth. Regardless, each chapter is geared to a generalist audience, making the variation among chapters approachable. Additionally, each chapter has sources cited to allow the reader to ascertain the validity of the sources and to facilitate further research.

Chapter authors were carefully sourced and vetted for relevant expertise. Ultimately, the top scholars who were retained have PhDs or other terminal degrees in such fields as criminal justice, criminology, law and legal studies, political science, sociology, international relations, emergency management, law enforcement, and human rights, among others. Only a few authors or coauthors were doctoral students at the time of submitting their chapters.

This book is organized into five parts. Part 1 provides an overview of the criminal justice system in sub-Saharan Africa, based on the experiences of a sample of three countries, namely, Kenya from eastern Africa, Nigeria from western Africa, and South Africa from the southern part of the continent. All three countries have a common history of British colonialism, and thus the trajectory of the development of their criminal justice systems—including policing and police reforms, judicial structures, and the prison system—reflects that common origin. Chapter 1 presents the criminal justice system of Kenya, where recent reforms have brought about strong independence and the separation of the arms of the government, to the extent that the judiciary can nullify presidential elections, as happened in 2017. According to the country's penal code, attempted suicide is considered criminal, and a person can be jailed for as long as ten years for "insulting modesty" by forcefully stripping another person naked. Chapter 2 addresses the criminal justice system of Nigeria, where a complex justice system features strong sharia law that guides the largely Muslim north, and Christian-style customary law that is practiced in the eastern and western parts of the country. In chapter 3, the criminal justice system of South Africa is presented. South Africa stands out because of the unique experience of apartheid, which allowed White rule to continue after independence, resulting in segregation between the majority Black indigenous population and the minority White settlers of British ancestry.

Part 2 focuses on the criminal justice systems found in East Asia and the Pacific region, using Australia, China, and Malaysia as the focal points. Chapter 4 provides a review of the Commonwealth of Australia, which is a constitutional monarchy, a parliamentary democracy, and a federation of states and whose early criminal justice system involved a White penal colony that uprooted indigenous people from their ancestral land. Although the justice system is still tilted against the first Australian people, much ground has been covered by way of transforming the criminal justice system in the country. Chapter 5 explores the justice system in China, where policing includes, among other branches, the "internet police," which enforces adherence to internet laws.[10] The country is also known for the use of "roundtable trials" for youthful or juvenile offenders, as opposed to the traditional courtroom setup, to remove the intimidating perception of a criminal trial. Chapter 6 focuses on the criminal justice system of Malaysia, where a balance between secular and religious law exists and where the Federal Constitution recognizes Islam as the religion of the federation. However, the constitution also allows for the practice of other religions, while Islamic courts retain jurisdiction over Islamic law.

Part 3 explores the criminal justice system in the twin regions of Europe and Eurasia. The selected countries from these regions include Italy, England, Wales, Poland, the Republic of Serbia, and Germany. Chapter 7 features Italy, where Napoleonic influence led to the replication of the French policing model—centralized, militarized, and repressive. Criminal law is used here as a tool to support state power by such means as using investigations not for securing convictions but as an avenue for the police to engage in intelligence gathering against antigovernment groups. Chapter 8 covers England and Wales, where the law does not require police officers to have reasonable suspicion to stop and search; rather, officers only need authorization from a supervisor. This has led the police to have disproportionately more encounters with racial minorities than with the White population, which puts minority children at an even greater risk of disproportionate targeting by the police. Chapter 9 covers the criminal justice system of Poland, where trials are adversarial and imprisonment remains below capacity, with a prison occupancy level of 85.4 percent as of 2020. Chapter 10 focuses on the Republic of Serbia, in which the justice system recognizes the lower limit of a juvenile as fourteen years of age and the upper as eighteen. In chapter 11, the justice system of Germany is explored. There, the maximum prison term is fifteen years; prisoners exercise the right to vote, and they can smoke, cook their own meals, wear their own clothes, and use mobile phones. Children below the age of fourteen cannot be held criminally liable.

Part 4 presents the criminal justice system in the largely Muslim region of the Middle East and in South Asia. Countries selected from this region include the Middle Eastern countries of Egypt, Iran, and Saudi Arabia and the South Asian country of Afghanistan. Chapter 12 focuses on Egypt, where joining the police service requires one not to plan to be married while enrolled in the academy. Egyptian trials are inquisitorial as opposed to adversarial, and thus judges become actively involved in fact-finding instead of remaining as passive arbiters. The justice system of Iran is presented in chapter 13. Here again, trials are inquisitorial, and harsh penalties—including execution—are meted out for such crimes as murder, incest, rape, sex between non-Muslim males and Muslim females, adultery, sodomy, and defamation to what is holy. Amputation is also practiced as a penalty for such infractions as waging war against God or his messenger, the penalty for which is the amputation of one hand and the foot of the opposite side. Chapter 14 covers Afghanistan, where a complex pluralistic legal system involves different traditions within a single political framework. Execution and other extreme punishments, such as flogging for alcohol consumption and stoning to death for adultery, are practiced. Strict adherence to Islamic law is expected, with the Quran—the holy text of Islam—being considered as the legal code. Chapter 15 examines the justice system of Saudi Arabia, where a branch of the police service called the Committee for the Promotion of Virtue and Prevention of Vice exists to enforce religious law and where the judiciary is based on Islamic law (sharia).

Part 5 includes countries from the region identified as the Western Hemisphere, which comprises North and South America. The countries selected from this region include the United States, Uruguay, Brazil, and Mexico. Chapter 16 focuses on the justice system in the United States, where the rights of accused persons are given protections that are found by some scholars to surpass the care and concerns showed to crime victims, incriminating evidence is thrown out if it is obtained illegally, and guilt confessions are dropped if the suspect was not warned about the consequences of making the confession beforehand.[11] Chapter 17 presents the criminal justice system of Uruguay, where trials can be either formal or abbreviated. When abbreviated, a sentence is meted out immediately after admission of guilt is secured. Chapter 18 examines the justice system in Brazil, a federation of twenty-six states and a federal district, where illegally obtained evidence is prohibited and crimes committed by persons in high-level federal positions are tried by the Federal Supreme Court. Finally, chapter 19 addresses the justice system in Mexico, a country that was colonized by Spain and where criminal sanctions were administered by the Catholic Church when state and religion were inseparable. Several police reforms have been initiated to address high levels of violence here, especially in the wake of the war on drugs.

Overall, this book is intended to inform and form a strong basis for future studies about the vast field of criminal justice and to encourage other collaborative works on topics that are germane to this field. Finally, this book will hopefully inspire those who study and work in the various components of the criminal justice system in different parts of the world in the unending search for a true solution to the problem of crime.

Notes

1. Johannes Knutsson and Jon Strype, "Police Use of Firearms in Norway and Sweden: The Significance of Gun Availability," *Policing and Society* 13, no. 4 (2003): 429–39, doi:10.1080/1043946032000105381.
2. Per Sevastik, "Rule of Law, Human Rights and Impunity: The Case of Afghanistan," *The Hague Journal on the Rule of Law* 12, no. 1 (April 2020): 93–145, doi:10.1007/s40803-019-00089-z.
3. F. Nagorcka, M. Stanton, and M. Wilson, "Stranded between Partisanship and the Truth? A Comparative Analysis of Legal Ethics in the Adversarial and Inquisitorial Systems of Justice," *Melbourne University Law Review* 29, no. 2 (2005): 448–77.
4. Mary K. Stohr, Anthony Walsh, and Craig T. Hemmens, *Corrections: A Text/Reader* (Los Angeles: Sage, 2019).
5. Code of Hammurabi, trans. L. W. King, Lillian Goldman Law Library, 2008, https://avalon.law.yale.edu/ancient/hamframe.asp.
6. Vesna Stefanovska, "Surveillance and Control over Incapacitation, Deterrence and Rehabilitation Effects of the Punishment," *Balkan Social Science Review* 11 (2018): 23–38.
7. Hilde Wermink, Robert Apel, Paul Nieuwbeerta, and Arjan Blokland, "The Incapacitation Effect of First-Time Imprisonment: A Matched Samples Comparison," *Journal of Quantitative Criminology* 29, no. 4 (2013): 579–600, doi:10.1007/s10940-012-9189-3.
8. Anne Teigen, "Juvenile Age of Jurisdiction and Transfer to Adult Court Laws," NCSL: National Conference of State Legislatures, April 8, 2021, https://www.ncsl.org/research/civil-and-criminal-justice/juvenile-age-of-jurisdiction-and-transfer-to-adult-court-laws.aspx.
9. Laws of Kenya, Cap. 8, Children Act, http://kenyalaw.org:8181/exist/kenyalex/actview.xql?actid=No.%208%20of%202001.
10. "Outlook Magazine: Unveiling the Mysterious Internet Police," Chinascope, accessed August 2, 2008, http://chinascope.org/archives/6151.
11. J. M. Mbuba, "The Criminal Is to Go Free because the Constable Has Blundered: Challenges of Law Enforcement in the Face of the Exclusionary Rule," *Free Inquiry in Creative Sociology* 36, no. 1 (2008): 55–62.

Part 1

SUB-SAHARAN AFRICA

CHAPTER 1

The Criminal Justice System of Kenya

POLICING, COURTS, AND THE PRISON SERVICES

Jospeter M. Mbuba

The Kenyan criminal justice system is a multifaceted organization comprising policing and law enforcement at various levels, an elaborate judicial agency that recognizes the African customary law and religious practices, and a penal system that consists of government prisons, police remand facilities, and a wide array of community-based corrections for adults as well as youthful offenders. The police organization is centralized with a chain of command that emanates from one national center of power—the inspector general of police. The country's judicial response to crime is guided by an elaborate act of Parliament that was codified into Cap. 75 of the Laws of Kenya and titled Criminal Procedure, and an equally expansive provision of criminal sanction known as the Penal Code and classified as Cap. 63 of the Laws of Kenya. The entire system and its implications are presented in this chapter.

Policing

Policing in Kenya is centralized. The National Police Service utilizes a national hierarchy that follows a single chain of command, tracing authority to a national chief executive: the inspector general of police.[1] The National Police Service comprises three agencies, namely, the Kenya Police Service, the Administration Police Service, and the Directorate of Criminal Investigations (DCI). The main functions of the Kenya Police Service include law enforcement, order maintenance, crime investigation, and apprehending of crime suspects. The Administration Police Service enforces the law and maintains order within the contexts of border patrol, the security of vital installations and government buildings, and support to government agencies in their administrative functions.[2] Like the other two police agencies, the DCI serves to maintain law and order and to detect and prevent crime. However, specific to the DCI are the provision of criminal intelligence and the investigation of serious crimes, including homicide, narcotics crimes, human trafficking, money laundering, and terrorism, among others. Both the Kenya Police Service and the Administration Police Service are headed by a deputy inspector general, while the DCI is headed by a director. The deputy inspectors general and the director are answerable to the inspector general.

CHAIN OF COMMAND

Both the Kenya Police Service and the Administration Police Service utilize parallel chains of command, which include the following ranks, from entry level to the topmost rank: constable, corporal, sergeant, senior sergeant, inspector, chief inspector, assistant superintendent, superintendent, senior superintendent, commissioner, assistant inspector general, deputy inspector general, and inspector general. While officers move up the chain-of-command ranks through merit and promotion, the top two positions of deputy inspector general and inspector general are constitutional offices whose bearers are hired competitively by the National Police Service Commission and appointed by the president.

POLICING SUPERVISION AND OVERSIGHT

Policing supervision is conducted by an independent civilian agency—the National Police Service Commission—whose personnel are non–police officers. The commission conducts police recruitment, training, deployment, and promotion while paying attention to gender balancing and regional policing differences. Some traditional African norms do not endorse the full equality of women to men, and there are cultural, religious, and familial considerations that affect female recruitment into the police service, thus necessitating a concerted effort to attract considerable numbers of women officers. To retain the few women who make it through the training, the commission considers the demands of the job in various policing units. Thus, women are more likely to be posted in diplomatic missions or at airports than to the Anti–Stock Theft Unit, which is a much more rigorous assignment.[3]

When complaints arise about the conduct of police officers, such complaints are investigated by the Internal Affairs Unit. If the nature of the allegation is too complicated for the unit, the complaint is taken to a civilian body—the Independent Policing Oversight Authority—whose role is to ensure police accountability by monitoring the way in which the police service deals with the public. The authority may recommend prosecution or other disciplinary actions against the accused officer, depending on the outcome of the investigation.

POLICE ORGANIZATION

There are two dimensions of police organization. The first is through police command bases, represented by police stations. An arrested person is taken to a police station for custody before being arraigned in court. If citizens arrest a crime suspect, they also deliver them to the nearest police station. Citizens in need of police services similarly go to police stations. Police stations are created by the inspector general of police. They are distributed across the country. A police station is headed by an Officer Commanding Police Station, mostly at the rank of inspector or chief inspector. Large police stations in expansive geographic areas with a sparse human population may also have auxiliary outposts called police posts. Densely populated urban areas may also have police posts, which are called patrol bases. Police posts and patrol bases are headed by noncommissioned officers, that is, corporals, sergeants, and senior sergeants.

The second dimension of police organization is the operational formation. The Kenya Police Service and the Administration Police Service are organized into units. The units are created by policy guidelines called Service Standing Orders, which are provided by the inspector general from time to time. The Kenya Police Service has such units as the Anti–Stock Theft Unit, Railway Police Unit, Kenya Police Airwing, General Service Unit, Traffic Law Enforcement Unit, and Kenya Police Dog Unit, among others. Examples of units in the Administration Police Service include Rural Border Patrol Unit, Security of Government Buildings Unit, Vital Installations and Strategic Points Unit, Rapid Deployment Unit, and Administration Police Peace Corps Unit.

The most conspicuous police unit is the Traffic Law Enforcement Unit, as it is the one that has the most contact with the public. The main function of this unit is to prevent traffic violations, such as overloading vehicles, speeding, drunk driving, reckless driving, and operating un-roadworthy vehicles on highways.[4] To compel motorists to stop for police inspection, traffic police officers can elect to use spiked metal-frame roadblocks across the road. If the roadblock is to remain in effect overnight, the police place lantern lamps by the barriers to warn approaching motorists. As an alternative to roadblocks, traffic police officers also position themselves at strategic points on highways where they stop approaching motorists, especially public service and commercial vehicles, for inspection.

POLICE PATROL

While the police conduct motorized patrols on the streets, air patrols (especially in crowded outdoor events), and marine vessel patrols in high seas, foot patrol remains the dominant method of patrol, at least in the eyes of the public, as that is what most people notice. Officers on foot patrol carry AK-47 assault rifles. The AK-47 is preferred because of its power, long range, accuracy, and general reliability under most conditions.[5] Most common police patrol vehicles are Land Rover and Land Cruiser pickup trucks. These are preferred for their ability to transport multiple suspects together and bulky contraband, such as drums of illegal alcoholic brews, to the police station.

The National Police Service also utilizes the strategy of community policing to encourage citizens' participation in crime prevention and general security. With respect to community policing, communities are organized into roughly ten households, called *nyumba kumi* (ten homesteads) in Swahili. Citizens are then encouraged to be familiar with the members of their sections and to report any suspicious behavior to the police. The effectiveness of this strategy varies widely; critics argue that it contravenes the constitutional provision that any citizen is free to live in any part of the country. However, supporters of the strategy find a greater value in the common good of the community.

The law permits anyone to arrest a crime suspect. According to the criminal procedure code, a police officer may arrest any criminal suspect with an order from a magistrate and a warrant of arrest.[6] An officer may also arrest a suspect without a warrant if the officer has reasonable grounds to suspect a person of having committed a cognizable offense or being about to commit one; if the officer witnesses a person committing a breach of the peace, that is, engaging in activities that may disturb the public tranquility; or if the officer witnesses a person who is preventing or about to prevent obstruction of police duty. Any private person can also arrest a person who commits a cognizable crime or is believed to have committed one as long as the arrested person is handed over to a police officer or to the nearest police station. Persons arrested without a warrant for crimes other than murder, treason, robbery with violence, or attempted robbery with violence may be released by the police on a police bond.

Judiciary

Kenya's judiciary was established by the constitution as one of the three state organs, the others being the executive and the legislature. The judiciary is the custodian of the justice system in the country. Its main functions include the administration of justice, the formulation of judicial policies, and the compilation of case law or landmark cases. The judiciary is headed by the chief justice, who is also the president of the Supreme Court, and a deputy chief justice, who serves as the vice president of the Supreme Court. There are two levels of courts in Kenya: the superior courts and the subordinate courts. Superior courts include the Supreme Court, the Court of Appeal, and the High Court. These are constitutional courts. Two other courts with the status of the High Court have also been established by Parliament by constitutional decree. They are the Employment and Labor Relations Court and the Environment and Land Court. The subordinate courts, which are referred to as such because they are under the control of the superior courts, include the Magistrates' Courts, Khadhis' Courts, the Court Martial, tribunals, and Small Claims Courts.

THE SUPREME COURT

Comprising seven judges, including the chief justice and the deputy chief justice, the Supreme Court is the apex court in the country. It is the final arbiter and interpreter of the constitution and, therefore, the court of last resort. The court has exclusive original jurisdiction to hear and determine disputes arising from presidential elections. It also has appellate jurisdiction to hear and determine appeals from all other courts and tribunals. Appeal cases that go to the Supreme Court are those that involve constitutional rights and matters of general public importance as certified by either the Supreme

Court or the Court of Appeal. When the certification is by the Court of Appeal, the Supreme Court may either accept or decline it. Other functions of the Supreme Court include rendering legal opinion to the national and county governments and state organs, and determining the validity of any declaration of a state of emergency.

COURT OF APPEAL

The Court of Appeal is a constitutional body created to hear appeals from the High Court and any other courts and tribunals. The court consists of a maximum of thirty judges and a minimum of thirteen, including the president of the court, who is elected by the judges of the court from among themselves according to seniority. In order to serve the whole country, the court is organized into six stations referred to as registries and situated in different regions. The registries include Nairobi, Mombasa, Nyeri, Kisumu, Nakuru, and Eldoret.[7] Each registry is headed by a presiding judge.

HIGH COURT

The High Court of Kenya has unlimited original jurisdiction in criminal and civil matters. In addition, the court has the jurisdiction to determine cases in which violation or denial of the right to fundamental freedoms is alleged. Moreover, the High Court hears appeals from all lower courts as well as decisions of tribunals and determines issues relating to the interpretation of the constitution. The court is headed by a principal judge and comprises judges who are appointed by Kenya's president on the recommendations of the Judicial Service Commission. Although there is room for as many as 200 High Court judges, by 2022, there were eighty-one.[8] The court is organized into stations that are dispersed across the country with nearly each county having one station. The High Court may be constituted for specific jurisdictions in the form of "divisions," which are established by the chief justice in consultation with the principal judge. Such divisions include Family and Children, Commercial and Tax, Admiralty, Civil, Criminal, Constitutional and Human Rights, Judicial Review Division, and Anti-Corruption and Economic Crimes.

Employment and Labor Relations Court

The Employment and Labor Relations Court is a superior court with the status of the High Court but with specific jurisdiction in matters of employment and labor disputes. Like the High Court, this court is also headed by a principal judge. This court has exclusive original and appellate jurisdiction on all cases regarding employment and labor relations between employers and employees, employers and trade unions, employers' organizations and trade union organizations, trade unions and their members, and the enforcement of collective bargaining agreements. With exclusive jurisdiction, it means that this court has the power to adjudicate these cases to the exclusion of all other courts in the country, save for appeals against court decisions, which are heard and determined by the Court of Appeal. The Employment and Labor Relations Court also has jurisdiction to hear appeals arising from the decisions of the Registrar of Trade Unions and local tribunals and commissions dealing with issues of employment and labor relations. Although the court is situated in Nairobi, the chief justice may designate any magistrate to hear employment and labor relations disputes on case-by-case basis anywhere in the country.

Environment and Land Court

The Environment and Land Court is a superior court with the status of the High Court. The Court has original and appellate jurisdiction over all disputes relating to environmental and land matters. The court has power to hear and determine cases of environmental planning and protection, land use, landownership, boundaries, taxes, valuations, minerals and other natural resources, and public and private land contracts, among others. The court may meet at any place and time as necessary. The chief justice also appoints magistrates on a case-by-case basis to adjudicate cases of environmental and land disputes across the country. If necessary, appeals against the decisions of such magistrates are referred to the Environment and Land Court.

MAGISTRATES' COURTS

A Magistrates' Court is a lower court subordinate to the superior courts in the country. Magistrates have various ranks: in ascending order of seniority, these ranks are resident magistrate, senior resident magistrate, principal magistrate, senior principal magistrate, and chief magistrate. While Magistrates' Courts have original jurisdiction over criminal and civil cases, the magistrate's rank determines the maximum cash value of the civil cases that they can hear. A resident magistrate can hear a civil case in which the value of the subject matter does not exceed 5 million Kenyan shillings (KSh), which is approximately U.S.$50,000, while a senior resident magistrate is capped at 7 million KSh (U.S.$70,000). A principal Magistrates' Court is limited to 10 million KSh (U.S.$100,000), and a senior principal magistrate can handle no more than 15 million KSh (U.S.$150,000). A chief magistrate's civil case value can go as high as 20 million KSh (U.S.$200,000). These values can be revised by the chief magistrate from time to time as inflation changes.

Magistrates' Courts also have jurisdiction on matters under African customary law, such as land under customary tenure; marriage, divorce, and dowry payments; seduction or pregnancy of unmarried women; enticement or adultery with married persons; children's guardianship, custody, and adoption; and intestate estates that are not governed by any law.[9] Although Magistrates' Courts have designated stations, a court session can be held anywhere within its geographic jurisdiction if critical evidence can be gathered only by doing so.

KHADHIS' COURTS

In matters of the administration of justice, Kenya recognizes the centrality of religious faith. Thus, given the large population of Muslims in the country, second only to Christians, the constitution allows for the creation of Islamic courts that exclusively hear cases relating to personal status, marriage, divorce, or inheritance when all the parties involved profess Muslim religion. Such courts are presided over by a *khadhi*, an Islamic leader appointed by the state. Khadhis' Courts are situated mostly in the parts of the country that have high concentrations of Muslims, mostly the coastal and northeastern regions. Although the criminal procedure and the rules of evidence are followed in the Islamic law in Khadhis' Courts, the chief justice provides direction as necessary. Witnesses are also heard without regard to their religious backgrounds. Khadhis' Courts are subordinate to the High Court.

TRIBUNALS AND SMALL CLAIMS COURTS

Tribunals are created by Parliament with judicial and, in some cases, quasi-judicial authority to supplement regular courts in the administration of justice. However, tribunals do not have the authority to mete out punishment. Most tribunals are subject to the supervision of the High Court. Examples include the Rent Restriction Tribunal, Transport Licensing Appeals Board, Water Appeals Board, Cooperative Tribunal, and Auctioneers Licensing Board, among others.

Small Claims Courts, however, are designated by the chief justice, who also sets the geographic jurisdiction of the court. The courts are presided over by an adjudicator who must be an advocate of the High Court of Kenya. To be an advocate of the High Court, a person must have a law degree, which, in Kenya, involves completing an undergraduate degree in law and attending the Kenya School of Law for admission into the bar. Small Claims Courts have authority over civil claims for loss or damage to property, compensation for breached contracts, personal injury, or such other claims as long as the involved sum of money is limited to 1 million shillings (roughly U.S.$10,000). This limit may be modified by the chief justice as the chief justice finds necessary. Appeals against decisions of Small Claims Courts can be made to the High Court. The outcome of such an appeal cannot be appealed further.

JUDICIAL INDEPENDENCE

Kenya's judiciary enjoys an unprecedented amount of independence from other branches of government, based on the new Kenyan Constitution that was passed in 2010. The decisions of the Supreme Court, which is the apex court, have wide-ranging ramifications across not only the judiciary but also the legislature and the executive. For example, the seven-judge Supreme Court nullified the results of the country's presidential elections in 2017 following an appeal by the then opposition leader, Raila Odinga, and ordered a repeat election—the first such ruling on the continent of

Africa.[10] Although Uhuru Kenyatta retained the presidency, the ruling made manifest the powers and independence of the judiciary.

LAW SOCIETY OF KENYA

To assist the government and the courts in matters relating to legislation, administration of justice, and the practice of law in Kenya, Parliament established the Law Society of Kenya. The society, whose membership is open to all advocates in the country and a select number of honorary members, ensures professionalism and safeguards appropriate standards in legal practice. The society assists the government in the legislation and administration of justice. It ensures that every person who provides legal services in the country meets the appropriate standards of training and observes professional conduct in keeping with the practice of law.

ADMINISTRATION OF JUSTICE: THE CRIMINAL PROCEDURE

Kenya's judicial process utilizes the adversarial system, in which the defense and prosecution parties are pitted against each other in front of an impartial court or judge. An accused person may be brought to court by either summons or warrant. If the summoned person is not available, the summons may be delivered to any adult family member or even the employer. If no one is available, the summons may be affixed to a conspicuous part of the homestead where the accused person is known to reside.[11] On arrest, a person can be bailed out either by the police through a police bond or by the court to await trial while not in custody.

The Kenyan Constitution offers the principles that should guide the administration of justice at the judicial level. Although it is almost obvious and therefore a natural expectation that justice should be done to all regardless of status, the Constitution goes further to decree that "justice shall be administered without undue regard to procedural technicalities." While it calls for the utilization of traditional dispute resolution mechanisms, the Constitution also warns against dispute resolution methods that are repugnant to justice and morality.

THE PENAL CODE

Laws that pertain to criminal offenses are aggregated into the Penal Code and legislated under Cap. 63 of the Laws of Kenya (Penal Code). Any act, attempt, or omission that is punishable by law is defined as an offense. Offenses are classified into two categories according to seriousness—felony and misdemeanor. The penal code defines felonies as any offenses declared by law as a felony or, if not declared, punishable with a prison term of three years or more or by death. A misdemeanor is simply "any offense which is not a felony." Some offenses are declared by law as misdemeanor and are punishable by three years or more. For example, "any person who unlawfully wounds or poisons another is guilty of a misdemeanor and is liable to imprisonment for five years."[12] According to the Penal Code, ignorance of the law does not provide a defense for any violation. However, a person who commits or omits an act under honest and reasonable but mistaken belief in the existence of facts is not criminally responsible for the act or omission.[13] There are other exceptions or acceptable defenses to criminal liability, including the inability to understand the consequences of behavior because of insanity, intoxication, and immature age, which absolves anyone below the age of eight years from criminal responsibility for any act or omission, and compulsion by others to commit crime.

The main forms of punishment include death, imprisonment, community service, fines, and forfeiture of property obtained fraudulently. However, there is controversy regarding the legality of the death sentence, with the Supreme Court ruling in 2017 that the death sentence is unconstitutional.[14] Although the death penalty remains in the books of law, the last execution was conducted in 1987. Additionally, a death sentence cannot be meted out to a person who "appears to the court" to have been below the age of eighteen at the time the offense was committed.[15]

Kenya's Penal Code closely safeguards cultural values with severe consequences for such violation. For example, the law provides that "any person who has carnal knowledge of any person against the order of nature; or has carnal knowledge of an animal; or permits a male person to have carnal knowledge of him or her against the order of nature is guilty of a felony and is liable to imprisonment for fourteen years."[16] An attempt to commit any of these acts attracts imprisonment for seven years.[17] The same law prescribes a punishment of imprisonment for five years for any two male persons who are involved, whether in public or in private, in "gross indecency." Similarly, in what the law regards as "insult to modesty," a person who forcefully strips naked another person and thereby insults the modesty of that other person commits an offense and, on conviction, is liable for imprisonment "for not less than ten years."[18] The penal code also punishes any form of behavior that may cause the death of a person, including oneself. It decrees that "any person who procures another to kill himself; or counsels another to kill himself and thereby induces him to do so is guilty of a felony and is liable for imprisonment for life."[19] According to the same law, a person who attempts suicide had better succeed, or the state will come after them: "Any person who attempts to kill himself is guilty of a misdemeanor."

The penal code is also highly intolerant of any form of violence, especially when the violence is used in the course of stealing. If any willful act leads to the death of a person, it is treated as murder, which, along with other acts such as treason, attracts a death sentence. While attempted robbery is punishable by imprisonment for seven years and robbery itself fourteen years, if the offender uses any form of violence, including striking or beating the victim; if the offender is armed with any dangerous or offensive weapon of any kind; or if the offender is in the company of one or more persons, the offender is sentenced to death, whether the robbery is successful or simply attempted. In the case of breaking and entering someone's house with felony in mind, which is referred to as housebreaking, the punishment is a prison term of five years. If the same is committed at night, which increases the likelihood of a confrontation with the home owner, it is termed burglary, and the penalty rises to seven years of imprisonment. The criminal act in this case is the act of entering someone else's dwelling place regardless of whether anything of value was stolen.

Most felonies in the country are punished by seven years of imprisonment. Examples of offenses that attract seven-year terms include possession of firearms, lying to the court while under oath to tell the truth, attempting to have carnal knowledge of a person against the order of nature, kidnapping, attempted robbery, forgery, and obstructing police officers. Other common sentence limits are three, five, and ten years, then life imprisonment and a death sentence.

Examples of offenses punishable by five-year imprisonment include possession of firearms, incitement to violence, assault with intent to steal, housebreaking, vandalism of government property, and conspiracy. Crimes that are punishable by ten years of imprisonment include foreign enlistment, rape, attempted defilement (molestation) of a child, indecent acts, incest, and threat to kill. Fourteen-year imprisonment terms are meted out to individuals who commit offenses such as robbery (which is enhanced to a death sentence if violence or threat of violence was also involved), defilement of idiots or imbeciles, attempts to procure abortion, stealing livestock, handling stolen goods, and attempting arson. Life imprisonment is reserved for such crimes as treason, rape of a child below the age of seven, inciting mutiny, aiding prisoners to escape, unlawful oaths, manslaughter, aiding suicide, arson, and rioting after a warning to disperse, among others.

Kenya Prisons Services

Prisons Services constitute a department within the Ministry of Interior and Coordination of National Government. Prisons are classified according to security levels, with maximum-security prisons housing the most dangerous criminals. By 2022, there were nine maximum-security prisons.[20] They include (1) Kamiti Maximum Security Prison, which is the largest prison in Kenya, housing an average of 1,800 inmates, located in Kahawa West in Nairobi County; (2) Shimo La Tewa Maximum Security Prison, located in Mombasa County and housing an average of 1,500 inmates; (3) Langata Women Maximum Security Prison, which is the largest women's prison, located in Langata, Nairobi; (4) Nairobi Remand and Allocation, which is in Nairobi along Enterprise Road; (5) Naivasha Maximum Security Prison, located in Nakuru County; (6) Manyani Maximum Security Prison, situated in Tsavo National Park in Taita County; (7) Nyeri Maximum Security Prison (commonly called Kingongo), located in Nyeri County; (8) Kisumu Maximum Security Prison (commonly called Kodiaga), located in Kisumu County; and (9) Kibos Maximum Security Prison, also in Kisumu County.

In addition to the nine maximum-security prisons, there are eighty-three medium- and low-level security prisons scattered across all regions of the country. Medium- and low-level security prisons house inmates who do not have a history of attempted escape from prisons and whose crimes are generally not dangerous. Table 1.1 shows the distribution of the prisons by region.

Table 1.1. List of prisons in Kenya by region

Nairobi region	*Central region*	55. Ngeria Prison
1. Nairobi Short Sentence Prison	27. Nyeri Medium Prison	56. Kapsabet Prison
2. Nairobi West Prison	28. Nyeri Women Prison	57. Kapenguria Prison
3. Kamiti Medium Prison	29. Thompson Falls Prison	58. Lodwar Prison
4. Kamiti Youth Correction and Training Center	30. Muranga Road	59. Kericho Main Prison
Prisons in the Coast Region	31. Maranjau Prison	60. Kericho Medium Prison
5. Shimo La Tewa Medium	32. Thika Main Prison	61. Kericho Women Prison
6. Shimo La Tewa Women Prison	33. Kerugoya Prison	62. Athi River Prison
7. Kwale Prison	34. Thika Women Prison	63. Maralal Prison
8. Kilifi Prison	35. Kiambu Prison	64. Rumuruti Prison
9.Malindi Prison	36. Ruiru Prison	65. Kajiado Prison
10. Hola Prison	37. Mwea Prison	66. Nanyuki Prison
11. Wundanyi Prison	*Nyanza region*	67. Narok Prison
12. Voi Remand Prison	38. Kisumu Medium Prison	68. Kabarnet Prison
13. Hindi Prison	39. Kisumu Women Prison	69. Eldama Ravine Prison
14. Taveta Prison	40. Nyamira Prison	70. Tambach Prison
15. Kingorani	41. Kisii Main Prison	*Eastern region*
Western region	42. Kisii Women Prison	71. Embu Main Prison
16. Kakamega Main Prison	43. Homa Bay Prison	72. Embu Women Prison
17. Kakamega Women Prison	44. Kibos Medium Prison	73. Machakos Main Prison
18. Bungoma Prison	45. Migori Prison	74. Machakos Women Prison
19. Shikusa Prisons	*Rift Valley region*	75. Meru Main Prison
20. Shikusa Borstal Institution	46. Naivasha Prison	76. Meru Women Prison
21. Busia Prison	47. Nakuru Main Prison	77. Kitui Prison
22. Vihiga Prison	48. Nakuru Women Prison	78. Uruku Prison
North Eastern region	49. Eldoret Women Prison	79. Isiolo Prison
23. Garissa Main Prison	50. Eldoret Main Prison	80. Marsabit Prison
24. Garrissa Medium Prison	51. Kitale Main Prison	81. Moyale Prison
25. Mandera Prison	52. Kitale Medium Prison	82. Kangeta Prison
26. Wajir Prison	53. Kitale Annex Prison	83. Makueni Prison
	54. Kitale Women Prison	

Source: J. M. Mbuba.

Moreover, by 2022, there were more than 100 publicly and privately operated rehabilitation centers for individuals whose behavior or actions are beyond their control for reasons such as mental incapacity and physical and physiological addiction to substances. While these may not fall under the purview of the Prisons Services and commitment may not be a result of judicial action, they are still correctional facilities to the extent that they aim at correcting behavior. Most rehabilitation centers are "total institutions," and clients do not have free movement in and out of the facilities. Mathari Hospital and Rehabilitation Centre on Muthaiga Road is a leading example. The total prison population in Kenya was reported at 52,979 as of March 2022.[21] Each prison is staffed by prison officers or warders, with one warder designated as "officer in charge." The officer in charge is responsible for the safety of prisoners and prison officers, safe custody of firearms and ammunition, and all storage of foods, clothing, and other supplies meant for use by prisoners.[22] In prisons where the number of prison warders is not sufficient to control the inmates, regular police officers may be deployed to perform the duties of prison officers for the desired duration. Once hired by the Prisons Services, an officer cannot quit the service or be absent without prior permission by the prisons commissioner or some other officer with the authority to grant such permission.[23]

Prisons hold three categories of people. These include convicted offenders who are serving a term of imprisonment; criminal suspects who must be detained while awaiting trial, otherwise referred to as remandees, or remand prisoners; and civil offenders or persons who have committed no criminal offenses but are guilty of civil violations, such as failure to maintain child support obligations or other forms of indebtedness. Civil offenders are also referred to as judgment-debtors.[24] According to the provisions of the Civil Procedure Act, the lender has to provide to the court convincing reasons as to why the judgment-debtor should be committed to a civil jail, including such reasons as probability of escape or concealment of property. The lender also has the obligation to pay the government for all the costs associated with keeping the judgment-debtor in jail. Commitment to a civil jail has been viewed as a method of punishing, humiliating, and shaming the judgment-debtor because of failure to pay a civil debt with the intention of inducing the debtor, the family, or friends to pay the debt.[25]

Juvenile Justice

Kenya's criminal justice system distinguishes the justice adjudication for children from the adult process. According to the Laws of Kenya, a child is defined as "any human being under the age of eighteen years."[26] Hearings in which the accused person is a child per the above definition are held in Children's Courts. A Children's Court is a subordinate court. The chief justice may appoint a magistrate to preside over cases involving children in any area of the country. Sittings of Children's Courts are held in different buildings or rooms or at different times from adult courts. Hearings in Children's Courts are not open to the public. They are restricted to officers of the court, parties to the case before the court, parents or guardians of the child before the court, authorized members of the press, and any other persons whom the court may authorize. The identity of a child before the court or that of the child's parents is held in confidence. Children who are not represented in court may receive legal representation in the form of a guardian ad litem (attorney appointed by the court to represent a child) at the state's expense if the court so orders.

Children's Courts may try a child for any offense except for allegations of murder or offenses in which the child is co-accused with an adult. No person under the age of eighteen years can be sent to prison. Indeed, the words "conviction" and "sentence" are barred from use in relation to hearings for children.[27] Children's Courts hear not only cases involving the violation of law by children but also cases of children's welfare, including custody cases in which there are parental disputes, as well as child maintenance. A court may make an order vesting the custody of a child to a parent or a guardian and provide specific directives about how custody is to be shared whereby more than one party is granted custody. Depending on the various circumstances that a child before the court may face, the court may order that a "person not awarded custody shall nevertheless have other rights and duties in relation to the child, other than the right of possession, jointly with the person who is given custody of the child."[28]

Children's Courts also hear cases involving children in need of care and protection. A child in need of care and protection is one who has no parents or guardians because the parents or guardians either are physically not present or are present but unable to provide for the child for various reasons, such as disability or terminal illness. A child may also be in need of care and protection if the child is pregnant, has been assaulted, is engaged in the use or trafficking of drugs, or has been sexually abused. Children in need of care and protection are housed in different facilities from children who are in custody for reasons to do with law violation.

Yet another category of children who come before the Children's Court are "escapees." These are children who run away from their parents or legal guardians or from institutions that have a legal responsibility to take care of the child. Such a child may be arrested, and the court may decide whether to send the child back to the parents or guardians or to some other agency, such as a rehabilitation center, a counseling facility, or any charitable children's institution as the court finds fit. In addition, Children's Courts hear cases of adoption of children, including hearing and determining adoption applications, making adoption orders, and imposing terms and conditions of adoption.

REHABILITATION OF YOUTHFUL OFFENDERS

A youthful offender is "a person who has been convicted of an offence punishable with imprisonment and has been found by the court, at the time of such conviction, to have attained the age of fifteen years but to be under the age of eighteen years."[29] Youthful offenders are sent to Borstal institutions for behavior corrections. The term "Borstal institution" was inherited from Britain, which colonized Kenya, and refers to "a kind of prison for young criminals, who were not old enough to be sent to ordinary prisons."[30] Borstal institutions are designed to be training facilities for purposes of rehabilitating youthful offenders. Each Borstal institution is supervised by a Board of Visitors, which appoints from among its members a committee to safeguard the welfare of youthful offenders in the institution, including conducting inquiries as to the age of Borstal inmates and their health and nutritional needs. Thus, although they house "children," that is, persons below the age of eighteen, Borstal institutions are under the administration of the Prisons Services and not the Children's Department. By 2022, there were two such facilities for male youthful offenders, namely, Shikusa and Shimo La Tewa,[31] and one for females, namely, Kamae Girls Borstal Institution, located inside Kamiti maximum-security prisons.[32] A youthful offender can remain in a Borstal institution up to a maximum age of twenty-one years.

In addition to Borstal institutions, children can also be committed to rehabilitation schools, detained in children's remand homes pending the court's determination of their cases, or sent to rescue centers if they are in need of help. Some of the main rehabilitation schools include Kabete, Kirigiti, Dagoretti, Getathuru, and Nairobi Children's Home. Others include Likoni, Kericho, Kakamega, Othaya, and Wamumu Rehabilitation Centers.

Notes

1. J. M. Mbuba, "Devolution without Devolution: Centralized Police Service Implications in a Decentralized Government in Kenya," *Africology: The Journal of Pan African Studies* 11, no. 8 (2018):165–81.

2. Laws of Kenya, 11A of 2011, National Police Service, accessed June 21, 2022, http://kenyalaw.org:8181/exist/kenyalex/actview.xql?actid=No.%2011A%20of%202011.

3. J. M. Mbuba, *Policing in Eastern Africa: A Focus on the National Police Service in Kenya* (Nairobi: LawAfrica, 2017).

4. Mbuba, *Policing.*

5. Mbuba, *Policing*, 56.

6. Laws of Kenya, Cap. 75.

7. The Judiciary of Kenya—Independent Custodian of Justice, accessed June 21, 2022, https://www.judiciary.go.ke.

8. Judiciary of Kenya.

9. Laws of Kenya, no. 26 of 2015, Magistrates' Courts Act.

10. Laura Smith-Spark and Farai Sevenzo, "Kenya Supreme Court Nullifies Presidential Election, Orders New Vote," CNN, September 2, 2017, https://www.cnn.com/2017/09/01/africa/kenya-election/index.html.

11. Laws of Kenya, Ch. 75, Sec. 82(1).

12. Laws of Kenya, Cap. 63, Penal Code (239).

13. Laws of Kenya, Cap. 63, Penal Code (12).

14. Sam Kiplagat, "What Supreme Court Ruling on Death Sentence Means," *Nation*, December 17, 2017, updated June 28, 2020, https://nation.africa/kenya/news/what-supreme-court-ruling-on-death-sentence-means—1246374.

15. Laws of Kenya, Cap. 63, Penal Code.

16. Laws of Kenya, Cap. 63, Penal Code (162).

17. Laws of Kenya, Cap. 63, Penal Code (162).

18. Laws of Kenya, Cap. 63, Penal Code (162).

19. Laws of Kenya, Cap. 63, Penal Code (225).

20. Venic Nyanchama, "List of All Prisons in Kenya and Where They Are Located," *Tuko*, September 3, 2021, https://www.tuko.co.ke/424121-list-prisons-kenya-located.html.

21. "Kenya," WPB: World Prison Brief, accessed February 9, 2022, https://www.prisonstudies.org/country/kenya.

22. Laws of Kenya, Cap. 90, Prisons Act.

23. Laws of Kenya, Cap. 90, Prisons Act (15).

24. Laws of Kenya, Cap. 21, Civil Procedure Act.

25. Justus Jeffery Olaka, "Our Terms of Civil Jail Defeat the Whole Idea of Justice," *Nairobi Law Monthly*, August 2, 2016, https://nairobilawmonthly.com/index.php/2016/08/02/our-terms-of-civil-jail-defeat-the-whole-idea-of-justice.

26. Laws of Kenya, Cap. 8, Children Act.

27. Laws of Kenya, Cap. 8, Children Act (189).

28. Laws of Kenya, Cap. 8, Children Act, 83(2).

29. Laws of Kenya, Cap. 92, Borstal Institutions.

30. *Collins Dictionary*, s.v. "Borstal," https://www .collinsdictionary .com/us/dictionary/english/borstal.

31. Horace Chacha, *Treatment and Social Reintegration of Offenders: Case Study of Shikusa Borstal Institution*, United Nations Asia and Far East Institute for the Prevention of Crime and the Treatment of Offenders, accessed February 15, 2022, https://www.unafei.or.jp/publications/pdf/13th_Congress/24_Kenya.pdf.

32. Walter Leitner International Human Rights Clinic, Law Clinic at Strathmore Law School, Wakilisha Initiative, and Clean Start, *Girls in Kenya's Juvenile Detention System: Recommendations for Abolition and Reform*, Leitner Center for International Law and Justice, accessed March 2, 2022, http://www .leitnercenter .org/wp -content/uploads/2020/12/Report -from-Strathmore-law-school.pdf.

CHAPTER 2

The Nigerian Criminal Justice System

AN OVERVIEW

Uche K. Kalu and Anita Kalunta-Crumpton

The Nigerian criminal justice system can be understood in terms of the deep cultural and ethnic diversity of the Nigerian nation-state.[1] The country is a multicultural and multiethnic society made up of several indigenous ethnic tribes. The three dominant tribes—the Hausa/Fulani, Yoruba, and Ibo ethnic tribes—occupy the three major geographical locations of north, southwest, and southeast, respectively. The different ethnicities ran their indigenous legal systems with peculiar criminal justice systems, which many scholars have described as informal tools of social regulation, before the advent of British colonial presence in the country. Notable among these were the systems found among the above-mentioned three dominant ethnic groups.[2] Although the various informal modes of social regulation were mostly unsystematic and trial by ordeal, the system worked in the various ethnic groups to maintain law and order and social harmony.[3]

With the advent of the British colonial administration came a series of constitutional developments, culminating in the introduction of what today could be referenced as the modern criminal justice system and the composite Nigerian legal system.[4] Therefore, the modern Nigerian criminal justice system, as an offshoot of the legal system, could be said to have come into existence through the colonial administration of the country.[5]

While the country is mainly divided along ethnic lines, there is also the element of deep-seated religious cleavages of the geopolitical groupings of the country.[6] While the north is mainly Muslim, the south is split further along Muslim and Christian creeds. In the southeast, Christianity holds strong, while the southwest is divided between the Christian and Islamic faiths. The country's unique religious heritage finds expression in the legal and criminal justice systems of the country, hence the presence of sharia law in the north and Christian-style customary law in the east and west.[7]

Therefore, an understanding of the complex religious segmentation of the country helps in understanding the legal system and, in a narrow sense, the criminal justice system.[8] The country runs a dual criminal law system—consisting of a Penal Code and Criminal Code—informed mainly by the country's foreign religious heritage. While the Penal Code, tailored toward sharia law and jurisprudence, operates in the mainly Muslim north, the Criminal Code, tailored toward Western continental jurisprudence, operates in the southern part of Nigeria. This unique dichotomy finds expression more in the lower judicial operational framework. The Customary and Sharia Courts, representing the lowest grade of courts in the judicial system, interpret questions of customs and sharia norms of the people at the lowest indigenous levels of dispute settlement.

To complicate issues further, one would be tempted to inquire into the utility of the Criminal and Penal Codes since these codes were enacted as sources of authority for crime control and penal enforcement beyond the boundaries of customary and sharia norms.[9] The answer is buried deep in the practical operation of the criminal justice system. Interestingly, though, regardless of the infusion of religion and custom into the criminal justice system, the Nigeria Police Force as one law enforcement agency enforces both the Criminal and Penal Codes separately in the two major geopolitical sections of the north and south of Nigeria. From this perspective, it is easy to understand why a suspect arrested by the police and arraigned in court in the north is charged under the Penal Code by the police, and a crime suspect in the south is charged under the Criminal Code in the south.

Law Enforcement

The advent of British colonial administration in the early eighteenth century brought with it for the first time a criminal justice system with components similar to parallels in the Western world but unfortunately tailored after Western cultural experiences.[10] The indigenous ethnic nationalities that make up the Nigerian nation had mechanisms in place for criminal justice administration. Paramount among the ethnicities was the need for security and social cohesion and hence the presence of various strong methods of local law enforcement and policing organized along the line of local vigilantes.[11] With the inception of British colonial rule, law enforcement shifted from local vigilantes to state-organized law enforcement, known as the Nigeria Police Force, as the first process point of the country's modern criminal justice system.[12]

Although the intent and purpose of this first Nigeria Police Force, from 1860 to 1914, was crime control, scholars argue that the agency was more of an instrument of the colonial suppression of ethnic rejection of colonial rule, the subjugation of ethnic dissention, and the perpetuation of British capitalist exploitation of extractive and commercial resources of the country than crime control.[13] The first so-called Nigeria Police Force did not come into full force until 1960, when Nigeria became a republic independent from British colonial rule. The force complemented the court system from then on. While the early period of independence saw a transfer of policing functions from the British colonial administration to Nigeria, the outfit arguably retained the paramilitary subterfuge of the country's colonial past and experience. The Nigeria Police Force from the post-independence era is more of a monolithic law enforcement outfit, with the inspector general of police at the top for the entire country, pursuant to the empowering law—the Nigerian Police Act of 1943—and its successive reenactments.[14] Under the inspector general of police are the various deputy inspectors general of police in charge of various departments of the police force.

Below deputy inspectors general are the assistant inspectors general of police in charge of the zonal police commands. The zonal police commands oversee clusters of states, and each state has a commissioner of police in charge who is under the inspector general of police. This is followed by the area police commands in each state and the divisional police commands, down to the police posts in the local government subunits.

POLICE FORCE: FUNCTIONS AND OPERATION

The primary functions of the Nigerian police from inception and as presently constituted are the maintenance of law and order through crime surveillance, as derived from the Constitution of the Federal Republic of Nigeria; they also include the enforcement of the Criminal Code that is operative in the south and the Penal Code that is operative in the northern part of the country. In addition to primary functions, the Nigeria Police Force has basic functions in the enabling law, including the enforcement of the Constitution of the Federal Republic of Nigeria and other laws enacted by the National Assembly, edicts made by the states, and executive orders and regulations made pursuant to the Constitution. They also prosecute criminals charged to court for violations of the Criminal and Penal Codes, and they have responsibility for the general internal security of the country.[15]

The Nigeria Police Force is monolithic in structure and command in the sense that authority is centrally local in one apex command from which power and authority are delegated from the inspector general of police vertically down to the lowest command or unit. A unique feature of the Nigeria Police Force is that there is only one police agency for the entire country, headed by the inspector general of police. Scholars argue that this operational feature of the Nigeria Police Force reflects the power and economic asymmetry of the country deliberately and systematically put in place by the powerful early oligarchy after independence.[16] Police systems all over the world are intended to protect the interest of every citizen within their jurisdictions without fear or favor. However, the opposite is the case in Nigeria, based on an analysis of the operations of the outfit cast against its intended functions. Instances of the poor being kept in custody for extended periods without trial abound, as do instances of the rich and superrich getting away with serious crimes even when arrested by the police.[17] The above stems from the quasi-prison function of the Nigerian police as a holding place of arrested suspects pending investigation and prosecution for both major and minor crimes.[18]

Growth in commerce and new tastes from economic growth and development saw an attendant explosion in crime and criminality that put a strain on police efforts to combat crime. Development in the cyberspace and dot-com technology brought erstwhile unknown cybercrimes to the domain of Nigeria law enforcement.[19] To tackle these novel developments effectively, Nigerian police came up with creative crime-fighting and law enforcement subunits, like Operation Fire for Fire and the Special Anti-Robbery Squad, which are charged with combating not only violent crimes, such as armed robbery, but also cybercrimes. Regardless of the noble intentions and objectives for setting up these subunits, corruption and abuse of power have become visible products of the subunits.

The Nigeria Police Force has been described as failing to achieve the functions for which it was instituted because of operational anomalies from corruption, poor equipment, poor salary structure, and nepotism in rank promotion, among other reasons.[20] An outfit in which promotion and posting are contingent on grease payments and whom you know in the upper command can hardly be trusted in terms of operational efficiency. In these ways, the Nigerian police outfit as an institution has been ridden with impunity and inefficiency.[21]

Judiciary

The history of the Nigerian judiciary can also be understood against the backdrop of the Nigeria historical development from the colonial era to the present.[22] The first appearance of what could be termed the modern court system in Nigeria appeared in 1863, with the British colonial establishment of four courts in the colony of Lagos to protect the British commercial interest and trade: Police Court, Criminal Court, Slave Court, and Commercial Court. Through the process of constitutional development from the British colonial administration, the judiciary came to be what it is today. The modern Nigerian judiciary can be traced back from 1960 when the country gained independence from the British government to the attainment of a republican status with the 1963 republican Constitution. Through a series of regime changes via military incursion into the democratic process, the Nigeria judiciary has gone through changes that brought the integrity and independence of the judiciary into question and under close scrutiny.[23] It would reasonably be inferred that the Nigerian legal system shows traces of the English commonwealth and English common law traceable through the country's historical evolution.

The Nigerian judiciary as a social institution of modern governance has its fair share of operational problems for a modern Third World judiciary, ranging from poor infrastructure to the poor emolument of judicial officers, which affect its independence. However, the judiciary remains one of the symbols of checks and balances in the Nigerian democratic process and is a safeguard against arbitrary rule.

The historical development of the Nigerian judiciary explains the mixture of English common law, sharia law, and customary law components of the judicial system. Basically, the judiciary interprets the Constitution and laws made pursuant to the Constitution, which include state edicts and executive regulations made pursuant to the Constitution. The judiciary also provides the mechanism for resolution of disputes between citizens against citizens and citizens against the state. In terms of structure, the Supreme Court, located in Abuja, is at the apex of the judiciary. The Supreme Court is made up of the chief justice of the federation as the head and twenty justices who are appointed by the president with the recommendation of the National Judicial Council and subject to confirmation by the Senate. Supreme Court justices enjoy lifetime tenure. A fundamental characteristic of Nigerian courts is the absence of the jury system; the presiding judge is the decider of facts and law.[24]

The Supreme Court is the final appellate court in the court dispute resolution process. Below the Supreme Court are the Courts of Appeal in various regions of the country, which hear appeals from the courts of first instance, the state High Courts. The states are organized into appellate regions overseen by Courts of Appeals. Appeals can be filed only from each state High Court to the appellate division under which the state falls and no other. The Courts of Appeals are intermediate appellate courts of the federal courts system of Nigeria. The appellate courts are located in the six geopolitical zones: north-central, northeast, northwest, southeast, southwest, and south-central.

The president of the Court of Appeals heads the Court of Appeals and is appointed for a tenure of four years by the president of the Federal Republic of Nigeria with the recommendation of the National Judicial Council and subject to confirmation by the Senate. Between the Courts of Appeals and the state High Courts are the Federal High Courts as courts of first instance on matters listed on the exclusive legislative list reserved for the federal government. At inception, the Federal High Court was known as the Federal Revenue Court. The court was a dictate of the federal system of government and was put in place to hear cases of federal revenue on the exclusive legislative list reserved for the federal legislature by the Federal Revenue Act of 1973. The court was renamed the Federal High Court pursuant to sections 228(1) and 230(2) of the second republican Constitution of 1979. The federal High Court is headed by a chief judge. In addition, the country is divided into federal High Court judicial divisions, with federal High Court judges presiding over federal High Courts within each judicial division.[25]

Below the appellate courts are the state High Courts, situated in demarcated judicial divisions of each state. The chief judge of the state is the head of each state judiciary. The governor of the state appoints each state chief judge and High Court judges, who sit alone to hear cases brought before the High Courts. The High Court judges are appointed by each state governor on recommendation by the state judicial service commission and subject to confirmation by the house of assembly of each state. The High Courts have original jurisdiction over civil and criminal cases that come under the residual and concurrent civil causes created by the Constitution and the specifically criminal violations in the Criminal and Penal Codes.

Below the High Courts of each state are the Magistrate Courts and Customary Courts. The Magistrate Courts are inferior courts of summary jurisdiction that entertain jurisdiction over criminal cases in a speedy manner. They are headed by a chief magistrate, who supervises the various magistrate courts in their jurisdiction. Magistrate Courts are created by the House of Assembly of each state, pursuant to section 6(4) of the 1999 Constitution of the Federal Republic of Nigeria, while the Magistrate Court of the Federal Capital territory is created by the National Assembly. Magistrate Courts exercise summary jurisdiction over all criminal cases except cases that attract a penalty of death. They exercise original limited jurisdiction over civil cases not exceeding 10 million Naira, as stipulated by the Constitution. The Magistrate Courts exercise appellate jurisdiction over Customary Courts below them.

The Customary Courts are in the south, and Sharia Courts are in the north. Because of the deep cultural and ethnic diversity of the Nigerian nation-state, Customary Courts and Sharia Courts were created and vested with adjudicatory authority and jurisdiction over issues of custom and native law in the various ethnic regions of the country.[26]

FUNCTIONS AND OPERATION OF THE JUDICIARY

The primary function of the judiciary, as stipulated in the Constitution, is the interpretation of the Constitution and laws made pursuant to the Constitution. The judiciary, through the courts, adjudicates disputes between citizens against citizens and between citizens and the states as the case may be. Aside from the adjudicatory function of the judiciary, the judiciary also serves as a watchdog against abuse of power by both the executive and the legislature. This it accomplishes through the power of judicial review of the acts of the other two branches of government.

Nigeria has an adversarial system of dispute resolution. The adversarial method remains a fundamental feature of the Nigerian court system, whereby litigants spar against each other through their lawyers in court according to procedural rules of court. The presiding judge, as the trier of fact and law, plays the role of an umpire and is expected to not descend into the arena of conflict between the litigants. This holds true in both civil litigation and criminal prosecution. Typically, in civil cases involving private citizens, the court's jurisdiction in the first instance is triggered by writ of summons or petition at the instance of the legally injured party asking or praying the court to mediate or make a determination as to the rights of the parties.

Legal remedies could be pursed through the hierarchy of the courts to the Supreme Court as the case may be. In its adjudicatory functions, the Nigerian judiciary is guided by the principle of judicial precedent, or stare decisis, whereby a lower court is bound by the decision of a higher court in a similar suit.[27] The principle of stare decisis, a prominent characteristic of the Nigerian courts, is an inherited characteristic from the British commonwealth.

Prison Service: Structure, Functions and Operation

The Nigerian prison service, presently known as the Nigerian corrections service, pursuant to Nigerian Corrections Service Act of 2019, constitutes the third arm of the Nigerian criminal justice system. The body is administered by the Ministry of Interior and Civil Defense, with headquarters in Abuja. A lot has been written about the Nigerian prisons, and a lot deserves to be written about the system, mainly because of its characteristic unsystematic profile. The governing law for the Nigerian prisons remains the Nigerian Corrections Act of 2019, which sets out the functions and philosophy underlying the Nigerian prison system to include ensuring the holding of convicted prisoners, the custody of inmates awaiting trial, rehabilitation, and the reintegration of offenders into society after serving their time in prison.[28] The law further compartmentalizes corrections into two broad classifications: custodial and noncustodial services. The Nigerian prison, despite developments in modern incarceration, has remained a relic of Nigerian colonial journey, as is evident in the centralized function of the agency into one monolithic, federal administration headed by the controller general of prisons. In other words, there are no state prisons or functions reserved for the states in the administration of the prisons in Nigeria.[29]

There are 145 prisons, eighty-three prison camps, ten prison farms, and two Borstal institutions for the detention of minors that make up the entire body of the Nigerian prison system. The prisons, as presently constituted, date back to the early seventeenth century, with the oldest being the Warri prison, built in 1805.[30] There are an estimated 68,551 prisoners housed in the 240 facilities spread across the country.[31]

Given that the prison system falls under the responsibility of the federal government, responsibility for prisoner welfare falls under the umbrella of the federal government. With the present arrangement, the reason for the detachment from modern correctional trends and reality is not far-fetched. Studies reveal that the Nigerian prisons lack modern recreational equipment and facilities and hospitals, so much so that the prisons are described as modern concentration camps that hold more unconvicted suspects than convicted criminals.[32] Specifically lacking are the criteria for housing convicted inmates and inmates awaiting trial, who constitute the bulk of the Nigerian prison population.[33]

The prison system has remained largely outdated and discordant with modern trends and philosophies of incarceration.[34] The functional composition of the Nigerian prisons that has spread across the country gives credence to the argument that the system has remained largely punitive and medieval in both structure and operation. It is mainly institutional in nature and form. Unlike the more developed Western model of incarceration that promotes alternatives such as community corrections, convicted felons in Nigeria are confined to one prison center or the other to serve punishment for violating societal norms that are enacted into law. The major functions of the prison service include protection of society and victims of crime, and reformation of the character of sentenced convicts. In reference to the latter responsibility, the prison system is expected to ensure the rehabilitation of offenders back into the society after serving sentences for crimes committed.

While in prison, convicts are expected to sober up through activities such as vocational training and training through religious instruction, which are designed to ensure character reformation while serving a just sentence for violation of law.[35]

Prior to serving time, convicted felons were once members of society and communities, and once their time is done, they are released back into society, where they are expected to lead normal lives alongside their fellow citizens. Rehabilitation serves the dual purpose of ensuring a soft landing for released prisoners and prevention of recidivism.[36] However, the question remains as to whether the Nigerian prison system lives up to the rehabilitation framework enshrined in the institution's empowering philosophy.[37]

A critical look at the operation of the Nigerian prison service today shows a bold imprint of the colonial legacy of incapacitation and retribution. Whereas the prison service serves as a warehouse for social deviants, prison congestion and a lack of standardized parameters for custody leave a question mark on the reformative and rehabilitative goals of the institution. Hardly any of the facilities hold inmates within their stipulated capacity. Overcrowding is a typical characteristic of Nigerian prisons.[38]

In the various prisons, evidence abounds of unsanitary conditions of convicts' living quarters. The prison houses are known super-spreaders of infectious diseases, such as tuberculosis and HIV, because of over-congestion and the poor welfare conditions of the various prison stations.[39] The institution is burdened with widespread corruption, mismanagement, incompetence, mistreatment of convicts, poor staffing, and the like.

Although several attempts have been recorded by successive regimes to change and reinvent the Nigerian prisons service, credible improvements remain illusory and elusive.[40] The Nigerian prison system remains more of a crime academy to which convicts go and then come back to society worse than they were prior to incarceration because of a lack of decisive steps to modernize the system.[41] Even though the country lacks a holistic, standardized method of record keeping to track the activities of released prisoners post-imprisonment, it is believed there is a high rate of recidivism among the ex-convict population.[42]

Much of the current state and conditions of the Nigerian prisons stems from the cultural stigma attached to convicts and serving time in prison. Prisoners are seen as social lepers by family, friends, erstwhile associates, and society at large. The same stigma endures with the convict post-imprisonment, so much so that the average ex-convict is left alone without a form of support system. This further explains the wholesale neglect of the prison system by policymakers of the country, who are charged with the responsibility of formulating policies that may improve the image of the prison system and, by extension, the operational conditions and welfare conditions of prisoners in the country. It is therefore argued that the operational framework and practical workings of Nigerian prison, as a vital arm of the criminal justice system, are antithetical to the avowed philosophy of rehabilitation and reformation of the character of convicts while serving time. It remains a fact that the Nigerian criminal justice system needs urgent reappraisal and realignment with the realities of modern societies compared with its Western counterparts.

Juvenile Justice

A discussion of juvenile justice in Nigeria first requires acknowledging that the statutory forms of administering justice to juveniles is rooted in English common law and its principles of due process and the rule of law. Likewise, the Nigerian justice approach to juveniles mirrors the doctrines of parens patriae and in loco parentis that currently guide juvenile justice in Britain and other Western societies. Both terms, which are Latin for "parent of the country" and "in place of the parents," respectively, are concepts that have origins in English common law.[43] In principle, the juvenile justice system assumes the authority of the parent of a child, thereby substituting itself for the natural parents in making decisions that, supposedly, serve the best interests of the child. With age as the mitigating factor, the conventional view that persons of a certain age have not developed adequate maturity of understanding of right and wrong and therefore cannot be held criminally responsible underlies the philosophy of rehabilitation over punishment in the approach to juvenile justice in present Nigeria, at least in principle.

However, the emphasis on the nonuse of adult-type punishment on young people was integral to the customary response to youth delinquency in precolonial Nigeria in that punishment was informal and restorative.[44] Some of the precolonial informal methods are used in parts of contemporary Igboland to resolve cases of a criminal and juvenile delinquency nature.[45] Taboos, including prohibitions aimed at instilling high moral standards in children, have been used to effect collective compliance with social norms in southwestern Nigeria.[46] These unwritten methods of social control of children and young people in precolonial Nigeria existed in the northern part of Nigeria. For example, the non-Muslim Hausa-speaking Maguzawa people frowned on the corporal punishment of children in favor of alternatives, such as reprimands and reintegrative shaming.[47]

COLONIAL NIGERIA AND THE DEVELOPMENT OF JUVENILE JUSTICE

With colonialism came the formalization and institutionalization of a structure for treating children and young people who violate laws governing offending behaviors. Like the social construction of child delinquency in nineteenth-century Britain, juvenile delinquency in African colonies was an invention of the 1940s, following the "late discovery of juvenile offenders and the criminalization of some African youth practices" by the colonists:[48]

> The development of an administrative and judiciary machinery legislated "juvenile delinquency" into existence: henceforth clearly identifiable as a social problem. Such a process was engineered in Lagos by the new Welfare Service set up during the Second World War. Lagos was not, however, unique, and specific judicial machinery for the "treatment of juvenile offenders" was also established in the French, Belgian, British and Portuguese empires in the 1940s and 1950s.[49]

While the age definition of a child for the purpose of punishment may have varied across precolonial southern and northern parts of Nigeria, the legislative response to juvenile delinquency in colonial Nigeria worked toward establishing an age status for designating children. The 1917 Prisons Ordinance provided segregated prison housing for children under the age of fourteen; the 1928 Native Children (Custody and Reformation) Ordinance and its amendment in 1932 specified fifteen and sixteen, respectively, as the age limit for a "child" status. However, in 1943, the Children and Young Persons Ordinance (CYPO), adapted from Britain's Children and Young Persons Act (CYPA) 1933, established two classifications of persons whom many contemporary societies would define as juveniles: a person under the age of fourteen is a child, and a person above fourteen and under the age of seventeen is a young person.[50]

Very few reformatories or schools were created in Nigeria by and during the 1930s in response to delinquency, which often took the form of street offenses, such as petty theft, pickpocketing, and extortion. The reformatories provided industrial training and formal education to juveniles in their care. A reformatory was built in Lagos in

1926 and housed boys convicted of an offense in Lagos, and an approved school in Enugu (eastern Nigeria) was established in 1933.[51] Perhaps the dearth of reformatories during these periods was, inter alia, reflective of the apathy of the colonial administration toward an issue that was, nevertheless, garnering press coverage as public concerns about street offenses among juveniles, including the involvement of young girls in hawking and prostitution, were increasing.[52] Such delinquent activities were not only prominent in Lagos but also notable in cities in southeastern Nigeria, such as Port Harcourt and Calabar.[53]

Reports written by David Faulkner—the first social welfare officer in the British colonial territory—in the early 1940s on the state of juvenile delinquency in Lagos highlighted the extent of the problem, with Lagos streets constituting a dangerous space for juvenile beggars, school dropouts, street trading, and hawking and prostitution by girls.[54] Faulkner's recommendations included the establishment of recreational facilities for boys and girls as a delinquency prevention measure and as an attractive alternative to the streets, and the creation of hostels for those who needed intervention. It was on the strength of his advocacy that the 1943 CYPO was passed. With an objective that underscored social welfarism, the CYPO paved the way for juvenile delinquency to fall primarily under the auspices of the social welfare service, which provided social workers who worked in partnership with probation and police officers. The social welfare presence was prominent in Lagos but had little or no existence in other regions of the country. Thus, the intersection of welfarism and juvenile delinquency in Lagos was not only evident in the welfare service department but also mirrored in the formation of juvenile-specific justice apparatuses—a Juvenile Court and a Juvenile Court police force—during the 1940s. These systems provided the Lagos social welfare service the mechanisms to put the CYPO into practice.[55]

While the welfare approach to juvenile delinquency lasted for the duration of colonial rule, it was not without criticisms, key of which alludes to the repressive, criminalizing, and postindependence consequences of the colonial administration of juvenile justice in Nigeria.[56]

JUVENILE JUSTICE IN INDEPENDENT NIGERIA

In the international scene, Nigeria acknowledges the vulnerability of juvenile offenders, as demonstrated in its position as a signatory to international conventions for the protection of juveniles, including the 1989 UN Convention on the Rights of the Child (UNCRC), which came into effect in 1990, and the 1990 African Charter on the Rights and Welfare of the Child (ACRWC).[57] Seemingly, the most important of the conventions, because of its comprehensiveness and international focus, is the 1989 UNCRC.

Both the UNCRC and the ACRWC define a child as any person under the age of eighteen. Both conventions mandate that children should not be subjected to the full weight of the law because they are less liable than adults for their actions. Articles 17 and 4 of the ACRWC outline special provisions for the treatment of child offenders in the juvenile justice system; for example, children are to be confined in segregated facilities, and juvenile trials are to be conducted outside the purview of the public and press. Likewise, Articles 3, 37, and 40 of the UNCRC prescribe age-appropriate leniency in the arrest, confinement, and overall treatment of children who break the law. Ultimately, the conventions call for an approach to the administration of juvenile justice that has the best interests of the child as its focus.

The structure of juvenile justice in contemporary Nigeria, at least in principle, is largely a mirror image of the country's colonial past and the effects of postindependence global influence. These are apparent in Nigeria's main legislations for children and young persons, including juvenile offenders. One is the CYPA, which was passed in 1943 as the CYPO and later underwent legislative amendments in subsequent years for implementation as laws at the state level.[58] The other is the 2003 Child Rights Act (CRA), enacted at the federal level and codified into law by most states.[59] This legislation is notable in that it is child-specific,[60] and it expands the human rights of children in Nigeria, including the protective rights of juvenile offenders in the juvenile justice system.

Both pieces of legislation have a strong foreign influence. The CYPA is a product of colonialism, while the CRA depicts a national alignment of child social welfare provisions with international standards. In line with the colonial framework, the CYPA was passed not only to provide for the social welfare of young people but also to cater to young offenders, including establishing courts that are specific to juveniles.[61] Contemporarily, the juvenile justice system is an integral component of the broader criminal justice administration in that it is processed through the main agencies of the criminal justice system—police, courts, and prisons.[62] At local, state, and federal levels, these agencies administer juvenile justice according to the federal and respective state laws and local policies. A notable indicator of the specialized nature of juvenile justice is that offenders are also entitled to access the services of local and state social welfare agencies that are significant players in the administration of juvenile justice.[63]

Provisions in the CYPA and the CRA pertaining to juvenile offenders prescribe juvenile justice processes from the point of arrest to imprisonment. Under these laws, alleged juvenile offenders arrested by the police should be released but with police discretion to release on recognizance except in certain circumstances, such as if the juvenile committed a grievous offense.[64] When the police consider it imperative to detain a juvenile prior to trial, the age status of the alleged offender must be considered in the decision, pursuant to the CYPA and the CRA. Pretrial custody remand of a juvenile should be in a remand home, in an approved institution, or in a prison where the juvenile should not be allowed contact with adult offenders/inmates.[65]

For a nonserious charge against a child, the CRA gives the police and others involved in the process wide discretionary authority to drop the charge or to avoid a court trial in exchange for community-based restorative and rehabilitative alternatives to punishment.[66] Social workers and probation officers are vital participants in the process in that the CRA stipulates that a report about the child and the alleged offense be presented to the court to guide judicial decisions. The goal to serve the best interests of the juvenile also means that these professionals may be among the few people allowed to be at the private trial of a juvenile.[67]

Court processing of juveniles is expected to conform to legislation. Under the CYPA, a designated Juvenile Court, presided over by a magistrate, should handle juvenile offending cases. Such cases should be heard at a venue different from the location for adult cases and at days and times different from those for adult cases.[68] The CRA is explicitly affirmative on the removal of children from the criminal justice process or the use of a punitive approach to juvenile justice. Thus, the legislation prohibits capital and corporal punishment of a child offender.[69]

Incarceration is also prohibited by the CRA, barring serious violent offenses against a person or repeated serious offenses that pose a threat to public safety. Otherwise, juvenile offenders should receive noncarceral corrections, such as supervision in the community under the care of a guardian or an official supervisor.[70] When incarceration is unavoidable pursuant to the CYPA, offenders should be housed in juvenile correctional institutions, such as Borstals, with a focus on the reformation of the offenders through vocational training and formal education.[71] This point is emphasized in the CRA mandate that punishment is not the goal of juvenile detention; as such, no incarcerated juvenile should experience any form of punishment, such as isolation.[72]

Criticisms abound that the administration of juvenile justice in Nigeria falls short of its national and international obligations to children, in part because of regional or state variations in the definition of a child and in how the offending laws that apply to children are interpreted. For example, the reenactment of clauses in the CYPA as state laws (i.e., Children and Young Persons Law) took "into account their socio-cultural, political and religious peculiarities."[73] Such variations seem to be an extension of the variations in the northern Nigeria Penal Code, the Sharia Penal Code in some states in northern Nigeria, and the southern Nigeria Criminal Code. Controversies over the issue of age of criminal responsibility illustrate this point.[74]

Alongside this overt ramification of federalism are deep-seated institutional barriers to an effective and efficient administration of juvenile justice across states in the country, such as deficiencies in policies, practices, administration, management, and economic resources.[75] Critics conclude that the administration of juvenile justice in Nigeria is a far cry from the spirit of care, protection, supervision, prevention, and rehabilitation expressed in the CYPA, the CRA, and related international conventions.

Conclusion

The complexity of the Nigerian system of justice for the adult and juvenile populations cannot be fully unraveled in a book chapter. Much of the complexity revolves around the ethos of federalism and the dual code structure under which the justice system operates. One could portray the unique and complex criminal justice system in one short phrase—unity in diversity. However, criminal justice was not alien to the indigenous Nigerian ethnic societies, considering that components of modern criminal justice existed in some form prior to British colonial rule.[76]

Notes

1. N. Okafo, "Law Enforcement in Postcolonial Africa: Interfacing Indigenous and English Policing in Nigeria," *International Police Executive Symposium*, Working Paper 7, May 2007, 4–23; H. A. Salihu, "Possibilities for the Incorporation of African Indigenous Procedures and Mechanisms of Dispute Resolution in the Administration of Criminal Justice in Nigeria," *Contemporary Justice Review* 23, no. 4 (2020): 354–72.
2. V. Saleh-Hanna, *Colonial Systems of Control: Criminal Justice in Nigeria* (Ottawa: University of Ottawa Press, 2008), http://library.oapen.org/handle/20.500.12657/31525; Salihu, "Possibilities"; Okafo, "Law Enforcement."
3. Okafo, "Law Enforcement"; Salihu, "Possibilities."
4. Okafo, "Law Enforcement"; Salihu, "Possibilities."
5. Okafo, "Law Enforcement."
6. Okafo, "Law Enforcement."
7. Okafo, "Law Enforcement."
8. Okafo, "Law Enforcement."
9. Okafo, "Law Enforcement."
10. Okafo, "Law Enforcement."
11. Okafo, "Law Enforcement."
12. Okafo, "Law Enforcement"; L. Ikuteyi and K. Rotimi, "The Image of Nigerian Police: Lessons from History," *Journal of Applied Security Research* 9, no. 2 (2014): 221–35.
13. Saleh-Hanna, *Colonial Systems.*
14. I. Chukwuma, "Police Transformation in Nigeria: Problems and Prospects," *Crime and Policing in Transitional Societies* (2000): 127–34, https://www.kas.de/c/document_library/get_file?uuid=092f7296-f4ec-371b-b5ce-c7bc0a678e1b&groupId=252038.
15. Chukwuma, "Police Transformation."
16. T. Akuul, "The Role of the Nigeria Police Force in Maintaining Peace and Security in Nigeria," *Journal of Social Science and Public Policy* 3, no. 7 (2001): 16–23.
17. Akuul, "Role."
18. Akuul, "Role."
19. Akuul, "Role."
20. Akuul, "Role."
21. Akuul, "Role."
22. J. Sofekun and N. Njoku, "The Court System in Nigeria: Jurisdiction and Appeals," *International Journal of Business and Applied Social Science* 2, no. 3 (2016): 18–29.
23. T. T. Aver and W. J. Orban, "Judiciary and Democracy, Issues in Contemporary Nigerian Society," *Global Journal of Arts, Humanities and Social Sciences* 2, no. 1 (2014): 85–95.
24. Sofekun and Njoku, "Court System."
25. Aver and Orban, "Judiciary."
26. Sofekun and Njoku, "Court System."
27. Sofekun and Njoku, "Court System."
28. K. S. Adebisi and O. O. Oyewo, "Prisons and Security Challenges in a Democratic Nigeria," *Research on Humanities and Social Sciences* 5, no. 6 (2015): 124–29.
29. Adebisi and Oyewo, "Prisons."
30. P. T. Ahire, "The Origin, Development, and Role of the Nigerian Prison System," *Annals of the Social Science Council of Nigeria* 7 (1995): 40–41.
31. Saleh-Hanna, *Colonial Systems.*
32. Ahire, "Origin."

33. C. Ndukwe and N. C. Iroko, "Nigerian Prison Service and the Challenges of Social Welfare Administration: A Study of Abakaliki Prison," *Journal of Policy and Development Studies* 9, no. 1 (November 2014): 20–28.

34. Ahire, "Origin."

35. F. Chukwudi, "Challenges of Reforms in the Nigerian Prison System: Lessons from USA and South Africa," *Journal of Social Sciences and Public Policy* 4, no. 9 (2012): 35–46.

36. J. Onyekachi, "Problems and Prospects of Administration of Nigerian Prisons: Need for Proper Rehabilitation of the Inmates in Nigerian Prisons," *Journal of Tourism and Hospitality* 5, no. 4 (2016): 1–14.

37. Onyekachi, "Problems."

38. Saleh-Hanna, *Colonial Systems.*

39. Chukwudi, "Challenges."

40. Ndukwe and Iroko, "Nigerian Prison Service."

41. Onyekachi, "Problems."

42. Onyekachi, "Problems."

43. For a review of these concepts, see R. A. Weisheit and D. M. Alexander, "Juvenile Justice Philosophy and the Demise of *Parens Patriae*," *Federal Probation* 52, no. 4 (1988): 56–64.

44. In reference to the Igbos of southeastern Nigeria, Onyeozili and Ebbe give an insightful account of informal and punitive but restorative ways through which deviant behaviors were socially controlled. See E. C. Onyeozili and O. N. I. Ebbe, "Social Control in Precolonial Igboland of Nigeria," *African Journal of Criminology and Justice Studies* 6, nos. 1–2 (2012): 29–43.

45. Onyeozili and Ebbe, "Social Control."

46. A. M. Afe, "Taboos and the Maintenance of Social Order in the Old Ondo Province, Southwestern Nigeria," *African Research Review: An International Multidisciplinary Journal, Ethiopia* 7, no. 1 (2013): 95–109.

47. M. Last, "Children and the Experience of Violence: Contrasting Cultures of Punishment in Northern Nigeria," *Africa: Journal of the International African Institute* 70, no. 3 (2000): 359–93.

48. L. Fourchard, "Lagos and the Invention of Juvenile Delinquency in Nigeria," *Journal of African History* 47, no. 1 (2006): 116.

49. Fourchard, "Lagos."

50. See Fourchard, "Lagos"; Center for Law Enforcement Education (CLEEN), *Rights of the Child in Nigeria: A Report on the Implementation of the Convention on the Rights of the Child by Nigeria*; and Center for Socio-Legal Studies (CFSS), *Juvenile Justice in Nigeria: A Report.*

51. Fourchard, "Lagos"; see also CLEEN, *Rights*, and T. Akintayo, "Options for Africa's Child Welfare Systems from Nigeria's Unsustainable Multicultural Models," *Sustainability* 13, no. 3 (2021): 1118, https://doi.org/10.3390/su13031118.

52. Fourchard, "Lagos."

53. Fourchard, "Lagos."

54. Fourchard, "Lagos."

55. Fourchard, "Lagos."

56. See Fourchard, "Lagos."

57. See African Union, African Charter on the Rights and Welfare of the Child, 1990, https://au.int/en/documents-45; United Nations International Children's Emergency Fund (UNICEF), Convention on the Rights of the Child, November 20, 1989, https://www.unicef.org/child-rights-convention; and World Health Organization, African Charter on the Rights and Welfare of the Child, 1990, https://www.who.int/hhr/African%20Child%20Charter.pdf.

58. See CLEEN, *Rights.*

59. See Akintayo, "Options."

60. According to the CRA, a child is a person under the age of eighteen years.

61. See CLEEN, *Rights*, and A. Abhulimhen-Iyoha and M. O. Oseghale, "Juvenile Justice Administration in Nigeria and Contemporary International Standards," *Journal of Law and Criminal Justice* 8, no. 1 (June 2020): 126–37.

62. CLEEN, *Rights*.

63. CLEEN, *Rights*.

64. See CLEEN, *Rights*; Abhulimhen-Iyoha and Oseghale, "Juvenile Justice"; and I. Ogunniran, "The Lock and Key Phenomenon: Reforming the Penal Policy for Child Offenders in Nigeria," *Justice Policy Journal* 10, no. 1 (2013): 1–20.

65. See CFSS, *Juvenile Justice*; CLEEN, *Rights*; Ogunniran, "Lock"; and Abhulimhen-Iyoha and Oseghale, "Juvenile Justice."

66. See Abhulimhen-Iyoha and Oseghale, "Juvenile Justice."

67. See A. Sa'ad, "Juvenile Justice in Nigeria," *Nigerian Journal of Sociology and Anthropology* 6, no. 1 (2008): 71–83.

68. See CLEEN, *Rights*, and Abhulimhen-Iyoha and Oseghale, "Juvenile Justice."

69. Abhulimhen-Iyoha and Oseghale, "Juvenile Justice."

70. Abhulimhen-Iyoha and Oseghale, "Juvenile Justice."

71. See CLEEN, *Rights*.

72. See Sa'ad, "Juvenile Justice."

73. Abhulimhen-Iyoha and Oseghale, "Juvenile Justice," 129.

74. See CLEEN, *Rights*; CFSS, *Juvenile Justice*; and Abhulimhen-Iyoha and Oseghale, "Juvenile Justice."

75. See Abhulimhen-Iyoha and Oseghale, "Juvenile Justice"; O. Atilola, G. Abiri, and B. Ola, "The Nigerian Juvenile Justice System: From Warehouse to Uncertain Quest for Appropriate Youth Mental Health Service Model," *BJPsych International* 16, no. 1 (2019): 19–21; B. O. Ajah and C. O. Ugwuoke, "Juvenile Justice Administration and Child Prisoners in Nigeria," *International Journal of Criminal Justice Sciences* 13, no. 2 (2018): 438–46; Ogunniran, "Lock"; CFSS, *Juvenile Justice*; and Sa'ad, "Juvenile Justice."

76. Saleh-Hanna, *Colonial Systems*; Okafo, "Law Enforcement."

CHAPTER 3

South Africa's Criminal Justice System

Sebastian Okello Wang'ombe

Policing and Law Enforcement

According to pioneer comparative police studies, varieties of policing can make the attempt to elaborate on similarities and differences in international police forces confusing. Every culture has its own distinctive system of establishing justice. The primary obligation of the state is to maintain peace and order. Modern police forces are organized to perform services related to "civil order control and deviance control."[1] These differences make sense when examining historical development in South Africa. Many countries, because of their high degree of centralization of governmental structure, have developed centralized police forces. Although this may be true in many countries in Europe, Africa, Asia, and South America, the United States stands apart with a decentralized system composed of almost 20,000 police forces.

The recent surge in interest in comparative justice has led to a number of publications chronicling at least some of the conventional differences between various styles of policing. Contemporary challenges to transnational policing have made the cooperation between police forces increasingly crucial. To understand how forces can work better, it is important to note the similarities and then detail how differences can be barriers to cooperation.

South Africa's criminal justice system has been in transition for a long period now because of the effects of the apartheid system, which was based on a rigid system of justice administration and an attempt to cope with massive changes resulting from the demise of the same system. The removal of apartheid created high expectations among the majority of the peoples of South Africa, specifically pertaining to the need for fair administration of justice to all, regardless of differences in color, ethnicity, race, and the economic status of the offender and the victims. In the area of national policing, there are optimistic expectations that there will be a removal of the oppressive control exerted by the former South African Police Force and that in its place will exist a new progressive paradigm of a partnership between the people and the government. The South African Police Force was initially focused as a state mechanism for ensuring internal civil social order. The focus has recently shifted from maintaining social order to a more traditional police mission that is centered on crime detection and prevention and community service.[2]

There is widespread doubt as to whether the police force will be able to shift its focus successfully and whether the police force has the skills required for this change in mission. The public view is that the police force is incapable of controlling crime, particularly violent crime. An increasingly garrison-like mentality at all levels of the community has stimulated the government and the private sector into formulating policy recommendations and toward restoring personal and property security. Meanwhile, the private security industry has rapidly expanded and currently employs more people than the police force.

Regardless of the policing model implemented, a new model incorporating community policing will be difficult to implement in the South African context. The Annual Plan of the South African Police Service for 2020–2021 reflects a twofold strategy of crime prevention and combating existing criminality. A key component of this plan is the use of community policing, defined as a set of interconnecting policies and programs introduced with success in various cities in the United States and worldwide that establishes a collaborative partnership between the police and the citizens. Although the concept of community policing has had several successes worldwide, the authors of the Annual Plan raise the question of whether this policing model is unconditionally exportable to the South African context. Theoretical views of crime and the change process affect the choice of organizational structures and methods for the successful introduction of community policing in South Africa. Given the escalation of criminal violence, the enormity of political and social change, and the unlikely prospect of rapidly meeting the high economic expectations of the newly powerful majority, the key question is about what organizational model is most conducive to managing continual, structural social change. If the model chosen is indeed a community policing model, the next question is whether it will be effective in the South African context.

Crime in South Africa

Crime continues to be a serious problem in South African society. Rates of crime and violence remain extremely high, and only the category of public violence (rioting, unlawful assembly, and so on) has abated significantly since the new democracy began. Violent crime has stabilized at high levels. Commercial crime remains at a high and sustained level. Comparisons to relatively peaceful societies, such as Sweden, New Zealand, Canada, and Denmark, show South Africa to be a violent place, with overall crime rates over double the world average. Even worse, South Africa may be the most murderous society on Earth, with a murder rate of between forty-five and seventy people per 100,000, exceeding the rates of countries such as Columbia, the Philippines, and Sudan.[3]

In Black communities, the murder rate may be as much as twenty times higher than in White suburbs. Active media coverage of crimes directed against individuals, such as car hijackings, add to public fears and perceptions of ineffective policing.

Crime was the most significant campaign issue in the November 1995 local elections. In a 1995 survey, the percentage of respondents rating the number one problem in South Africa was a dramatic 46 percent for crime, followed by 18 percent for unemployment, 4 percent for housing, and 2 percent for poor education.[4]

Current crime statistics show that the ratio of crime per 100,000 people has either decreased or stabilized since 1994. Only the incidence of rape has increased. This increase could be because of an increase in the number of rapes or because of changes in South African society that make it more likely that rape will be reported.[5]

High crime is also affecting productivity and the economy in the business sector. The incidence of crime in the business context is three times higher than in the personal or domestic sphere, with the dominant form of crime being truck and van hijacking, a violent act distinguished from simple theft by the threat of harm to drivers. Crime dominates the decisions of small businesses regarding investment and expansion.

When viewing growth of crime and prevention strategies in South Africa, unique and complicating factors exist. South African history is dominated by colonialism, racism, apartheid, and repressive labor policies. The economy was built on systematically enforced racial division in every sphere of society, including official segregation in education, health care, welfare, transportation, and employment. One need only compare the Black townships, which lack even basic infrastructure, to prosperous, well-resourced White suburbs to realize the breadth of the inequality extant in South African society.

Income distribution in South Africa is racially distorted and ranks as one of the most unequal in the world. Even in the economic heart of the country, Gauteng Province, unemployment is at 46 percent among Blacks. One thousand rural people per month migrate to the cities of Johannesburg and Pretoria, only to become squatters. The economy has been able to absorb only 5 percent of the estimated 300,000 per year entering the job market. Estimates of the growth of gross national product required for such assimilation are 56 percent annually, about double the current rate. The apartheid-based marginalization of Black youth and the slow growth of the job market have led to increases in numbers of youth "at risk" for criminal behavior.[6]

Responding to Crime

Responses in South Africa to instability and crime have ranged from arguments over statistical accuracy to vigilantism. Suburban Whites have turned homes into garrisons, complete with vicious dogs, razor wire, and armed guards summoned by panic buttons. Common concerns resulting in a sense of general lawlessness include the high numbers of firearms in society, the growth of organized crime, increased white-collar crime and its attendant economic effects, increased gender violence, intergroup conflict, vehicle theft and hijacking, and corruption in the justice system.

The new democracy is struggling to overcome a racially based, disproportionate distribution of criminal justice resources, which had concentrated on the criminalization of political protest and activity. Insufficient and ill-equipped crime detection and prevention personnel, outdated systems, and fragmented departments contribute to a system that has been unable to cope with the demands created by the need to provide services to all the people since the 1994 National Unity Government took office.

The government, in May 1995, decided to develop the first National Crime Prevention Strategy (NCPS). The resulting document stated that any successful crime prevention strategy must be based on information and analysis, must contain multiple substrategies involving multiple agencies (both public and private), and must require the breaking down of the concept of crime into specifics that would allow for crimes to be attacked with specific strategies.

The NCPS proposed four pillars of action for implementing the overall strategy: strengthening the criminal justice system, designing crime-resistant governmental systems (e.g., identity documents and vehicle registration system), creating educational crime prevention programs aimed at youth in schools, and strengthening South Africa's regional security. Community policing was specifically recommended as a goal for restructuring the South African Police Service.

To that end, the Government of National Unity's Reconstruction and Development Program recommended the establishment of policing programs that cut across divisional and agency lines, including the establishment of Community Safety Centers that could accommodate personnel from multiple departments, such as police stations, clinics, day care centers, and courthouses; each center could render one-stop services in a safe and secure environment. Future provisions of the plan include establishing satellite stations where the different role players would be placed under one roof in decentralized service points.[7]

A ten-point police transformation program was launched in February 1995. The plan included human resources management changes to accommodate police unionization and to improve the work environment, new basic and field training of a full year (up from six months) for recruits, and a service-wide training project, called "Ubuntu," to expose more than 146,000 police officers to the new policing philosophy of the South African Police Service.

Police search and seizure powers and emergency action powers were reduced. Military-style ranks were abolished. The police reserve has been deemphasized, and steps have been taken to make policing a more attractive professional career option.

South African Judiciary

Before the dawn of democracy in South Africa, the judicial system functioned as part of the apartheid legal order and was perceived as contributing to the legitimization of this order. The Westminster system of government, in which the legislature was supreme over the other branches of government, resulted in the judiciary upholding and sustaining the discriminatory and unjust laws. The courts were confined to interpreting and enforcing legislation. They could not consider and determine the substantive legality of acts of Parliament.

The year 1996 was a defining moment in South Africa's history, as its Constitution went through a thorough consultative process culminating in its certification and adoption by the Constitutional Court and by the Parliament. It entrenched a democratic state founded on the values of constitutional supremacy, equality, and rule of law, among others. The relevant provision relating to the judiciary is Section 165 of the Constitution, which vests the courts with judicial authority and provides for an independent and transformed judiciary that delivers high-quality justice to all without fear, favor, or prejudice. These courts are subject only to the Constitution and the law, which they must apply impartially. This is a crucial provision of the postapartheid Constitution, which protects constitutional democracy. Section 165 further provides that no person or organ of the state may interfere with the functioning of the courts, and it enjoins organs of state, through legislative and other measures, to assist and protect the courts in order to ensure their independence, impartiality, dignity, accessibility, and effectiveness. The Constitution also outlines its vision for establishing a judicial system suited to the requirements of the new Constitution.[8]

To this end, the president of South Africa established the Office of the Chief Justice as a national department, responsible for rendering support to the judiciary and the chief justice as head of the judiciary. This was a commendable step by the South African government. It fulfilled the transformative imperatives demanded by the Constitution in a path toward a judiciary-led court administration system in recognition of the need to enhance judicial independence as espoused in Section 165 of the Constitution. The final goal of the judiciary was the creation of a revitalized court administration structure located within the judicial branch of government.

The Constitution of South Africa assigns the responsibility of establishing and monitoring norms and standards for judicial officers to the chief justice as the head of the judiciary. To this end, there is gazettement of the norms and standards for judicial officers in order to enhance optimal and effective performance by the courts. Positive developments since the implementation of norms and standards have underscored the understanding that judicial independence and judicial accountability are intrinsically intertwined. For this reason, from January 2014, judges have been required by the Constitution to disclose their financial interests in order to eliminate any perception of conflict of interest that might affect judicial independence.

THE JUDICIAL SYSTEM

In South Africa, the courts are vested by the Constitution with judicial authority, and they are independent and subject only to the Constitution and the law, which they must apply impartially and without fear, favor, or prejudice. The Constitution outlines the structure of the courts as follows:

1. Constitutional Court
2. Supreme Court of Appeal
3. High Court of South Africa, consisting of nine divisions
4. Specialist Courts: Land Claims Court, Labor Court, Labor Appeal Court, and Competition Appeal Court

5. Any other court established or recognized in terms of an act of Parliament, including any court of a status similar to either the High Court of South Africa or the Magistrates' Courts
6. Magistrates' Courts

THE CONSTITUTIONAL COURT

The Constitutional Court is the highest court in South Africa. It was established in 1994 in South Africa's Interim Constitution. The court is situated at Constitution Hill, Braamfontein, in Johannesburg. It comprises the chief justice (who is its head), the deputy chief justice, and nine other judges. The court may decide constitutional matters and any other matter if it grants leave to appeal on the grounds that the matter raises a constitutional issue or an arguable point of law of general public importance. The court is the final arbiter of the constitutional validity of decisions taken by the president. It is the final court that decides on the constitutional validity of laws made by Parliament and legislatures. Generally, the court sits as an appeal court, but in certain limited circumstances, it may sit as a court of first and final instance. Any matter before this court must be heard by at least eight judges.

THE SUPREME COURT OF APPEAL

The Supreme Court of Appeal is the successor to the Appellate Division of the Supreme Court of South Africa, which was first established in 1910. The name of the court was changed by the 1996 Constitution. The Supreme Court of Appeal comprises the president, deputy president, and as many judges of appeal as may be determined by an act of Parliament. This court functions only as a court of appeal. It decides appeals from the High Court, Land Claims Court, and Electoral Court. Although it previously had jurisdiction in labor and competition matters, it no longer has such jurisdiction. Appeals from the Labor Appeal Court and Competition Appeal Court go to the Constitutional Court rather than to the Supreme Court of Appeal.

THE HIGH COURT OF SOUTH AFRICA

The High Court of South Africa consists of as many divisions as may be determined by an act of Parliament. Each division consists of a judge president and one or more deputy judges as determined by national legislation. The High Court of South Africa has inherent jurisdiction to hear any case that is not assigned to another court by an act of Parliament. Each division of the High Court has jurisdiction in its own area over all persons residing or present in that area. It has the power to declare legislation constitutionally invalid, but its order is subject to confirmation by the Constitutional Court. Courts of a status similar to that of the High Court are the following specialized courts:

1. Electoral Court, which adjudicates electoral disputes
2. Labor Court, which adjudicates certain labor disputes
3. Labor Appeal Court, which hears appeals from the Labor Court
4. Competition Appeal Court, which deals with appeals from the Competition Tribunal
5. Land Claims Court, which deals with matters on the restitution of land rights that people lost as a result of racially discriminatory land laws

MAGISTRATES' COURTS

Regional and District Magistrates' Courts together comprise the so-called lower courts. These courts are a vital part of the legal system, as they are where ordinary people come into contact with the justice system. Magistrates are appointed by the minister of justice and correctional services on recommendations of the Magistrates' Commission. Regional Magistrates' Courts deal with more serious cases than do the ordinary (District Courts) Magistrates' Courts, which deal with such cases as murder, rape, armed robbery, and serious assault. They can sentence a person convicted of murder or rape to life imprisonment. A Regional Magistrates' Court can impose a maximum fine of R 300,000. They also have civil jurisdiction to the extent that they can hear divorce matters. The District Courts deal with less serious cases. Unlike the Regional Courts, they cannot try cases of murder, treason, rape, terrorism, or sabotage. They can sentence a convicted person to a maximum period of three years in prison or a maximum fine of R 100,000.[9]

Correctional and Rehabilitation Services

The history of corrections is also a history of experimentation, but few methods of punishment have surpassed the almost universal popularity of incarceration. For hundreds of years, prisoners have been incarcerated in dungeons, on fetid prison hulks, in gulags and concentration camps, at boot camps, on deserted islands, and, most recently, in penitentiaries. Although involuntary confinement is the most familiar characteristic of corrections, countries around the world have made increasing inroads into finding alternatives to the warehousing of inmates.

HISTORICAL OVERVIEW

The Department of Correctional Services (DCS) is mandated to place offenders in a secure, safe, and humane environment and to ensure that rehabilitation and successful reintegration programs are implemented. This mandate derives from the Correctional Services Act of 1998 (Act 111 of 1998), the Criminal Procedure Act of 1977 (Act 51 of 1977), the 2005 White Paper on Corrections in South Africa, and the 2014 White Paper on Remand Detention Management in South Africa. As prescribed in these legislative actions, DCS has to contribute to maintaining and promoting a just, peaceful, and safe society by correcting offending behavior in a safe, secure, and humane environment that allows for optimal rehabilitation and reduced repeat offending.[10]

DCS acknowledged the development of rehabilitation services as a key starting point in the direction of a crime-free South Africa. In 2001, amendments were made to the Correctional Services Act 111 of 1998. The Correctional Services Amendment Act 32 of 2001 was instituted to implement the principal act fully as well as to be more compliant with the provisions of the Constitution. Central to the Amendment Act were the following topics:

- The treatment of prisoners
- Accommodation of disabled offenders and gender considerations
- Disciplinary procedures for prisoners
- New parole systems
- Treatment of child offenders
- The use of firearms and other nonlethal incapacitating devices

The *Mvelaphanda Strategic Plan for 2002–2005*, adopted by DCS in October 2001, put rehabilitation at the center of all DCS activities. In South Africa, in addition to the various strategies undertaken to manage the challenge of overcrowding, which is an occurrence throughout the world, prototype designs for the construction of a cost-effective new generation of prisons were instituted. The so-called new-generation prisons were intended to offer DCS the ability to carry out the rehabilitation mandate effectively within the principles of unit management, which was identified as the missing component in the transformation of the South African prison system. This is an approach that makes provision for the following:

- The division of the prison into smaller manageable units
- Improved interaction between staff and prisoners
- Improved and effective supervision
- Increased participation in all programs by prisoners
- Enhanced teamwork and a holistic approach
- The creation of mechanisms to address gangsterism

This approach will not be workable while overcrowding persists in the incarceration of violent offenders. The prisoner-to-population ratio will remain high, and overcrowding will remain the norm for most prisons.[11]

EXPANSION OF PRISONS FROM 1910

Significant developments of correctional law occurred in the period immediately after the Union of South Africa. The Department of Prisons formed part of the Department of Justice for a number of years. The British occupation for the Transvaal and the Orange Free State (OFS) Republics in 1900 led to a major reorganization of the penal systems in these provinces.

THE PRISON SYSTEM OF THE CAPE

Jan van Riebeeck, during his stay at the Cape, followed a policy regarding the punishment of criminals that had its roots in seventeenth-century Dutch judicial practice. The full panoply of penalizing measures was presented as a brutal and public demonstration. This judicial system inevitably had an influence on various aspects of judicial practice, the penal system, and the administration of justice in South Africa. The kind of punishment used for offenders was directed at the body, such as public executions by firing squads and public crucifixion. The imprisonment of convicted persons and the use of such persons for manual labor did not appear to be prioritized. Convicted persons were occasionally held in chains in the Dutch East India Company's slave lodge and made to labor in public projects. An attempt was made to extract labor from convicts deported to Robben Island. Deportation removed criminals from a society that did not have much interest in their welfare.

Only after the Fort and the Castle were built in the Cape was detention possible. Incarceration was reserved mainly for debtor prisoners who were condemned or awaiting trial and judgment. Some of the cruel forms of punishment were abolished during the eighteenth century, which led to the expansion, however informal, of imprisonment. The extant small places of detention were overpopulated with people held for minor offenses. Places of detention were also erected for people who had to serve longer sentences. During this period, the whole prison system was extremely disorganized and made no reference whatsoever to rehabilitation.

The most significant reformations pertaining to punishment occurred after the British occupation of the Cape from 1795 to 1803. In 1795, the orientation of the penal system toward physical harm began to decline. Punishment that resulted in physical suffering was abolished and replaced with "incarceration for a fixed period proportionate to the heinousness of the offence."[12] In 1807, the slave trade was abolished, and full emancipation occurred in 1834. Penal policy began to develop in the Cape. Slavery was a form of imprisonment, and the abolition of slavery caused the supply of labor on farms to suffer. A rudimentary pass system for indigenous inhabitants, later a well-known feature of apartheid, was introduced. Those who abused the system were put to work as prisoners.

The role of the state as the provider of unskilled Black labor for the mines through the penal system became manifest. Another aspect of penal policy that emerged in the 1880s was the first systematic attempt to segregate prisoners along racial lines. In 1888, the Act to Consolidate and Amend the Law Relating to Convict Stations and Prisons (Act 23 of 1888) was passed by the Cape Parliament. There was a shift to unite all places of confinement under a single prison system. There was also an introduction of gender-based classification and a proviso for the separation of different categories of offenders—for example, awaiting-trial offenders.

THE PRISON SYSTEM OF NATAL

For a substantial period, there was no true prison in Natal. In 1849, a brick building was established with a provision for ten communal cells. By 1907, because of the increasing offender population, this had increased to 260 cells. A prison was completed in 1863 with an initial number of twenty-five cells. This had expanded to 158 by 1907. The prison conditions were deleterious and unhygienic. Prisons were overcrowded, and there were fundamental shortcomings in the system. A recurrent problem was that of escapes and attempted escapes. Because of the overcrowded conditions in prisons, there was no question of classification. Corporal punishment was common and included the use of whips. Objections were raised against the use of this instrument, however, and the cane replaced the whip. There was no question of reform at this juncture because of the lack of scientific knowledge of crime causation and the inadequate facilities in the existing institutions.

In 1887, a tripartite classification system of "Europeans" (colored), "Indian," and "Native" (African) was adopted by government notice. This had a ripple effect in terms of segregated accommodation for prisoners. Prior to the Union in 1910, there was no major penal reform in Natal.

THE PRISON SYSTEM OF THE OFS AND TRANSVAAL

There is insufficient research into the development of the early prison system in both the OFS and the Transvaal. It emerged that in both the OFS and the South African Republic (Transvaal), the early Republican periods were characterized by low priority being given to the development of a prison system or a legislative framework to encompass it.

In the OFS, the first prison was introduced in Bloemfontein after 1854. By 1873, there were thirteen other institutions. The prison system used in the Cape and Natal was also applied here after the British occupation in 1902. The conditions in the prisons of the OFS were extremely inadequate. Although commissions were appointed to investigate prison conditions, nothing could be done about the matter due to limited funds for this purpose and the widespread poverty that prevailed in the Republic.

The Constitution at that time provided that prisoners had to do hard labor in public. During the 1840s and 1850s, offenders were made to build roads and, later, ships. These prisoners, who were sentenced to hard labor, had to be chained, and further provisions were made for sentencing prisoners to work for a maximum of five years under contract to a civilian with or without remuneration and with or without prior imprisonment. Section 6 of the Constitution (Constitutie van die Oranje Vrystaat) stipulated that if a prisoner refused to comply with the discipline, they could be sentenced to corporal punishment of not more than twenty-five lashes.

The first prison in Pretoria was built in 1865, and by 1893, there were already thirty-three penal institutions in the Transvaal. The British system was also applied here. In 1894, the system of internal discipline was reorganized, and the local *landdrost* was given exclusive jurisdiction to try cases of infringements of prison regulations. He could impose corporal punishment of up to twenty-five lashes; imprisonment of up to twelve months, with or without hard labor; or solitary confinement, with or without reduced rations, of up to seven days. The British occupation of the OFS and the Transvaal in the mid-1900s resulted in a reorganization of the penal systems of both territories. A Commission of Inquiry into conditions at the Fort in Johannesburg, one of the main prisons in the Transvaal, revealed that the prison system was inadequate and needed changes. The resultant reform to prison in the OFS and the Transvaal was the introduction of indeterminate sentences. Section 9 of the Criminal Law Amendment Act 38 of 1909 made provision for indeterminate detention to be hard labor for prisoners who had been declared by a court to be habitual criminals. Thus, the early part of the twentieth century saw the prison system regulated mainly by various Provincial Ordinances. The British occupation of the Transvaal and OFS Republic in 1900 led to a major reorganization of the penal systems in these provinces.[13]

AFTER THE UNION OF SOUTH AFRICA

In 1910, the year of the unification of South Africa, there was an endeavor to create a penal and prison policy for the country as a whole. This attempt was embodied in the Prisons and Reformatories Act of 1911 and in the institution of a Department of Prisons. This act repealed, either wholly or in part, all the legislation concerning the penal system, which had been in force in the four colonies before unification—that is, 1902–1910. As the title implies, the Prisons and Reformatories Act (Act 13 of 1911) sanctioned the responsibility of the management of reformatories onto the prison system. Courts started playing an increasing role in the development of prison law, inter alia, with findings that it was unlawful to detain prisoners awaiting trial in solitary confinement and the ruling that prisoners who felt they had been unfairly treated in prison had the legal right to approach courts of laws for intervention.

A Prison Board was instituted under Section 45 of the Prisons and Reformatories Act (Act 13 of 1911) to guarantee more effective treatment of convicts and prisoners and to provide better direction concerning the conditions in which prisoners should be granted remission of sentence. Section 25(3) of the new act made provision for the isolation of prisoners awaiting trial and their subjection to mechanical restraint "if the isolation or restraint is requested by the police authorities in the interests of justice." This period saw the introduction of a system that allowed for the remission of part of a prison sentence subject to good behavior on the part of the prisoner and the system of probation that allowed for the early release of prisoners, either directly into the community or through an interim period in a work colony or similar institution. Certain elements contained in the Prisons Act have formed an integral part of the present prison policy.

With regard to rehabilitation, although there was much speculation, little has materialized. Within the prison system, punishment for transgressions was extremely severe and harsh. It included whipping, solitary confinement, dietary punishment, and additional labor. The law prescribed racial segregation within the prison, and throughout the country, it was rigorously enforced. Prisons that were built in the twentieth century are still operational. These prisons were not designed for the rehabilitation of offenders but for the more cardinal purpose of keeping prisons foremost as places for punishment. To a considerable extent, the system that was set up by the 1911 Act remained captive to its own legal and social history. It was designed to imprison offenders, and efforts were made to segregate prisoners along racial lines. Undoubtedly, this led to the overcrowding of prisons because a majority of the general population consisted of non-Whites. In May 1910, there were 4 million Africans, 500,000 coloreds, 150,000 Indians, and 1,275,000 Whites in South African prisons. Whenever imprisonment was used, it was imposed disproportionately against the poor, the powerless, the marginalized, or those whom the repressive government deemed expedient to eliminate from society.

The Prisons and Reformatories Act (Act 13 of 1911) consolidated earlier colonial legislation, and strict segregation was enforced throughout the system. Thus, some of the most punitive features of prison systems of the four colonies survived unscathed. The development of the prison system was closely linked to the progressive institutionalization of racial discrimination in South Africa, starting from the time when widely enforced "pass laws" were introduced for Africans in the 1870s to the elaboration of an official theory and systematized practice of apartheid following the victory of the National Party in the election of 1984.[14]

Juvenile Justice in South Africa

Juvenile justice and child rights have been a subject of deep concern in South Africa. This concern has its roots in the immediate past of the country, when virtually all aspects of human and social life were based on and driven by a philosophy of institutionalized racial and other discrimination. The concern came to the fore during the protest and struggle against this system that was waged by children and adults and following mass political detentions of children in the 1970s and 1980s without trial and in violation of age-old due process of the law. In 1994, there were close to 2,000 children awaiting trial in South African prisons and police cells in grave conditions. This heightened concern has been manifested in the fact that one of the first goals announced by State President Nelson Mandela on taking office was to empty the prisons of children. Indeed, one of the early postapartheid legal reform measures was an amendment to Section 29 of the Correctional Services Act. The amendment provided that children under fourteen years of age awaiting trial could not be held for longer than twenty-four hours and that children between fourteen and eighteen years could not be held for longer than forty-eight hours.

Notwithstanding the fact that systematic mass violations of children's rights in the social, cultural, and economic realms, in addition to the political and civil realms, have been common in the recent past, there has until recently been little attention paid to the rights of children in South Africa. Indeed, the Convention on the Rights of the Child and several other instruments of international standards for children and adults were recognized in South Africa only following the installation of the Government of National Unity. Notably, the Convention on the Rights of the Child, ratified by both houses of Parliament on June 16, 1995, was the first international human rights treaty to be ratified since the installation of a nonracial government.

In the arena of juvenile justice, although there have been legal provisions for dealing with children in conflict with the law, these have been limited and are still scattered across four main statutes dealing with criminal procedures, probation services, child care, and correctional services. Within these four statutes, young offenders have been legislated for mostly under the Criminal Procedure Act of 1977 within narrow prosecutorial and due process orientations. The South African system for dealing with young offenders has been deemed inappropriate. Many of these statutes have been or are being amended in line with the provisions of the Convention on the Rights of the Child, particularly Articles 2, 3, 37, and 40, many of which have been entrenched in South Africa's new Constitution and its Bill of Rights. They are also being amended with reference to international standards for dealing with children in conflict with the law, juveniles deprived of their liberty, and juvenile delinquency, such as the Beijing Rules, the UN Rules for the Protection of Juveniles Deprived of their Liberty, the Riyadh Guidelines, and the African Charter on the Rights and Welfare of the Child in addition to the Convention on the Rights of the Child.

Despite the substantial progress being made toward meeting minimum standards, the criminogenic context in which juvenile justice exists is a negative one, and reports have suggested that the situation is not improving. According to the Department of Welfare, child and youth crime is on the increase. According to data from the DCS, the number of children awaiting trial in prisons and prison cells has been steadily increasing. The number of children awaiting trial in prisons and police cells increased from 537 at the end of July 1996 to 698 at the end of September 1996 and from 788 at the end of March 1997 to 931 at the end of May 1997. Furthermore, the number of children sentenced to imprisonment rose by 29.9 percent between July 1996 and July 1997. Alarmingly, the imprisonment of children aged from seven to fourteen years, many for economic offenses, has risen by 400 percent and accounts for by far the greatest imprisonment increase among all age groups. In addition, crimes committed by children and youth have become more violent, including offenses such as murder, rape, and armed robbery. The overwhelming majority of children arrested for such crimes happen to be Black children.[15]

The first attempt to reform inmates in South Africa has its origins in 1882, when the first reformatory was established. The Porter Reformatory was established not in the industrial heartland of the Northern Cape or Witwatersrand but in the commercial and agricultural hinterland of the Cape Colony. The main correctional program in the reformatory facility was placement of youth offenders on apprenticeship. However, not all youth offenders who were arrested were placed in the reformatory facility; youth offenders who were found pilfering and stealing stock from the farms were whipped or fined and released. Youth offenders who committed violent crimes were incarcerated together with adult prisoners.

During the 1850s, William Porter, the then attorney general of Cape Colony, emphasized that more focus should be placed on the offenders' social environment rather than taking delinquency as an innate attribute that cannot be treated. Porter's suggestion led to massive changes in correctional models, which now had to include schooling and training in agriculture. Porter's reformatory facility was redesigned to serve two main purposes. First, it had to remove the youth offenders from their degrading surroundings. Second, it had to separate juveniles from adult offenders in order to bring them within the ranks of wage earners so that they could become valuable assets to the colony. Methods for correcting youth offenders changed dramatically in the 1890s, when the colonial government took over these institutions and appointed a schoolmaster to head them. Youth offenders in these institutions were subjected to the same unyielding work routine and socialization. They were drilled into docility by a timetable characterized by military discipline. Later, industrial training was introduced, especially tailoring, carpentry, and blacksmithing. However, the purpose of these programs was never met, as there was a lack of trained instructors and equipment. During the weekend, religious instruction was also introduced.

Moreover, because of overcrowding, a lack of classification, and a militarized management style, the youth offenders developed subcultures that had some autonomous authority that was against the institution's authority. This caused a lot of conflict and violence in the institutions. There was also a lot of segregation based on color and race. White youth were channeled to industrial training, while Black youth were channeled to manual labor, such as gardening, milking, tendering cows, and working with horses. White youth also enjoyed extra privileges, such as going to bed at 8:00 p.m. instead of 6:00 p.m. They also had access to small libraries during their extra time. By the end of the century, as the Cape increasingly became industrialized, the focus on juveniles also shifted northward. In 1900, provision was also made in the Porter system for the detention of juvenile offenders across Orange River Colony and the Transvaal. In the early 1990s, rehabilitative models also shifted and borrowed from positivist criminology. Interest shifted to the investigation of youth offenders' social environments and especially to their family backgrounds.[16]

In South Africa, by May 31, 2021, there were fifty-five children in remand detention, 5,105 juveniles awaiting trial, and 1,503 juveniles sentenced. Between 2019 and 2020, there were 2,058 juveniles already sentenced and 3,724 in remand. Furthermore, the South African government, through the Department of Social Development, has a blueprint for the rehabilitation of juveniles in the form of a policy framework and a national action plan. This provides a clear path for addressing the problem of juvenile delinquency. The six key strategies of the action plan involve strengthening the capacities of families who take care of orphans and vulnerable children, rehabilitating hard-core delinquents through institutionalization, mobilizing community-based interventions, providing support and protection to orphans and vulnerable children, ensuring regular access to social services by all children regardless of their social status, and ensuring that legislation, policy, and programs are in place to assist the most vulnerable members of the society.

UNICEF INTERVENTIONS

UNICEF's program of cooperation in South Africa is, in essence, knowledge-intensive cooperation. The program is based on five strategies, namely, advocacy/networking, social policy development, capacity building, child-focused monitoring, and the demonstration of effective approaches for dealing with basic social services. UNICEF assistance for the process of reforming juvenile justice has been at various levels.

First, and less directly, there has been substantial advocacy and financial and technical assistance for the establishment and development of the National Prosecuting Authority (NPA) process. This assistance dates from the early 1990s to 1995, when UNICEF provided catalytic support for situation analyses, social mobilization and child rights promotion, and policy development objectives. This assistance was intended to identify and highlight the plight and specific problems of children, including children in conflict with the law, and to build consensus and understanding around the principles of the Convention on the Rights of the Child before the signing and ratification of the convention. Some major outcomes of this assistance were the following:

- The formation and organization of a broad alliance of child rights activists, advocates, politicians, and researchers and child and youth service workers in various areas of child rights, including juvenile justice
- The production of the first national situation analysis of children and women in South Africa, which supported the establishment of a national consensus on various problems and on proposed policy and legal measures for the benefit of children and youth, including the ratification of the Convention on the Rights of the Child and the introduction, improvement, and augmentation of services for children and youth in various areas, including juvenile justice
- The formulation of an NPA outline, which was handed over to the new Government of National Unity shortly after its installation in April 1994, for adoption and for further development within formal governance mechanisms (This outline included actions for children in conflict with the law.)
- The integration of children's issues, including juvenile justice issues, in the Reconstruction and Development Program White Paper
- The establishment in December 1994 of an interministerial Core Cabinet Committee on the NPA to oversee and ensure the development, implementation, and monitoring of an NPA (This included responsibility for ensuring ratification of the Convention on the Rights of the Child.)
- The establishment in January 1995 of a standing technical steering committee to work regularly on matters of the NPA (This standing committee is composed of representatives from various national departments, representatives of all provinces, and representatives of nongovernmental organizations and UNICEF.)
- The formation of NPA sectoral working groups (with intersectoral participation) on key sectors, such as justice, education, children in especially difficult circumstances, health and nutrition, and water and sanitation
- The formation of standing intersectoral provincial NPA working groups

Second, and more directly, UNICEF, in addition to ongoing advocacy and networking activities, has provided the following assistance for areas concerning juvenile justice:

- Ongoing technical and advisory assistance for the NPA working group on justice and welfare concerning policy and programmatic issues relating to children in conflict with the law and juveniles deprived of their liberty
- Modest financial and advisory assistance to the South African Litigation Centre on the juvenile justice project (This has included the development of an awareness package aimed at eliciting public input and participation in the development of juvenile justice legislation and public workshops to discuss the proposals in the juvenile justice issues paper.)
- Modest advisory assistance to the Inter-Ministerial Committee on Young People at Risk, specifically the subcommittee on juveniles awaiting trial, which is working on issues such as the monitoring of juveniles awaiting trial through police-based systems and facilitating experience exchanges with Namibia
- Financial assistance for the National Institute for Crime Prevention and the Rehabilitation of Offenders to undertake research on prosecutorial attitudes toward diversion (This research is expected to be useful in the formulation of new juvenile justice legislation and the development and the expansion of diversion programs in addition to providing input for advocacy.)[17]

Lessons and Conclusions

The South African experience in the area of juvenile justice makes clear that not only does it take a whole village to raise a child, as the African saying goes, but it takes a whole society in its many dimensions, forms, and constituents to bring to fruition the rights of children, including those rights of children in need of special protection.

The first lesson that can be drawn from the South African experience is that it is important to underpin integrated, multisectoral national plans and programs with intersectoral, interdepartmental, and intersocietal planning and monitoring processes.

The second lesson is that the management of these processes stands to benefit a great deal from the deep involvement of child rights advocates and activist specialists in the area of child protection law. It has become increasingly clear in South Africa that, while mainstreaming goals and child-centered reform initiatives into the development plans and work processes of government departments and agencies is essential, this mainstreaming needs to be supported, strengthened, and, in many cases, catalyzed by committed nongovernmental organizations and child rights activists.

The third lesson is that a one-off political commitment and developing a sole "process" to address the plight of children who are in conflict with the law and juveniles who are deprived of their liberty may not be sufficient. The fourth lesson is that it is essential to have an effective monitoring mechanism that regularly provides data, in quantitative and qualitative terms, on practices and quality so as to inform policy and program development. The fifth lesson is that there is a need to sensitize the actors in the area of juvenile justice and the public about the importance of a restorative approach to juvenile justice that focuses on setting wrongs right through healing and accountability, through learning processes, and through efforts to reintegrate juveniles into society in ways that are in line with the Convention on the Rights of the Child and the Beijing Rules.

The South African experience shows the importance of and need for a juvenile justice system through which contradictions, gaps, and weaknesses in legislation regarding children who are in conflict with the law and juveniles who are deprived of their liberty can become more apparent and more easily addressed. A coherent and unified system is instrumental since it would bring together various pieces of legislation and illuminate the different actors and their complementary roles in this trans-sectoral arena. It would also help to establish understanding and to foster intersectoral, interdepartmental collaboration. Finally and critically, it could, through multilevel causal analyses, help clarify the responsibilities and the relationships among the various actors and their actions, lending itself to the wider implementation of the Convention on the Rights of the Child and helping to reveal the truth that juvenile justice objectives related to both crime-related justice and social justice can be attained only through the development and implementation of informed social and economic policies, legal reforms, and specialized educational programs.

Notes

1. African National Congress, *52nd National Conference Resolutions 2007*, 2007, http://www.anc.org.za/ancdocs/conference52/resolutions.html.
2. E. Pelser and J. Rauch, *South Africa's Criminal Justice System: Policy and Priorities*, 2001, https://www.files.ethz.ch/isn/104998/southafricascriminal.pdf.
3. P. Gastrow and M. Shaw, "In Search of Safety: Police Transformation and Public Responses in South Africa," *Daedalus* 130, no. 1 (2001): 259–75.
4. J. D. Iwarimie, *Criminology: The Study of Crime*, 3rd ed. (Owerri: Imo State Spring Field, 2003).
5. L. Siegel, *Criminology*, 8th ed. (Belmont, CA: Cengage Learning, 2022).
6. South African Republic, Promotion of Equality and Prevention of Unfair Discrimination Act, February 9, 2000, https://www.gov.za/sites/default/files/gcis_ document/201409/a4-001.pdf.
7. National Crime Prevention Strategy (1995).
8. C. E. Stone and H. H. Ward, "Democratic Policing: A Framework for Action," *Policing and Society* 10 (2000): 11–45.
9. "The South African Judiciary," Constitutional Court Justices of South Africa, June 2014, https://www.judiciary.org.za/index.php/documents/ publications/ category/55-judiciary-publications?download=218:the-south-african-judiciary.
10. South African Republic, Criminal Procedure Act 51 of 1977, April 21, 1977, https://www.justice.gov.za/legislation/acts/1977-051.pdf.
11. *Mvelaphanda Strategic Plan (2002–2005)* (Pretoria: Government Printer, 2002).
12. E. O. Mavulele, *Transformative Reform Process of South African Prison System* (Pretoria: Greenwood Publishing Group, 2008).
13. F. T. Murenga, "An Analysis of South African Prison System," master's thesis, Egerton University, 2010.
14. T. Leggett, "Just Another Miracle: A Decade of Crime and Justice in Democratic South Africa," *Social Research* 72, no. 3 (2005): 581–604.

15. Department of Correctional Services, *Progressive Reports, 1996–2000* (Pretoria: Government Printer, 2000).

16. K. H. Maurice, *Comparative Juvenile Justice Systems: Children in Conflict with the Law* (Nairobi: Zee and Cee, 2020).

17. "How Does the Criminal Justice System Work?" South African Government, accessed June 20, 2022, https://www.gov.za/faq/justice-and-crime-prevention/how-does-criminal-justice-system-work.

Part 2

EAST ASIA AND THE PACIFIC

CHAPTER 4

The Australian Criminal Justice System

FEDERAL AND STATE JURISDICTIONS

Mark F. Briskey and Samuel M. Makinda

This chapter examines the judiciary, policing, and corrective services that constitute the Australian justice system. A critical overview of this system from the initial White settlement in 1788 to now reveals at least three crucial elements. The first is that the establishment of Australia as a White penal colony, which uprooted indigenous people from their ancestral land, was representative of the initial criminal justice system. The second is that the system has been so transformed and become so accommodating that its broad objectives, which are cosmopolitan, include the championing of racial equality, gender equality, marriage equality, and other fundamental rights. The third element is that as of early 2022, the Australian justice system is heavily tilted against the first Australians, who are disadvantaged in many respects and incarcerated in large numbers.

But what are the origins of the Australian justice system? How is it organized across the country in the federal and state spheres of government? What challenges has the system faced over the years, and how has it addressed them? What methods of criminal justice has the Australian system adopted? These and similar questions guide this chapter's analysis.

The Commonwealth of Australia is a constitutional monarchy and parliamentary democracy. It is also a federation of six states—New South Wales (NSW), Queensland (QLD), South Australia (SA), Tasmania (TAS), Victoria (VIC), and Western Australia (WA)—and two major mainland territories—the Australian Capital Territory (ACT), in which Australia's capital city of Canberra is located, and the Northern Territory (NT).

Its written Constitution, which came into effect on January 1, 1901, establishes the institutions and prescribes the functional framework of Australian national politics.[1] While many of the institutions, rules, and procedures for the Australian federal government can be described through direct reference to the Constitution, some of the most vital features of government, such as the office of prime minister, are not mentioned in the written Constitution.[2] The Constitution sets out to limit the powers of government over the people, though this is somewhat diminished because of the continuing responsibilities of the powers that the states have reserved to themselves and the constitutional safeguards that prevent the federal government from encroaching on the states.

The Australian Constitution provides that all new legislation passed in Parliament be tested against its own constitutional clauses. The High Court has the power to declare any legislation unconstitutional and therefore invalid if it is inconsistent with the provisions of the Constitution. It can also rule in situations in which executive action clearly transgresses the rights of citizens.[3] The states and territories hold legislative powers for the administration of criminal justice within their jurisdictions. They have separate and independent systems of police, courts, prisons, juvenile institutions, and other corrective and treatment services. Therefore, Australia has no single criminal justice system. This analysis begins with the judiciary.

The Judiciary in Australia

As much of the state-based judicial systems in Australia are similar, this chapter provides a comprehensive focus on just two of them: the QLD and NSW systems. This will, in turn, offer a more in-depth appreciation of the history, organization, and operations of the justice system in Australia within the available space. The following account of these two states' judiciary systems incorporates most of the features and characteristics of the judicial systems in the other Australian states and territories.

There is no general power in the Australian Constitution that allows the Commonwealth Parliament to enact uniform criminal laws for the whole country.[4] Until the 1970s, the Commonwealth had relatively little involvement with criminal law, as the existing legislations were usually tied to trade and commercial matters. There were also a few legislative measures that protected the Commonwealth from fraud. The two recent major expansions of federal laws have been on terrorism and illicit drugs, with national security having become a priority area in criminal law since the 9/11 terrorist attacks in the United States.

The Australian judiciary operates within the doctrine of separation of powers. This doctrine underpins the Australian democratic structure and its inherent system of checks and balances. Under this system, the Parliament enacts the laws, which are implemented by the executive and interpreted by the judiciary. However, unlike in the United States, there is a limited fusion between the executive and legislature because the cabinet in Australia straddles the executive and the Parliament.

The judiciary is separate from both the executive and the legislature. The Australian Constitution allows the judiciary independence in interpreting and applying the law without interference. This judicial independence is supported by constitutional guarantees of tenure and recompense. In Australian federal jurisdictions, judicial officers are appointed by the government, and they cannot be removed from office unless incapacity or misbehavior is proven. Moreover, to support judicial independence, the remuneration of judicial officers cannot be reduced while they hold office.

THE HIGH COURT OF AUSTRALIA

Chapter III of the Australian Constitution establishes the High Court. It also empowers Parliament to create other federal courts and to vest federal judicial power in state and territory courts within three primary federal courts. The High Court, which comprises seven judges, is the highest and final court of appeal. Over the years, it has played a crucial role in expanding the scope of human rights. It was established in 1903 and deals with matters relating to many issues, including disputes on the meaning of the Constitution as well as final appeals in civil and criminal matters from all courts in Australia. It did not become the final court of appeal until the right to appeal to the Privy Council in the United Kingdom was gradually ended between 1968 and 1986. The Privy Council (Limitation of Appeals) Act 1968 and the Privy Council (Appeals from the High Court) Act 1975 ended appeals to the Privy Council from the High Court. However, this right of appeal remained with state courts until the enactment of the Australia Acts, both state and federal, in 1986.

The High Court's transformative power was demonstrated in 1992, when it agreed with Eddie Mabo, who challenged the legal fiction that aboriginal and Torres Strait Islander peoples had no rights to their ancestral lands. By agreeing with Mabo that indigenous people had tenure in some areas, the High Court overturned the doctrine of terra nullius.[5] Moreover, several eminent jurists from the High Court have undertaken significant international roles. For example, Justice Michael Kirby, a former judge of the High Court of Australia from 1996 to 2009, was appointed chairperson of the UN Commission of Inquiry in the Democratic People's Republic of Korea from 2013 to 2014.[6] Earlier, former Chief Justice of the High Court Owen Dixon was appointed as UN mediator in the India–Pakistan Kashmir dispute in 1950.[7]

FEDERAL COURT OF AUSTRALIA

The Federal Court, established in 1976, is ranked at the same level as supreme courts at the state/territory level. It deals with matters on a range of subjects, including bankruptcy, corporations, industrial relations, native title (a result of the Mabo case), taxation, and trade practices. Its decisions have also played important roles in transforming Australia's social, economic, and financial sectors. This court also hears appeals from some judgments of the Federal Circuit and Family Court, with the exception of family law decisions.

THE FEDERAL CIRCUIT AND FAMILY COURT OF AUSTRALIA

The Federal Circuit and Family Court (FCFC) started operations on September 1, 2021. It is an amalgamation of two courts that had jurisdiction over family law matters, the Family Court of Australia and the Federal Circuit Court of Australia, which now exist as two divisions within one administrative structure.

Since its establishment in 1976, the Family Court has been a specialist court dealing with family issues, including divorce, parenting disputes, and division of property. This Court is notable in that it was subject to a series of violent attacks over a five-year period during the 1980s when a bomber killed one judge, killed another judge's wife, attempted to kill another judge, and bombed court buildings.[8] This was the first time a judge had been targeted in Australia. It was only relatively recent forensic evidence that related in the successful conviction in 2020 of the bomber, who was sentenced to the term of his natural life.[9] The Family Court faced these problems partly because of its role in upholding gender equality and, thereby, in transforming Australia's social structure.

The Family Court's counterpart—the Federal Circuit Court—deals with matters relating to family law and child support, administrative law, admiralty law, bankruptcy, copyright, human rights, industrial law, migration, privacy, and trade practices. Prior to 2013, the Federal Circuit Court was referred to as the Federal Magistrates Court. At that time, the titles of "chief federal magistrate" and "federal magistrate" were changed to "chief judge" and "judge," respectively. Under the 2021 administrative structure, the FCFC became the only Australian federal court with jurisdiction over all issues related to family law.

NSW State Court System

Sydney, in NSW, was the site of the first British colonial settlement in Australia. The British did not recognize the indigenous inhabitants and introduced the doctrine of terra nullius, meaning that the country was uninhabited prior to colonization. Unsurprisingly, the main colonial source of revenue was crown land, so it was considered essential that the colonial government had control of land without any concern for the rights of the indigenous inhabitants.[10] From the moment the first fleet landed at Botany Bay in NSW, land was at the center of the struggle between indigenous Australians and the settlers, as it would be in all subsequent colonies in Australia.[11]

Although the High Court's judgment in the 1992 Mabo case overturned terra nullius, in the same judgment, the High Court accepted the 1788 British assertion of sovereignty and asserted that, from that time, there was only one sovereign power and one system of law in Australia.[12] NSW was founded as a penal colony for prisoners from the United Kingdom and their accompanying military guards. The death penalty, which was widely used in the colonial era, was abolished in NSW in 1955, though some provisions for it with regard to piracy and treason were not fully abolished until 1985. The last person executed in NSW was John Kelly, in 1939, for murder.[13]

The NSW justice system is two tiered and consists of lower and higher courts. The lower courts include the Local Court and Children's Court. The Local Court, referred to as a Magistrates Court in some other Australian jurisdictions, deals with the majority of criminal charges against adult offenders. The Local Court also holds committal hearings for indictable serious criminal matters to decide on whether individuals should be committed to trial. Some indictable matters may be determined by the Local Court if the defendant so elects. The Local Court also encompasses a function as a Children's Court involving primarily juvenile offenders aged between ten and seventeen years. In some circumstances, charges against offenders aged eighteen years or over may be heard before the Children's Court. Local and Children's Court proceedings are conducted by a magistrate. There are no juries in either of these courts.

NSW HIGHER COURTS

The District Court and the Supreme Court, including the NSW Court of Appeal, constitute the NSW Higher Courts. The District Court deals with more serious offenses committed by both juveniles and adults. District Court proceedings are presided over by a District Court judge. The District Court hears trials, sentencing matters, and appeals against decisions made in the lower courts. In most cases in which the accused person pleads not guilty, trials are held before a judge and jury. If the jury delivers a verdict of guilt, then the judge determines an appropriate penalty. In some circumstances, the accused may elect to be tried before a judge, forgoing a jury. When a person admits guilt, there is no jury trial, and the matter proceeds to sentencing.

The Supreme Court conducts trials before a judge and jury for a few offenses that are more serious than those that are heard in the District Court, such as murder. As in the District Court, in certain circumstances, the accused may elect to be tried by a judge without a jury. The Supreme Court judge may also adjudicate without a jury on certain offenses, particularly those that carry heavy fines. The Court of Criminal Appeal, which is a special division of the Supreme Court, hears appeals against convictions and sentences from the District Court and from the Supreme Court. An appeal is conducted in the presence of three Supreme Court judges. The Court of Criminal Appeal is the ultimate court of appeal for criminal matters in NSW.

As an alternative to entering the court system, juveniles charged with relatively minor offenses may be dealt with by a system of formal police cautions. Cautions to juveniles are issued by senior police officers in the presence of the offenders and their parents or guardians.

QLD State Court Systems

The QLD judicial system includes a range of courts, such as the Magistrates Court, District Court, Supreme Court, Children's Court, and a number of specialized courts that deal specifically with indigenous Australians and domestic violence, among other issues.[14] These courts hear civil and criminal cases. Civil cases in Australian jurisdictions may be described as disputes between two or more persons or organizations whereby one sues the other, usually for compensation for a harm done or a loss that was sustained. Criminal cases involve offenses against the broader community, ranging from littering to murder.

Magistrates Courts can hear cases in 131 locations throughout QLD, while the Supreme and District Courts sit in eleven and thirty-eight locations, respectively.

Judges also travel regularly throughout the state to hear cases in towns and remote areas. QLD is Australia's second-largest state in landmass and by comparison is about 2.4 times larger than the U.S. state of Texas. This means that a travel circuit for a judge can take up considerable time in travel and execution of court duties.

THE SUPREME COURT OF QLD AND THE COURT OF APPEAL

The Court of Appeal is a division of the Supreme Court of QLD and hears all appeals from the Supreme and District Courts and tribunals. It does not hear entire cases or have a jury. This court only adjudicates on the subject of the appeal. It comprises three or five judges of the Supreme Court who hear arguments by the opposing sides and decide whether an error of law was made or some crucial fact was overlooked in the original hearing. The Court of Appeal hears both civil and criminal cases. In an appeal hearing, a judge makes all decisions.

The Court of Appeal may decide to dismiss an appeal or to uphold the decision of a lower court or tribunal; if a decision is upheld, then nothing changes. Alternatively, the Court of Appeal may allow the appeal and set aside the decision of the lower court and make a different decision in its place or order a retrial. If an application is to appeal against a sentence, the Court can increase or decrease the length of the sentence. If the Court is considering increasing the sentence on appeal, it will inform the applicant so that that person may withdraw the application. If the QLD attorney general appeals, then the sentence may be increased.[15]

The trial division of the Supreme Court hears the most serious criminal cases, including murder, manslaughter, and serious drug offenses. This division also hears all civil matters involving amounts over AUD$750,000, which is about the equivalent of U.S.$535,950.

QLD CRIMINAL AND CIVIL TRIAL

The outward features of an Australian trial would be familiar to many common law jurisdictions around the world. In a criminal trial, a jury of twelve people selected at random is subject to peremptory challenges by the defense and prosecution solicitors or barristers. Barristers are independent advisers in law and advocacy who specialize in dispute resolution; they hold the requisite training both to anticipate a likely range of outcomes and to choose the most prudent path for their client and their client's solicitor or lawyer. Following jury selection in a criminal trial, the jury then hears the facts of the case and decides whether an accused receives a verdict of guilty or not guilty. A judge makes all other decisions, including penalties. If a criminal trial is held without a jury, then the judge decides whether an accused is guilty. Evidence against the accused is presented by the prosecutor from the Office of the Director of Public Prosecutions. The person charged with the offense and accused of its commission is referred to as the "accused." In Australian criminal trials, including those in QLD, the accused may be represented by a solicitor and/or a barrister.

Some senior barristers in Australia receive what is referred to as "silk," which designates them as Queen's Counsel (QC) in the past or as Senior Counsel (SC) now, with this designation providing a public identification of their outstanding service as advocates.[16] As with other high-performing legal advocates in other common law jurisdictions, Australian barristers can earn thousands of dollars a day for their services and, like the late Chester Porter QC, become known nationally during high-profile trials.[17]

In a civil trial, the evidence against the defendant is presented by the plaintiff, who is the person or organization that commenced the civil proceeding and who may be represented by a solicitor and/or a barrister. The defendant, known as the "respondent," is the person whom the civil proceeding is brought against and who may also be represented by a solicitor and/or barrister. In a civil trial, a judge makes all decisions, including orders that one party pay another or perform certain actions to rectify a problem. On rare occasions, a civil trial may be held with a jury of four people whose task is to answer any question of fact put to it by the judge.

Persons who may attend an Australian court trial include the judge's associate, who assists the judge with proceedings, which may include reading out the charges, calling the names of prospective jurors, and reading documents to the court. Other Australian court personnel common to QLD and other Australian states include the bailiff, who calls witnesses and asks for their oath or affirmation before giving evidence, ensures the good order of the jury, and announces the beginning and end of the court session. Additionally, depending on the matter being heard in criminal and civil trials, numerous witnesses may provide evidence on behalf of either party. Interpreters are also commonly used in Australian courts to assist proceedings. In a criminal trial involving transnational drug smuggling, for example, there may be interpreters and translators required to assist the accused, provide translations of intercepted communications in foreign languages for the court, or translate documents being presented as evidence.

The public and media may attend these proceedings, unless the reporting is restricted because of the nature of cases with, for example, children involved or in other situations, as ordered by the judge. In some criminal matters, courts have been closed if there are national security implications, though these rulings can be contested thanks to an October 2021 decision overturning a government bid to have evidence hidden at trial in the case of an Australian intelligence officer and his lawyer.[18]

QLD DISTRICT COURT

A District Court deals with serious criminal offenses such as rape, armed robbery, serious assaults, and fraud. It is the first court in the hierarchy that involves a jury. This court also has a role in hearing appeals from cases decided in the lower Magistrates Court as well as on disputes involving amounts between AUD$150,000 and AUD$750,000. Unlike a criminal case, a civil action can be commenced and heard in the District Court without first being heard in the Magistrates Court. The majority of appeals against decisions decided in the Magistrates Court are also heard in the District Court. There are eight District Courts throughout QLD, with about forty District

Court judges.[19] The District Court hears more than 7,000 criminal and 1,000 civil matters each year. District Court judges also periodically visit QLD regional centers.

QLD MAGISTRATES COURT

The Magistrates Court is the first level of the QLD Courts system and hears about 95 percent of court cases, both criminal and civil. There are around 130 locations where Magistrates Courts may sit. A person charged with a criminal offense must be brought before the Magistrates Court as soon as possible after being charged. Unlike the Supreme and District Courts, Magistrates Courts have no jury. Therefore, the magistrate makes all decisions in criminal matters, including any penalty, and in civil matters, including an order that one side pay the other money or perform certain actions to rectify a problem.

The Magistrates Court deals with a range of offenses, including less serious offenses, such as traffic infringements, shoplifting, disorderly behavior, and driving under the influence of alcohol, as well as more serious offenses, such as burglary, assault, fraud, and some drug offenses. When the offense is more serious, the magistrate may commit the case to a higher court for sentence or trial. The Magistrates Court deals with civil cases if the amount in dispute is $150,000 or less as well as with some minor family law matters, domestic violence matters, and federal matters, such as those covered by the Customs Act 1901, the Social Security Act 1991, and the Taxation Act 1953.

QLD DRUG COURTS

Drug Courts treat offenders who have severe substance-use disorders that have contributed to their offending behavior. The QLD Drug and Alcohol Court may order that adult offenders be supervised and undertake treatment to address their drug and/or alcohol dependency issues and criminal offenses. The Drug and Alcohol Court commenced in QLD's state capital, Brisbane, on January 29, 2018, with the objectives of providing a judicially supervised, therapeutically oriented, integrated treatment regime in order to reduce the level of criminal activity associated with substance abuse and to reintegrate the sufferer into the community.[20]

QLD CORONERS COURT

In Australian states, coroners are responsible for investigating reportable deaths. In QLD, this duty is within the Coroners Act 2003. Coronial inquests are not held for every death; however, for certain categories of deaths, such as deaths in custody, an inquest is required. The overarching focus of Australian Coroners Courts is to determine what happened and to make recommendations in order to prevent similar deaths in the future.

THE MURRI COURT IN QLD

Some Australian states have established specialized courts for First Nations people. In QLD, this is the Murri Court, which links aboriginal and Torres Strait Islander defendants to cultural and support services that help prevent reoffending. "Murri" is a demonym for the indigenous peoples of QLD and northern NSW. Murri Courts feature the involvement of elders or respected persons from the community who are present in the courtroom to guide defendants and to assist magistrates in understanding cultural matters attached to the defendant and their offense. The Murri Court also seeks to increase Aboriginal and Torres Strait Islander people's confidence when having interactions with the criminal justice system and to help reduce their overrepresentation within correctional settings.[21]

QLD SPECIALIST DOMESTIC AND FAMILY VIOLENCE COURT

A Specialist Domestic and Family Violence (DFV) Court adjudicates exclusively on civil and criminal matters as well as culturally responsive Aboriginal and Torres Strait Islander DFV matters. These DFV Courts feature magistrates with expertise in DFV issues and a specialist DFV Court registry office, where specialist court staff offer support, information, and domestic and family violence programs for victims and perpetrators.

QLD MENTAL HEALTH COURT

The Mental Health Court decides the state of mind of people charged with criminal offenses. This court's primary objective is to decide whether an alleged offender was of unsound mind when committing an offense. It also determines whether the alleged offender is fit to undergo a trial. Additionally, this court not only hears appeals from the Mental Health Review Tribunal but also inquires into the lawfulness of a patient's detention in authorized mental health facilities.

CHILDREN'S COURT OF QLD

In QLD, criminal matters involving children are dealt with in the Children's Court of QLD (CCQ). This court is constituted by either an appointed CCQ judge or other District Court judge if a CCQ judge is unavailable. Alternatively, it may be constituted by an appointed CCQ magistrate or other magistrate if a CCQ magistrate is unavailable. The CCQ also hears matters involving child protection and certain adoption cases. It is important to note that the CCQ is not the same as the Family Court of Australia, which is a federal court dealing with other family-related matters.

All CCQ proceedings in the Magistrates Court are heard in a closed court; only people directly involved in the case may be present, and no information identifying a juvenile defendant can be published.[22] Some matters involving juveniles are heard in the District Court by the CCQ, including those involving serious crimes.

Policing in Australia

Like the judiciary and the correctional system, police services and cognate agencies fall into national, state, or territory jurisdictions. These jurisdictional boundaries date back to the second half of the nineteenth century and have been modified over time through the enactment of police acts and regulations throughout the colonies and, later, states and territories.[23] This jurisdictional feature of Australian policing and law enforcement differentiates policing in Australia from many other countries, including the United Kingdom, from which Australian policing models were drawn.

Another significant difference that distinguishes the Australian model is its primary centralization of policing within state jurisdictions rather than on a municipal basis as in the United States. Australia does not have county, city, or localized policing as the United States does. Neither does Australia have the equivalent of police departments attached to institutions such as universities and colleges, which in the United States often have their own campus police. In Australia, the state police undertake all these functions, and the federal police, in a uniformed capacity, have a small community policing role in the Australian Capital Territory and several other small jurisdictions.

However, policing in Australia is similar to policing in other jurisdictions throughout the world. As with other modern policing services, the primary duties of Australian policing services are the prevention, detection, and investigation of crime and the maintenance of civil order. Depending on location, police in Australia may also perform a diverse range of other duties for their states, from the issuance of stock permits to court duties; prosecuting summary offenses; driver's license testing; fisheries, firearm, and wildlife inspection duties; and other cognate roles. Between 2020 and 2021, Australian police forces were also involved in ensuring that Australians observed the restrictions relating to COVID-19. All police services in Australia, except for the Australian Federal Police (AFP) and other federal entities, are controlled by state and territory governments, usually under a minister of police. Uniformed and plainclothes police in Australia carry sidearms, pepper spray, handcuffs, and other defensive and offensive equipment—from Tasers to protective vests and clothing—as deemed necessary for their duties.

The AFP, with assistance from state police services, also undertakes peace and stabilization missions with members of the Australian Defence Force. A notable long-term mission in this regard was the Regional Assistance Mission to the Solomon Islands between 2003 and 2017 to restore peace after conflict between ethnic militant groups.[24] Australian police returned at the request of the Solomon Islands government in late November 2021 to help authorities quell the violent rioting and civil disorder that left several people dead and substantially damaged infrastructure.[25]

The federal police role in investigating terrorism, drug offenses, and several other federal offenses means that, occasionally, AFP and state police, while investigating an offense within their jurisdiction, will discover crimes outside of their jurisdiction. In

Australia, "application of laws" legislation allows for the assessment or examination of multi-jurisdictional crimes in the course of an investigation. The history of Australian policing features a great deal of cooperation in the form of joint crime investigation and intelligence collection task forces that have both formal legislative status and informal arrangements, such as memorandums of understanding. The centralization of much criminal intelligence, for example, is conducted by the Australian Criminal Intelligence Commission.[26]

Australian police services also include numerous specialized units. Undercover police are part of covert operations. Stock Squad police specialize in the large-scale theft of cattle, sheep, and other rural commodities. Special operations and weapons units undertake the resolution of events with a high propensity for violence. Technical units install listening devices and transport serious offenders. Specialized child-sex-offender units investigate online offenders. Water police and Air Wing police address matters pertaining to marine and aviation issues, respectively. Other specialized police provide witness security, forensics, family liaison, hostage negotiation, and UN peacekeeping services. Some specialized police serve in long-term deployments to Australian embassies and high commissions in order to expedite transnational crime investigations and capacity-building ventures with host government agencies.

Australian policing, like other modern police services, has introduced a raft of developments from recommendations made in the findings of royal commissions as well as being introduced by progressive police administrators to address issues of technology, domestic violence and the murder of Australian women, and community policing. Australia has embraced the concept of community policing from the 1970s. The premise of community policing is that the community should be involved in questions of policing needs in consultation with the police. In several Australian jurisdictions, this move to proactive policing that derives from community needs is visible in the establishment of neighborhood watch programs, police shop fronts, police youth clubs, electronic alert systems, surveys, and police–community consultation forums on a range of issues from community policing needs to assessments of police effectiveness. Although community policing has been criticized as being tokenistic in several jurisdictions, a number of community policing initiatives, as well as the move away from a reactive "fire brigade" policing model, have had a few positive outcomes.

Another way in which federal and state policing agencies in Australia and those in other countries have made developments is through the adoption of innovative intelligence-led policing approaches to preventing as well as supporting the investigation of crime. The objective of intelligence-led policing is to move from a "'reactive' or 'prosecution-directed' mode of policing" to more proactive methods.[27] Under this model, widely adopted in the United Kingdom and other jurisdictions around the globe, the underlying premise is that "crime intelligence should guide operations rather than operations dictating intelligence-gathering priorities."[28] Australian policing agencies also undertake joint-agency transnational criminal intelligence operations. A recent notable success involving the AFP and the U.S. Federal Bureau of Investigation was Operation Ironside, a three-year covert investigation in which the encrypted communications of organized crime were targeted. The operation resulted in the arrest of 224 Australian offenders alleged to be members of the Australia-based Italian mafia, outlaw motorcycle gangs, Asian crime syndicates, and Albanian organized crime in every mainland state of Australia. It also led to the seizure of 3.7 tons of drugs, 104 weapons, and AUD$52 million. Additionally, the AFP saved many lives after passing intelligence to state policing agencies on twenty death threats.[29]

AUSTRALIAN CORRECTIONAL SYSTEM AND PUNISHMENT

In 1788, Australia began as a penal colony for British convicts who were sentenced to deportation. With the loss of the American colonies and prison hulks of Britain overflowing, Britain decided to settle the Australian continent that had been explored by Captain James Cook nearly twenty years previously. Strategically, the British also wished to secure the Australian continent from the French, who had been exploring its coast. Louis François Marie Aleno de Saint Aloüarn laid claim to territory in WA in 1772. The transportation of convicts to the Australian continent continued until British reformers increasingly attacked the ethics and practice of the convict system, especially from the 1830s.[30]

In Australia in the nineteenth century, as many as eighty persons per year were hanged for crimes such as burglary, sheep stealing, forgery, sexual assault, and even, in one case, "being illegally at large" as well as for murder and manslaughter. This was at a time when the population of Australia was in the hundreds of thousands rather than its 2021 population of nearly 26 million.

Since the federation of the Australian colonies into the Commonwealth of Australia in 1901, only 114 persons have been legally executed in Australia.[31] The death penalty was officially abolished in 1973. In 2010, the Commonwealth Parliament passed the Crimes Legislation Amendment (Torture Prohibition and Death Penalty Abolition) Act. This act amends the Death Penalty Abolition Act 1973 (Commonwealth) to extend the current Commonwealth prohibition on the death penalty to all states and territories. This amendment foreclosed the possibility of any individual state jurisdiction reintroducing the death penalty. It also prohibited the Commonwealth from deporting or allowing to be extradited a prisoner to another jurisdiction if that prisoner might face the death penalty.[32] This became a contentious issue between the QLD state government and the U.S. state of Alabama, where the QLD government sought a guarantee from Alabama that it would not execute U.S. citizen Gabe Watson for the drowning death of his wife, Tina, on their honeymoon in 2003.[33]

PUNISHMENT IN AUSTRALIAN CORRECTION SYSTEMS

Even though the period between 2002 and 2016 saw substantial reductions in a number of major categories of crime in Australia, including murder, robbery, burglary, breaking and entering, and motor-vehicle theft, the rate of imprisonment in Australia grew by 36 percent, which may have been the result of changes in policing policy, especially regarding domestic violence and drug crimes.[34]

In March 2021, Australia had 42,908 persons incarcerated in state and nonstate prisons, representing an imprisonment rate of 167 per 100,000 of a complete Australian population of 25.7 million.[35] Of those incarcerated, 7.7 percent were female, and 17.1 percent were foreign prisoners imprisoned in a total of 111 institutions throughout Australia, of which eighty-five were government operated, nine were privately operated, four were transitional institutions, twelve were "court cell" centers (prisoner cell blocks contained within larger court complexes), and one was a periodic detention center.[36]

Australian corrections provides for diverse forms of orders and restrictions other than imprisonment for convicted persons. As with many modern jurisdictions, an appropriate sentence is considered in conjunction with the principles of sentencing, aggravating factors in the commission of the crime that the individual is being sentenced for, and any mitigating factors presented to the judges and magistrates. All of these factors are considered in a method known as "instinctive synthesis," which was explained by the High Court in the matter of *Anthony Masken Varcarian v. the Queen.* Instinctive synthesis was described in that case as an approach "whereby the sentencing judge weighs all the competing factors and arrives at one final sentence, as opposed to an approach whereby the judge quantifies the individual factors leading to a final determination."[37] For less serious offenses, Australian courts, depending on the jurisdiction, can issue fines, order compensation, or impose a community service order requiring the convicted person to complete a specified number of hours of volunteer work in the community.

The purpose of punishment in the Australian criminal justice system was explored in the matter of *Veen (No. 2)* (1988) 164 CLR 465. The case is a significant decision in Australian criminal law, as it is an authority for the principles that apply when sentencing is undertaken by a court. The High Court explained that the purposes of punishment may overlap, and they act as a "guidepost" for assisting a judge in providing an appropriate sentence. "The purposes of criminal punishment," according to the High Court,

> are various: protection of society, deterrence of the offender and of others who might be tempted to offend, retribution and reform. The purposes overlap and none of them can be considered in isolation from the others when determining what is an appropriate sentence in a particular case. They are guideposts to the appropriate sentence but sometimes they point in different directions.[38]

One of the most difficult areas of criminal justice decision making on punishment policy concerns the age of criminal responsibility and determining fair and appropriate attention in the transition from childhood, adolescence, and maturity. In addition, children's courts and juvenile detention centers in NSW and QLD have developed specific legal rules for carefully differentiating the position of young persons and children within the criminal justice system. The minimum age of criminal responsibility is an ongoing contentious issue in Australia, as is the imposition of criminal responsibility above that age, especially with regard to young offenders' appreciation of the wrongness of their acts.

Australian jurisdictions have held that the statutory minimum age of criminal responsibility be ten years of age. The common law maximum of doli incapax notes that a child between the ages of ten and fourteen years is incapable of committing a criminal act, though this is a rebuttable presumption. Young persons between the ages of fourteen and seventeen or eighteen years, depending on jurisdiction, may be held fully responsible for their criminal acts but can be given alternative criminal punishment compared to the punishments given to adults who commit the same offenses.[39] Even without criminal liability, young offenders may still be subject to court-ordered welfare measures, such as "care and control" orders, along with a range of other orders in relation to residence, contact, supervision, and assessment.[40]

Conclusion

One way of gaining a broad picture of the administration of criminal justice in Australia is by examining the judiciary, police, corrections, and punishment since White settlement in 1788. Although the colonial criminal justice system legitimized the dispossession of indigenous Australians, the system has been substantially transformed and now champions racial equality, gender equality, marriage equality, and other fundamental freedoms. Nonetheless, indigenous Australians remain disadvantaged and continue to be incarcerated in large numbers.

Although Australia has federal- and state-based systems of justice that are in some distinct ways different, these systems also have much in common. The Murri Courts demonstrate that Australian jurisdictions have adopted progressive developments in order to address the unique cultural and societal needs of indigenous Australians. With regard to policing in Australia, which is similarly undertaken by state and federal systems, there is evidence of the increasing technological sophistication that provides room for creative and effective responses to organized crime and similar criminal activities.

Notes

1. Parliamentary Education Office, *Australian Constitution*, 2021, https://peo .gov .au/understand -our -parliament/how -parliament -works/the -australian -constitution/australian -constitution.

2. G. Maddox, *Australian Democracy in Theory and Practice*, 5th ed. (London: Pearson Longman, 2005), 57.

3. Maddox, *Australian*, 57.

4. D. Brown, D. Farrier, L. McNamara, A. Steel, M. Grewcock, J. Quilter, M. Schwartz, T. Anthony, and A. Loughnan, *Criminal Laws: Material and Commentary on Criminal Law and Process of New South Wales* (Sydney: Federation Press, 2020), 27.

5. High Court of Australia, *Mabo v. Queensland* (No. 2) (1992) HCA, 23, https://legalheritage.sclqld.org.au/mabo-v-queensland.

6. M. Kirby, "The Honourable Michael Kirby AC CMG," https://www.michaelkirby.com .au.

7. High Court of Australia, "Portraits of Chief Justices and the First Bench," 2021, https://www.hcourt.gov.au/artworks/portraits-of-chief-justices/sir-owen-dixon.

8. A. Dale, "Shaken to Its Foundations: The Family Court Bombings," *LSJ Online*, 2021, https://lsj.com.au/articles/shaken-to-its-foundations-the-family-court-bombings.

9. Dale, "Shaken."

10. G. Blainey, *The Story of Australia's People: The Rise and Fall of Ancient Australia* (New York: Viking, 2020), 353–54.

11. R. Broome, *Aboriginal Australians: A History since 1788*, 5th ed. (Sydney: Allen and Unwin, 2019), 283.

12. Australian Institute of Aboriginal and Torres Strait Islander Studies, "The Mabo Case," 2021, https://aiatsis.gov.au/explore/mabo-case.

13. I. Potas and J. Walker, "Capital Punishment," in *Trends and Issues in Crime and Criminal Justice*, no. 3 (Canberra: Australian Institute of Criminology, 1987), 2.

14. Queensland State Government, "About the Court of Appeal," 2021, https://www.courts.qld.gov.au/courts/court-of-appeal/about-the-court-of-appeal.

15. Queensland State Government, "About."

16. Australian Bar Association, "What Is a Barrister: Specialist Advocate and Advisor in Law?," 2021, https://austbar.asn.au/for-the-community/what-is-a-barrister.

17. New South Wales Bar Association, "Vale Chester Alexander Porter QC (1926–2021)," https://nswbar.asn.au/the-bar-association/publications/inbrief/view/08b347d11316f1372f3414b4c453bb7b.

18. C. Knaus, "Bernard Collaery Hails 'Victory for Justice' as Court Overturns Bid to Keep Evidence Hidden at Trial,'" *The Guardian*, October 7, 2021, https://www.guardian.com/australia-news/2021/oct/07/bernard-collaery-hails-victory-for-justice-as-court-overturns-bid-to-keep-evidence-hidden-at-trial.

19. Queensland Law Society, "Understanding Queensland's Court System," 2021, https://www.qls.com.au/For-the-community/Legal-brochures/Understanding-Queensland-s-court-system.

20. Queensland State Government, "About."

21. Queensland State Government, "About."

22. Queensland State Government, "Children's Court," 2021, https://www.courts.qld.gov.au/courts/childrens-court.

23. M. F. Briskey and S. M. Makinda, "Law Enforcement and Policing in Australia: State and Federal Systems from the 'Convict Night Watch' to 'Problem-Oriented Policing,'" in *Global Perspectives in Policing and Law Enforcement*, ed. J. M. Mbuba (Lanham, MD: Lexington Books, 2021).

24. Regional Assistance Mission Solomon Islands (RAMSI), 2017, https://www.ramsi.org.

25. Australian Broadcasting Corporation, "Prime Minister Scott Morrison Says More AFP Personnel Being Sent to Solomon Islands as Calm Returns," 2021, https://www.abc.net.au/news/2021-11-28/scott-morrison-afp-peacekeepers-solomon-islands-honiara-looting/100656874.

26. Australian Criminal Intelligence Commission, 2021, https://www.acic.gov.au.

27. Martin Innes, Nigel Fielding, and Nina Cope, "'The Appliance of Science?': The Theory and Practice of Crime Intelligence Analysis," *British Journal of Criminology* 45, no. 1 (2005): 41.

28. J. Ratcliffe, *Intelligence-Led Policing* (New York: Routledge, 2016), 6.

29. Australian Federal Police, "AFP Led Operation Ironside Smashes Organised Crime," 2021, https://www.afp.gov.au/news-media/media-releases/afp-led-operation-ironside-smashes-organised-crime.

30. M. Roe, "1830–50," in *A New History of Australia*, ed. F. K. Crowley (Melbourne: William Heinemann, 1976), 90–91.

31. Potas and Walker, "Capital Punishment," 2.

32. Law Council of Australia, "Policy Agenda–Death Penalty," 2020, https://www.lawcouncil.asn.au/policy-agenda/human-rights/death-penalty.

33. T. Thompson and C. Crawford, "Gabe Watson May Be Prosecuted in Alabama If Queensland Government Assured of No Death Penalty," *Courier Mail*, 2010, https://www.couriermail.com.au/news/queensland/gabe-watson-may-be-prosecuted-in-alabama-if-queensland-government-assured-of-no-death-penalty/news-story/18a696917aad07bbd3ae10e849e02507.

34. Don Weatherburn, "Australian Imprisonment 2002–2016: Crime, Policing and Penal Policy," *Australian and New Zealand Journal of Criminology* 51, no. 4 (2018): 537–59.

35. University of London, "Institute for Crime and Justice Policy Research, World Prison Brief: Australia," 2021, https://www.prisonstudies.org/country/australia.

36. University of London, "Institute."

37. High Court, *Anthony Masken Varcarian v. the Queen* (2005).

38. *Veen (No. 2)* (1988) 164 CLR 465.

39. G. Urbas, "The Age of Criminal Responsibility," Australian Institute of Criminology, 2000, https://www.aic.gov.au/sites/default/files/2020-05/tandi181.pdf.

40. Urbas, "Age."

CHAPTER 5

The Criminal Justice System in China

ORGANIZATION AND FUNCTION

Yunyun Yang, Han Wang, Pingping Huang, and Mengliang Dai

This chapter introduces policing in China via an overview of the history of China's current police system, organization, and law enforcement. Then it introduces the judicial system in China, with a special focus on its organization and functions. It then describes the penal system in China, the organization of its multiple bodies, and some critical issues about this system. Finally, this chapter focuses on the juvenile justice system in China, as this system illustrates the larger justice system's operations and major practices.

The Police System

A BRIEF HISTORY OF THE POLICE SYSTEM

Different institutions and officials have long maintained public order in China, and these institutions and officials have been integrated into government and the military forces at all levels.[1] The Chinese Communist Party (CCP) built the current police system in China. Early public security agencies took on some wartime characteristics and went beyond traditional policing functions.[2] The earliest public security organ, the Central Intelligence Agency (*zhongyang teke*), was established in 1927 to protect the CCP Central Committee and its leaders during the civil revolution; to gather and send intelligence to revolutionary base areas; to punish spies, traitors, and moles; and to establish secret contacts and radio stations. In 1931, the State Political Security Bureau (*zhengzhi baoweiju*) was established, and its mission centered on secret agents and counterrevolutionaries. It also initially carried out specialized work, such as political reconnaissance, criminal investigation, preliminary examination, public security administration, security, and reform through labor. In February 1939, the CCP Central Committee decided to create the Social Affairs Department (*shehui shiwubu*) within the CCP's senior organizations, which it structured in subagencies such as investigation, public security, intelligence, cadre protection, and the Central Guard Corps. After establishing the People's Republic of China (PRC), the Social Affairs

Department was terminated, and a new public security system was created by officials at the First National Conference of Senior Public Security on October 15, 1949, with the Ministry of Public Security (MPS) as the central public security organ. The MPS became an important member of the State Council, and it laid a foundation for the dual leadership of the public security system.

On December 14, 1949, the Chinese police force was formally renamed as the People's Police. In the 1950s, the People's Police played an important role in controlling counterrevolutionaries, and hundreds of thousands of brigands and spies were arrested. It also cleaned up social conduct by organizing antidrug campaigns and shutting down brothels. While the PRC was experiencing the Great Proletarian Cultural Revolution during the 1960s and 1970s, the legal system and public security agencies were destroyed. After the downfall of the Gang of Four, in 1976, policing work was gradually restored. Following several functional reforms and institutional restructuring, the People's Police system has gradually taken shape, with Chinese characteristics.

Organization

CENTRAL PUBLIC SECURITY ORGAN

According to Article 3 of the Organic Administration Regulation of Public Security agencies, the MPS—the central public security organ—leads and commands national public security work. Currently, its leaders include one minister, six vice ministers, one team leader of discipline inspection and supervision, and one director of its political department. The minister is one of the five state councilors. The MPS consists of the following twenty-two units: the general office, the information command center, the research center, supervision and auditing, personnel and training, propaganda, criminal investigation, economic crime investigation, public order administration, counterterrorism, food and drug crime investigation, the secret service, railway public security, network security protection, prison and detention house administration, logistics, traffic administration, legal affairs, equipment finance, international cooperation, narcotics control, and scientific and technical information.[3]

LOCAL PUBLIC SECURITY AGENCIES

The Chinese administrations consist of five levels, namely, the central, provincial, prefectural, county, and township levels, ranking from the highest to lowest levels, respectively. Each establishes corresponding public security agencies. Local public security agencies are under the leadership of a higher public security organ, the CCP Committee, and the government of the corresponding level. Furthermore, local public security agencies usually imitate the structure of the MPS; hence, a public security system is set up from central to local levels. Table 5.1 depicts the general model of the public security agencies from highest to lowest rank.

Table 5.1. The public security system in China

Level of administration	*Types*	*Notes*
Central	Ministry of Public Security	The central public security organ
Provincial	Public Security Department/ Bureau (*gong'an ting/ju*)	Public security departments in twenty-three provinces and five autonomous regions
		Public security bureaus in four centrally administrated municipalities
Prefectural	Public Security Bureau (*diji gong'an ju*)	In each prefecture-level city and autonomous prefecture
County	Public Security Bureau (*xianji gong'an ju*)	In each county-level city, county, and autonomous county
Township	Public security subbureaus and police stations (*paichusuo*)	In each township and autonomous township

Source: Yunyun Yang, Han Wang, Pingping Huang, and Mengliang Dai. Although the term for the county-level public security agency is the same as the prefectural-level agency, the prefectural-level agency has authority over the county-level agency.

POLICE CATEGORIES

The People's Police includes public security agencies, state security agencies, prisons, the administrative organizations of education through labor, and the judicial police of the People's Courts and the People's Procuratorates. When people discuss the police, they refer to the public security agencies that undertake the task of maintaining national and public security and that are under the leadership of MPS, with a total number of 2 million police officers.[4] The police are divided into the following twelve categories: (1) Public security police (*zhi'an jingcha*) have the tasks of preventing, detecting, and stopping illegal activities; maintaining public order in public areas; and managing special trades and dangerous goods. (2) Household registration police (*huji jingcha*) oversee household registration, domestic migration, and identity cards. (3) Criminal police (*xingshi jingcha*) are responsible for criminal investigations and the analysis of criminal cases. (4) Traffic police (*jiaotong gong'an*) maintain traffic order and manage vehicle and driver activities. (5) Forest police (*senlin gong'an*) protect forests and wild animals, plant resources, and the ecosystem and maintain public order in forest areas. (6) Foreign affairs police (*waishi jingcha*) are responsible for immigration affairs. (7) Economic criminal police (*jingji fanzui zhencha jingcha*) investigate financial crimes, economic fraud, and other economic criminal cases. (8) Internet police (*wangluo jingcha*) supervise public information–network security and crack down on cybercrimes. (9) Narcotics police (*jidu jingcha*) are responsible for matters and criminal cases involving drugs. (10) Police inspectors (*jingwu ducha*) are police supervisors and are referred to as the "police in the police." (11) Railway police (*tielu gong'an*) ensure primarily the safety of railway transportation. (12) Civil aviation police (*minhang gong'an*) draft rules about civil aviation security, gather intelligence, decide on and issuing prewarning levels, and deal with illegal interference in civil aviation security crises.

Although auxiliary police are not official civil servants in China, their functions in policing affairs cannot be ignored. In some provinces, the number of auxiliary police surpasses that of police officers. For example, there were 101,000 police officers and 182,000 auxiliary police officers in Jiangsu Province in 2020.[5] According to the Opinions on Regulating the Administration of Auxiliary Police Personnel of Public Security Agencies, which the General Office of the State Council issued in November 2016,

> the auxiliary police personnel refer to the personnel recruited in accordance with the law and managed and used by the public security agencies to perform the duties prescribed in these measures and the labor contract without the status of the People's Police, mainly including clerical and auxiliary police personnel. But the following personnel are not included, such as personnel recruited by public security agencies but engaged in catering, cleaning, security and other work, social volunteers and other mass prevention and mass treatment forces.[6] (Article 3)

However, auxiliary police personnel do not possess the qualifications of law enforcement, so they perform their duties under the command and supervision of the public security police and cannot carry out law enforcement alone or use weapons, which Article 4 and Article 11 clearly regulate.[7]

LAW ENFORCEMENT OF PUBLIC SECURITY AGENCIES

Criminal Law Enforcement

Public security agencies perform the first procedures of criminal proceedings. According to the Procedures for Handling Criminal Cases by Public Security agencies,

> the basic functions and powers of the public security agencies in criminal proceedings include to file, investigate and conduct preliminary trials of criminal cases in accordance with the law, deciding on and implementing compulsory measures. (Article 3)

Generally, the principle of localization administration (*shudi guanli*) is carried out in criminal cases, which means that public security agencies at the county level investigate criminal cases that occur within their jurisdiction. However, prefectural-level public security agencies should deal with some major cases, including (1) crimes endangering state security, (2) crimes of terrorist activities, (3) crimes involving foreign elements, (4) economic crimes, (5) organized crimes, and (6) transregional crimes.

As a supplement to localization administration, the public security organ at a higher level can investigate criminal cases under the jurisdiction of the public security organ at a lower level if deemed necessary. The latter can request that the former exercise jurisdiction over a criminal case that it considers to be greatly important.[8] The main measures of investigation include (1) interrogating criminal suspects; (2) questioning witnesses; (3) inspecting and examining criminal locations; (4) conducting a search of relevant places of criminals, criminal suspects, and persons who may be hiding criminals or criminal evidence; (5) impounding material evidence and documentary evidence; (6) investigating suspects' financial accounts and freezing them when necessary; (7) requesting expert evaluation; (8) asking for victims', witnesses', and criminal suspects' identification; (9) conducting technical investigations; and (10) finding those wanted for arrest. Public security agencies can, by law, adopt compulsory methods in order to restrict the personal freedom of criminal suspects and defendants, including detention pending trial, residential surveillance, detention, and arrest.

Administrative Law Enforcement

Because public security agencies are important administrative organizations in China, the scope of the administrative law enforcement's public security activities is wide, involving every aspect of social life. The scope of public security administrative law enforcement includes the following aspects: (1) public security administration, such as the management of public order management, residents' registration, entry and exit of ports, fire control, road traffic control, and computer safety supervision; (2) public security administrative penalties, including warnings, fines, confiscation, temporary seizure, and the revocation of permits, licenses, and other documents as well as administrative detention and orders to stop production and business; (3) public security administrative coercive measures to restrict specific counterparts from exercising certain rights or forcing them to perform certain obligations[9] and to limit property rights in accordance with legal powers and procedures, including mainly compulsory measures that restrict personal freedom, such as compulsory restraint, compulsory drug rehabilitation, and compulsory treatment on the counterpart, in addition to and sealing up, distraining, and freezing the counterpart's property; and (4) public security administrative compulsory execution, including mainly compulsory detention, compulsory summons, repatriation, compulsory transfer, compulsory deduction, compulsory demolition, performance on behalf, and compulsory payment.

Law Enforcement Supervision

Public security law enforcement is under multiple levels of supervision by legally authorized organizations (i.e., the legal department, the discipline inspection department, the supervision department, and the letters and visits department, among others), citizens and social organizations over the performance of duties, and functions, powers, and the observance of disciplines by public security agencies and police.

Law enforcement contains both external and internal supervisions. In internal law enforcement supervision, the inspection system from central to county level is under the guidance of Regulations on Inspection of Public Security agencies, which the State Council promulgated on June 20, 1997, and revised and put into effect on

October 1, 2011. To ensure the successful implementation of inspection, the MPS has an inspector general, who concurrently serves as a deputy minister. Internal supervision also includes a legal department supervision system, which implies that the public security agencies' legal departments at all levels are responsible for the legal work of public security agencies and the supervision of internal law enforcement. Additionally, internal supervision entails a public security administrative reconsideration system, in which any citizen, judicial persons, or other organization that refuses to accept the specific administrative sanctions that the public security organ promulgates can apply for administrative reconsideration from the government of the same administrative level or from a public security organ of higher level, as based on the Administrative Reconsideration Law. Finally, internal supervision includes the public security compensation system, which offers financial compensation in misjudged cases, according to the 2012 State Compensation Law of PRC.[10]

There are five forms of external supervision of public security agencies, namely, supervision of the state power organ, administrative supervision, procuratorial supervision, administrative litigation, and social supervision systems. Organizations of state power, the government, and public security agencies at higher levels can exercise supervision via inspection, examination, and investigation. Furthermore, procuratorial organizations, through legal procedures, can supervise activities such as investigating and executing criminal punishment. Administrative supervisory organizations can conduct supervision through such administrative supervisory procedures as inspection and investigation. The supervisory body can conduct supervision through special supervisory procedures, while other social subjects can conduct supervision in the form of criticism, suggestion, appeal, report, and accusation.

The Judicial System

The Chinese judicial system has four levels: Supreme, Higher, Intermediate, and Basic People's Courts. The Supreme People's Court is the highest court of the PRC, and the local People's Courts at all levels consist of Higher People's Courts, Intermediate People's Courts, and Basic People's Courts. In addition, the established special People's Courts include Military Courts, Maritime Courts, Intellectual Property Courts, Financial Courts, Forestry Courts, and Internet Courts.

SUPREME PEOPLE'S COURT

As the highest trial organ and supervising organ, the Supreme People's Court (SPC) oversees the trial practices of the local People's Courts and special People's Courts at all levels. It reports its work to the National People's Congress (NPC) and its Standing Committee. The right of appointment and removal of the president and vice president as well as members of the trial committee of the SPC lies with the NPC.

Jurisdiction

The SPC has jurisdiction for cases of first instance as the law prescribes and as it deems cases to be under its jurisdiction. It also has jurisdiction in appellate cases from the Higher People's Courts and in cases that are filed in accordance with the provisions of the Standing Committee of the NPC. Additionally, its jurisdiction extends both to retrial cases that are filed in accordance with trial supervision procedures and to death penalty cases for which the Higher People's Courts submit requests for approval.

Internal Organization

The SPC consists of thirty-one divisions, including the General Office, the Political Department, the Research Office, the Trial Administration Office, the Supervision Bureau, the Bureau of International Cooperation, the Judicial Equipment Administration Bureau, the Party Committee, the Retired Cadre Bureau, the Information Bureau, the Case Filing Tribunal, Criminal Adjudication Tribunal No. 1–5, Civil Adjudication Tribunal No. 1–4, the Adjudication Tribunal for Environment and Resources, the Administration Adjudication Tribunal, the Trial Supervision Tribunal, the Compensation Committee Office, the Enforcement Bureau, and six Circuit Courts.

Circuit Courts are the SPC's standing judicial organizations and branch offices. The judgments, rulings, and decisions that the Circuit Courts render are the SPC's judgments, rulings, and decisions. According to the Provisions of the SPC on Several Issues concerning the Trial of Cases by the Circuit Courts, the Circuit Courts try or handle several types of cases that the SPC should accept and try within the circuits. Among these cases are major and complicated first-instance administrative cases nationwide and first-instance civil and commercial cases with nationwide significance. Additionally, the Circuit Courts handle appeal cases that are filed against an administrative or civil and commercial judgment or ruling that a Higher People's Court renders as a court of first instance. It also tries cases in which a party files an application for retrial against an effective administrative or civil and commercial judgment, ruling, or mediation paper that a Higher People's Court renders. Criminal petition cases and cases that are retried according to the statutory authority also fall under the Circuit Courts' jurisdiction, as do cases in which a party applies for reconsideration after refusing to accept the decision about a fine or detention that a Higher People's Court makes. Circuit Courts also have jurisdiction in cases in which a Higher People's Court requests the SPC to render a ruling or to make a decision on jurisdiction issues. Cases in which a Higher People's Court requests to extend the time limit of a trial are also taken up by Circuit Courts. Additionally, Circuit Courts take on civil and commercial cases and judicial assistance cases related to Hong Kong, Macao, and Taiwan. Finally, Circuit Courts also have jurisdiction over other cases that the SPC finds should be tried by the Circuit Courts.

On October 23, 2014, the Fourth Plenary Session of the 18th Central Committee of the CCP was held. It indicated that the SPC needed to establish Circuit Courts in order to improve the allocation of judicial functions and powers and to

Table 5.2. List of six Circuit Courts

Circuit Courts	*Date*	*Location*	*Jurisdiction areas*
First	January 28, 2015	Shenzhen City	Guangdong, Guangxi, Hainan, and Hunan
Second	January 31, 2015	Shenyang City	Liaoning, Jilin, and Heilongjiang
Third	December 28, 2016	Nanjing City	Jiangsu, Shanghai, Zhejiang, Fujian, and Jiangxi
Fourth	December 28, 2016	Zhengzhou City	Henan, Shanxi, Hubei, and Anhui
Fifth	December 29, 2016	Chongqing City	Chongqing, Sichuan, Guizhou, Yunnan, and Tibet
Sixth	December 29, 2016	Xi'an City	Shaanxi, Gansu, Qinghai, Ningxia, and Xinjiang

Source: Yunyun Yang, Han Wang, Pingping Huang, and Mengliang Dai.

carry out pilot reforms in separating judicial from executive power. Table 5.2 shows the Circuit Courts' establishment dates and territories. For example, the first Circuit Court was established on January 28, 2015, in Shenzhen City, Guangdong Province, with circuits of Guangdong Province, Guangxi Zhuang Autonomous Region, Hainan Province, and Hunan Province.

HIGHER PEOPLE'S COURT

The Higher People's Courts are the highest-level courts at the provincial level and include twenty-two Higher People's Courts of provinces, five Higher People's Courts of autonomous regions, and four Higher People's Courts of municipalities that are directly under the central government. The Higher People's Courts have responsibility over (1) cases of first instance under their respective jurisdictions, as the law prescribes; (2) cases of first instance for which the People's Courts at lower levels submit requests for trial; (3) cases of first instance of which the SPC designates the jurisdiction; (4) appellate cases that the Intermediate People's Courts judge and make rulings; (5) retrial cases filed in accordance with the trial supervision procedures; and (6) death penalty cases for which the Intermediate People's Courts submit requests for approval.

INTERMEDIATE PEOPLE'S COURTS

The Intermediate People's Courts are the second-lowest level local courts and include 288 Intermediate People's Courts of municipalities that are directly under the jurisdiction of provinces or autonomous regions. Of these, fifteen Intermediate People's Courts were established within municipalities directly under the central government; there are twenty-nine Intermediate People's Courts of autonomous prefectures, and seven Intermediate People's Courts were established for prefectures in provinces or autonomous regions. The Intermediate People's Courts have jurisdiction over (1) cases of first instance under their jurisdiction as the law prescribes, (2) cases of first instance for which the Basic People's Courts submit requests for trial, (3) cases of first instance of which the Higher People's Courts designate jurisdiction, (4) appellate cases in which the Basic People's Courts judge and make rulings, and (5) retrial cases filed in accordance with the trial supervision procedures.

BASIC PEOPLE'S COURTS

The Basic People's Courts are the lowest-level courts and consist of People's Courts of counties and autonomous counties, People's Courts in cities not divided into districts, and People's Courts of municipal districts. There are about 2,800 Basic People's Courts across China. The Basic People's Court may set up People's Tribunals, which is an integral part of the Basic People's Court. The rulings of the People's Tribunal are that of the Basic People's Court.

SPECIAL PEOPLE'S COURTS

According to Article 15 of the Organic Law of the People's Courts of the PRC, the special People's Courts include Military Courts, Maritime Courts, Intellectual Property Rights Courts, Financial Courts, Railway Transport Courts, Internet Courts, and Forestry District Courts. The Standing Committee of the NPC prescribes the setup, organization, functions, powers, and appointment and dismissal of these courts' judges.

The special courts in China are not without problems. For example, according to the Organic Law of the People's Courts, the Standing Committee of the NPC prescribes establishing special courts, yet it only issues decisions on establishing Maritime Courts, Intellectual Property Rights Courts, and Financial Courts. Moreover, except for Military Courts, special courts lack a complete three-level court structure; Maritime Courts, Intellectual Property Rights Courts, Financial Courts, and Internet Courts have only a one-level structure.

Military Courts

Chinese military reform was implemented in November 2015 at a plenary session of the Central Military Commission's Central Leading Group for Military Reform. The newly formed Political-Legal Commission of Central Military Commission adjusted and built the Military Courts of the whole army in June 2016. Subsequently, on June 29, 2016, the SPC issued the levels and substitute characteristics of Military Courts, of which the Chinese People's Liberation Army (PLA) Military Court is the Higher Military Court. As shown in figure 5.1, the Intermediate Military Courts included PLA Eastern Theater Command, Southern Theater Command, Western Theater Command No. 1, Western Theater Command No. 2, Northern Theater Command, Central Theater

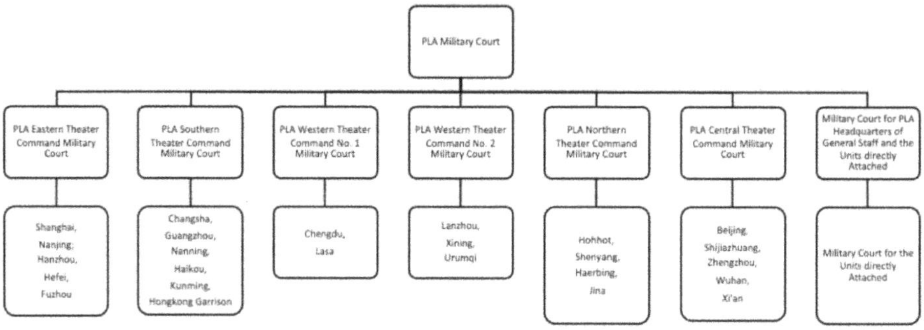

Figure 5.1 Organization of Military Courts. *Source:* Yunyun Yang, Han Wang, Pingping Huang, and Mengliang Dai.

Command, and Military Court for PLA Headquarters of General Staff and the Units Directly Attached. Each Intermediate Military Court consists of one to six Basic Military Courts. For example, the Southern Theater Command Military Court includes six Basic Courts and Military Court for PLA Headquarters of General Staff, and the Units Directly Attached has only one Basic Court. There are twenty-six Basic Military Courts, which are mainly in charge of hearing criminal cases involving servicemen.

Maritime Courts

To meet the needs of maritime transport development, economic relations, and trade with foreign countries, the Standing Committee of the NPC issued a decision on November 14, 1984, establishing Maritime Courts in costal port cities. There are eleven Maritime Courts, one each in Daliang, Tianjin, Qingdao, Nanjing, Shanghai, Ningbo, Xiamen, Guangzhou, Haikou, Beihai, and Wuhan. The SPC decides the establishment, alteration, and abolition of the Maritime Court. The Standing Committee of the People's Congress of a city where a court is located will appoint or remove the president of a Maritime Court based on a proposal submitted by the chairperson of the Standing Committee of the People's Congress.

Each Maritime Court is equal to an Intermediate People's Court and consists of several divisions. For example, the internal departments of the Tianjin Maritime Court include a political department, a detachment of judiciary police officers, a general office, a research office, an enforcement bureau, a Circuit Tribunal, the Qinhuangdao Dispatched Tribunal, the Caofeidian Dispatched Tribunal, an Integrated Tribunal, and the complaint and filing division.[11] The Maritime Courts have jurisdiction over maritime cases and maritime trade cases of first instance, and they do not handle criminal cases or other civil cases. To be specific, according to Provisions of the SPC on the Scope of Cases to Be Accepted by Maritime Courts (2016), Maritime Courts accept (1) cases concerning maritime tortious disputes, (2) cases concerning disputes over maritime contracts, (3) cases relating to disputes over developing and utilizing oceans and water areas leading to sea and environmental protection, (4) other cases concerning disputes over maritime affairs, (5) maritime administrative cases, and (6) cases concerning special maritime procedure.

Intellectual Property Rights Courts

To promote implementing the national strategy of development that innovation drives and to strengthen the judicial protection of intellectual property rights, the Standing Committee of the NPC passed a decision on August 31, 2014, establishing Intellectual Property Rights Courts. The courts are established in Beijing, Shanghai, and Guangzhou. On December 26, 2020, the fourth Intellectual Property Rights Court, the Intellectual Property Rights Court of the Hainan Free Trade Port, was established. Moreover, twenty-one Intellectual Property Rights Tribunals have been established since 2017,[12] which are internal organizations. The Intellectual Property Rights Court has jurisdiction over such civil or administrative intellectual property cases as those involving patents, new varieties of plants, integrated circuit layout designs, and highly technical knowledge. The Higher People's Court will try an appeal against a judgment or ruling of an Intellectual Property Rights Court for the first instance at the place where the Intellectual Property Rights Court is located. The Intellectual Property Rights Court reports to the Standing Committee of the Municipal People's Congress in the nearest jurisdiction.

Financial Courts

There are two Financial Courts. The Shanghai Financial Court was formally established on August 20, 2018. The second, the Beijing Financial Court, was established on March 18, 2021. According to Rule on the Jurisdiction of the Shanghai Financial Court, which was authored by the SPC, the Shanghai Financial Court is mainly responsible for financial civil and commercial cases, such as disputes involving securities, futures, trusts, insurance, negotiable instruments, letters of credit, financial lending contracts, bank cards, financial lease contracts, entrusting financial contracts, and items pawned.

Railway Transport Courts

According to the SPC, all Railway Transport Courts were integrated into the national court system by the end of June 2012. Before 2012, all Railway Transport Courts were under the purview of the Ministry of Railways. On July 17, 2012, the SPC issued several provisions on the jurisdiction of Railway Transport Courts, namely, that they should accept criminal cases, including crimes (1) committed within railway work areas, such as stations, freight yards, and transportation command institutions; (2) aimed at railway lines, locomotives, communications, electricity, and other railway equipment and facilities; and (3) committed by employees of railway transport enterprises in the course of carrying out their duties. Meanwhile, the Railway Transport Courts also have jurisdiction over some civil cases related to railway transportation, security, and property, such as disputes over contracts on transport, railway passengers, baggage, and packages. The two levels of the Railway Transport Courts comprise seventeen Intermediate Courts and fifty-eight Basic Courts.[13]

Forestry District Courts and Internet Courts

There are four Intermediate Forestry Courts and twenty-two Basic Forestry Courts. Their tasks include protecting the forests, addressing cases involving sabotage of forestry resources, and handling serious responsibility cases and cases involving foreigners. Moreover, to maintain network security and order and to meet the people's diverse judicial needs, three Internet Courts—one each in Hanzhou, Beijing, and Guangzhou—have been established since August 2017. The Internet Courts are responsible for specific types of internet-related first-instance cases, such as disputes over internet shopping and service contracts, infringement on internet copyrights, and internet domain names. The Internet Courts try cases online, and the acceptance, service, mediation, evidence exchange, pretrial preparation, court trial, judgment pronouncement, and other litigation tasks are completed online.

The Penal System

A BRIEF HISTORY OF THE PENAL SYSTEM

The earliest judicial administrative agency of the CCP is the Central People's Committee of Justice (*zhongyang sifa renmin weiyuanbu*), which exercises overall leadership over the judicial organizations and is in charge of detention and reformatory (or prison) centers. It was created when the CCP established the Chinese Soviet Republic in November 1931. In 1932, the People's Central Committee of Justice established the earliest labor reformation house (*laodong ganhuayuan*). The Committee stipulated that the labor reformation house would guard and educate all prisoners who violated Soviet decrees so that such prisoners would become useful members of society after their sentence expired. With the establishment of the PRC, forcing prisoners to reform themselves and become new people became the legal basis of criminals' rehabilitation, which the Common Program of the Chinese People's Political Consultative Conference (*zhongguorenmin zhengzhixieshanghuiyi gongtonggangling*) set in September 1949. The Third National Public Security Conference, held in 1951, decided to organize prisoners across the country to carry out labor reform. The meeting passed the Resolution on Organizing the Rehabilitation of Prisoners through Labor, which made clear arrangements for such matters as the management system, funding sources, armed detention, and labor projects. The large-scale criminal reform across the country thus began.[14] In September 1954, the State Council of the PRC promulgated and implemented the Regulations of the People's Republic of China on Labor Reform, indicating that the PRC's prison laws and regulations had entered a stage of orderly and standardized development.[15] In February 1982, the MPS promulgated the Detailed Rules for the Prisons' Reform-through-Labor Teams, containing seven chapters and 137 articles, and stipulated for the first time prisoners' rights and obligations in the form of laws and regulations. In December 1994, the Prison Law of the PRC was promulgated and implemented.

CATEGORIES OF SANCTIONS

Both punishment and rehabilitation dominate the rationales of Chinese penology.[16] According to Prison Law Article 3, to transform prisoners into law-abiding citizens, a prison must follow the principle of combining punishment with reform and education with labor. The Chinese correctional system's ultimate mission, according to the notice that the State Council published in 1995, is to reform criminals.

Two categories of sanctions exist in China: principal punishments and supplementary punishments. Principal punishments include public surveillance (*guanzhi*), criminal detention (*juyi*), fixed-term imprisonment, life imprisonment, and the death penalty. The term of public surveillance is no less than three months and no more than two years. Criminals sentenced to public surveillance are subject to community correction. The term of criminal detention is no less than one month and no more than six months. The public security agencies in criminal detention centers execute the sentence of a criminal sentenced to criminal detention. These centers are facilities similar to jails, but the local public security agencies administer them. In addition to housing criminals who are sentenced to criminal detention, these centers also house individuals who are awaiting the courts' sentencing or whose remaining sentence is less than three months. The duration of fixed-term imprisonment is no less than six months and no more than fifteen years. Criminals sentenced to fixed-term imprisonment or life imprisonment are to have their sentences executed in correctional facilities that the Ministry of Justice administers. The death penalty includes immediate execution and a two-year suspension of execution.

Supplementary punishments include fines, deprivation of political rights, and confiscation of property. These punishments can be imposed independently of the principal punishments. According to criminal law, "in imposing a fine, the amount of the fine shall be determined by the court according to the circumstances of the crime. . . . If the person sentenced is unable to pay the fine in full, the court may collect whenever the person is found in possession of the executable property."[17] The term of deprivation of political rights is no less than one year and no more than five years. According to Article 54, the

> deprivation of political rights is deprivation of the following rights: (1) the right to elect and the right to be elected; (2) the right to freedom of speech, of the press, of assembly, of association, of procession, and of demonstration; (3) the right to hold a position in state organizations; and (4) the right to hold a leading position in a state-owned company, enterprise, or institution or people's organization.

All of the property the criminal personally owns can be confiscated. According to Article 59, "If all property is confiscated, the necessary living expenses shall be reserved for the criminal individual himself and his dependent family members." Table 5.3 presents the organizations responsible for implementing different criminal penalties in China.

Table 5.3. Organizations that implement different criminal penalties

Organization		*Penalties*
Courts		Fines Confiscation of property Death penalty
Public security agency		Criminal detention Fixed-term imprisonment (the remaining sentence is less than three months) Deprivation of political rights
Department of Justice	Prison	Fixed-term imprisonment, life imprisonment, and death penalty with a two-year suspension of execution
	Community corrections	Public surveillance, probation, parole, and temporarily serving a sentence outside an incarceration facility

Source: Yunyun Yang, Han Wang, Pingping Huang, and Mengliang Dai.

PRISON

The "World Prison Population List," published in November 2018, reported that there were 1.65 million prisoners in China.[18] The Ministry of Justice holds sentenced prisoners in 683 prisons, including forty-one prisons for females and twenty-eight reformatories for juvenile delinquents.[19]

REHABILITATION

In the past, the mechanisms by which criminals could be reformed were referred to as the Three Major Reforms (*sandagaizao*), which were regulatory, education, and labor reform.[20] In 2018, the minister of justice proposed Five Major Reforms (*wudagaizao*) as the new pattern of reforming criminals, adding two new means to the previous mechanism: political and cultural reform.

According to *Legal Daily*, which is the official newspaper of the Political and Law Committee of the CCP, political reform must use Communist ideology and the Communist Revolutionary tradition of the CCP to "wash the minds of criminals and occupy their ideological realm."[21] This reform is currently the top priority. Regulatory reform emphasizes the role of strict norms, security infrastructure, and monitoring systems in regulating inmates' behavior. Educational reform refers to providing inmates with education, including legal and vocational education. Culture reform is intended to eliminate inmates' bad habits and enhance their identification with Socialist core values. Labor reform organizes inmates to work in positions on specific labor projects. The labor projects assigned to inmates depend largely on the prison's location.[22] Importantly, the labor projects are chosen with the intention of reforming criminals instead of creating profits.[23]

PENALTY REDUCTION

Both principal punishments and supplementary punishments apply to reducing penalties. Penalty reduction involves two circumstances: the inmate's sentence "may" be reduced or "shall" be reduced. According to Article 78 of the Criminal Law, inmates sentenced to public surveillance, criminal detention, fixed-term imprisonment, or life imprisonment may have their sentences reduced if they earnestly observe the regulations of the prison, accept reform, truly repent, or perform meritorious service. A reduced sentence will occur if the inmate performs any of the following meritorious services: (1) stopping someone from engaging in major criminal activities, (2) reporting on verified major criminal activities inside or outside the prison, (3) making inventions or major technological renovations, (4) risking his or her life to save others, (5) fighting natural disasters or mitigating grave accidents, or (6) making other major contributions to the state or society. Importantly, penalty reduction should be treated as a reward rather than as an inmate's legal right.[24]

According to Prison Law Article 30, prisons will make the recommendation to the court for reducing a sentence. After reduction, the actually executed term of criminal penalty shall not be (1) less than half of the original term of criminal penalty, if public surveillance, criminal detention, or fixed-term imprisonment is imposed; (2) less than thirteen years, if life imprisonment is imposed; or (3) less than twenty-five years, if the death penalty with a reprieve imposed on a convict is legally reduced to life imprisonment on the reprieve period's expiration, or less than twenty years, if it is reduced to imprisonment of twenty-five years on the reprieve period's expiration.

RELEASE AND RESETTLEMENT

According to Prison Law Articles 35, 36, and 37, prisons will release prisoners and issue them a certificate of release when they have completed the service of their sentence. The local government will assist the released prisoner in resettling, and the public security agency will register the residence of the released prisoner. If a person released after serving a sentence has lost his or her ability to perform labor and has no statutory supporters or basic source of income, the local government will offer the person relief. In 2017, approximately 518,000 people used resettlement institutions across the country, with a successful resettlement rate of 95 percent.[25]

COMMUNITY CORRECTION

Statistics in 2017 showed that there were 700,000 offenders serving sentences in the community, and the rate of reoffending during the correction period had been maintained at a relatively low level of about 0.2 percent.[26] In December 2019, the 15th Meeting of the Standing Committee of the 13th National People's Congress passed the Community Correction Law of the PRC, which came into effect on July 1, 2020. According to Article 2 of the Community Correction Law, a convict who is sentenced to public surveillance, probation, or parole or who is permitted to serve temporarily a sentence outside an incarceration facility will be subject to community correction.

PUBLIC SURVEILLANCE

Offenders who are sentenced to public surveillance are not required to undergo a period of incarceration. According to Article 39 of the Criminal Law, such offenders must report on their activities to the local authority that is responsible for surveilling the offender, and they must obtain approval from that authority in order to change their residence or to depart from the city or county. However, there is no specific regulation in the Community Correction Law regarding offenders who are sentenced to public surveillance. In judicial practice, because of controversy regarding its applicable object and its lack of deterrence, the courts often replace the sentence of public surveillance with probation, and it is consequently marginalized in community corrections work.[27]

PROBATION

According to Article 72 of the Criminal Law, a suspended sentence will be announced if the offender is under the age of eighteen, is pregnant, or attains the age of seventy-five. Probation may also be awarded if the offender is sentenced to imprisonment of no more than three years and (1) the circumstances of the crime are minor, (2) he or she shows repentance, (3) he or she is not likely to commit any crime again, and (4) announcing the probation will not have any major adverse impact on the community where he or she lives. For offenders sentenced to criminal detention, the probation term is between two months and one year. For offenders sentenced to a fixed sentence, the term is between one and five years. Recidivists and ringleaders of criminal gangs will not be awarded probation. Offenders with a suspended sentence must report their activities periodically to the community correction institution and take part in the public welfare labor that the institution arranges. According to Article 28 of the Community Correction Law, if offenders violate the regulations or law in their probation term, the community correction institution may submit a request for revoking probation.

PAROLE

Per Article 81 of the Criminal Law, an inmate who is sentenced to fixed-term imprisonment can qualify for parole after serving half of the term of the original sentence. For a convict sentenced to life imprisonment, the term is no less than thirteen years. Eligibility for parole depends on whether the inmate has earnestly observed the prison rules, accepts reform, shows true repentance, and is unlikely to commit any crime again. Recidivists and convicts sentenced for no less than ten years or life imprisonment for murder, rape, robbery, abduction, arson, explosion, dissemination of hazardous sentences, or organized violent crime will not be paroled. The period of parole in the case of fixed-term imprisonment is the term that has not been completed, and the period in the case of life imprisonment is ten years. The offender must observe laws and regulations, report on all activities regularly, and obtain permission before changing residence or leaving the city. If the offender fails to abide by the regulations and provisions, the community correction institution may submit a request for parole revocation.

TEMPORARILY SERVING A SENTENCE OUTSIDE AN INCARCERATION FACILITY

Criminals sentenced to fixed-term imprisonment or criminal detention can, according to Article 254 of the Criminal Procedure Law, temporarily serve their time outside the prison if temporary execution outside prison will not harm society and if they have a serious illnesses and need to be on parole for medical treatment, are pregnant or breastfeeding their own babies, or cannot take care of themselves. As soon as the above circumstances no longer pertain, the offender will be sent to prison promptly if there is any remaining sentence to serve. For these offenders, because of the hardships they encounter, the community correction institution will assist them instead of forcing them to do public service.[28]

MODELS OF COMMUNITY CORRECTION

Shanghai launched the earliest pilot reform in community corrections in 2002. The Shanghai model emphasizes the participation of nongovernmental organizations (NGOs) and community forces in the community correction process.[29] Shanghai established a municipal community corrections office to lead the city's community corrections work, cooperating with the private nonprofit organizations through purchasing their social services and participating in the psychological consultation, education, and vocational training projects that these private organizations provide. NGOs also recruit volunteers to provide educational assistance, temporary housing, and work for "homeless, unaccompanied, unemployed" corrections subjects.[30]

The Beijing model of community correction emphasizes the governmental and judicial administration's force in the process of community correction.[31] To monitor correction subjects strictly, Beijing transferred many prison officers to judicial offices with the intention of improving the community corrections institutions' ability to address emergencies. The government also recruited "coordinators" to assist with community corrections work, and it established government-run education centers to conduct intensive vocational training and to provide the offenders temporary accommodations.

Throughout the years, the Beijing model has gradually become the dominant model across the country.[32] In other words, the government dominates the community corrections work and advocates the participation of NGOs and communities. In 2017, judicial and administrative agencies across the country recruited 673,000 volunteers and 84,000 social workers to work in community corrections, and they have established 676,000 community corrections groups. There were also 2,305 community service bases, 9,265 education bases, and 8,229 employment bases established through cooperation between local government, relevant enterprises, and social organizations in order to provide services such as vocational training and psychological corrections for offenders engaging in community service.[33]

The Juvenile Justice System

In a sense, the juvenile justice system is the fundamental way to prevent and reduce violations and crimes.[34] It comes from a critical reflection and reform on the effectiveness of traditional criminal justice. Yet its ideas, principles, systems, and procedures differ in many ways from those of the adult justice system. This section provides a brief overview of the juvenile justice system's operations and major practices related to this system in China.

PROCESSING OF THE JUVENILE OFFENDER

The criminal procedure involving minors applies to the cases in which minors are suspected of committing crimes. The procedures include filing, investigating, prosecuting, trying, and executing juvenile criminal cases when juveniles are investigated for criminal responsibility according to the law. Because juvenile justice focuses on minors' return to society and normal life, education and protection is primary in the handling of juvenile offenders through public security agencies, the People's Procuratorates, and the People's Courts.

PUBLIC SECURITY AGENCIES AND JUVENILE CRIMINAL JUSTICE

In the juvenile criminal justice procedure, the public security agencies' main task is investigating criminal cases, specifically case filing and investigation. The public security agencies have the power to decide whether to file a case under its jurisdiction against a minor; to investigate all aspects of the case; to decide on the criminal suspect's custody, on bail pending trial, on the surveillance of the suspect's residence and place of detention, and on the purpose of the investigation; and to arrest the juvenile suspect or defendant for the approval or decision of the People's Procuratorate and the People's Court. The power to withdraw cases is another task of the public security agencies. If the public security agencies find that the juvenile suspect should not be prosecuted, they will cancel the case. A public security organ's withdrawal of a case does not require approval from the People's Procuratorate. Referral for prosecution is another power by which a public security organ can request the People's Procuratorate to initiate public prosecution in a juvenile criminal case in which the investigation has ended and the suspect cannot be prosecuted directly. In the filing procedure of juvenile criminal cases, the public security agencies must focus on the year, month, and day of birth of the suspect to determine whether the suspect has reached the age of criminal responsibility.

THE JUVENILE PROCURATORIAL ORGAN

The juvenile procuratorial organ is set up within the People's Procuratorate to address juvenile cases. The Regulations of Shanghai Municipality on the Protection of Juveniles, formed in 1987, included special juvenile procuratorial institutions in the provisions for the first time.[35] By the end of 2019, 1,566 People's Procuratorates had established independent juvenile procuratorial institutions and case-handling teams of juvenile procurators, accounting for 45.36 percent of the total number of procuratorates.

The juvenile prosecution organizations have the power to review the juvenile justice cases that the public security agencies transfer for prosecution and to decide whether to initiate public prosecution according to the law. On the one hand, the juvenile prosecution organizations listen to the opinions of the parents, defenders, and other legal representatives of the juveniles as well as to minor victims and their legal representatives. On the other hand, the legal representatives of juvenile suspects should be notified and present when suspects are interrogated. If the juvenile procuratorial organizations consider it necessary to arrest a juvenile in a criminal case, they may decide to arrest them. In such a case, the public security agencies would immediately implement the decision to arrest.

The application of arrest measures should be limited for the juvenile suspect and defendant per Article 280 of the Criminal Procedure Law. To ensure the cautious use of arresting measures, the juvenile prosecution organizations make comprehensive assessments of the social risks of the juvenile suspect's criminal activity according to the nature, circumstances, subjective malignancy, presence of guardianship, social assistance conditions, and whether the suspect accepts guilt and punishment.

THE JUVENILE COURTS

The Juvenile Courts exercise judicial power on behalf of the state in juvenile justice procedures and hold responsibility for the trial and adjudication of juvenile criminal cases. Since the People's Court in Shanghai Changning District established the first collegial panel specialized in hearing juvenile criminal cases in China in October 1984, the Juvenile Courts have continued to grow. By the end of May 2021, more than 1,800 Juvenile Courts had been established in courts across the country.[36] On December 7, 2020, the 1,820th meeting of the Judicial Committee of the SPC adopted an interpretation of the Criminal Procedure Law, which then came into force on March 1, 2021. Article 550 of the judicial interpretation states that in cases in which the defendant is under the age of eighteen when committing the alleged crime and under the age of twenty when the People's Courts file a case, the suspect will be tried by the trial organization of juvenile cases. The juvenile trial organization can try the following cases: (1) criminal cases involving school students who were under the age of twenty-two when the People's Court files the case against them; (2) cases involving rape, indecency, maltreatment, abandonment of minors, and other criminal cases infringing on minors' personal rights; and (3) other cases that are more appropriate for the trial organization of juvenile cases to try. If there are juvenile defendants in a joint crime case or other criminal cases involving minors, the president will decide whether the juvenile trial organization will hear the cases according to the actual situation of the Juvenile Court.

Although the Juvenile Court notifies the juvenile defendant's legal representative to be present during interrogation and hearing, when trying juvenile crimes involving negligence or criminal cases in which suspects may be sentenced to a penalty of no more than five years' imprisonment, the Juvenile Court may set up court seats in a manner suitable for the characteristics of minors. Many courts use roundtable trials to try juvenile cases in order to eliminate juvenile defendants' panic and resistance, to help juvenile defendants better and more easily accept the judgment results, and to be more conducive to educating judges of teenagers. If a Juvenile Court convicts a juvenile defendant, it will explain the conviction to the juvenile defendant after it pronounces the sentence. To educate juvenile defendants about the terms of a conviction, participants in the proceedings, other suitable adults, social investigators, and psychological counselors can participate.

JUVENILE CORRECTIONAL INSTITUTIONS

If, after trial, the Juvenile Court finds that the juvenile defendant is guilty and sentenced to criminal punishment, the juvenile correctional institution executes the criminal punishment. According to the Prison Law, executing criminal punishments for juvenile offenders focuses on education and reform; the labor of juvenile offenders conforms to the characteristics of minors and focuses on a learning culture and production skills. The juvenile correctional institution cooperates with the state, society, schools, and other educational institutions to provide necessary conditions for juvenile offenders to receive compulsory education. Juvenile offenders who have reached the age of eighteen and whose remaining term of imprisonment does not exceed two years will still be punished in the juvenile correctional institution for the remainder of their sentence.

Chapter 5 of the Law on the Prevention of Juvenile Delinquency further details the juvenile correctional institution's responsibilities. To prevent minors from committing crimes again, (1) minors who execute sentences in the juvenile correctional institution will be detained, managed, and educated separately from adults; (2) the juvenile correctional institution will strengthen legal education for juvenile offenders and carry out vocational education according to the actual situation; and (3) for minors released from prison, the juvenile correctional institution will notify their parents or other guardians in advance to take them back on time, and it will assist in implementing resettlement, assistance, and education measures, among other services.

For juvenile offenders newly admitted to the juvenile correctional institution, the juvenile correctional institution carries out admission education, including admission to the law, code of conduct, and discipline education. For criminals who are about to complete their sentences, the juvenile correctional institution educates them in terms of situation, policies, discipline, and how to abide by the law; provides guidance in terms of employment and returning to school; and provides necessary skills training. The juvenile correctional institution sets up education buildings, laboratories, libraries, sports venues, and other teaching facilities with the necessary equipment for learning—from books to art and sports equipment. Each administrative area sets up conversation rooms, reading rooms, and activity rooms.

Based on the term of imprisonment, types of crimes committed, and prisoners' sex, the juvenile correctional institution detains and manages them separately. The female People's Police manages female juvenile offenders. Juvenile offenders' reform performance is treated differently in terms of such factors as activity scope, communication, meetings, receiving goods, leaving to visit relatives, assessment, reward, and punishment.

CURRENT PRACTICES

In view of the fundamental differences between the purpose and function of juvenile justice and adult justice and considering minors' physical and mental characteristics, the unique systems in the juvenile justice process provide a specific protection and assistance mechanism to help minors avoid the negative effects of simple punishment on their personality formation.

SOCIAL INVESTIGATION SYSTEM

The social investigation system refers to the public security and judicial organizations in handling juvenile criminal cases to investigate not only the facts of the cases but also the physiological and psychological characteristics, personality characteristics, growth experience, social interaction, causes of crime, monitoring education, and post-crime performance of the juvenile suspect and defendant. Social investigation figures out the causes and conditions of juvenile delinquency by investigating and analyzing the personality, quality, life experience, and environment of the juvenile delinquent suspect and defendant.[37]

In dealing with juvenile criminal cases, the public security agencies, the People's Procuratorates, and the People's Courts can, following Article 279 of the Criminal Procedure Law, investigate growth experience, causes of crime, and guardianship education of the juvenile suspect or defendant, according to the circumstances. The public security and judicial organizations can conduct and produce the social investigation report or entrust it to other subjects, such as judicial administrative organizations,

Communist Youth League organizations, and other social organizations. The defender can also submit written materials reflecting the minors' overall situation. The social investigation report and other materials reflecting the minors' overall situation will be examined and can be used as a reference for examining and approving arrests and prosecutions. Cross-examination is conducted in court proceedings, and the social investigation report can be used as a reference for court education and sentencing.

At present, a social investigation pattern that public security agencies dominate, procuratorial organizations supplement, and entrusted investigations support is gradually taking shape. Through careful examination of social investigation reports, these organizations can grasp the growth experience, criminal causes, psychological characteristics, and conditions of helping and educating a young criminal suspect and then promote the implementation of personalized handling and precise assistance.

SYSTEM FOR LEGAL REPRESENTATIVES AND APPROPRIATE ADULT PRESENCE

The system for legal representatives and appropriate adult presence allows a third party to intervene in the litigation process to help minors understand and complete litigation activities. This goal of this special criminal litigation system is to protect minors' rights and interests and to provide them with relief. Article 281 of Criminal Procedure Law and Article 110 of the Law of the PRC on the Protection of Minors state that in order to interrogate minor criminal suspects and defendants and minor victims and witnesses, the public security agencies, the People's Procuratorates, and the People's Courts lawfully must notify their legal representatives and ask that they be present. If it is impossible to notify the legal representative, if the legal representative cannot be present, or if the legal representative is an accomplice, the People's Court may also notify other appropriate adult relatives, representatives of the minor's school or units (*danwei*), grassroots organizations in the place of residence, or the organization for protecting minors and request that they or one of their representatives be present and record the relevant information.

Other adult relatives, representatives of their schools or units (*danwei*), grassroots organizations in their places of residence, or juvenile protection organizations are usually referred to as "other appropriate adults." The legal representatives present at the scene can exercise the litigation rights of juvenile suspects and defendants on their behalf, and they will not damage the minor suspect's legitimate rights and interests. If a juvenile criminal suspect explicitly refuses to attend, then the People's Procuratorate may grant permission for a suitable adult other than the suspect's legal representative to attend the case and, after soliciting the juvenile suspect and defendant's opinions, will notify the other appropriate adults to be present. If the legal representatives or other persons present believe that the case handlers have infringed on the minors' legitimate rights and interests during interrogation and trial, they can put forward their opinions. The legal representative or other persons present can receive the interrogation and court proceedings transcripts to read and relate to the minor, and they will sign, seal, or stamp on the transcripts for confirmation.

LEGAL AID SYSTEM

The juvenile legal aid system is the state's provision of free or reduced-price legal services to minors who need to use legal remedies to protect their legal rights from infringement but who are unable to pay legal service fees because of their inherent vulnerability. This system ensures that the rights that minors receive by the law can be effectively realized. According to the Article 278 of the Criminal Procedure Law, if the juvenile suspect or defendant does not trust the defender, then the People's Courts, the People's Procuratorates, and the public security agencies notify the legal aid agency to appoint a lawyer to provide the minor with a defense. On September 16, 2020, the Ministry of Justice and the China Bar Association issued the guidelines for legal aid services for minors for trial implementation. Article 5 of these guidelines stipulates that when legal aid institutions assign juvenile cases, they should give priority to assigning those who are familiar with minors' physical and mental characteristics and their legal business. In the case of female minors, assigning females to handle them has priority. For major social significance or difficult and complex cases, legal aid institutions can guide and assist those responsible for legal aid in seeking necessary support from the case-handling authorities.

When conditions permit, legal aid institutions can establish a team of lawyers for providing legal aid to minors. The principles of legal aid for minors are to provide help that is of greatest benefit, to give special and priority protection to minors, to respect their personal dignity, to take advantage of the laws in ways that are sensitive to the characteristics of their individual physical and mental health development, to listen to minors' opinions, and to uphold the principle of combining protection with education. In recent years, the procuratorial organizations and judicial administrative organizations have established and improved working mechanisms, gradually improved the coverage and specialization level of legal aid, unblocked channels for legal aid, actively promoted establishing professional legal aid lawyers for juvenile criminal cases, and provided legal aid to juvenile suspects. The unified application system was established within the subsystem of selecting and implementing procurators for minors in July 2018; as of December 2019, the procuratorial organizations have supplied legal aid for juvenile delinquency suspects 37,823 times.[38]

CONDITIONAL NONPROSECUTION SYSTEM

The conditional nonprosecution system is the nonjudicialization of disposing criminal cases that should have entered the criminal procedure, which some countries call "turning disposal." If conditional nonprosecution is applied, the following four conditions should also be met: (1) minors under the age of eighteen are involved in implementing crimes stipulated in Chapter 4 (crimes against citizens' personal and democratic rights), Chapter 5 (crimes against property), and Chapter 6 (crimes against social management order) of the specific provisions of the Criminal Law; (2) according to the crime's specific facts and circumstances, minors can be sentenced to fixed-term imprisonment of no more than one year; (3) the crime's facts are clear, and the evidence is true and sufficient, which meets the conditions for prosecution; and (4) the minor shows repentance.

Before making a decision on conditional nonprosecution, the People's Procuratorate listens to the opinions of the public security agencies, victims, juvenile suspects, and their legal representatives and defenders; they then make and attach to their decision a written record. If the victim is a minor, the People's Procuratorate listens to the opinions of the victim's legal agent and agent ad litem. The inspection period is more than six months and less than one year, calculated from the date when the People's Procuratorate made a decision on conditional nonprosecution.

In the period of trial with conditional nonprosecution, the People's Procuratorate supervises and inspects juvenile suspects. If a juvenile suspect has committed a new crime in the trial period or if there is another crime to be prosecuted before deciding not to prosecute conditionally, the People's Procuratorate transfers the case to the investigating organ for investigation. If these conditions are not met during the trial period, the People's Procuratorate makes a decision not to prosecute. According to a white paper, the procuratorial organizations around the country applied 32,023 cases of conditional nonprosecution to juvenile delinquency suspects; in 2019, there were 7,463 juvenile delinquency suspects, 85.6 percent more such suspects than were recorded in 2014.

CLOSED TRIAL SYSTEM

In the closed trial system, when the People's Court hears juvenile criminal cases, the court is not allowed to publish the name, age, occupation, address, and photos of juvenile defendants for news media reporters. Relevant international laws, such as Rule 8 of the United Nations Standard Minimum Rules for the administration of juvenile justice (Beijing Rules)[39] and Article 40 of the United Nations Convention on the Rights of the Child,[40] clearly stipulate the protection of children's special right to privacy. Article 285 of the Criminal Procedure Law stipulates that cases in which the defendant is under the age of eighteen at the time of trial will not be tried in public. However, with the consent of minor defendants and their legal representatives, the school that the minor defendant attends and the organization in charge of the minor's protection can send representatives to the court. For minors who embark on a path of crime, punishment is only a means, and education and protection are the purpose. Therefore, a closed trial aims to safeguard such minors' reputation, respect their personality, protect their self-esteem, and prevent unnecessary mental trauma to them that may result from an open trial.

CRIMINAL RECORD SEALING SYSTEM

To prevent minors who have completed their sentences and are released from custody from being discriminated against when they return to school, enter a higher school, or obtain employment, the Eighth Amendment to the Criminal Law stipulates that those who were under the age of eighteen at the time of committing a crime and were sentenced to a penalty of no more than five years of fixed-term imprisonment do not have to report to the relevant units that they have received criminal punishment when they join the army and obtain employment. Article 286 of the Criminal Procedure Law stipulates the criminal record sealing system. According to the provisions, if a person who committed a crime was under the age of eighteen at the time the crime was committed and is sentenced to a penalty of no more than five years' fixed-term imprisonment, the relevant offender's record is sealed. When criminal records are sealed, they are not provided to any unit or individual except as needed by judicial organizations or relevant units in accordance with state regulations. A unit that makes inquiries according to law keeps the criminal records confidential.

To better implement the criminal record sealing system, the relevant judicial interpretations have refined their specific operation: Articles 62 through 66 of the Provisions of the People's Procuratorate on Handling Juvenile Criminal Cases stipulate that if a person is under the age of eighteen at the time of committing a crime and is sentenced to a penalty of less than five years of fixed-term imprisonment, then the People's Procuratorate seals criminal records after receiving the effective judgment of the People's Court. The People's Procuratorate seals the juvenile delinquency records, files, and other relevant materials. They keep them encrypted, establish a special juvenile delinquency archive, and implement a strict custody system. If a judicial organ or relevant unit needs to inquire about criminal records, it submits a written application to the People's Procuratorate that sealed the records, and the People's Procuratorate makes a decision within seven days on whether to grant permission. After the juvenile criminal records are sealed, they are not unsealed without legal reasons and legal procedures.

Notes

1. Yanlong Han and Yigong Su, 中国近代警察史 [Modern Police History in China] (Beijing: Social Sciences Academic Press, 2000).
2. Tao Xu and Nan Yang, "Chinese Policing: Its History from a Legal Perspective," in *Comparative Policing from a Legal Perspective*, ed. Monica den Boer (Cheltenham: Edward Elgar, 2018), 363–79.
3. See https://www.mps.gov.cn.
4. According to the MPS, there are more than 280,000 women police officers nationwide, which accounts for 14.3 percent of all police officers. See https://baijiahao.baidu.com/s?id=1693631857150487535&wfr=spider&for=pc.
5. See https://www.sohu.com/a/394992478_170282.
6. The tasks of auxiliary police almost cover all aspects of official police. For more details, refer to https://baike .baidu .com/item/关于规范公安机关警务辅助人员管理工作的意见/20243648?fr=Aladdin.
7. See https://baike .baidu .com/item/关于规范公安机关警务辅助人员管理工作的意见/20243648?fr=Aladdin.
8. See http://www.liaoningxinhe.com/article-72887-191570.html.

9. The measures of reeducation through labor and asylum and education were abolished in 2013 and 2019, respectively. On December 28, 2013, the Standing Committee of the National People's Congress adopted the decision to abolish the provisions of laws on reeducation through labor. On December 28, 2019, the 15th Session of the Standing Committee of the 13th National People's Congress adopted the Decision of the Standing Committee of the National People's Congress on Abolishing Legal Provisions and Systems concerning Asylum and Education.

10. See http://www.gov.cn/zhengce/2010-04/30/content_2602244.htm.

11. See http://entjhsfy .chinacourt .gov .cn/article/index/id/M8xNNzAwNDAwNiACAAA.shtml.

12. See http://www.court.gov.cn/zixun-xiangqing-4349.html.

13. It includes Nanjing, Suzhou, Chengdu, Wuhan, Hanzhou, Fuzhou, Jinan, Shenzhen, Qingdao, Hefei, Changchun, Ningbo, Tianjin, Zhengzhou, Changsha, Xi'an, Nanchang, Lanzhou, Urumqi, Haikou, and Xiamen.

14. Y. Li, "Xinzhongguo jianyu 70 nian gaizao zuifan de chenggong fazhan zhi lu" [The successful development road of reforming criminals in New China prisons in 70 years], Ministry of Justice, December 20, 2019, http://www .moj .gov .cn/organization/content/2019 -12/20/zgjygzxhxwdt_3238369.html.

15. Li, "Xinzhongguo."

16. Richard J. Terrill, "China," in *World Criminal Justice Systems: A Survey* (7th ed.), (Amsterdam: Elsevier, 2009), 492–595.

17. Criminal Law of the PRC, Articles 52, 53.

18. This included sentenced prisoners only, and the total number of prisoners in pretrial detention and other forms of detention was unknown. R. Walmsley, "World Prison Population List" (12th ed.), 2018, https://www.prisonstudies.org/country/china.

19. Walmsley, "World."

20. Zhiliang Wang and Yuan Yuan, 监狱学理论与实务 [Theory and practice of penology] (Beijing: China Legal Publishing House, 2015).

21. H. Sun, "Jianxing 'wudagaizao,' goujian xuexiaohua jianyu" [Practicing the 'five major reforms' and building a new school-style prison], *Legal Daily*, January 14, 2020, http://www.moj.gov.cn/Department/content/2020-01/06/606_3239235.html.

22. Terrill, "China."

23. Z. Hu and H. Wang, "Jianxing wudagaizao xingeju yao shuli wugeyishi" [Practicing the new pattern of five major reforms must establish five consciousnesses], Ministry of Justice, January 14, 2019, http://www.moj.gov.cn/organization/content/2019-01/14/zgjygzxhxwdt_226642.html.

24. Zongxian Wu, 监狱学导论 [Introduction to Penology] (Beijing: Law Press, 2012).

25. China Law Yearbook Editorial Department, 中国法律年鉴2017 [Law Yearbook of China 2017] (Beijing: Press of Law Yearbook of China, 2018).

26. China Law Yearbook Editorial Department, *Law Yearbook*.

27. Ping Wang, Xianbing He, and Fangfang Hao, 社区矫正制度研究 [A Study of Community Corrections] (Beijing: China University of Political Science and Law Press, 2014).

28. Zongxian Wu, 社区矫正制度导论 [Introduction to Community Corrections] (Beijing: China Renmin University Press, 2011).

29. Jing Zhang, 社区矫正法的立法意义与执法难点 [The legislative significance and difficulties of enforcement of Community Correction Law], *Chinese Criminology Review* 4 (2020): 6–17.

30. Zhang, "Legislative."

31. Wang et al., *Study*.

32. Zhang, "Legislative."

33. China Law Yearbook Editorial Department, *Law Yearbook.*

34. G. Yu and S. Xu, "Overview of Juvenile Justice System," in *Theory and Practice of Juvenile Justice System*, ed. G. Yu and S. Xu (Beijing: China People's Public Security University Press, 2012), 1–20.

35. J. Yao, "Juvenile Justice Organization System," in *Growing Up: The Construction of the Juvenile Justice System*, ed. J. Yao (Beijing: China People's Public Security University Press, 2003), 83–121.

36. See http://www.court.gov.cn/zixun-xiangqing-308231.html.

37. Meijing Li and Gaofeng Jin, 我国未成年人社会调查制度 [Social investigation system of minors in China], in *Juvenile Delinquency and the Innovation of Juvenile Justice System*, ed. Meijing Li and Gaofeng Jin (Beijing: China People's Public Security University Press, 2014), 88–120.

38. See https://www.spp.gov.cn/xwfbh/wsfbt/202006/t20200601_463698.shtml#1.

39. According to Rule 8 of the United Nations Standard Minimum Rules for the administration of juvenile justice (Beijing Rules), the right of juvenile offenders to privacy should be respected at all stages in order to avoid harm to minors that may result from improper publicity or naming (Rule 8.1); in principle, information that may lead to the recognition of a juvenile offender shall not be published (Rule 8.2).

40. According to Article 40 of the United Nations Convention on the Rights of the Child, children's privacy is fully respected at all stages of the proceedings (Rule VII).

CHAPTER 6

Introduction to the Criminal Justice System in Malaysia

Yik Koon TEH

Malaysia gained independence from British rule in 1957, when it was Malaya. In 1963, Malaya, Sabah, Sarawak, and Singapore became Malaysia; Singapore left the federation in 1965. The Malaysian criminal justice system is inherited from the British. However, it has evolved into its own system. This chapter discusses how the criminal justice system has evolved into its current form. It focuses on policing and law enforcement, the judiciary, and the correctional system and concludes with an overview of the prevailing challenges facing the system.

Brief History

Malaysia was formed in 1963 after a long history of being colonized by both Asian and Western countries. Hence, the development of its criminal justice system is greatly influenced by the colonial rulers. From the seventh century, Malaysia was ruled by the Buddhist Sri Vijaya Empire; the Hindu Majapahit Empire gained control in the fourteenth century. Islam was introduced to the Malays by traders from India and the Arabian Peninsula after Melaka (Malacca) was established as a port in the fourteenth century. In 1403, the Malay Sultanate was established when Parameswara, a prince from Palembang, established the Malacca Sultanate. He and his people converted to Islam, and Islamic principles were gradually absorbed into the existing legal system, which consisted of "animistic traditions, Malay *adat* (customs), Hindu and Buddhist feudal and princely traditions."[1] The Undang-Undang Melaka (Law of Melaka), the first compilation of law in the Malay Sultanate, was written between 1446 and 1456.[2] Another important legal code was the Undang-Undang Laut Melaka (Maritime Laws of Melaka).

During the Malay Sultanate period, the sultan or, in his absence, the *bendahara* (chief minister) had absolute power in meting out sentences, while the *temenggung* (equivalent to the chief of security) acted as the chief of police. Apart from the *temenggung*, all the *penghulu* (local chiefs) also maintained their own police or *mata-mata* (eyes of the state).[3]

The Portuguese colonized Melaka, the oldest Malay Sultanate, in the sixteenth century. The Portuguese relied on the military to administer the state, and policing work was carried out by the Portuguese soldiers.[4] As Melaka was already a cosmopolitan society, the Portuguese used the *capitan*[5] system in their administration of the different ethnic groups. Each ethnic group was placed under a leader who performed the institutional role of the police. Leading citizens were appointed as magistrates with civil and criminal jurisdiction.[6] Appeals could be made to the chief justice. However, there was no separation between the judiciary and the executive, as the chief justice had to apply to the governor for his advice and approval of verdicts in criminal cases that were triable in his court. Punishments meted out by the Portuguese—including torture, imprisonment in dungeons, and executions—were brutal.[7]

In the seventeenth century, the Dutch captured Melaka from the Portuguese. The Dutch initially relied on the existing military system and continued with the *capitan* system. However, as the European population started to grow, a police force called the Burgher Guard was established. The Burgher Guard, an amateur organization, was managed by Dutch citizens living in Melaka and by the natives, who were employed in the lower ranks. The Burgher Guard was answerable to the Council of Justice, members of which were selected from the Dutch community in Melaka, and they functioned as investigating officers as well as magistrates. The Dutch allowed Islamic law and Malay customs to be applied to cases involving the locals. The penghulus continued to perform their policing duties, and the Dutch continued the brutal punishments of the Portuguese. Sentences for offenders included crucifixion, "breaking wheel," having their hands chopped off, and being inhumanely flogged.[8]

The British took control of Prince of Wales Island—currently known as Penang Island—in the eighteenth century when Captain Francis Light was sent by the British East India Company to the island for trade purposes in 1786.[9] He was given the rank of superintendent and instructed to maintain the security of the island himself.[10] Initially, he relied on the Bengali sepoy (soldiers) who came with him from India to carry out the task. As the sepoys were not reliable in their duties, he appointed leaders among the Malays, Chinese, and Chulias (southern Indians) and gave them the title of captain.[11] Their roles were similar to those of a magistrate in adjudicating petty cases, while the serious cases were brought before the superintendent. Each captain was assisted by five peons, whose role was similar to that of a constable, namely, to look after the security of a few districts. These peons could be regarded as the first regular policemen in British Malaya.[12] In addition to their main role as law enforcement, they had other administrative roles, such as controlling the water supply, registering births and deaths, preventing fires, and overseeing prisons. Captain Light repeatedly requested assistance from the East India Company in establishing an official police force, but his requests were ignored.[13] In 1800, following the publication of a report by Colonel Arthur Wellesley—later the Duke of Wellington—titled "Memorandum on Pulo Penang," an English barrister named John Dickens was appointed as the first judge and magistrate of the island. The law for the island was at that time to be "the law of the different peoples and tribes of which the inhabitants consist, tempered by such parts of the British law as are of universal application."[14]

On March 25, 1807, the island was granted the first Charter of Justice[15] by the British Crown, which enabled the island to establish a proper court of judicature, which consisted of the governor, three counselors, and a recorder, all of whom acted as judges. It also entailed a more efficient and effective police force, as legal enforcement could be carried out with a proper set of laws. This was the beginning of the acceptance of English common law and modern policing in Malaysia. A high sheriff, a deputy sheriff, and high constables were appointed among the Europeans, while petty constables were recruited among the Asians.[16] Recruitment of special constables in the island started in 1836 to quell the riots of the secret societies among the Malays and Chinese.[17]

The British expanded their control to Singapore in 1819 and to Melaka in 1825. Sir Thomas Stamford Raffles acquired Singapore for Britain, but he did not succeed in setting up an efficient police force there. The situation improved considerably by early 1840s, when the sitting magistrate served as the superintendent and was assisted by three European constables, an assistant constable, fourteen officers, and 110 police.[18] After the British took over Melaka from the Dutch, a Council of Justice meeting held in July 1827 created a police force and appointed a superintendent of police, or chief police officer.[19] He was assisted by two European constables, four headmen of the Burgher Guard, twenty-eight peons, and twenty-one penghulus. The brutal Dutch punishment for offenders was replaced with a more "humane" British system.[20]

The British united Singapore, Melaka, and Prince of Wales Island to form the Straits Settlements in 1826. In 1827, the second Charter of Justice was issued, which was reported to be similar to the first charter and was only an extension of the jurisdiction of the court in Prince of Wales Island to Melaka and Singapore.[21] However, there was no separation of powers between the judiciary and the executive, nor was there a move to unite the police of the three states.[22] The third Charter of Justice was introduced in 1855 to "restructure the administration of justice" so that the increasing judicial workload could be managed.[23] The court was divided into two divisions: Penang as one division and Melaka and Singapore as another division. The introduction of the Indian Police Act of 1856 allowed the local government in the Straits Settlements to appoint a commissioner and a deputy commissioner of police for each town or station.[24] This allowed the police force to be on a more regular footing.

After 1867, the Supreme Court was established, and judicial functions were finally taken away from the executive branch.[25] The Indian Penal and Criminal Procedure Codes were adopted with some modifications. The Civil Procedure Code was also introduced. The Civil Law Ordinance introduced English law relating to businesses by land and sea, corporations, and banks and banking. Magistrates at the time could be British, Malay, Chinese, or Eurasian. The Court of Appeal was introduced, and certain appeals could be brought to the Privy Council.

In 1871, the Police Force Ordinance was introduced to the Straits Settlements. This ordinance brought the police force of the colony under the control of an inspector general who was stationed in Singapore. The inspector general was assisted by superintendents, assistant superintendents, inspectors, other officers, and constables at each of the settlements.[26] This was the beginning of the development of the Royal Federation of Malaya Police. Prison duties were still under the purview of the police.

The Supreme Court was reorganized in 1873. The four Supreme Court judges were now the chief justice, the judge of Penang, a senior puisne judge, and a junior puisne judge.[27] A criminal court known as the Court of Quarter Sessions, which was presided over in Singapore by the senior puisne judge and in Penang by the junior puisne judge, was also established together with the Court of Appeal.

The Courts Ordinance was passed in 1878 to amend the constitution of the civil and criminal courts. Among the provisions were the establishment of the inferior courts and appeals to be heard by the Supreme Court. The courts established by the ordinance were as follows:

- Supreme Court of the Straits Settlements
- Courts of Requests at each settlement
- Courts of Two Magistrates at each settlement
- Magistrates' Courts at each settlement
- Coroners Courts at each settlement
- Justices of the Peace[28]

By 1895, British control had extended to Perak, Selangor, Negeri Sembilan, and Pahang, which the British formed into the Federated Malay States (FMS). A common judiciary was introduced to establish a common court of appeal called the Court of the Judicial Commissioner, which was the highest court.[29] In 1905, it was replaced by the Supreme Court, which was established by the respective state legislation and had jurisdiction only in the respective state. It was only in 1918 that the federal Supreme Court was established in the FMS by federal legislation. Kedah, Perlis, Kelantan, Terengganu, and Johor came under British control between 1909 and 1914. They formed the Unfederated Malay States (UFMS). Each state had its own judiciary, Supreme Court, and Constitution of the Courts.[30]

When the FMS was formed in 1896, the police force from Perak, Selangor, Negeri Sembilan, and Pahang were made contingents of the FMS police.[31] Harry Syers was appointed the first commissioner of police of the FMS. The first official police force was reportedly established in Selangor in late 1870s; this force was reformed by Syers and given the title of the Selangor Military Police Force.[32] Among the FMS police forces, the Perak Armed Police, reformed by Captain Tristram Speedy and Captain Paul Swinburne, was reported to be outstanding. It was "an organization recognizable as the ancestor of the Royal Federation of Malaya Police."[33] In 1897, the supervision of the Prisons Department was separated from the police and placed under the deputy inspector of prisons.[34] In 1903, the Police Force Enactment brought the whole police force under the control of the commissioner. A new training scheme for probationers for the officer ranks was introduced, and a police depot was established to centralize training.[35]

FMS enacted its first Criminal Procedure Code in 1935 and its first Penal Code in 1936. In 1938, the titles of the gazetted officer ranks of the FMS were replaced with those used in the Straits Settlements and most parts of the British Empire. "Commissioner of police" became "inspector general," "deputy commissioner" became "superintendent," and "assistant commissioner" became "assistant superintendent."[36]

After the Japanese occupation from 1942 to 1945, the British named the police force the Civil Affair Police Force. Administration of the police in the whole of Malaya was centralized under this force.[37] In 1946, the force was renamed the Malayan Union Police Force.[38] In 1948, after the Straits Settlements, the FMS and the UFMS were brought together under the Federation of Malaya, and the police force was renamed again, this time as the Federation of Malaya Police Force. In the same year, the Courts Ordinance introduced a new structure of inferior courts, which comprised the Sessions Courts, Magistrates' Courts, and Penghulus' (Headmen) Courts.[39] As for the Superior Courts, they consisted of the Court of Appeal and High Court, which was under a chief justice.

Women were recruited into the police force during the Malayan Emergency, starting in 1948, when the Communist Party of Malaya tried to take over the country.[40] However, it was only in 1955 that the Women Police Force was formally established. When Malaya gained independence from the British in 1957, the Federation of Malaya Police Force was granted the title of the Royal Federation of Malaya Police by the *agong* (king). The court system, excluding Islamic courts, became matters under the legislative powers of the Federation.

After Sarawak and Sabah joined Malaya to form Malaysia in 1963, the Sarawak Constabulary and North Borneo Armed Constabulary were absorbed into the Royal Malaysia Police (RMP).[41] The Federal Constitution was amended and the court system restructured to include Sabah and Sarawak. Provision was also made for the establishment of the Federal Court, the highest court, and the introduction of a lord president. However, Singapore left Malaysia to become independent in 1965. The Police Act came into force in 1967.

At present, criminal cases in Malaysia continue to be bound by the Criminal Procedure Code (Act 593) and the Penal Code (Act 574), which were enacted by the FMS and have been amended over the years to serve the needs of the moment. The Federal Constitution recognized Islam as the religion of the Federation, "but other religions may be practiced in peace and harmony in any part of the Federation."[42] As such, Syariah (sharia) Courts, which are under state jurisdiction, have jurisdiction only over "Islamic law, and personal and family law of persons professing the religion of Islam, which includes, inter alia, matters such as betrothal, marriage, divorce, legitimacy, dowry, maintenance, adoption, succession, and religious endowments."[43]

Organization and Structure of the RMP

As of 2021, the RMP consists of more than 137,000 police and civilian personnel who are headed by the inspector general of police.[44] The RMP has seventeen police ranks within the two main categories of senior police officers and junior police officers and constables.

Senior police officer ranks include, in order from highest to lowest authority, inspector general of police (four-star), deputy inspector general of police (four-star), commissioner of police (three-star), deputy commissioner of police (two-star), senior assistant commissioner of police (one-star), assistant commissioner of police, superintendent of police, deputy superintendent of police, assistant superintendent of police, inspector, and probationary inspector. Junior police officers and constables include, in order from highest to lowest authority, subinspector, sergeant major, sergeant, corporal, lance corporal, and constable. Support groups that assist the RMP in its duties include the Polis Tambahan (extra police constables), Sukarelawan Polis (police volunteer reserves), Polis Bantuan (auxiliary police), police cadets, and civil servants.

The structure of the RMP consists of four levels: the headquarters or federal level, located at Bukit Aman in Kuala Lumpur; the state level; the district level; and the station level.[45] The headquarters is the administrative center for the entire police force and also the office of the inspector general of police and his deputy.

The RMP is divided into ten main departments:

1. Management Department: responsible for the general management and administration of the RMP.
2. Criminal Investigation Department: investigates criminal cases and arrests and prosecutes offenders.
3. Narcotics Crime Investigation Department: investigates and prosecutes cases related to drug trafficking and drug abuse.
4. Logistics and Technology Department: provides support services to the RMP related to finance, communication, information technology, transportation, armaments, and asset and supply management.
5. Internal Security and Public Order Department: enhances effective enforcement and maintains public order and national security. Its functions include land and maritime security and suppressing violence. As such, it must cooperate with other enforcement agencies, such as the Malaysian Armed Forces and Malaysian Maritime Enforcement Agency. It has five branches: the General Operations Force, the Special Operations Force, the Marine Operations Force, the Federal Reserve Unit, and the Air Operations Force.
6. Special Branch: collects and processes information and security intelligence.
7. Commercial Crime Investigation Department: investigates, arrests, and prosecutes white-collar criminals.
8. Integrity and Standards Compliance Department: strengthens the integrity of the police and ensures that police officers perform their tasks in accordance with standards.
9. Crime Prevention and Community Safety Department: responsible for strategizing and implementing initiatives to lower crime rates and to raise public awareness about security.
10. Traffic Enforcement and Investigation Department: ensures the safety and comfort of road users and investigates and takes action against irresponsible drivers.[46]

Organization of the Courts

The present structure of the Malaysian court system is shown in figure 6.1.

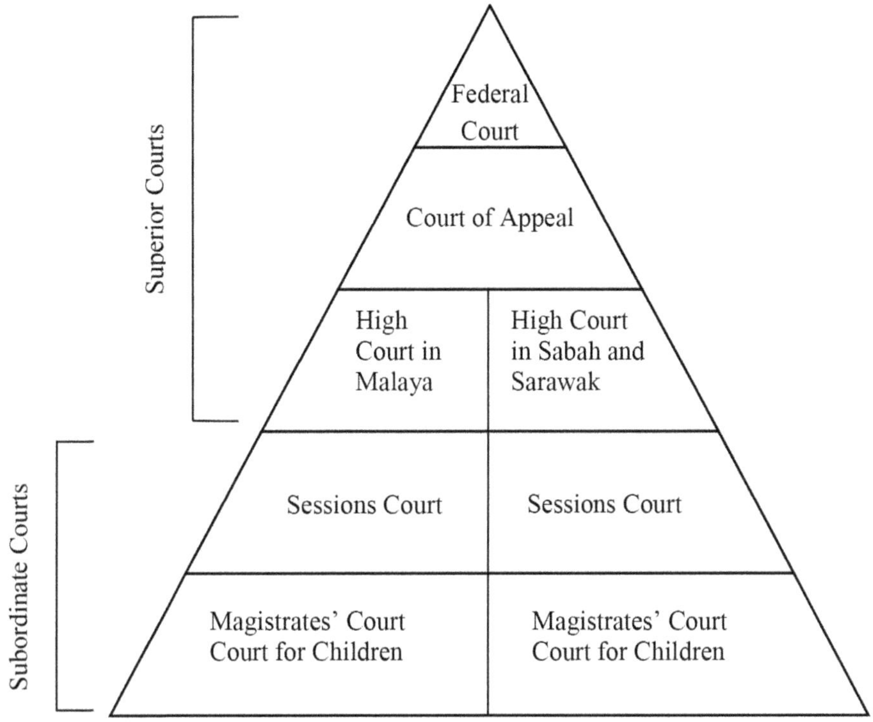

Figure 6.1. Structure of the Malaysian Court System. *Source: Yik Koon TEH*

Generally, there are two types of trials in Malaysia: criminal and civil. The hierarchy of courts, which entails an appeal system, begins with the Magistrates' Court, followed by the Sessions Court, High Court, Court of Appeal, and Federal Court. The Penghulu Court was abolished on March 1, 2013, by the Subordinate Courts (Amendment) Act 2010. The Sessions Court and the Magistrates' Court, as the two subordinate courts, are governed by the Subordinate Courts Act of 1948, while the superior courts, which consist of the High Court, the Court of Appeal, and the Federal Court, are governed by the Courts of Judicature Act of 1964. Article 121 of the Federal Constitution provides for two High Courts: the High Court in Malaya and the High Court in Sabah and Sarawak. This created two separate parallel systems for the states in Peninsular Malaysia and the two Borneo states of Sabah and Sarawak. There is no jury system in Malaysia, as it was abolished on January 1, 1995. The senior-most judge is the chief justice of the Federal Court of Malaysia, who is also known as the chief justice of Malaysia, followed by the president of the Court of Appeal, the chief judge of Malaya, and the chief judge of Sabah and Sarawak.

Outside the court hierarchy are the state Syariah Courts; the Native Courts of Sabah and Sarawak, which have jurisdiction on matters of native law and custom; and the Special Court, established in 1993, which has jurisdiction over cases involving the rulers of the states and the *agong*.

The Malaysian Correctional System

Among the punishments listed in the Criminal Procedure Code that could be awarded to the offenders are death sentence, whipping, imprisonment, fines, police supervision, and good-behavior bonds. The death penalty, which can be handed out only by the High Court, is carried out by hanging. Pregnant women and minors may not be punished with a death sentence. Instead, their sentences are reduced to life imprisonment. Whippings may not be executed in installments and should not exceed twenty-four strokes for an adult or ten strokes for a "youthful offender" between the ages of eighteen and twenty years. The rattan cane used in whippings should not be more than half an inch in diameter. Women cannot be sentenced to whipping, nor can men who have been sentenced to death. Exclusion from whipping also applies to men whom the Court considers to be more than fifty years old, although there are notable exceptions to this exclusion. Men more than fifty years old can be whipped if they are sentenced to whipping for the following reasons:

- Rape (Penal Code Section 376)
- Carnal intercourse against the order of nature on another person without the consent, or against the will, of the other person (Penal Code Section 377c)
- Sexual connection with another person by the introduction of any object or any part of the body, except the penis into the vagina or anus of the other person without the other person's consent (Penal Code Section 377ca)
- Inciting a child under the age of fourteen years to any act of gross indecency with the offender or another person (Penal Code Section 377e)

Juvenile Justice in Malaysia

The Child Act of 2001 (Act 611) is the principal legislation regarding juvenile offenders. Under the act, a child is defined as a person under the age of eighteen years who has attained the age of criminal responsibility. As stipulated in Penal Code Section 82 (Act 574), "Nothing is an offence which is done by a child under ten years of age." Therefore, juvenile offenders are those who are ten years old and younger than eighteen. However, there are exceptions; for example, Penal Code Section 83 stipulates that "nothing is an offence which is done by a child above ten years of age and under twelve, who has not attained sufficient maturity of understanding to judge of the nature and consequence of his conduct on that occasion." Additionally, the Child Act enforces strict privacy on the identity of the child who has been arrested.

The Court for Children has the jurisdiction to try all offenses except for offenses punishable with death or for other "grave crimes," such as murder, offenses under the Firearms (Increased Penalties) Act of 1971, and offenses under the Dangerous Drugs Act of 1952, which are punishable with imprisonment for more than five years or with death. These more serious offenses are tried at the High Court. If a child commits a crime together with an adult, the trial will also be heard in the adult criminal court rather than the Court for Children. Per Child Act Section 83(4), however, the adult court must "exercise in respect of the child all the powers which may be exercised under this Act by a Court for Children" and must consider the probation report before exercising the powers conferred.

In general, after a child has been arrested, the arresting police officer will immediately inform a probation officer and the child's parents or guardians. A copy of the charge and other information necessary will be passed to the probation officer in order to enable a probation report to be prepared or obtained (Child Act Section 87). The child will be brought before a Court for Children within twenty-four hours (Child Act Section 84). If it is not possible to bring the child to a Court for Children, then the child will be brought before a magistrate who may direct the child to be remanded to a detention facility until the child can be brought before the Court for Children. It is compulsory for the child's parents or guardians to be present at court during all the stages of the proceedings unless the court is satisfied that it would be unreasonable to require the attendance of the parents or guardians (Child Act Section 88).

When the child is brought to the Court for Children, the court will determine whether it is in the child's best interest to be removed from association with any undesirable person or whether the release of the child would be detrimental to justice (Child Act Section 84[3]). If the court decides to release the child, then it will do so on a bond, with or without sureties, that is executed by the child's parents or guardians or by another person responsible for the child for an amount that, in the opinion of the court, will secure the attendance of the child on the hearing of the charge. If the child is not released while awaiting trial, then the court has the power to order the child to be detained in a police station, police cell, or police lockup that is separate from adult offenders or, if necessary, in a mental hospital (Child Act Section 86). In addition, female offenders will be put under the care of women.

If the child does not plead guilty to the offense committed, the Court for Children will then hear the evidence of the witnesses in support thereof. The witness may be cross-examined by or on behalf of the child. Children who conduct their own defense may be assisted by their parents, guardians, relatives, or other responsible persons (Child Act Section 90). For children who are not legally represented or assisted in their defense, the court will proceed to question the child and witnesses in order to bring out the truth of the matter. If the court finds that the child is not guilty, the court will record an order of acquittal. However, if the child is proven to be guilty, the court will, before deciding how to deal with the child, consider the probation report prepared by the probationary officer.

Depending on the severity of the case, per Child Act Section 91, the Court for Children could administer the following punishments for children who are found guilty:

1. Admonish and discharge the child
2. Discharge the child on his executing a bond to be of good behavior and to comply with such conditions as may be imposed by the court

3. Order that the child to be placed in the care of a relative or other fit and proper person
   a. for such period to be specified by the court
   b. with such conditions as may be imposed by the court
4. Order the child to pay a fine, compensation, or costs
5. Make a probation order under Child Act Section 98
6. Order the child to be sent to an approved school or a Henry Gurney School
7. Order the child, if a male, to be whipped with not more than ten strokes of a light cane
   a. within the Court premises
   b. in the presence, if the child desires, of the parents or guardians of the child
8. Impose on the child, if he is at least fourteen years old and the offense is punishable with imprisonment and subject to Child Act Section 96(2), any term of imprisonment that could be awarded by a Sessions Court

In Malaysia, Section 97 of the Child Act stipulates that no death sentence can be meted out to juvenile offenders. Instead, the juvenile offenders are to be detained in a prison at the pleasure of either the *agong*, if the offense was committed in the Federal Territory of Kuala Lumpur or the Federal Territory of Labuan, or the sultan or the Yang di-Pertua Negeri (ruler of the state), if the offense was committed in the state.

Children, their parents, their guardians, and any other aggrieved party who are not satisfied with the judgment of the Court for Children may appeal to the High Court against such finding or order in accordance with the provisions of the Criminal Procedure Code relating to criminal appeals to the High Court from Magistrates' Court.

Current Challenges Facing the Criminal Justice System

Over the years, the RMP has been accused of not being efficient in bringing down crime rates and not addressing police brutality, custodial deaths, discrimination against non-Bumiputeras (nonindigenous people), corruption, and undue political influence.[47] The Royal Commission to Enhance the Operation and Management of the RMP was set up in 2005 and recommended setting up the Independent Police Complaints and Misconduct Commission (IPCMC) as an external oversight body that would ensure good governance in the RMP.[48] However, the recommendation was not taken up by the then Barisan Nasional (National Front) government, as there was strong objection from the police force. Moreover, the Barisan Nasional government worried about losing police votes to opposition parties in future elections.[49] Instead, a watered-down Enforcement Agency Integrity Commission, which could investigate but not take action, was implemented.[50] The negative perception and mistrust toward the RMP continued.

When the Pakatan Harapan (Alliance of Hope) government took over in 2018, the Prime Minister's Department published the National Anti-Corruption Plan

2019–2023 (NACP) to curb corruption in the country, particularly after high-profile political corruption cases, such as one involving a former prime minister. The NACP also reported that 57 percent of respondents to a 2017 survey by Transparency International perceived that police officers were corrupt and that the police force was the most corrupt government agency.[51] Consequently, one of the strategies of the NACP was to introduce the IPCMC to address integrity issues and to curb misconduct among the police. The Pakatan Harapan government had a first reading of the IPCMC bill in Parliament in July 2019 and a second reading in October 2019 before referring it to a special committee for further review. It was tabled in Parliament after the review, but the Pakatan Harapan government lost control of the government, and the Perikatan Nasional (National Alliance) coalition came into power in 2020. The Perikatan Nasional coalition had no interest in considering the IPCMC. Instead, it was replaced with the Independent Police Conduct Commission (IPCC) bill; the first reading of the IPCC bill in Parliament was in August 2020. The Human Rights Commission of Malaysia (SUHAKAM), the human rights non-governmental organization Suara Rakyat Malaysia (or Suaram) (Voice of Malaysian People), the Malaysian Bar, and Human Rights Watch voiced their concerns about the IPCC. They believed that the IPCC did not capture the essence of the IPCMC bill of 2019 and the 2005 Royal Commission's recommendations. The IPCC, as an alternative to the IPCMC, lacked both independence, as commissioners could be police officers and government appointees, and the disciplinary powers to deal with police misconduct.[52] Without the IPCMC, the RMP will continue to be negatively perceived by the public.

It has also been alleged that corruption has permeated the judiciary. A former Court of Appeal judge, Hamid Sultan Abu Backer, wrote a sixty-three-page affidavit in February 2019 alleging "judicial interference" in court cases. He alluded that "the contents of my affidavit are prima facie to expose constitutional and judicial misconduct before the [last general] election and also after the election, which is continuing without abate, as there is sufficient material to purportedly say top judges are continuing to mislead the public by conniving not to expose judicial crimes."[53] For example, he claimed that "certain members of the judiciary have been aiding private parties to defraud the government."[54] He also alleged that judges could be called to the chambers of top judges and briefed on what to do.[55] Hamid Sultan further alluded that he was suspended for six months by the Judges' Ethics Committee for following his conscience.[56] His persistent call for a royal commission of inquiry (RCI) in the judiciary unfortunately was not taken up by the chief justice.

Firdaus Ramlan, former magistrate in the state of Kelantan, was sentenced to three years' imprisonment in 2009 for accepting bribes. His confession in February 2021 brought to light the extent of corruption in the judiciary in Malaysia[57] and lent further credibility to Hamid Sultan's allegations. Firdaus Ramlan alleged that the corrupt system was an "open secret." When he reported for duty on his first day as a young magistrate, middlepersons or brokers had already approached him on behalf of offenders, offering him as much as 10,000 ringgit (approximately U.S.$2,500) per case. Firdaus Ramlan identified a middleperson as a senior police officer who had access to the magistrates in the courthouse. This confession, in conjunction with Hamid Sultan's revelations, increased public support for the RCI in the judiciary. However, the RCI is still not forthcoming.

Finally, there has been an increasingly strong movement to abolish the death penalty. The movement has been supported by members of Parliament, the Human Rights Commission of Malaysia,[58] and the Malaysian Bar.[59]

Notes

1. Shad Saleem Faruqi, "Malaysian Legal System—An Introduction," *University of Malaya Law Review*, November 27, 2017, https://www.umlawreview.com/lex-in-breve/malaysian-legal-system-an-introduction.
2. Richard Winstedt, "The Date of the Malacca Legal Codes," *Journal of the Royal Asiatic Society of Great Britain and Ireland*, issue 1–2 (April 1953): 33.
3. Patrick Morrah, "The History of the Malayan Police," *Journal of the Malayan Branch of the Royal Asiatic Society* 36, pt. 2, no. 202 (1968): 8.
4. Halal Bin Hj. Ismail, Samsudin Bin Ali, Abd. Latif Bin Yahaya, Selamat Bin Sainayune, and Ruziah Vinti Abdullah, *Sejarah Bergambar Institusi Polis di Malaysia* [Pictorial History of the Police Institution in Malaysia] (Kuala Lumpur: Persatuan Muzium Negara [National Muzium Association], 1994), 3.
5. *Capitan* is a Spanish word, and, according to Morrah ("History," 12), the system was introduced by the Portuguese. The local spelling is *kapitan*.
6. Richard Winstedt, *Malaya and its History* (London: Hutchinson University Library, 1966), 96.
7. Winstedt, *Malaya*, 96.
8. Morrah, "History," 29–30; Winstedt, *Malaya*, 96.
9. Halal et al., *Sejarah*, 7.
10. Halal et al., *Sejarah*, 7; Morrah, "History," 15.
11. Morrah, "History," 18.
12. Morrah, "History," 18.
13. Morrah, "History," 21.
14. Winstedt, *Malaya*, 97.
15. Halal et al., *Sejarah*, 8; Morrah, "History," 25.
16. Morrah, "History," 25.
17. Halal et al., *Sejarah*, 10; Morrah, "History," 39–40.
18. Morrah, "History," 34–35.
19. Morrah, "History," 30–31.
20. Winstedt, *Malaya*, 96.
21. L. A. Mills, Constance M. Turnbull, and D. K. Bassett, "British Malaya 1824–67," *Journal of the Malayan Branch of the Royal Asiatic Society* 33, pt. 3, no. 191 (1960): 84.
22. Morrah, "History," 28.
23. Tun Abdul Hamid Mohamad and Adnan Trakic, "The Reception of English Law in Malaysia and Development of the Malaysian Common Law," *Common Law World Review* 44, no. 2 (2015): 126.
24. Morrah, "History," 37.
25. Winstedt, "Malaya," 98.
26. Morrah, "History," 40.

27. Y. A. A. Tan Sri Dato' Abdul Hamid Omar, "Administration of justice in Malaysia," *The Denning Law Journal* 2, no. 1 (1987): 3.
28. W. Napier, "An Introduction to the Study of the Law Administered in the Colony of the Straits Settlements," *Malaya Law Review* 16, no. 1 (July 1974): 4–51.
29. Tun Abdul Hamid, "Reception," 3.
30. Tun Abdul Hamid, "Reception," 4.
31. Morrah, "History," 89.
32. Morrah, "History," 52–55.
33. Morrah, "History," 61.
34. Morrah, "History," 90.
35. Morrah, "History," 100.
36. Morrah, "History," 144.
37. Halal et al., *Sejarah*, 121.
38. Halal et al., *Sejarah*, 123–25.
39. Tun Abdul Hamid, "Reception," 6.
40. Halal et al., *Sejarah*, 143.
41. Halal et al., *Sejarah*, 101, 111.
42. Federal Constitution Section 3(1).
43. Yvonne Tew, "The Malaysian Legal System: A Tale of Two Courts," Georgetown University Law Center, 2011, https://scholarship.law.georgetown.edu/cgi/viewcontent.cgi?article=2944&context=facpub.
44. The Official Portal of Royal Malaysia Police, "*Mengenai Polis Diraja Malaysia* (About RMP)," https://www.rmp.gov.my/infor-korporate/polis-diraja-malaysia.
45. The Official Portal of Royal Malaysia Police, "*Struktur* (Structure)," https://www.rmp.gov.my/infor-korporate/polis-diraja-malaysia.
46. The Official Portal of Royal Malaysia Police, "*Jabatan-jabatan* (Departments)," https://www.rmp.gov.my/infor-korporate/polis-diraja-malaysia.
47. Yik Koon TEH, "The Challenges of the Royal Malaysia Police," in *Global Perspectives in Policing and Law Enforcement*, ed. Jospeter M. Mbuba, 217–19 (Lanham, MD: Lexington Books, 2021).
48. Nadhrah A. Kadir and Kamaruzaman Jusoff, "Strategic Management and Improvement of the Malaysian Police from the Perspective of the Royal Commission Report," *Journal of Law and Conflict Resolution* 1, no. 4 (September 2009): 76, https://www.researchgate.net/publication/252974205_Strategic_management_and_improvement_of_the_Malaysian_Police_from_the_perspective_of_the_Royal_Commission_Report.
49. Faisal Asyraf and Zikri Kamarulzaman, "How Does the IPCMC Affect Police Votes?," *Malaysiakini*, August 23, 2020, https://zh.malaysiakini.com/news/539664.
50. *Malaysiakini*, "IPCMC Is Here—But Does It Have Bite?," July 19, 2019, https://www.malaysiakini.com/news/484490.
51. Prime Minister's Department, *National Anti-Corruption Plan 2019–2023* (Putrajaya: Prime Minister's Department, 2019).
52. *Malaysiakini*, "IPCC Bill: Suhakam Concerned over Lack of Independence, Conflict of Interest," August 27, 2020, https://www.malaysiakini.com/news/540302; *Malaysiakini*, "HRW Accuses PM of 'Spitting in Face' of Royal Commission on Police," August 28, 2020, https://www.malaysiakini.com/news/540441.
53. *Malaysiakini*, "Senior Judge Willing to Reveal More in RCI, but Regrets CJ's Reluctance," February 21, 2019, https://www.malaysiakini.com/news/464039.
54. *Malaysiakini*, "Shocking! Judge Claims Judiciary Involved in Swindling Public Funds," February 15, 2019, https://www.malaysiakini.com/news/464034.

55. *Malaysiakini*, "Senior Judge—Harapan Win Rattled Judges, but Now 'Business as Usual,'" February 15, 2019, https://www.malaysiakini.com/news/464045.

56. V. Anbalagan, "I Have Lived Up to My Oath of Office, Says Suspended Judge on Retirement Day," *Free Malaysia Today*, August 27, 2021, https://www.freemalaysiatoday.com/category/nation/2021/08/27/i-have-lived-up-to-my-oath-of-office-says-suspended-judge-on-retirement-day.

57. Faisal Asyraf, "Justice Gone Wrong: Jailed for Graft, Ex-Magistrate Shares His Story," *Malaysiakini*, February 5, 2021, https://www.malaysiakini.com/news/561772.

58. *Free Malaysia Today*, "Abolish Death Penalty, Suspend Pending Executions, Say Groups, MP," October 10, 2021, https://www.freemalaysiatoday.com/category/nation/2021/10/10/abolish-death-penalty-suspend-pending-executions-say-groups-mp.

59. *Free Malaysia Today*, "Malaysian Bar Renews Call to Abolish Death Penalty," October 10, 2020, https://www.freemalaysiatoday.com/category/nation/2020/10/10/malaysian-bar-renew-calls-to-abolish-death-penalty.

Part 3

EUROPE AND EURASIA

CHAPTER 7

The Criminal Justice System of Italy

Giulia Fabini and Alvise Sbraccia

Each criminal justice system (CJS) can be represented as a set of integrated agencies involved in protecting public safety from threats posed to legal interests that legal systems identify as being superior. Such superiority is implied by the fact that the laws defining the scope of penalties have the maximum sanctioning capacity, being capable of exercising on those who violate them the highest level of institutional coercion. In the rule of law, therefore, the state's power to punish must be carefully determined by the law. In Italy, the principles identified by the Constitution should be reflected in the provisions of the Criminal Code.[1] This is somewhat paradoxical, as the constitutional charter of the Italian Republic (1948) was promulgated after the Criminal Code was created (1933), which happened during the fascist dictatorship (1922–1943). The necessary adjustment process was carried out not by producing a new Criminal Code but through a series of transformations accompanying the seventy-six-year history of democratic Italy.

Regulatory evolutions have also influenced the organizational structures of the various segments of the CJS. Such evolutions include the process of attributing responsibilities to different civil and military police forces, such as the state police, finance police, Carabinieri, and prison police;[2] the functioning of the criminal sector of the judiciary, which is increasingly contaminated by administrative mechanisms; the structure of prison circuits; and the establishment of juvenile justice as a subsystem.

The fundamental pillar of the Italian penal system, which is clearly influenced by political-cultural canons of criminological positivism,[3] is the notion of social dangerousness. The influence of criminological positivism on the Italian penal system is possible only because of contaminated definitions of terms from the social sciences on the one hand and from psychiatry and legal formulations on the other. For example, the Italian sanctioning system has a double-track structure that entails convictions for transgressors who are aware of the criminal rules and security measures for those who are dangerous but cannot be indicted because of personal deficits. However, the matter cannot be resolved by identifying the possible balance between the areas of technical knowledge involved in the definition of social dangerousness. The latter is the result of historical and political contingencies that are related to control cultures.[4] In this sense, following a critical criminology approach, the CJS can be identified not as a set of integrated agencies that have as their reference point a formally understood principle of legality but rather as a field of forces within which organized players compete to reach hegemonic positions related to their ability to direct criminal selectivity. The latter, in brief, also refer to social and media representations and to the practices of control agencies, which contribute to identifying the behaviors, persons, and social groups in any given historical moment that are labeled as being socially dangerous. This historical and cultural variability produces internal enemy archetypes that are reflected in waves of moral panic, which provoke criminal policy responses that play on the repressive mechanisms that we now attribute to the notion of criminal populism.[5] A cyclical trend such as this is characterized by the need to formulate political responses based on the identification of emergency criminal phenomena, which require exceptional reactions.[6]

In the fascist era, social dangerousness was attributed mainly to the area of political dissent, but the republican history has configured a criminal policy that is constantly pursuing different forms of emerging dangerousness. The enemies to be tackled by the CJS have therefore taken on different traits over the years. The subversive figure characterized a phase of intense political conflict in the country (1968–1982). More recently, drug addiction and petty crime have been identified as social phenomena to be combated through the penal system as they have been in the rest of the Western world. Particularly stringent special legislation was introduced in the 1990s to address the Mafia "emergency." At the same time, migrant criminalization was fueled by discursive constructions that are typical of crimmigration,[7] in which illegal immigrants are characterized archetypally dangerous "predators" and potential "terrorists."

The Italian CJS constantly sees itself addressing difficult challenges. Some criminal organizations are so strong that they battle with the state for a monopoly on the use of force in several territorial areas. This conflict between the state and Mafia organizations has led to high rates of economic crime and political corruption.[8] Although these issues are not excluded from public debate and therefore fall within the scope of the fight against crime, the mechanisms for identifying and contrasting social dangerousness still appear to be anchored to the sphere of illegality at a lower level and are deprived of systemic consistency and, therefore, are useful for fueling cycles of social alarm.

Policing and Law Enforcement

A BRIEF HISTORY OF POLICING AND LAW ENFORCEMENT

The creation of a centralized police organization in Italy was prompted by popular unrest following the country's unification in 1861. Because of Napoleon's influence, the Italian police organization replicates the model of the French police: it is centralized, militarized, and able to use repressive power. In Italy, from the beginning of the organized police force, the police were highly dependent on the political power of government.[9] The two main police forces, the Carabinieri (CC) and the Polizia di Stato (state police [PS]), compete to maintain order and public security, bearing witness to a dualism of power that incomprehensibly survives to the present day.[10] King of Sardinia Vittorio Emanuele I established the Corpo dei Carabinieri Reali, an ancestor of today's CC, in 1814; they became part of the Royal Army in 1861 with the unification of Italy; like the French *gendarmerie*, they were intended to be widespread across the country and to be responsible for public security and for defending the nation's boundaries. King Carlo Alberto of Sardinia established the Corpo delle Guardie di Pubblica Sicurezza, a forerunner of today's PS, in 1852. Similar to the French *police nationale*, they were responsible for security and public order in the country's larger towns and cities. In those days, the threat to security and public order took the shape of idles, vagrants, beggars, loose women, players, and recidivists whom, as in present times, the police were called on to monitor, control, and select for punishment. Under fascism, Mussolini first unified the two forces and then separated them: the Corpo dei Carabinieri remained faithful to the king, while the Corpo delle Guardie answered to the government.

ORGANIZATION OF POLICING AND LAW ENFORCEMENT

Italy has often been called "the state with too many police forces." There are four main bodies operating nationwide: the CC, the PS, Polizia Penitenziaria (PP), and Guardia di Finanza (GDF). Alongside these, local police forces serve municipalities and provinces. The large number of personnel in the Italian police force is unparalleled in Western Europe. This sizable police force is the responsibility of many ministries and is therefore marked by internal diversification and a lack of coordination.[11]

The different police forces have largely similar responsibilities in terms of the territories they control and the scope of their actions. This gives rise to overlaps and can complicate coordination, particularly with regard to coordination between the PS and the CC. The PS employs approximately 98,500 people and reports to the Ministry of the Interior. It has general responsibilities but focuses mainly on security and public order, particularly in larger towns and cities. The CC, which comprises 110,000 units, answers to the Ministry of Defense. It also has general responsibilities in terms of security and public order, although coordination is the responsibility of the PS. However, the CC is found not only in large cities but in rural areas as well. The main difference between the PS and the CC is that the PS is a civil police force, while the CC is a military police force. The PS, which has been part of the army since 1854, just like the CC, underwent a "democratization" process during the 1970s—a period of tense political struggle and terrorism (from grassroots and from the state) that ended with the 1981 reform that converted the PS from a military to a civilian force.[12] However, in 2005, when compulsory military service was abolished, preferential routes were introduced for the PS in order to employ personnel from the military. This may have led to a remilitarization of the PS and has had repercussions on its operations and the way in which it handles public order in Italy's towns and cities.

The CC and the PS are not the only police forces active in urban settings for security reasons. Local police forces also play a role in this field. Unlike the CC and the PS, which are national forces, the local police forces serve municipal, provincial, or metropolitan authorities and operate only within their local areas. Originally used in traffic control, their activities have expanded over time, as has their importance in public debates since the 1990s in matters of security and decorum in urban settings.[13]

The PP and the GDF are the two other national police forces, each with specific tasks. The PP is a civil police force that reports to the Ministry of Justice and operates inside prisons. The GDF is a military police force that answers to the Ministry of Economy and Finance and has general competence in economic and financial matters.

OPERATIONS OF POLICING AND LAW ENFORCEMENT

The main concern of postmodern police forces relates to aspects that produce social alarm.[14] Italian police forces are constantly called on to deal with phenomena that are presented as "emergencies," which, as such, cannot be dealt with using ordinary tools but necessarily require the use of extraordinary instruments. Police activity is often celebrated as the action of "crime fighters" against specific enemies, which change over time. What does not change is the police's selective and discretionary use of power, especially in terms of criminal policies that focus on the "exception" and the "emergency."

Italian police forces have used special powers and reinforced organizational structures to combat the political violence of leftist and rightist political groups in the 1980s, organized crime in the early 1990s,[15] and, from the second half of the 1990s, the emerging issue of street crime in large cities and towns. The alarm around microcriminality in the 1990s is inextricably linked to the so-called invasion of illegal immigrants. In Italy, the police are responsible for every aspect of immigration control—from controlling, detaining, and repatriating illegal(ized) migrants and asylum seekers to permitting their legal entry by issuing residency permits. As a result, the law on immigration might be implemented strategically in order to prevent and repress crime rather than to control borders and so as to provide the police with additional discretionary power during patrolling activities for territorial control rather than for border control.[16]

The police also govern the penitentiary system, accounting for more than 80 percent of its personnel. Their approach to this system favors repressive forms of detention, which contradicts the law's stated rehabilitative intention for prisons. They do so by building a public discourse identifying inmates as responsible for the deterioration of Italian prisons.[17]

The management of public order in Italy sheds light on the connection between political power and police practices,[18] while the connection with legal procedures is rather weak: mediation practices between the police and protesters during political demonstrations follow no standardized procedure but are conducted informally. There are no clear limits on political police gathering information about demonstrators.[19] The limits on the use of force during demonstrations are not formalized, and the proper use of the means available to the police is established not by law but by police manuals.[20]

The Judiciary in Italy

ORGANIZATION OF THE JUDICIARY

Like the police, the judiciary also implements a process of selectivity during trials and, in doing so, contributes to the social construction of crime. There are three main players in the judicial system—judges, public prosecutors (PMs), and lawyers—each playing different roles in the process while sharing part of the same legal culture.[21]

Criminal matters are dealt with by ordinary magistrates, including judges, who can exercise judicial power, and PMs, who act as investigators. In both cases, they must be autonomous and independent of legislative and executive powers. For this reason, ordinary magistrates are regulated by a self-governing body, the Supreme Judicial Council (Consiglio superiore della magistratura [CSM]), which is headed by the president of the Italian Republic, who is an ex officio member of the CSM.

Magistrates can be professional or honorary. Professional members of the judiciary are recruited through a public competitive exam that is administered by the minister of justice; once appointed, professional members of the judiciary serve for life and cannot be removed except by the CMS as a serious disciplinary measure. Honorary judges (justices of the peace [JOPs]) are lawyers who pass a public exam that is less competitive than the exam that professional magistrates must pass. Honorary magistrates serve for a maximum of eight years, work at piece rate, and have jurisdiction over minor crimes. They do, however, have jurisdiction over migration issues, such as immigration detention, illegal entry, and disregarding a removal order. The role of the JOP in migration control could be considered paradoxical, with a minor judge being granted responsibilities for aspects as crucial as individuals' personal liberty, even in the form of administrative detention. The fact that JOPs validate the great majority of decisions made by the police highlights their lack of independence and autonomy from the executive power.[22]

The PM performs investigative duties in the judiciary and decides whether to file criminal charges or to dismiss a case. This decision will depend on the severity of the specific case and on the priority attributed to it, which is usually decided on the basis of a subjective evaluation, one that takes into consideration the punishment established by the law, the need to prosecute the crime in a timely fashion, the legal priority of the violated right, and the social alarm connected to the specific crime. Discretionary decisions of this nature are made at both individual and office levels.[23]

Lawyers may either be independent or act as court-appointed attorneys, depending on the defendant's economic situation, with clear differences in the quality of the defense.

Decisions made by the judge in Ordinary Courts and Juvenile Courts at first instance can be reviewed by the Court of Appeal. JOPs operate in the lower courts, and their decisions can be appealed before judges in the Ordinary Courts. The third-instance jurisdiction is exercised in all cases by the Court of Cassation. The courts have territorial responsibility and are distributed across various districts in Italy: 140 courts, 404 offices of the JOPs, twenty-six regional Courts of Appeal, the Supreme Court of

Cassation, and the Constitutional Court, which is located in Rome. Judicial decisions may differ, depending on the courts.

FUNCTIONS OF THE JUDICIARY

Measures restricting personal liberty *praeter delictum* have solid roots in Italy and have never been abandoned. The dangerousness concept originates primarily from discretionary police practices, and the positive school justifies the concept legally and ideologically. The presence of regulatory offenders, with indeterminate and vague contours, within a criminal system fundamentally inspired by the "objective criterion of the fact" has become a structural element, which has its roots far back in the history of Italy's legal system. It has the effect of creating spaces in which the discretionary power of social control operators, primarily the police and the magistrates, see such power increase. On one side, criminal law demonstrates its symbolic force; on the other, criminal law and administrative law interweave in practices of control, from the actions of the police to those of judges and magistrates, producing new practices of control that are less spectacular but perhaps more effective.

In the illegal immigration control system, the use of the administrative law facilitates interventions on the sphere of the migrant's personal freedom beyond the guarantees imposed by criminal law. At the same time, because of the symbolic and material power of criminal law, there is considerable overlap between who can be considered criminal migrants, illegal(ized) migrants, and enemies.

In governing political conflicts, criminal law is used both as an exhibition of state power (e.g., in one case, a trial for property damage during political demonstrations resulted in twenty-year penalties)[24] and to instigate investigations whose strategic purpose is not to result in convictions but to allow police to gather intelligence about certain groups as a strategic element aimed not so much at convicting but at producing police knowledge on suspects by way of investigation. Alongside criminal law, preventive administrative measures are regularly used to limit activists' freedom of movement. These measures have been used to weaken political groups. In this sense, the increasing use of administrative law in criminal policies in Italy threatens the judiciary's power and meaning in favor of the executive with respect to the constitutionally guaranteed rights to a fair trial and to the right to a defense.

In the 1990s and 2000s, the judiciary also played an important role in raising concerns about security. Mayor-sheriffs at the time created new regulations in illogical response to the perception that insecurity was rampant. These strategies were a way to dispose of police work and to combat what was deemed—rather arbitrarily—to be indecorous or uncivil behaviors, prioritizing such cases over those about dangerous and criminal acts of a more serious nature. The result was that courts were backlogged with cases that, in the eyes of judges and PMs, were not severe, urgent, or high priority. The practical effect of social alarm was therefore sometimes diminished because judges imposed paltry penalties, acquittals because of the minor nature of the offense, or dismissals.[25]

Because the category of dangerousness is changeable and responds to social alarms of the moment, new "dangerous" persons continue to take shape or return to the fore.

Today, in the aftermath of the so-called refugee crisis, judges and attorneys find themselves playing a secondary role in the criminalization mechanisms of asylum seekers through the persecution of alleged traffickers[26] and sympathizers. In some cases, these end up with convictions, such as the thirteen-year sentence recently given to Mimmo Lucano, former mayor of Riace, in southern Italy.[27] Other cases result in acquittals, as in the famous case of Carola Rackete and the Sea's Watch. However, that trial, with its delays and significant media exposure, has a criminalizing effect, symbolically and materially.

CRIMINAL PROCEDURES

Entitlement to a fair trial is guaranteed by the Italian Constitution. A trial must include a debate of reasonable duration between equal parties before an impartial third party, the judge. Criminal procedures play a core role in criminalization processes, as it is this stage that decides what criminal proceedings are brought before the judge, how an act should be classified, and whether to acquit or convict the defendant. Throughout these steps, numerous legal and nonlegal elements are taken into consideration by the people involved.

The social construction of migrants' criminality in criminal procedures provides an example of what, when, and how nonlegal elements affect the judicial decision and of the police's influence on the judiciary. In general, there are four main steps involved in evaluating a defendant's personal responsibility: confirmation of the arrest by the prosecutor and the decision about the indictment, the validation hearing, the decision about precautionary measures, and the trial. Confirmation of the arrest is almost automatic as long as the validation request—the second step—is made within twenty-four hours of the arrest. For the validation request, the PM requests precautionary measures against suspects if there is a risk of absconding, a risk of repeated crimes, or a risk of interference with police investigations. This decision, which constitutes the third step, is made prior to the fourth step—the trial—in which procedural facts are established.

Empirical research reveals that during trial, the evaluation of the defendant's personality, reliability, and dangerousness is crucial. Such an evaluation is performed in relation to the defendant's previous criminal record, any aliases, and any regular job and accommodation.[28] Similar elements are taken into account by the JOP during validation hearings for immigration detention. Empirical research shows that migrants' illegality is not sufficient to justify their detention, yet the JOP mobilize the rhetoric of migrants' dangerousness, constructed on evidence produced by the police—including elements hinting at their social marginality and unreliability[29]—to attempt such a justification. Moreover, hearings are rapid, lasting just a few minutes, and JOPs base their decisions almost exclusively on evidence produced by the police. This is not helped by the fact that lawyers for migrants are often court appointed, assigned the day before the trial, and able to read the pleadings only a few minutes before, usually without having the opportunity to talk with clients. These findings reveal the judiciary's diminished autonomy and power compared to the executive's, particularly in relation to certain types of offenders.

The Correctional System

A BRIEF HISTORY OF THE CORRECTIONAL SYSTEM

In republican Italy, the main mechanism for regulating the detention rate was a combination of amnesties and pardons, clemency measures that characterized the criminal policy of the United Kingdom and the Italian fascist regime.[30] In the period after World War II, prisons were used as a way to contain social conflict that was linked to the civil war that contributed to the disintegration of the fascist regime. Even during this time, the overall capacity of the prison system has always stood at around 50,000 units. This implies that, even if penal legislation adopts repressive imprisonment policies, the detention rate cannot exceed 100 per 100,000 Italians. Italy has illegally restricted the rights of prisoners by compromising hygiene conditions in prisons, which constitutes torture. In 2010, Italy was sanctioned in that regard by the European Court of Human Rights (ECHR) in the case of *Torreggiani v. Italy*, which cited Italy's systemic failure to respect the minimum standard of three square meters of space for each prisoner.

Aside from that ECHR ruling, the Italian penal system has always been structured on the basis of alternating between an ordinary increase of incoming flows into prisons, measures that reduce the release rate (e.g., raising mandatory minimums and penalizing recidivism), and "emergency" measures aimed at decongesting prisons. With the last pardon (2006), around 20,000 people were released from prison, almost a third of the population held at the time, taking the prison population well below the threshold of 50,000. In short, mass incarceration plans and hypotheses have always clashed with restrictions determined by the failure to build new prisons. This can be attributed to the political cultural configuration of the context.[31] For example, interventions have often been driven by the Vatican to decrease the number of prisoners. This led the state and its various governments to make a largely symbolic response by increasing their focus on punishing what they consider to be real criminal emergencies. This focus is then emphasized by the media. The deterrent function of imprisonment has therefore been implemented historically in Italy through tangible detention conditions that are extremely problematic in the context of a democratic state.

The custodial purpose of the prison system of the Italian fascist regime has therefore survived in a prison sector strongly marked by institutional violence and pervasive misery, effectively circumventing for almost thirty years the constitutional precept that, since 1948, has encouraged the philosophical and operational principle of reeducation. The two major reform processes[32]—which oriented the penal system toward rehabilitation, introduced the first alternative measures, and established a reward system for good conduct—were the result of an alliance between the political prisoners of the struggles of the 1970s and common prisoners who were becoming politicized. Their alliance produced an extraordinary wave of prison riots and demands for improvements in prison living conditions, which received the support of a good part of public opinion at the time. The state's strategic response, against the risk of losing control of the prison system, was thus implemented in a dialectic between reform and revolt. The dominant reward–punishment logic became part of the new framework of individual prisoner rehabilitation, expanding special detention mechanisms for the most dangerous inmates. However, the beneficial and progressive effects of the reforms were largely offset by gradually more aggressive penal legislation, which in the 1990s had already produced a dramatic increase in prison overcrowding, particularly by virtue of a rapid incarceration process for migrants.

ORGANIZATION OF THE CORRECTIONAL SYSTEM

The Italian prison system now consists of 191 institutions, which are distributed across the country. Although some metropolitan prisons are approaching a capacity of 1,000 units, most Italian prisons are much smaller, some containing fewer than 100 prisoners. From an administrative perspective, the sector is governed by the Penitentiary Administration Department (DAP), which is structured into regional departments and is one of the fundamental sectors of the Ministry of Justice. This structure includes almost all prison staff, including educators and institute directors—both of which are few in number—as well as prison police officers, who make up an autonomous police force in the prisons. These prison police have supervisory and administrative duties, supplementing the understaffed civilian workforce. From a functional perspective, in the same ministerial structure and beyond the formalized hierarchical scale, the prison police are a hegemonic force in the prison system. Their trade union is highly influential, and Italy holds the record for the lowest ratio of inmates to guards in continental Europe (1.67 inmates for each guard compared to 2.5 prisoners in France and 3.7 in Spain). Doctors, nurses, and teachers in prisons are employed by local administrations in health and education sectors. Training, rehabilitation, recreation, and sports activities are coordinated by educators but implemented by associations and cooperatives in the respective field.

After the recent closure of the psychiatric-judicial hospitals, smaller mental health facilities and resettlement prisons opened across the country. Additionally, in 1998, a circuit was established for the administrative detention of illegal foreigners. However, the main distinction between prisons remains the one between Case di Reclusione (CR), which house prisoners serving a sentence longer than five years, and Case Circondariali, which holds inmates during pretrial detention or inmates with sentences of less than five years. This differentiation is not applied rigidly because, on one side, there are few CR. On the other side, transfer requests arise for disciplinary, judicial, and safety reasons; this includes the principle of territorialization of the sentence, which legitimizes requests by inmates to serve their sentences close to their families' homes. Based on this basic distinction, the Italian prison system has undergone, in the past forty years, an intense functional differentiation process that has been carried out through the establishment of specific detention sectors and through an informal circulation mechanism.

CORRECTIONAL SYSTEM OPERATIONS

After the last pardon, in 2006, the growth rate of the prison population increased rapidly, from 50,000 after the pardon to 68,000 prisoners by 2010. The Italian government thus found itself having to reduce pretrial detention, and by 2015, the number of detainees had dropped to 52,000. However, structural trends toward incarceration took the population back to 61,000 prisoners by 2019. As of 2021, measures linked to pandemic risks in prisons have led to a reduced population of 53,000 inmates. The fluctuations clearly indicate the political nature of "emergency decongestion" measures. These fluctuations are not linked to the relationship between criminality and immigration. In fact, despite the persistence of incoming population flows into the country, the share of foreigners in prisons has remained stable for more than twenty years, at a third of the incarcerated population. More precisely, the population has decreased from 37.5 percent in 2007—the peak of the population of foreigners in Italian prisons—to 32.3 percent in 2021.

The majority of these prisoners[33] live in medium-security prions, while a few hundred inmates benefit from lower-security institutions. The reconfiguration of special high-security prisons now sees around 750 persons, who are subject to the strictest treatment.[34] High-security facilities can house 7,000 people who are second-level affiliates of organized crime who are involved in illegal drug trafficking, referred to as AS3; eighty people who have been convicted of crimes related to terrorism and subversion, particularly of an anarchist or jihadist nature, referred to as AS2; and 300 people who are Mafia affiliates who are known to be dangerous or those who are leaving prisons where torturers were held, referred to as AS1. These high-security prisons consist of accentuated affliction conditions and are based on a conceptualization of criminals as enemies,[35] in which external contact is limited and opportunities for rehabilitation and internal sociability are reduced. These prisons are the legacy of the special regimes of the past, which, in the twentieth century, were applied to political prisoners who had promoted prison riots. After the Mafia attacks in the early 1990s that targeted senior institutional figures, including politicians, magistrates, and police, these special prisons were brought back in the context of the fight against the Mafia. Their reintroduction reconfigured the conceptualization of the most dangerous of the internal enemies while maintaining a stringent detention mechanism for the AS2 class of politicized and radicalized persons.[36] The state justifies these more stringent prisons as a way to incentivize "informants": inmates in high-security prisons can leave by providing information on subversive organizations. The pragmatism of this justification remains legally unresolved.

The distinctions among different security levels of prisons have overlapped with the creation of specific circuits and sections, including those for informants, perpetrators of severe social crimes, drug addicts, those with psychiatric illnesses, transsexuals, and sex offenders. Italy has four institutions for women prisoners, who make up 5 percent of the total prison population. Most women prisoners are housed in small sections within men's prisons and thus have limited access to rehabilitation opportunities. Alongside these circuits that have been formally established by the DAP, there are others that respond to the informal organizational and managerial needs of "punitive" and "rehabilitation-oriented" institutions, which are not recognized at the level of the legal system. It also includes the establishment within these individual institutions of areas of increased supervision (e.g., limiting the number of hours that inmates can spend outside their cells) or sections to which people are assigned (according to criteria that are not generalizable insofar as they are informal) on the basis of common ethnicity, religion, language, or national affiliation. This trend toward differentiation or "penitentiary individualism" can be seen as compromising the universality of sentencing. Additionally, such systemic adaptations tend to create detention environments in which the highest levels of material and relational deprivation are concentrated. Often, these spaces have the highest rates of self-harm and the greatest consumption of psychotropic drugs.

One benefit of this differential organization—which focuses on a logic of reward and punishment, a pillar of Italy's institutional prison culture—has been that prison conflicts have remained low since the 1980s. During the COVID-19 pandemic, however, the dialectic between revolt and reform reemerged. The fear of contagion from the pandemic in an overcrowded system was compounded by anger against government decisions to prevent exposure from external visitors, such as relatives, volunteers, and teachers. This led to a wave of prison riots in early 2020 that involved at least a quarter of national prisons, with hundreds of injuries, thirteen deaths, and millions of euros of damage. Following the explosion of such conflicts, the executive implemented deflationary measures, allowing approximately 8,000 people to leave the prison system—yet another "emergency" measure that allowed the system to survive.

Juvenile Justice

STRUCTURE OF THE JUVENILE JUSTICE SYSTEM

In the architecture of the Italian Ministry of Justice since 1934, legal matters concerning minors are dealt with by an autonomous judicial sector of juvenile courts that deal with civil proceedings (e.g., adoption and fostering) and criminal proceedings. There is also an autonomous juvenile prison sector. The earliest juvenile correctional facilities were established during the monarchy in 1891. The most restrictive sanctions for juvenile offenders are imposed in juvenile prisons (IPM) and by ministerial community structures. In 2009, juvenile justice was incorporated into the administrative sector of external criminal execution, which manages probation mechanisms and alternative measures to imprisonment for adults.

The reform that resulted in this organizational structure consolidates an earlier reform of the juvenile penal system that was imposed by Italian Presidential Decree 448 of 1988. This legislative innovation introduced an advanced juvenile penal procedure in Italy that focuses on a destigmatizing and progressive juvenile justice system. In this system, detention is just one form sanction for juveniles; other forms include probation and criminal mediation institutions. These sanctions have proven resilient in the face of fluctuating concerns about security "emergencies" that some moral entrepreneurs have pushed. Since the mid-2000s, the seventeen Italian IPMs have consistently housed an average of 10,000 minors, fluctuating between 500 and 375 prisoners on any given day.

Since the early 2000s, in Italy's adult penal system, there has been no correlation between an increase in alternatives to detention and a decrease in incarceration. On the contrary, both different punitive methods and incarcerations have grown, resulting in an overall growth in the number of people in the penal system.[37] However, in the juvenile CJS, the progressive nature of punitive methods that decrease imprisonment—such as probation, home detention, and criminal mediation—and the focus on restorative justice are now having an effect on the adult CJS and undermining the traditional prison-centered approach typical of the national punitive culture. A 2014 regulatory innovation (l. 117\2014) is emblematic of this effect. It allows for juveniles to serve their sentences in IPMs until the age of twenty-four, an increase from twenty-one, which was the prior limit. This change has in fact reduced the tendency to empty juvenile prisons, resulting in problems for facilities that must now manage rehabilitation and interaction plans for persons at drastically different stages of mental and physical development, namely, those aged between fourteen (the Italian threshold for criminal liability) and twenty-four (an age at which someone may have already consolidated criminal profiles). This issue should be considered in the context of selective mechanisms that define the sociodemographic characteristics of minors who are subjected to different forms of penal control.

FUNCTIONS OF THE JUVENILE JUSTICE SYSTEM

The criminalization process of migrants and ethnic minorities—which has literally revolutionized the Italian penal system structures since the 1990s—has also been anticipated in the juvenile penal sector. As with the adult CJS, juvenile defendants, convicts, and detainees are more likely to be from the southern regions of the country or foreigners. Additionally, many alternatives to imprisonment for juveniles have a paradoxical effect for minority groups. Methods of rehabilitation—such as home detention, mediation, probation, limitation periods, and positioning in residential communities—tend to build on social and familial structures that are often more easily available to native Italians than to foreigners. This dynamic can translate into institutional racism in judicial decisions and procedures as well as discrimination against persons who have fewer resources because of the migratory movements that they have experienced—including as children of migrants—or because of their positioning at the lower levels of the social hierarchy.[38]

The duty of prisons to contain forms of social marginality thus reflects—particularly with regard to juvenile justice—its composition along the lines of color and ethnicity. The official data and recent reports[39] reveal that the most acute levels of criminal and, above all, prison overrepresentation have concerned mostly the Roma minority (consisting of groups with and without Italian citizenship by virtue of older or newer migratory flows) and foreign minors—often unaccompanied—originating mostly from the regions of the Maghreb, Nigeria, Eastern Europe, and Central and South America, particularly Ecuador. For the Roma people, the criminalization process appears to be correlated to segregation in camps deriving from housing policies broadly applied in Italy. This is a radical form of ghettoization that is legitimized by discursive practices focused on the essentialization of a culture that is presumed to be predatory and nomadic.[40] For foreign minors, the structures of opportunity[41] appear to be limited by the orientation of migratory policies and difficult access in the labor market, factors that result in social exclusion that is weakly compensated for by welfare structures and connected to the involvement of these minors in vast sectors of informal economies, with high rates of exploitation, and of illegal economies, particularly street drug dealing, theft, and receiving stolen goods. In the 2010s—as in countries with more consolidated traditions of incoming migratory movements[42]—the type of criminalized minor who has participated in illegal economies has been partially replaced by a subjectivity having the same ethnic origins but now permanently present in the country—the now full-blown incidence, in criminal justice statistics, of so-called second generations. The forms of discomfort, discrimination, and social subordination that they experience appear to be related to reactive forms of deviance that could probably be contained through a quicker mechanism of recognition of rights, namely, a faster acquisition of citizenship. Foreigners have constantly comprised half of the detained juvenile population since the early 2000s.

Finally, underrepresented natives in the juvenile CJS tend to originate from the most problematic urban suburbs that are hardest hit by the continuing economic crisis and the gradual reduction in welfare services. Therefore, precisely in a sector in which the most advanced forms of criminal diversion and decreases in prison population have taken shape, the selective penalization of the most vulnerable and now broadly ethnicized sector of the population seems to be intensifying. A further political push toward criminal sanctions and prison as an extreme rationale, supported by an abolitionist orientation at least with regard to juvenile justice, could facilitate practices of social inclusion and pathways to exit from social marginality.

Notes

1. Article 27 of the Constitution states that "criminal responsibility is personal. The defendant is not considered guilty until definitively sentenced. Punishment cannot consist in inhuman treatment and must aim at reeducating the convicted. Death penalty is prohibited."
2. G. Fabini and A. Sbraccia, "Criminal Policies in Action," in *Global Perspectives in Policing and Law Enforcement*, ed. J. M. Mbuba (Lanham, MD: Lexington Books, 2021), 99–114.
3. M. Pifferi, *The Limits of Criminological Positivism* (London: Routledge, 2021).
4. D. Garland, *The Culture of Control* (Chicago: University of Chicago Press, 2000).
5. See S. Cohen, *Folk Devils and Moral Panics* (London: Routledge, 2002), and J. Pratt, *Penal Populism* (London: Routledge, 2006).
6. It is not by chance that one of the most important contemporary scholars of the state of exception at the international level is Giorgio Agamben, an Italian philosopher who has reflected on the oxymoron of the normalization of the exception. See Giorgio Agamben, *State of Exception* (Chicago: University of Chicago Press, 2003).
7. M. van der Wouden, V. Barker, and J. van der Leun, "Crimmigration in Europe," *European Journal of Criminology* 14, no. 1 (2017), https://doi.org/10.1177/1477370816639814.
8. F. Allum, I. Clough-Marinaro, and R. Sciarrone, *Italian Mafias Today: Territory, Business and Politics* (Cheltenham: Elgar, 2019).
9. S. Tuzza, *Il dito e la luna: Ordine pubblico tra Polizia e potere politico, un caso di studio* (Milan: Meltemi, 2021).

10. D. Bertaccini, *La politica di polizia* (Bologna: Bononia University Press, 2009).

11. M. Di Giorgio, *Per una polizia nuova: Il movimento per la riforma della Pubblica Sicurezza (1969–1981)* (Rome: Viella, 2019).

12. Di Giorgio, *Per una polizia.*

13. R. Selmini and S. Crocitti, "Controlling Immigrants: The Latent Function of Italian Administrative Orders," *European Journal on Criminal Policy and Research* 23 (2017): 99–114.

14. S. Palidda, *Polizia postmoderna: Etnografia del nuovo controllo sociale* (Milan: Feltrinelli Editore, 2000).

15. A. Stille, *Excellent Cadavers: The Mafia and the Death of the First Italian Republic* (New York: Vintage, 1996).

16. G. Fabini, "'These Are Crimes for Poor People and Sex Workers!' Reading Europe through Immigration Crimes and Local 'Frames of Dangerousness,'" *Etnografia e ricerca qualitativa* 3 (2017): 415–34.

17. Fabini and Sbraccia, "Criminal Policies."

18. Tuzza, *Il dito e la luna.*

19. D. Della Porta, "Police Knowledge and Protest Policing: Some Reflections on the Italian Case," *Policing Protest: The Control of Mass Demonstrations in Western Democracies* 6 (1998): 228.

20. E. Gargiulo, "Ordine pubblico, regole private: Rappresentazioni della folla e prescrizioni comportamentali nei manuali per i Reparti mobile," *Etnografia e ricerca qualitativa* 8, no. 3 (2015): 481–512.

21. V. Ferrari, *Diritto e società: Elementi di sociologia del diritto* (Bari: Laterza, 2004).

22. M. Mastromartino, E. Rigo, and M. Veglio, "Lexilium. Osservatorio sulla giurisprudenza in materia di immigrazione del Giudice di Pace: Sintesi rapporti 2015," *Diritto immigrazione e cittadinanza* 2 (2017), https://www.dirittoimmigrazionecittadinanza.it/allegati/lexilium/84-sintesi-ricerca/file.

23. C. Sarzotti, *Processi di selezione del crimine: Procure della Repubblica e organizzazione giudiziaria* (Milan: Giuffré, 2007).

24. X. Chiaramonte, *Governare il conflitto: La criminalizzazione del movimento No Tav* (Milan: Mimesis, 2019). This was what happened in the trial for the crime of "damage and looting" against the No Tav movement, a protest movement that has, for twenty years, objected to the construction in Val Susa of the high-speed line that would connect Turin and Lyon.

25. Sarzotti, *Processi di selezione del crimine.*

26. These are often migrants who, as they are steering the makeshift boats when they arrive at the Italian coast, are taken for "traffickers."

27. C. Caprioglio, F. Ferri, and L. Gennari, "La colpa di Lucano: Una lettura della condanna oltre la criminalizzazione della solidarietà," *SSQC Online*, https://wp.me/p7JYW5-16J.

28. F. Quassoli, "Migrant as Criminal: The Judicial Treatment of Migrant Criminality," in *Controlling a New Migration World*, ed. V. Guiraundon and C. Joppke (London: Routledge, 2001), 150–70.

29. G. Campesi and G. Fabini, "Immigration Detention as Social Defence: Policing 'Dangerous Mobility' in Italy," *Theoretical Criminology* 24, no. 1 (2020): 50–70.

30. C. De Vito, *Camosci e Girachiavi* (Rome: Laterza, 2009); G. Geltner, *Italian Prisons in the Age of Positivism: 1981–1914* (London: Bloomsbury, 2019).

31. M. Cavadino and J. Dignan, *The Penal System: An Introduction* (London: Sage, 2007).

32. Institution of the penitentiary system (1975) and the Gozzini law (1986).

33. With regard to the statistical composition of prisons (judicial and sociodemographic variables), see https://www.giustizia.it/giustizia/it/mg_1_14.page?selectedNode=0_2. Historically, by virtue of the essentially colonial dynamic of national unification, imprisoned natives come mainly from the southern regions of the country. Southern Italians have also been broadly

criminalized as a result of domestic migrations toward the richer and more industrialized north-central areas. The criminalization of natives now takes shape above all in the peripheral areas of large cities and is still largely present in the south and on the islands of Sardinia and Sicily. Conversely, the incoming prisoner flows of foreign citizens are focused mainly in the north-central areas (close to 50 percent of detainees compared to 32 percent for the national average).

34. Art. 41bis, convicted of mafia crimes.

35. D. Linhardt and C. Moreau de Bellaing, "The 'Enimization' of Criminal Law?," *International Political Sociology* 13, no. 4 (2019): 447–63.

36. D. Ronco, A. Sbraccia, and G. Torrente, *Prison De-Radicalization Strategies, Programmes and Risk Assessment Tools in Europe* (Rome: Antigone Edizioni, 2020).

37. Z. Gallo, "Punishment, Authority and Political Economy: Italian Challenges to Western Punitivity," *Punishment and Society* 17, no. 5 (2015): 598–623.

38. A. Sbraccia, *More or Less Eligibility: Theoretical Perspectives on the Imprisonment Process of Migrants in Italy*, CIRSDIG Working Paper 31, https://www.cirsdig.it.

39. Data and themed analyses of an institutional nature are available at https://www.giustizia.it/giustizia/it/mg_12_4.wp. To access independent reports, we recommend https://www.ragazzidentro.it.

40. P. Saitta, "Immigrant Roma in Sicily," *Romani Studies* 20, no. 1 (2010): 17–45.

41. R. Cloward and L. Ohlin, *Delinquency and Opportunity* (New York: Free Press, 1960).

42. A. Portes and R. G. Rumbaut, *Legacies* (Berkeley: University of California Press, 2001).

CHAPTER 8

The Criminal Justice System in England and Wales

Timi Osidipe, Nenadi Adamu, and Jonathan South

Of the four countries that make up the United Kingdom, Scotland and Northern Ireland have separate criminal justice systems (CJSs), while England and Wales share a CJS. In England and Wales, the criminal justice institutions are the police, His Majesty's Prison and Probation Service (also known as the National Probation Service [NPS]), the Crown Prosecution Service (CPS), and the Criminal Courts. We begin this chapter with a brief history of the development of the CJS in England and Wales and then provide a brief history and description of the roles and functions of the police, the NPS, the Criminal Courts, and youth justice in England and Wales.

The Historical Background of the CJS in England and Wales

The current organization, role, and functions of the CJS in England and Wales—which dates back to the twelfth century—are intertwined with ideological influences that have precipitated changes in the twentieth and twenty-first centuries. Broadly speaking, the CJS in England and Wales investigates and tries suspected criminals and punishes and rehabilitates people who are convicted of committing a crime.[1] In recent years, the CJS in England and Wales has been strengthened in the areas of rule of law, due process, judicial and police accountability, victim support, prison and probation reforms, human rights, and restorative justice thanks to policy interventions and legislation and the influence of advocacy campaigns by civil society organizations.

In England and Wales, the CJS is managed by the Home Office and the Ministry of Justice (MoJ). The Home Office is responsible for formal policing,[2] which is primarily the purview of forty-three different Home Office or territorial police forces. Other, smaller organizations also perform policing functions; these include the British Transport Police, which covers the rail network, and the Civil Nuclear Constabulary. The National Crime Agency, along with local forces, tackles serious and organized crime. The MoJ is responsible for prison and probation services through His Majesty's

Prison and Probation Service, Criminal Courts, tribunals, and services for victims of crime, children, and vulnerable people.

The multiagency nature of the CJS today also involves a range of other public bodies and agencies in the delivery of services. These include the National Criminal Justice Board—which is chaired by the justice minister and whose members include key CJS stakeholders—which oversees the CJS's multiagency-based delivery of services,[3] while the Local Criminal Justice Board is responsible for management at the local level.

Independent inspectorates are responsible for driving improvements, effectiveness, efficiency, and public confidence in the CJS. These inspectorates include His Majesty's Crown Prosecution Inspectorate, His Majesty's Inspectorate of Constabulary and Fire and Rescue Services, His Majesty's Inspectorate of Prisons, and His Majesty's Inspectorate of Probation. Additionally, the Police and Justice Act 2006 established the Criminal Justice Joint Inspection for the Constabulary, the CPS, probation, and prisons.

The current structure of criminal justice institutions in England and Wales has been influenced by the modernization of the public sector and by new principles of public management, neoliberalism, and business management. The common use of buzzwords such as "what works," "evidence-based policy," "efficiency," "accountability," and "performance" was part of the means by which this modernization agenda reflected the broader ideas of a lean government or public sector, market principles, and the promotion of fiscal austerity. Changes were effected in the areas of management, functions, and delivery of services in the form of, for example, the introduction of private prisons and policing, the active involvement of volunteer participation, and the creation of agencies. Through these developments, criminal justice, which was free from the influence of the economy and politics and managed exclusively by the state, became exposed to the prescriptions of the market and of a privatization agenda.[4]

Despite these changes, the focus on adversarial justice and the primacy of the common law remain part of the CJS in England and Wales, as an examination of policing in England and Wales reflects.

Policing in England and Wales

Modern-day policing in England and Wales has strong ties with developments in England in 1829. The Metropolitan Police Force was formed in 1829. Sir Robert Peel, home secretary at the time, said of the "new police" that "at the outset . . . the object to be attained is the prevention of crime."[5] Indeed, Peel later told Parliament, "I want to teach people that liberty does not consist in having your house robbed by organised gangs of thieves."[6] Crime prevention was, clearly, at the heart of Peel's vision for policing in England and Wales.

Furthermore, one of the Peelian principles that still inform views of policing in England and Wales is that "the police are the public and the public are the police," which suggests that the public should be involved in policing rather than have it be that policing is something done to the population. If this is the case, there are certainly styles and approaches that the police can take that would enable community involvement rather than constrain it. Presently, however, the role of the police is largely to punish offenders rather than to investigate and prevent possible crimes, to maintain order both symbolically and by force, and to protect the public. Modern policing is now frequently a problem-solving exercise that uses or applies mainly criminal law in an attempt to resolve issues related to maintaining order and protecting the public. Questions that remain to be answered include how to reduce or control crime rates and what the police should and should not control. To use crime as the metric by which the police force is measured is to overlook the other work that the police do that is not related to crime, such as peacekeeping issues or addressing deep social inequalities and differences.

Some may consider stricter punishments and mass incarceration to be the ultimate forms of crime prevention, but critics of that stance observe that these approaches are often "poorly orientated to correctionalist goals."[7] Others may look at the diverse complexities of crime requiring situational consideration, such as target protection, deterrence, surveillance, and other specific approaches, as ways to reduce opportunity and manage prolific offenders. Issues beyond police control that can cause crime include welfare, work, the nature of society, politics, and policy initiatives. This has helped to create a problem of normalized high crime rates and acknowledgment of the limitations of criminal justice. On the latter point, there is not "any settled confidence in the capacity of the criminal justice state to control crime and provide law and order, no matter what framework it adopts."[8] This normalization of crime can make the role of the police more difficult not only in reducing crime rates; inconsistent policies and public attitudes also greatly affect their effectiveness in tackling crime rates.

Although one way of trying to simplify and understand how the police operate within the CJS is to understand police work as broadly a matter of responding to incidents, investigating incidents, and preventing crime and disorder, another way to understand police work is in a temporal fashion, as in investigating past events, responding to current incidents, and preventing future crime or harm by managing risks and threats. In a more developed system, the roles and functions of policing could be understood as crime control and investigation, crime reduction, order maintenance, peacekeeping, a social service, emergency response, and state/national security.[9] The work of the police is complex, and few universal theories or models will be wholly successful in describing it; indeed, some of the police functions listed above, such as mental health and welfare, may not actually operate within criminal justice at all.

Ultimately, policing sits within the wider CJS in England and Wales; it not only relies on other agencies but also must be clear about exactly where and how it features in preventing, investigating, and responding to crime within that infrastructure. Police forces in England and Wales do not conduct that work in isolation from the community, state, and public or private bodies, and they are frequently required to work with others to achieve their goals. The police are one body working within the CJS, and as more demands are placed on the police force, it has become more difficult to place them at the start, middle, or end of the system or process. Because understanding what it is that the police do is essential to discussions about assessing, measuring, and improving the work that they do, it is one of the important challenges facing police officers and criminal justice scholars and students. If we fail to identify that work, we will also be unable to identify whether other organizations would be better equipped, resourced, or trained to undertake some of that work. We broadly understand the police to be a formal agent of social control, which applies the specific laws of the jurisdiction it covers.[10] This is the case for policing not only in England and Wales but around the world as well.

Comparatively, one issue that is frequently cited as a key difference in policing between England and Wales and the United States is that police officers are not routinely armed in England and Wales, although there is a growth in Taser use alongside batons and incapacitating sprays. Just as significant, however, is that policing in England and Wales is more centrally controlled, so all forty-three forces operate in a similar fashion in terms of how they work and operate, how they are governed and monitored, how they recruit and train, the equipment they use, and how they operate with other bodies in criminal justice. There is also one main legislative framework, so there are not as many regional differences as in the United States. It is perhaps because of this that there is a more connected and consistent approach to criminal justice than in the United States.

Legislation also significantly affects the complexities of police staffing. The numbers of police regularly change because of staff departures, retirement, and recruitment, but since 2010, government cuts and austerity measures have led to a reduction in the workforce. However, between 2019 and 2020, there was an increase in the combined workforce of police officers, police civilian staff, and designated officers or police and community support officers (PCSOs), the last of whom have a community-facing role with limited powers. The latest numbers include 132,467 police officers, 74,572 police staff, and 9,115 PCSOs, which is an annual increase of 5.5 percent.[11] In 2018–2019, spending on policing in England and Wales was approximately £13.3 billion.[12] While there has been a decrease in central government funding, there has also been growth in local funding, called the police precept, which is levied by council tax increases authorized by the police and crime commissioner for that area.[13] This follows a devolution of power away from central government toward local democracy, following the introduction of elected police and crime commissioners, as part of the Police Reform and Social Responsibility Act 2011. As part of their role and in line with a neoliberal reform process and marketization of policing, the local police and crime commissioner is also responsible for the commissioning of services to support and run alongside the police service in a practice under the umbrella of policing plurality.

Cost is just one factor in how the police decide to respond to reports of a crime. Their decision to investigate a reported crime or to close an investigation without taking any further action will be based on cost, policy, the likelihood of identifying a suspect, and the effect of the investigation on victims. If a suspect of a crime is identified, the police will decide whether to deal with it by way of a diversion or a restorative approach, such as a fine, caution/warning, or community-based resolution, especially if the suspect had no or little criminal history. Restorative approaches that seek to involve the victim, such as letters to victims or reparation measures, can also be used by police in certain situations. In other cases, the police can choose to charge the offender, who then has to attend a Juvenile, Magistrates', or Crown Court, depending on the circumstance. In recent times, the police have had to make such decisions in conjunction with the CPS, or at least they have had to follow the advice and guidance of the CPS about whether there is sufficient evidence to proceed or gaps and weaknesses in evidence. This can lead to conflict between the two agencies, but it is an initiative that has been put in place to improve the prosecution system, its cost-effectiveness, and the effect on stakeholders. This is not necessarily due to poor police practice because evidence and witnesses in some cases can be difficult to find, and there can be significant pressure on officers conducting an investigation. Such issues, alongside poor prosecution rates, can lead to dissatisfaction with the police or the criticism of the police as having a "Janus face" because the police can rarely satisfy everyone.[14]

It would be difficult for a discussion of policing in England and Wales to bypass issues of stop and search, which is a highly contested practice in the United Kingdom. Police officers can use stop-and-search powers to search someone whom they have reasonable grounds for believing is in possession of something relating to an offense, such as stolen goods, weapons, items used for committing an offense or using drugs, and the like. Officers can use reasonable force to detain that person, who technically may not have committed an offense. Although legislation and other policing strategies have been developed to limit and control power, stop and search remains a part of policing that is subjective and can involve individual discretion. Section 60 of the Criminal Justice and Public Order Act 1994 does not require that officers have suspicion in order to stop and search someone. Rather, the officer can be authorized by a senior officer to manage the public safety threat of disorder and violence. There are issues of disproportionate stops and searches in Black, Asian, and other minority ethnic groupings; for every White person in England and Wales, there were six searches per 1,000 people, but for Black people, the figure was fifty-four for every 1,000 people.[15] Almost half of the stops and searches in England and Wales in 2020 took place in London, so it cannot be said that those figures are representative of every police force area. One often-cited case is that of the Dorset Police, who stopped and searched Black people at a rate twenty-three times higher than they did White people.[16] These figures indicate that there are fracture lines in both the reality and the perception of the way in which police operate with all community groups and what this means for fairness of the CJS. This is significant insofar as public perception of stop-and-search practices is one of the measurements of legitimacy, trust, and confidence that a local community has in its police force.

Traditional models of policing may situate the police at the start of the criminal justice process—before courts, prison, and probation. However, there are times when police will be involved in many different aspects of the CJS. Some people may come into contact with the CJS by virtue of being a victim or witness and interact differently with the police as compared to the way that a suspect does. Suspects will have certain rights and entitlements afforded to them by the Police and Criminal Evidence Act 1984 (PACE) and the Human Rights Act 1988. Not all suspects are arrested; many now attend a voluntary interview because they do not meet the threshold for arrest found under Code G of PACE 1984. Sometimes the police will manage suspects or convicted offenders within the community through various orders and notices, notably for crimes in the areas of domestic abuse, sexual assault, violence against the person, child-related offenses, and terror-related offending. A growth in partnership work or a multiagency approach to policing may well mean that police officers work alongside other professional bodies to prevent and investigate crime and to support those who come into contact with the CJS.

Probation

The probation service began as a mission of the Church of England Temperance Society in the nineteenth century. It received official recognition through the Probation of First Time Offenders Act 1886. Appointment as a probation officer was based on Christian beliefs and character, and by 1906, there were 123 missionaries working as probation officers.[17] The 1907 Probation of Offenders Act led to government involvement, as Magistrates' Courts were advised to appoint and pay probation officers, who were to "advise, assist and befriend" offenders.[18] By 1907, 143 missionaries were working as probation officers.[19] The Criminal Justice Act 1925 made the role officially part of the CJS and made the appointment of probation officers by courts mandatory.[20]

From the 1930s through the 1990s, the probation service went through reforms that led to changes in duties, responsibilities, and management. For example, in 1938, the Home Office assumed responsibility for the probation service.[21] The 1967 Criminal Justice Act introduced the Parole Board and suspended sentences. However, the Parole Board became an independent, executive, nondepartmental, public body on July 1, 1996, under the Criminal Justice and Public Order Act 1994.[22] The Criminal Justice Act 1972 had established Community Service Orders, which is a form of a community sentence. The 1991 Criminal Justice Act set national standards for supervising offenders in the community; more recently, the 1998 Crime and Disorder Act enabled multiagency partnership between the Parole Board and other agencies and institutions.[23]

Notably, until the mid-1970s, the probation service's approach to offending was based on treatment and rehabilitation models.[24] However, this changed following the electoral victory of the Conservative Party in the 1979 general election. The Conservative government rhetoric of law and order was matched by the rhetoric of retributive justice, which included the use of such words as "prison works" and "just deserts."[25] The change from rehabilitation and treatment models to retribution and deterrence reflected the reemergence of classical rational theories of crime and New Right ideology in CJS in the late 1970s.[26] For example, the 1907 cannon of advising, assisting, and befriending was replaced with the Community Service Orders, introduced by the Criminal Justice Act 1972, which directed probation to supervise and manage offenders. Additionally, the introduction of the National Standards by the Criminal Justice Act 1971 overrode probation officers' discretion, particularly in the practice of enforcement and breach of requirements within an order.[27]

The probation service in England and Wales is responsible for a core set of duties that emphasizes offender and sentence management along with the management of accredited programs (e.g., building better relationships and the use of the Horizon program, which works with men convicted of sexual offenses), unpaid work, and structured interventions.[28] Offender management entails public protection, reducing offenses, facilitating and enforcing proper punishment, ensuring awareness about the effects of crime on victims and the public, and rehabilitating offenders through cognitive behavioral therapy (CBT). Various CBT tools are used, including the Offender Management System, which assess criminogenic needs based on eight factors: attitude; thinking and behavior; alcohol misuse; drug misuse; lifestyle; relationships; education, training, and employment; and accommodation.[29]

Historically, there have been four generations of probation service assessments. The first generation (1900–1970s) was characterized by practitioner discretion and judgment and the second generation (1970s–1990s) by actuarial scales that were based on data. The third generation (1990s–2000s) focused on risk assessment, specifically using CBT, while in the fourth generation (2000s to the present), assessment has been based on Risk Need Responsivity (RNR).[30] RNR is a model used to assess and treat offenders. RNR is based on three core principles based on the "whom," "what," and "how" of assessment and treatment. "Whom" is about accessing the likelihood of reoffending. "What" targets the type of intervention, while "how" addresses the delivery of intervention.

It has been during this fourth generation that the NPS in England and Wales was created, resulting from the Criminal Justice and Court Services Act 2000. The act set out the following aims of the NPS: the protection of the public, the reduction of reoffending, the proper punishment of offenders, ensuring offenders' awareness of the effects of crime on the victims and the public, and the rehabilitation of offenders.[31] Other significant changes to probation services at the time, under the New Labour government, included the Criminal Justice Act 2003, which introduced a single community order with twelve possible requirements, such as curfew, exclusion from certain areas, compulsory unpaid work, and supervision. Additionally, the Multi-Agency Public Protection Arrangements (MAPPA) were established around this time in each of the forty-two criminal justice areas in England and Wales. The MAPPA, alongside the Integrated Offender Management (IOM)—a multiagency program involving the police and other agencies—highlights the role of probation in public protection. While the MAPPA focuses on protecting the public and victims of crime from sexual and violent offenders, the IOM is focused on prolific and problematic offenders within communities.[32] In July 2008, the National Offender Management Service was created.[33] The backdrop to this was the 2003 Carter report "Managing Offenders, Reducing Crime: A New Approach," a correctional review that recommended end-to-end service in offender management, competition from providers in the private and voluntary sectors, and a purchaser/provider split (i.e., a service delivery model that separates the purchasers who are the service providers from the suppliers of goods).[34]

More recently, the Transforming Rehabilitation approach, launched by the coalition government in 2010, led to the privatization of some aspects of the probation service. In a consultation paper titled "Breaking the Cycle: Effective Punishment, Rehabilitation and Sentencing of Offenders," five main reforms were proposed: extending rehabilitation to offenders released from short-term sentences, introducing a network of seventy local resettlement prisons, inviting providers from the voluntary and private sectors, introducing the Payment by Result program, and creating a new NPS.[35] The adoption of these reforms led to the division of the probation service into, on the one hand, an NPS—divided into seven geographic areas—that dealt with the most serious offenders and provided advice to the courts and, on the other hand, twenty-one community rehabilitation companies (CRCs) run by private and/or third-sector organizations contracted to deliver community sentences for lower-risk offenders.[36] This led to the creation of the NPS and the CRCs in June 2014.[37] Central to the operation of the CRCs is the idea that payment would be made based on how they managed to reduce reoffending. However, the failure to transform rehabilitation led the government to terminate the CRCs' contracts and reverse the decision to split the probation service into two agencies. The unified model was introduced in June 2021; it merged the NPS and the CRCs across twelve regions, including Wales.[38] The NPS in this model is still be able to commission some services from private and/or third-party sectors. The NPS would be responsible for the delivery of unpaid work, accredited programs, other interventions, and resettlement services.[39]

Youth Justice

The youth justice system in England and Wales dates back to the work of the Royal Philanthropic Society in 1792.[40] In the nineteenth century, a total of six legislative and policy interventions and reforms were introduced by the government, including the 1847 Juvenile Act, the 1854 Reformatory School Act, and the 1854 Youthful Offenders Act. At the beginning of the nineteenth century, there was no distinction between juvenile and adult offenders within the CJS. This changed with the Children Act 1908, which established a separate Juvenile Justice Court.[41] Of importance is the significance of the social, economic, and political changes on the conceptualization and understanding of youth offending at this time. For example, youth crime and justice in the late eighteenth and nineteenth centuries must be understood within the context of broader changes, such as the transition from an agrarian system to the Industrial Revolution. More specifically, juvenile delinquency itself was being reconceptualized by philanthropic and religious reformers collectively known as "child savers."[42]

The approach to youth justice in the twentieth century was dynamic. Thirty-four legislative acts and policy directions shaped youth justice at that time, starting with the 1901 Youthful Offenders Act and ending with the 1999 Anti-Social Behavior Orders. The Juvenile Courts were renamed in 1992 as the Youth Courts by order of the 1991 Criminal Justice Act. The youth justice system went through four key phases of reforms following World War II: the welfare phase (1940s–1970s), the justice phase (early 1980s–1992), the punitive phase (1993–2008), and the pragmatic phase (2009 to the present).

In the welfare phase, the approach to youth justice was based on the notion that youth crime should be viewed from an inclusive lens that focuses on a child's social and personal situation.[43] The need for a welfare-based approach was central to the 1933 Children and Young Persons Act, which mandated courts to take children's welfare into account.[44] The idea of welfarism was also reflected in the 1963/1969 Children and Young Persons Act. By the 1980s, like with the development of probation in

England and Wales, the focus on welfarism in youth justice was displaced by a movement toward a justice model that emphasized punishment.

The subsequent punitive phase (1993–2008) developed following the murder of James Bulger—a two-year-old killed by two ten-year-old boys in Liverpool in 1993. The media response and public outcry led to a more punitive turn and response to youth crime and, in some ways, to the politicization of youth justice.[45] Several significant changes to youth justice came about with the passing of the 1998 Crime and Disorder Act, which introduced youth offending teams, a multiagency approach to delivering youth justice services at the local level. The youth offending teams include probation officers, social workers, police officers, health workers, and education workers.[46] Presently, the term "youth justice teams" has been replaced by "youth justice services." The 1998 Crime and Disorder Act also abolished doli incapax—the notion that it is possible to be incapable of doing harm—for children aged ten years and older; the 1963 Children and Young Persons Act had classified those aged ten to seventeen years old as children. Finally, the act also created the Youth Justice Board (YJB), a nondepartmental public body that oversees, monitors, and leads the youth justice system in England and Wales.[47]

Following the punitive phase, youth justice in England and Wales since 2009 has been in a pragmatic phase, one characterized by hybrid strategies involving actuarial issues, risk reduction, protection of the public, restorative justice, welfarism through treatment, CBT, and diversionary techniques. For example, Key Elements of Effective Practice, developed by the YJB, provides a robust approach to youth offending and crime.

One feature of today's youth justice in England and Wales is the distinction between Youth Courts, which only deal with children in trouble, and Family Proceeding Courts, which were established with the passing of the Children Act 1989 and deal with care matters.[48] Youth Court proceedings are held in the buildings of Magistrates' Courts, although some other courts have different provisions in terms of dedicated courtrooms. Youth Courts can hear cases on theft and burglary, drug offenses, and antisocial behavior, among other matters. However, serious crimes can be passed from Youth Court to the Crown Court. The Youth Court operates on an adversarial system, just like the adult court does. Children are to be accompanied to court by either a parent or a guardian. Unlike with Magistrates' Courts, Youth Court proceedings are not open to the public,[49] but Youth Courts are similar to Magistrates' Courts in that their cases are presided over by three lay magistrates or a single district judge who have the power to sentence children. Sentences passed at the Youth Court are based on the consideration of such factors as age, criminal records, seriousness of the crime, and whether the child pleads guilty. Examples of sentences that can be given in Youth Court are community sentences (i.e., a referral order or youth rehabilitation order) and detention and training orders for children aged between twelve and seventeen years for as much as two years. It must be noted that the first half of the detention and training orders are to be served in custody, while the second half are to be served in the community.[50] Between April 1, 2020, and March 31, 2021, 50,784 children were arrested; 18,649 of those arrests ended up in court, and 12,217 received a sentence.[51]

A major challenge currently facing the youth justice system is how it is failing Black children. A Black child is 18 percent more likely to be stopped and searched than she would be if she were of another race. Similarly, Black children are 15 percent more likely than other children are to be arrested and 12 percent more likely to be cautioned or sentenced. Thirty-four percent of children in custody or remand and 29 percent of the youth custody population are Black.[52] Research also suggests that Black children also face further discrimination once they enter into the CJS with regard to remand and sentencing.[53] The disproportionality of Black children in the CJS has been linked to policing practices and issues around suspicion. According to the YJB and the MoJ, ethnic disproportionality is seen at many stages of the youth justice system, with the proportion of Black children in the system rising over the past ten years from 18 to 29 percent.[54]

The Structure and General Functioning of the Courts in the United Kingdom

The courts generally operate under the auspices of the executive arm of the MoJ—His Majesty's Courts and Tribunal Services—in matters of public and private law. Matters of public law are usually criminal cases, as they are seen to affect the public and are classed as an offense against the state. Such trials take place in the Magistrates' Courts and Crown Courts, depending on the offense. For matters classified as issues of private or civil law, the onus remains on affected individuals to seek redress from the court, usually at the county or High Court level. Therefore, the role of the court hinges on the distinction between criminal and civil cases, as civil law compensates individuals who have suffered or experienced loss, in order to restore them, usually through financial compensation to the offended party such that they would have been if they had not experienced the injury or harm. Criminal law, in contrast, focuses on prohibiting certain behaviors and maintaining law and order in the interest of the general public. Civil matters are cited using the names of the individuals or organizations that are party to the case and take the form of *Name v. Name*, while criminal law citations are usually *R v. Defendant's Surname*, where "R" stands for "Rex" or "Regina"—the monarch as the state's representative.

THE CRIMINAL COURT SYSTEM

Criminal proceedings begin with the decision to prosecute, and the CPS is the principal prosecution authority. It works on a local level through thirteen "areas" across England and Wales under the leadership of Chief Crown Prosecutors (CCP). It also serves a fourteenth virtual area, called CPS Direct, which is also led by the CCP and provides after-hours services to the police. Once the police have investigated a crime and a decision has been made to charge, the appropriate documentation is passed on to the CPS, which then decides based on two tests—evidential and public interest—that are set out in the Code for Crown Prosecutors. Prosecutions typically begin in the Magistrates' Courts, and cases are then classified as offenses triable only on indictment, which are serious cases such as murder; offenses triable summarily, which are cases labeled as such by statue that can be tried only by magistrates and not by jury; offenses triable either way, which are also created by statute and in which the accused chooses to be tried either summarily or on indictment; and summary, in which there are multiple offenses that are both triable summarily and indictable.

The Criminal Courts have two main functions: dealing with criminal cases and ensuring a fair trial. In dealing with cases, the Criminal Courts hear arguments both for and against the accused before determining guilt and selecting the appropriate sentence when necessary. When the accused pleads not guilty, the courts have a duty to consider the evidence that is presented and then reach a decision. In Magistrates' Courts, this is done by the magistrates; in the Crown Court, it is done by the jury under the guidance of the trial judge, who at the start of proceedings provides the jury with a summary of the case. The prosecution has a duty to prove beyond reasonable doubt that the alleged offense has been committed. The role of the defense is to cast doubt on the allegations in the hopes of demonstrating that the burden of proof has not been sufficiently satisfied; when that burden has not been met, the defendant is acquitted. However, when the defendant pleads guilty, the function of the court is to determine the appropriate sentence, taking pleas in mitigation on behalf of the accused into account.

Ensuring a fair trial is one of the fundamental tenets of the due process model of criminal justice. In this model, there is an emphasis on strict adherence to the criminal justice procedure and on the use of evidence so that all accused people have a fair trial, as is their right. The crime control model's principal concerns are security and public protection. There are tensions between a due process model and a "crime control" model, which has recently been the focus of criminal justice in England and Wales.[55] For example, both models are based on different principles. In the crime control model, criminal procedures, which are in place to ensure fairness for the accused, are sometimes compromised. Regardless of the model used, the courts in England and Wales are charged with articulating and following the rules of fairness for a trial, and these rules influence what the courts can accept as evidence and disclosure in a criminal trial.

THE CRIMINAL COURTS

Magistrates' Courts

There are two types of Magistrates' Courts in operation in England and Wales: the District Judge Magistrates' Courts and the Lay Justices' Courts. The Magistrates' Courts rely heavily on laypersons who volunteer to serve because magistrates are often people who come from the community that is affected by alleged criminal activity. Of the two types of Magistrates' Courts, the Lay Justices' Courts are usually made up of three laypersons called justices of peace, who receive legal advice on criminal cases, which they determine from the justices' clerk, who is a qualified barrister or solicitor with a minimum of five years' experience. The District Judge Magistrates' Courts, by contrast, are run by district judges who are legally qualified and sit individually rather than in groups of three.

The Magistrates' Courts have responsibility over most noncustodial issues, such as fines and traffic offenses. Committal proceedings in Magistrates' Court were once a formal stage in the criminal procedure. These proceedings gave magistrates a way to be certain that there was a legitimate case for the defendant to answer to before moving the case to the Crown Court, but issues with publicity made it difficult to find an independent jury that had never heard of cases. These sorts of proceedings were abolished, and from January 2001, all cases that are indictable are now automatically sent to the Crown Court for trial, following a simple appearance before the Magistrates' Court. In 2013, the need for committal proceedings was abolished for offenses that could be tried by indictment or summary. Section 49 of the Criminal Procedures and Investigations Act 1996 provides that all accused persons must enter a plea, either guilty or not guilty, before a Magistrates' Court.[56]

Crown Courts

The Crown Courts deal with the most serious crimes—those tried on indictment. There are seventy-seven court centers, and the court is divided into three tiers according to the hierarchy of judges presiding over cases in the courts. The first-tier courts are presided over by High Court judges, Circuit Court judges, and part-time judges known as recorders. These first-tier judges deal with the full range of criminal cases and High Court civil cases. These judges have higher levels of security and can therefore preside over difficult criminal cases and prisoners by having access to higher levels of security. The second-tier courts differ from first-tier courts only insofar as they do not deal with civil cases. In third-tier courts, only circuit judges and recorders preside.

Cases heard in Crown Courts are divided into three classes according to severity. Class 1 cases are for the most serious crimes, such as murder and treason. These cases are heard by a High Court judge. Class 2 cases are also for serious crimes, including rape; circuit judges hear these cases under the authority of a presiding judge. Class 3 cases involve all other, less serious offenses. These cases are heard by a circuit judge or recorder.

The Crown Court can also sentence a case heard in the Magistrates' Court when the magistrates believe that their powers of sentencing are insufficient. This is based on the rationale that the more serious the offense, the more senior the judge deciding on it should be. The Crown Court will also hear appeals from the Magistrates' Court.

CRIMINAL PROCEDURE

The Criminal Procedure Rules are a creation of Section 69 of the Courts Act 2003. Rule 1.1(1) of the Criminal Procedure Rules states that the core objective of the Criminal Courts is to ensure that criminal cases are dealt with justly, to give the accused the presumption of innocence, to ensure that the procedure is as fair as possible to allow an accurate determination of guilt or innocence, and to ensure that the consequences of conviction are adequate and proportionate to the circumstances and severity of the offense.

There are two ways to commence prosecution of a case. The first is by arrest without a warrant, and the second is through the prosecutor presenting allegations to the magistrate and the accused being summoned to answer the allegation. The police are the only agency with the authority to commence prosecution with a charge.

Conclusion

The CJS in England and Wales has changed greatly in recent years in terms of both management and delivery of services. These changes reflect what is happening in these countries' social, economic, and political spheres. More important, the adoption of neoliberal principles and the mainstreaming of political ideologies are reflected in the current approach to the CJS. Hence, it is not surprising to find words such as "multiagency," "joined up," "scrutiny," "accountability," "performance," "strategic management," "targets," and "inspections," among others, in some CJS policy statements and legislation.

Notes

1. National Audit Office, "Efficiency in the Criminal Justice System," 2016, https://www.nao.org.uk/report/efficiency-in-the-criminal-justice-system, 5.
2. National Audit Office, "Departmental Overview 2019–2021, Ministry of Justice, 2021," https://www.nao.org.uk/wp-content/uploads/2021/01/Departmental-Overview-2019-20-Ministry-of-Justice.pdf.
3. National Audit Office, "Efficiency in the Criminal Justice System."
4. K. Albertson, M. Corcoran, and J. Philips, "Introduction: Marketization and Privatisation in Criminal Justice: An Overview," in *Marketization and Privatisation* (Bristol: Polity Press, 2020), 1–14.
5. Peel, 1829, in T. A. Critchley, *A History of Police in England and Wales* (London: Constable and Company, 1978), 52.
6. Peel, 1829, in Critchley, *History*, 54.
7. D. Garland, *The Culture of Control* (Oxford: Oxford University Press, 2011), 14.
8. Garland, *Culture*, 108.
9. M. Davies, *Criminal Justice*, 5th ed. (Harlow: Pearson Longman, 2015).
10. Bittner focused on the legal use of force when considering the role of the police, while Johnston and Shearing use a much wider consideration in a set of programs to promote peace while managing a wide range of threats to individuals, communities, or our ways of life. L. Johnston and C. Shearing, in E. McLaughlin and J. Muncie, *The Sage Dictionary of Criminology*, 3rd ed. (London: Sage, 2013), 319; Bittner, in McLaughlin and Muncie, *Sage*, 319.
11. Office of National Statistics, "Population Estimates for the UK, England and Wales, Scotland and Northern Ireland Mid-2020," 2020, https://www.gov.uk/government/statistics/

police-workforce-england-and-wales-30-september-2020/police-workforce-england-and-wales-30-september-2020.

12. Office of National Statistics, "Population Estimates."

13. Institute for Government, https://www .instituteforgovernment .org .uk/publication/performance-tracker-2019/police.

14. R. Reiner, *The Politics of the Police*, 4th ed. (Oxford: Oxford University Press, 2010), 17.

15. Home Office, "Police Workforce England and Wales September 2020," 2020, https://assets.publishing.service.gov.uk/government/uploads/system/uploads/attachment_data/file/956449/police-workforce-sep20-hosb0321.pdf.

16. Home Office, "Police."

17. W. H. Chui and M. Nellis, "Creating the National Probation Service: New Wine, Old Bottles," in *Moving Probation Forward: Evidence, Arguments and Practice* (Harlow: Pearson Longman, 2003), 1–18.

18. Chui and Nellis, "Creating."

19. P. Strickland and G. Berman, *The Offender Management Bill*, Research Paper 06/62 (London: House of Commons Library, 2006), 8.

20. Davies, *Criminal.*

21. *The Guardian*, "Timeline: A History of Probation," 2007, https://www .theguardian .com/society/2007/may/02/crime.penal.

22. B. Rodin, *The Parole System of England and Wales*, Briefing Paper 8656 (London: House of Commons Library, 2019), 4.

23. See, for example, K. Bird and M. Ward, *Probation in Europe: England and Wales* (Utrecht: CEP, Confederation of Europe, 2021).

24. Chui and Nellis, "Creating."

25. Chui and Nellis, "Creating," 6.

26. R. White and F. Haines, *Crime and Criminology*, 4th ed. (Oxford: Oxford University Press, 2018); J. Deering and M. Feilzer, "Hollowing Out Probation? The Roots of Transforming Rehabilitation," *Probation Journal* 66, no. 1 (2019): 3–24.

27. Deering and Feilzer, "Hollowing."

28. https://www.gov.uk/government/organisations/probation-service/about.

29. Bird and Ward, *Probation*, 7; His Majesty's Inspectorate of Probation, "Assessment," 2020, https://www .justiceinspectorates .gov .uk/hmiprobation/research/the -evidence -base -probation/supervision-of-service-users/assessment. See also Deering and Feilzer, "Hollowing."

30. His Majesty's Inspectorate of Probation, "Assessment."

31. https://www.legislation.gov.uk/en/ukpga/2000/43/part/I/chapter/I/enacted.

32. HM Prison and Probation Service, "MAPPA Guidance," 2021, https://view.officeapps.live .com/op/view.aspx?src=https%3A%2F%2Fassets.publishing.service.gov.uk%2Fgovernment%2Fuploads%2Fsystem%2Fuploads%2Fattachment_data%2Ffile%2F1035787%2FMAPPA_Guidance_November_2021.odt&wdOrigin=BROWSELINK.

33. J. Bardens and G. G. Grimwood, *Introducing "Payments by Results" in Offender Rehabilitation and Other Reforms* (London: House of Commons Library, 2013), https://researchbriefings.files.parliament.uk/documents/SN06665/SN06665.pdf.

34. Bardens and Grimwood, *Introducing.*

35. Bardens and Grimwood, *Introducing*, 9.

36. J. Beard, *Contracting Out Probation Services*, Briefing Paper 06894 (London: House of Commons Library, 2019); J. Beard, *Unification of Probation Services* (London: House of Commons Library, 2019).

37. Beard, *Contracting*; Beard, *Unification.*

38. Beard, *Contracting*; Beard, *Unification.*

39. Beard, *Contracting*; Beard, *Unification.*

40. T. Bateman, "Youth Justice," in *An Introduction to Criminal Justice*, ed. J. Harding, P. Davies, and G. Mair (London: Sage, 2017), 346–65.

41. T. Bateman and N. Hazel, *Beyond Youth Custody: Youth Justice Timeline* (London: Big Lottery Fund, 2014); B. Goldson, "Excavating Youth Justice Reform: Historical Mapping and Speculative Prospects," *Howard Journal* 59, no. 3 (2020): 317–34.

42. H. Hendrick, "Histories of Youth Crime and Justice," in *Youth Crime and Justice: Critical Issues*, ed. B. Goldson and J. Muncie (London: Sage, 2004), 3–16. See also A. M. Platt, *The Child Savers: The Invention of Delinquency* (New Brunswick, NJ: Rutgers University Press, 2009). For a more detailed review of the historical and social-structural contexts of the emergence of youth justice system in England and Wales, see Hendrick, "Histories."

43. Hendrick, "Histories."

44. See, for example, Bateman and Hazel, *Beyond Youth Custody.*

45. See, for example, Bateman, "Youth Justice."

46. See Section 39(1) of the Crime and Disorder Act 1998.

47. Youth Justice Board for England and Wales, "Youth Offending Teams: Making the Difference for Children and Young People, Victims and Communities," 2015, https://assets.publishing.service.gov.uk/government/uploads/system/uploads/attachment_data/file/445271/Board_Visits_Final_Report.pdf.

48. Bateman and Hazel, *Beyond Youth Custody.*

49. H. Pidd, "How Do Youth Courts in England and Wales Function?," *The Guardian*, 2019, https://www.theguardian.com/society/2019/nov/03/how-do-youth-courts-in-england-and-wales-function, 2019.

50. https://www.gov.uk/courts/youth-courts.

51. Youth Justice Board for England and Wales and Ministry of Justice, *Youth Justice Statistics: 2020/21* (London: Ministry of Justice, 2022), https://assets.publishing.service.gov.uk/government/uploads/system/uploads/attachment_data/file/1054236/Youth_Justice_Statistics_2020-21.pdf.

52. Youth Justice Board for England and Wales and Ministry of Justice, *Youth Justice Statistics.*

53. Youth Justice Board for England and Wales, "Ethnic Disproportionality in Remand and Sentencing in the Youth Justice System: An Analysis of Administrative Data," 2021, https://assets.publishing.service.gov.uk/government/uploads/system/uploads/attachment_data/file/952483/Ethnic_disproportionality_in_remand_and_sentencing_in_the_youth_justice_system.pdf.

54. Youth Justice Board for England and Wales and Ministry of Justice, *Youth Justice Statistics.*

55. M. Partington, *Introduction to the English Legal System* (Oxford: Oxford University Press, 2021).

56. https://assets.publishing.service.gov.uk/government/uploads/system/uploads/attachment_data/file/931173/Criminal-procedure-and-investigations-act-1996.pdf.

CHAPTER 9

The Criminal Justice System and Criminal Process in Poland

Monika Baylis

The Polish criminal justice system (CJS) links strictly to the legality principle based on a division of power between the legislature and the executive and judicial authorities. Its establishment and development have often been driven by various social, economic, and political changes that occurred since Poland's foundation in 966. In this chapter, the origins of modern Polish CJS and how this development was achieved are analyzed. This includes the nature of pragmatic approaches used by different actors involved in democratic policing and the Polish criminal process as well as the concepts of Polish legal culture and "adversarial procedure," centralized and decentralized models of democratic policing, and the penal system. This highlights the importance of various factors that can affect the process of delivering social and criminal justice in the transnational state system. The chapter finishes with a brief conclusion to prompt critical thinking concerning the role of the state, law, research, and society in democratic Poland.

Development of the Polish Legal Culture and System in Democratic Poland

The democratic system of the Republic of Poland is represented by a president who is a head of state. The Polish state is based on government that consists of various cabinet offices managed by the Council of Ministers and led by a prime minister. The president appoints the cabinet according to the proposals of the prime minister, typically from the majority coalition in the Sejm. The president is elected by general election every five years. However, the judicial system plays an important role in decision making,[1] which is often influenced by Polish legal culture[2] and the history of the country itself.[3]

Poland was founded in 966 as an independent kingdom with elected monarchs, but it has faced four partitions since 1772.[4] These powers influenced the Polish adversarial model over that time,[5] while the role of the state[6] in public and private life was and still is evident.[7] The same narrative is present in different publications of various political and international stakeholders that helped to shape the current Polish legal system before, during, and after World Wars I and II, communism, and capitalism, leading the modern Poland to become a democratic country.[8] This complex process faced various challenges (i.e., the struggle for constitutionalism,[9] cultivating an understanding of democracy,[10] and the economic and political trends and shifts linked to the process of polarization[11]), defined as legal and extralegal factors. These elements also influenced and established legitimate professionalism in policing in Poland[12] along with the process of criminalization in the country.[13]

The process of criminalization is a broad concept, meaning that various actors can define it differently because of political stands, culture, social changes, the academic understanding of it (i.e., theoretical stances of criminology: critical criminology, imaginative criminology, comparative criminology, and so on), or the role of the state.[14] In the Polish context, this process often relates to a legal doctrine of the past or the present[15] that is viewed as consisting of specific changes made by the state over different criminal procedures (i.e., the Polish Code of Criminal Procedure).[16] This includes the debate over the roles of participants in trials, such as prosecution, defense, and adjudication that shall be impartial,[17] and how the Polish CJS shall deal with any type of criminality.[18] However, some Polish academics argue that the concept of impartiality forms the basis of the principle of an adversarial model that is frequently recognized as the direct participation of two different parties who have rights to fight with the opposing side for a positive outcome for themselves.[19] This highlights the role of the adversarial model when it comes to the process of administering the law and justice and the process of adjudication that links to the act of judgment made by a specific court or tribunal. Both elements form the basis of decision-making processes of law enforcement in the Polish context.[20] However, this can be problematic in terms of securing the impartiality or objectivity of the decisions or judgments made in the Polish CJS,[21] particularly in the highly centralized legal and policing system.[22] For the purpose of this chapter, the focus is first on the judiciary system that is part of CJS in Poland in order to support the existing argument that the judicial sector and the state play essential roles in shaping Polish law and criminal proceedings in the country. However, the focus of discussion reflects recent judicial changes conducted by the Polish government in 2015 in order to narrow the scope of the analysis and cover the most current developments related to this topic, thus covering the years 2015–2022.

The Polish Justice System and the Constitution: Courts and Tribunals (2015–2022)

In Poland, there are different types of courts and tribunals that are organized in a hierarchical order to reflect their powers and importance within the Polish CJS. These are the Supreme Court (Sad Najwyzszy [SN]); the Common Court (Sad Powszechny); the Administrative Court (Sad Administracyjny), including the Supreme Administrative Court; and the Military Court (Sad Wojskowy). For example, the Common Courts deal with civil and criminal cases,[23] whereas Military Courts look after the cases related mainly to active-service Polish military members; thus, they are often defined as Specific Courts (Sady Sczegolne).[24] Additionally, the judicial system in Poland offers a dual approach to administering the law because of the presence of two tribunals: the Constitutional Tribunal (Trybunal Konstytucyjny [TK]) and the Tribunal of the State (Trybunal Stanu).[25] Both tribunals have different roles. The TK scrutinizes the constitutionality of Polish legislation,[26] whereas the Tribunal of the State oversees the work of people who hold the highest offices in the Polish state. These are the president of the Republic of Poland, members of the government, and other senior state officials.[27] However, when it comes to the process of administering justice in this country, the vital key player is the head of the SN, who oversees the work of the courts in general. The head of the SN is also in charge of the Extraordinary Review and Public Affairs Chamber.[28] This indicates that the role of the head of the SN is crucial in terms of the effectiveness of each court regardless of its statues; however, many argue that there are other factors that can affect the impartiality of the legal system in this country. First, the head of the SN is appointed by the president of the Republic of Poland for a term of six years. Second, although the head of the SN is selected from various candidates proposed by the General Assembly of the Judges of the SN,[29] the process is rarely openly questioned by other actors (i.e., public organizations and private institutions) who are also part of the CJS in Poland. Third, there is a limited amount of empirical evidence about the process of the selection of the head of the SN or different judges. This demonstrates a direct dependence of the head of the SN on the head of state, highlights the hermetic nature of the Polish legal system in general, and suggests questions about whether the system can really be transparent, which can be crucial in terms of ensuring the accountability of actors that represent a democratic state in any organization.[30]

The process of ensuring the accountability of the people who represent the democratic system has been evident in the Polish public and political domain since the introduction of democracy in Poland in 1989,[31] when some cases of miscarriage of justice or wrongful convictions occurred.[32] One example is the case of Tomasz Komenda, who spent eighteen years in a Polish prison and was accused of murdering a young woman in 1996.[33] This shows that the Polish legal system is being viewed through the effectiveness of the political system and CJS itself. Also, it could be argued that the Polish legal system is more reactive than proactive in nature and relies on the public trust and human reactions, which may play an important factor when it comes to assessing the role and functions of each public legal institution and the decision-making process of judges involved in each case. This can be seen in the case of the Komenda, who was awarded PLN 12 million of compensation from a District Court in Opole after being released from prison in 2018 with the decision of the SN.[34]

The public trust and human reaction are broad in nature,[35] but they are often evident in various forms (i.e., negative or positive attitudes and behavior toward the organizations that represent the Polish CJS or official reports published by United Nations or Amnesty International) and linked to their legitimacy and procedural justice.[36] Both concepts have been present during public demonstrations and in the political debate that have taken place in the Polish media, prompting the Polish Parliament or European Parliament to make changes in the law.[37] The changes in law considered mostly the following: to protect basic human rights (i.e., the report of the UN Subcommittee on the Prevention of Torture in 2018 or the case of *Doroz v. Poland*, which was passed to the European Court of Human Rights in Strasbourg in 2020) or to prevent corruption in the Polish state.[38]

Moreover, some Polish scholars and practitioners of law (i.e., lawyers) argue that when it comes to administering procedural justice, making a judgment when being a judge—regardless of the hierarchy of the court—always links to the process of decision making and can be complex because of Polish law[39] or the broad definition of judgment. For example, a judgment can be a decree, order, decision, writ of execution, or decision on the determination of costs or expenses by an officer of the court (*referendarz sadowy*).[40] Additionally, the definition of the judgment can include provisional and protective measures that are ordered by such a court or tribunal without the defendant being summoned to appear, unless the judgment containing the measure is served on the defendant prior to enforcement.[41] This means that the ultimate power lies in hands of both actors, who shall follow the Polish law as created by the Polish government.[42] However, this can be problematic, especially in a highly centralized model in which the government can implement legal and policy changes that can undermine the independence of the judiciary. This topic has been recently questioned by various actors who argued that the independence of the judiciary was effectively terminated by radical reforms carried out by the Law and Justice Party (Prawo i Sprawiedliwosc [PIS]) since 2015.[43] The political party won the mandate to rule in democratic Poland and was the first one to introduce radical restructuring of the justice system in this country.[44] The process included taking over a number of state institutions, including public media and the cultural sector, and, more important, the PIS terminated the independence of the judiciary and judges by making them dependent on direct political control.[45] This could be seen as a radical replacement of cadre in key positions, including the president of the TK and legally elected judges, who were replaced with party loyalists. This allowed the Polish government to establish control over the courts, meaning that constitutional control over the government's action was removed.[46]

In addition, the PIS initiated a restructuring of the ordinary courts, the National Council of the Judiciary (Krajowa Rada Sadownicza [KRS]), and the SN. The new KRS has the power to control almost all appointments to the body that is responsible for appointing and disciplining judges. Also, a new Disciplinary Chamber of the SN was established. Both these institutions are controlled by the executive and can be seen as another tool to exert control over judges, including their dismissal.[47] The government's control was also magnified by the fact that the function of the prosecutor general was linked with that of the minister of justice.[48] Because the changes were unconstitutional, numerous demonstrations took place in Poland, but they were ignored by Polish authorities.[49] As a result, the European Union, of which Poland has been a member since 2004, has expressed its concerns regarding the legal reforms by issuing a directive in 2019 that linked the funds received by the Polish government to its maintenance of democratic standards. This started a conflict between the Polish government and the European Union and the people of Polish society, who began to question the policies and legal changes made in their own country.[50] However, it is difficult to discuss this further, as the topic is still fresh in the public and political domains. Also, there is a limited amount of empirical evidence related to it. A similar view could be presented when it comes to the past and current changes regarding the role and the functions of the Public Prosecution Office/Service in Poland. Again, for the purpose of the chapter, the current prosecution model and changes proposed in 2016 will be the primary focus of examination.

The Role of the Public Prosecution Office/Service (2016–2022)

Similar to the Polish judicial system, the Polish procuracy (Prokuratura) evolved over many centuries after having been developed only since the Polish nation regained its statehood, in 1918.[51] Before World War II, following the French model, it was subordinate to the Ministry of Justice, whereas during the era of communism, it was organized according to the Soviet system, meaning it was dependent on a highly centralized political system.[52] However, the state of dependency remained despite the fall of communism, which could be seen in its structure.[53] For example, from the 1950s, the Public Prosecution Office was the main public institution that was run by the General Prosecution Office (Prokurator Generalny), which was in charge of other prosecution offices, namely, the National Prosecution Office (Prokuratura Krajowa) and Prosecution Offices (Prokuratorzy). This was changed in 2016 with the introduction of the Law of the Prosecutor's Office, which initiated structural reforms in the prosecution model. This resulted in the Public Prosecution Office being linked with the Ministry of Justice, thereby establishing the National Prosecution Office, which ultimately replaced the Public Prosecution Office. Also, the Law of the Prosecution Office of 2016 created regional prosecution offices (*prokuratury regionalne*), which have replaced the prosecution offices that dealt with appeals. This law has also removed the military unit that was responsible for some prosecution offices in Poland, and a new public body was established called the Institute of National Remembrance (Instytut Pamieci Narodowej [IPN]).

The main role of the National Prosecution Office is to oversee the accountability and integrity of the prosecution offices. The National Prosecution Office is managed by the general prosecutor (Prokurator Generalny). The main function of the public institutions is to conduct criminal prosecutions under the supervision of the Ministry of Justice and in accordance with Polish criminal and civil law.[54] The role of the IPN is to research and popularize the modern history of Poland and to investigate crimes committed from November 8, 1917, to July 31, 1990,[55] including World War II and communism. However, it could be argued that both these public bodies are under the control of the state, especially since the Ministry of Justice is a supreme, one-person authority of the governmental administration[56] and the PIS amended the existing law of the IPN in 2018 to remove the influence of academia and the judiciary on the IPN. The legal changes also empowered the organization to defend the "good name of Poland" by prosecuting anyone who publishes false information that dishonors or harms the Polish nation.[57] This shows again that the process of administering the law is interdependent with the Polish state, and it highlights the role of politicians and the centralized model in general. Similarly, the role and functions of the Polish police in democratic Poland[58] can be seen as collaborating with the National Prosecution Office by gathering evidence and preparing cases before prosecutors and judges make a final judgment during criminal proceedings.[59] However, the focus in the next section of this chapter will be mainly on the recent changes and issues related to the topic, thus discussing their development since the creation of the New Police (Policja), which occurred in 1990.

The New Police (1990–2022)

The Polish police was formally created during the interwar period of 1918–1939. The formation was highly centralized and hierarchical, and at that time, it was seen as an independent public organization.[60] However, similar to the Polish judicial system and Polish procuracy, various administrative and legislative changes occurred over time that were driven by social, economic, and political factors.[61] These aspects have shaped the role and functions of this institution.[62] For example, one major event was the beginning of Polish capitalism in 1989,[63] which prompted the introduction of the most important piece of legislation in the Polish policing system: the Police Act of 1990. At that point, the New Police was established.[64]

The Police Act of 1990 was created by the Polish government to improve the newly established democratic system and is still used by the organization to justify its powers and support its accountability.[65] The act also forms the police structure and the model of policing used in this country. Both are based on a centralized and hierarchical approach, reflecting its original approach from 1918 to 1939.[66] Therefore, the Polish police service consists of the Main Headquarters of Polish Police, located in Warsaw, the capital of Poland. The headquarters oversees sixteen regional command units that are managed by their respective commanders. Each unit has its own subdivisions that are in charge of various activities. For example, some of them deal with crime prevention, criminal investigations, traffic control, aviation service, and counterterrorism, reflecting the complex nature of their work and policing in this country.[67] However, the Polish police service does not work on its own because there are other public organizations that assist Polska Policja. These are the Central Bureau of Investigation, the Internal Bureau of Police Conduct, the Central Subdivision of the Counter-Terrorism Unit, the Central Forensic Laboratory of the Police, and the City Guards Formation. All of them perform different functions, which is evident not only in the way that they are dressed but also in how they are trained and which powers they can use when dealing with criminals or the Polish public.[68] Therefore, it has been argued that the policing model starts to reflect a decentralized one, especially when some regional police command units also rely financially on a local council system,[69] which indicates that a partnership model is also used in this country. The police command units are represented by police officers of various ranks whose duty is to "protect and help" Polish society.[70]

As of January 1, 2019, the Polish police employed approximately 100,000 police officers and 12,000 civilians,[71] and this number has remained stable according to data from March 1, 2021.[72] However, some issues have been identified by various scholars, different organizations, and the Polish public in terms of applying procedural justice by the police. For example, the police faced allegations about the use of force, ignorance, and favoritism when securing public demonstrations[73] or providing safety to local politicians who gather to perform their duties.[74] Also, the codependent relationship between the media and the police was questioned, along with the police brutality that was shown on Polish television channels, such as TVN in 2017, after the case of Igor Stachowiak dominated the public and political domains in 2016.[75] Police brutality was again raised as a concern in 2021 with three new cases being discussed by the public and Polish politicians, namely, the deaths of Bartosz Sokolowski, Dmytro Nikiforenko, and Lukasz Lagiewka.[76] This implies that the police training and education provided by the organization itself in the form of various police training centers and schools[77] may not be effective after all and should be evaluated again.[78] This includes the introduction in 2018 of additional body cameras, which have been bought for PLN 9,208,940 by the chief commander of Polish police, the head of Polish police. The funds came from the Program of the Modernization of Polish Public Services, which provided funds to the police, Customs and Border Services, State Fire Service, and Government Protection Bureau from 2017 to 2020.[79] Although the three new cases related to the deaths of Sokolowski, Nikiforenko, and Lagiewka are still under investigation by the National Prosecution Office, this argument could be supported by other, similar incidents and reports under the review of the Polish Ombudsman (Rzecznik Praw Obywatelskich).[80]

The Polish Ombudsman oversees cases that infringe the Human Rights Act of 1998. It is managed by the Commissioner for Human Rights, who may examine cases and lodge a last-resort appeal with the SN in a penal case.[81] This offers additional help for victims and the families of victims who might face or have faced brutality at the hands of Polish police officers or other public organizations that deal with criminal or deviant behavior in the Polish context. However, the police service itself can also investigate the behavior of police officers because there is an internal unit that deals with various complaints made by the Polish public. This department, called the Complaint Office, is located in the Main Headquarters of the Polish Police in Warsaw.[82] This demonstrates that there are different avenues that can be taken by the public to search for justice, but some officials and scholars argue that police accountability and transparency should be studied further to improve its work in general.[83] This includes studying different models of policing used in this country (i.e., community or neighborhood policing[84] and intelligence-led policing[85]), especially when the interdependence of the Polish police on the Polish government is strongly evident through the role of the minister of interior affairs and administration, who selects and oversees the work of the chief commander of the Polish police, despite the fact that the Police Act of 1990 states that the police service should be free of political influence and act independently. Also, the same minister of interior affairs, with the Polish Parliament, decides how much public money shall be spent on improving the police in Poland, which again magnifies the role of politicians and decisions made by them when it comes to public safety and spending related to it.[86] Perhaps this shall be resolved by introducing an independent body in which the major voice would be given to local communities and victims. However, the question still remains as to who would fund such an institution and which part of the Polish law should be amended, especially since the legal system in Poland is complex and still relies on the process of simple judgment. This can be seen in the correctional/penitentiary system in this country, which is represented by the Polish prison and probation service. In the next section, the focus is on the Polish prison and probation service, specifically on the time following the fall of communism (i.e., from 1989 to the present).

The Prison and Probation System (1989–2022)

The penitentiary system in Poland consists of various institutions called "prisons" that house criminals convicted of serious crimes.[87] The current prison population rate per 100,000 inhabitants is 183, and as of July 2020, 4 percent of those prisoners are female. The official capacity of the prison system is 81,127, and the occupancy level is 85.4 percent as of July 31, 2020.[88] The prison service is a uniformed and armed formation, similar to the Polish police, and its system has been supported by two main pieces of legislation: the Criminal Executive Penal Code of 1997 and the Act of 9 April 2010 on Prison Service. There are other provisions that complement these two items of legislation. These are the minister of justice's ordinance on the organizational rules of the execution of imprisonment from 2016 and the minister of justice's ordinance on the organizational rules of pretrial detention from the same year.[89] In charge of the Polish prisons are directors of the units, who deliver the service according to these specific legislative items and internal policies established by them. This implies that the system is decentralized in practice; however, because the Polish penitentiary system is governed by the minister of justice,[90] the role of the state and the law is highlighted again. This can be magnified by the fact that the directors of the prison service are overseen by the general director, who is nominated by the prime minister via application by the minister of justice.[91] The general director of the prison service leads the Central Board of Prison Service and is responsible for fifteen circuit inspectors of prison service, who are in charge of the penitentiary units in their jurisdictions. However, the directors coordinate the prison service and different activities conducted in it. For example, they supervise schools and the medical units that run inside the system, they ration the available financial resources, they decide how the staff shall be trained and educated, and they determine the number of work sites in each prison unit.[92]

In Poland, the prisons can be organized as closed units, semi-open units, and open units.[93] They differ among themselves in terms of the level of security, the level of isolation of inmates, and the rights and duties connected with inmates' opportunities to move inside and outside the unit.[94] In this country, inmates can stay in units for young offenders, for people serving their sentence for first time, for recidivists, and for people serving military arrests. Also, the prisoners can be attached to units that represent one of three types of systems: the program system (the so-called program ward), the therapeutic system (the so-called therapeutic ward), or a regular system (the so-called regular ward).[95] Each program system guides the prisoners in their "structured activities." For example, a prisoner in the program system works with a tutor to map out a plan. Then the plan is submitted to a penitentiary commission for final approval.

The therapeutic system offers prisoners support from psychologists, therapists, and educators to manage their needs, especially when its units are occupied by people with nonpsychotic mental disorders or sexual disorders and other mental health issues. This includes people who are disabled or addicted to drugs or alcohol. However, this system is only for people who have been diagnosed previously and who will stay in the unit only for the duration of the therapy. The therapy can include different methods: psychotherapy, pharmacotherapy, addiction therapy, therapy meetings, and so on.[96] The execution of imprisonment is guided by main rules that are divided in the following categories: allocation, meals, visits, gender, and "N" status.[97]

The rule of allocation forms the basis of where and for how long to place the offender, which is explained in Article 100 of the Executive Penal Code. According to this piece of legislation, each prisoner shall be placed, if possible, in the prison units that are allocated close to their homes or places of social rehabilitation. This legal requirement is valid only in the period of six months before the end of the prisoner's sentence. The only exception to this rule is when prisoners have permanent custody of their children. In addition, the rule of allocation is based on the stage of criminal proceedings, whether the prisoner has yet been tried, and the prisoner's gender. For example, in the Polish context, untried prisoners are separated from those who have been sentenced, and according to Article 86(1) of the Polish Executive Penal Code, male prisoners are kept separate from female prisoners.[98] However, in some cases, this rule can be changed, as there are prisons that have both male and female wards.[99]

The rules about meals address various aspects of looking after prisoners. These are the content of meals, which should be prepared and planned according to the prisoner's age; dietary requirements, religion, or culture; and the frequency of the meals provided (i.e., prisoners have a right to have a meal three times a day). The food standards and types of diets are determined by ordinance of the Ministry of Justice.[100]

The rule of visits deals with the length of allowed visits to inmates and their frequency. According to Article 105a of the Executive Penal Code, each visit can last for sixty minutes, and the frequency of the visits depends on the type of prison (i.e., its security level). For example, the open prison has no limitations as to the number of visits, whereas in the closed prison, only two visits per month are allowed.[101] However, prisoners who are at least twenty-one years old are entitled to one additional visit per month. The visits are supervised by a prison guard, and if the visitor is not a relative or another person close to the prisoner, then a consent form is needed from the prison director.[102] Also, prisoners who hold permanent custody of their children are allowed to have an additional visit with their children,[103] and if the behavior of prisoners improves, then they can also be awarded additional time or visits.[104] The visits usually take place in rooms that are specially designed according to the needs and status of the prisoner. For example, prisoners who are perceived as being dangerous may be able to be seen only through glass and with an additional number of guards.[105]

The rules about gender address the needs of males and females in terms of how they perform gender in their ordinary life (e.g., if they are parents or if they are going to become parents).[106] This means that, in practice, the female prisoner is allowed to see her child or look after her newborn in specifically arranged child care premises that offer facilities for grooming and education classes, services from qualified personnel (e.g., pediatricians, psychologists, or nurses), cooking, and sanitary or infirmary activities.[107]

Prisoners' "N" status links to the presence of aggressive behavior or whether a prisoner poses a high risk of such behavior to others. This status is frequently used for a prisoner who may escape from prison. Therefore, in practice, the prisoners are kept in closed units that consist of maximum technical security cells. The cells are rooms in which all furniture and equipment is firmly fixed to the walls and floor of the cell. The cells are monitored by closed-circuit television.[108] However, prisoners' age plays an important role in terms of their allocation, as dictated by Polish law. Therefore, prisoners who are viewed as minors (i.e., they are criminally responsible after they turn seventeen years old) should be placed in Houses of Corrections, and this decision is made by the judge, who represents Family Courts in Poland.[109] This reflects the welfare approach when it comes to the juvenile justice system, which is based on providing support to young persons in various forms (i.e., educational, psychological, and social measures) to prevent demoralization or committing crime in the future.[110] This approach changes to some extent when young people turn seventeen because automatically, if there are no other issues identified with their mental health, they are usually placed in prison units for young offenders. This is supported by the Executive Penal Code, which states that the person should be kept separately from older prisoners, but this again could depend on education, meaning that sometimes they could share a cell with an older person.[111] Additionally, the age of the person can influence what type of disciplinary sanctions shall be used in the prison service. This mirrors a similar approach used in the Polish judiciary, prosecution, and policing system, highlighting the role of age when it comes to criminal responsibility in Poland. However, these sanctions are different in each context. For example, in the prison system, the sanctions may include reprimands; withholding rewards; barring the prisoner from participating in any cultural, educational, or sporting event; or serving a life sentence or spending a specific amount of time in prison.[112] However, in the context of policing, this links to powers of arrest, detention, stop and search, and so on.[113] This demonstrates that different language and processes are used in each organization to reflect their structure, functions, and legal powers available to them. Also, this again magnifies the complexity of Polish law. Nevertheless, similar arguments regarding the rules of punishment can be used in the context of the probation system in Poland, which plays an important role in the Polish CJS.

The Polish probation system mirrors the Anglo-American system and is based on the idea that individuals should be given a chance to redeem themselves.[114] The Probation Service is a government agency and is closely tied to the structure of the courts of ordinary jurisdiction and subordinated to the Ministry of Justice.[115] In the Polish model, the system is divided into probation and parole.[116]

Probation and Parole

Probation refers to a period of time before a person is sent to prison, whereas parole is the period of time after a defendant is released from prison.[117] Probation is a sentencing decision made by a judge, and parole is an administrative decision made by a penitentiary court. Both must abide by conditions or risk revocation, meaning that they are similar in terms of mechanisms used to reintegrate a defendant into society.[118] The mechanism is based on the principles of humanitarianism, which are focused on ensuring and respecting human dignity.[119] Therefore, the provisions prohibit the use of torture and inhumane, degrading treatment or punishment of the sentenced person.[120]

In Poland, the Probation Service and the Prison Service are separate organizations that are responsible for different tasks. However, they collaborate if needed, which is codified in the Polish legal system (i.e., the Executive Penal Code and the Probation Officers Act). In the Probation Service, it is a probation officer who looks after the offender by performing various duties (e.g., supervising and managing offenders to make sure that they do not break the law, conducting home visits, and performing curfew checks). All these activities link to three main measures connected with putting offenders to a test (i.e., trial). These are conditional discontinuation of proceedings, probation (a conditionally suspended sentence), and parole (a conditional release from prison after serving a part of the sentence).[121] Also, there are other, optional sanctions that can be imposed on offenders. These are the obligation to inform the court or probation officer about the course of the trial period, to apologize to victims, to maintain other persons whom offenders are burdened with, to perform paid work, to study or undertake vocational training, to refrain from abusing alcohol or drugs, to undertake additional therapy, and so on. However, if prisoners fail to carry out a specific requirement and they have no reasonable excuse for not doing so, then usually they will receive a warning, but if this does not work, then they will return to court for having breached the suspended sentence. This also usually influences their future rights for parole or can result in having parole revoked, as parole is in the hands of the court.[122] This again highlights the role of human judgment and criminal law in the Polish CJS. It would be useful to comment further on the specific idea, but there is limited empirical evidence surrounding it, and to the extent that there is academic debate, it focuses mainly on the severity of the sanctions imposed on the offender,[123] the role and broad nature of the definition of punishment in Polish law,[124] the inhumane conditions of Polish prisons and the overused probation system,[125] and the changing political discourse.[126] Therefore, more empirical research should be conducted in each sector of the Polish CJS in order to understand why certain decisions are made. This approach would help improve the system itself—its performance and decision-making style and recommendations for it[127]—as well as its transparency and accountability if we want to perceive Poland as democratic country.[128] This includes studying each organization's occupational culture, and the Polish government should provide more funding to various training centers and academic institutions to create interdisciplinary knowledge[129] and to develop further an evidence-based approach.[130]

Conclusion

This chapter presented and discussed the origins of the modern Polish CJS and how its development was achieved. This also includes the nature of pragmatic approaches used by different actors involved in democratic policing and the Polish criminal process. Hence, the following concepts have been covered: Polish legal culture and "adversarial procedure," centralized and decentralized models of democratic policing, and the penal system. This has highlighted the importance of various factors (i.e., political, social, legal, economic, and human) that can affect the process of delivering social and criminal justice in the transnational state system, which is evident in Poland. The chapter concluded with an argument that the Polish CJS links strictly to the legality principle, based on a division of power between the legislature and the executive and judicial authorities that needs to be explored further in order to understand various issues faced by each actor and factors that drive the decision-making process in general. This approach would create new knowledge that could improve the transparency and accountability of the CJS. This includes the democratic system in Poland, which, according to the Constitution of the Republic of Poland of 2 April 1997 Article 175(1) and Article 183, shall be independent.

Notes

1. United Nations Office on Drugs and Crime, *Country Review Report of Poland* (New York: United Nations, 2016).

2. Polish legal culture is defined as legal "personality," which consists of its hereditary traits, values, principles, and practices. A. Ryan, "Comparative Procedural Traditions: Poland's Journey from Socialist to 'Adversarial System,'" *International Journal of Evidence and Proof* 20, no. 4 (2016): 305–25, https://journals.sagepub.com/doi/pdf/10.1177/1365712716655169.

3. J. Markiewicz, "Kszaltowanie sie Polskiego Systemu Prawa Sadowego i Jego Tworcy w Okresie Miedzywojennym 1919–1939" [The development of legal court system and its makers during the years of 1919–1939], *Teka Komisji Prawniczej Lubelskiego Oddziału Polskiej Akademii Nauk* 2010: 113–22, https://www.tkp.edu.pl/wp-content/uploads/2020/03/TKP_III_2010_113-122_Markiewicz.pdf.

4. A. Korobowicz, "Judicial Reform in the Kingdom of Poland in 1876," *Russian Law Journal* 2, no. 4 (2014): 91–103; J. B. Perkins, "The Partition of Poland," *American Historical Review* 2, no. 1 (October 1896): 76–92, https://www.jstor.org/stable/1833615?seq=1#metadata_info_tab_contents. Perkins wrote that the country was divided among different political powers (i.e., Austria, Russia, and Prussia).

5. Ryan, "Comparative Procedural Traditions."

6. The Polish state is represented by the government, which consists of the Sejm and the senate (Senat). Rozdzial IV, Sejm I Senat, Article 95 [Chapter IV: The Sejm and the Senate, Article 95], Sejm Rzeczypospolitej Polskiej, accessed March 8, 2022, https://www.sejm.gov.pl/prawo/konst/polski/4.htm; "Rozdzial III Zrodla Prawa" [Chapter III: Sources of law], Prezydent.pl, accessed March 8, 2022, https://www.prezydent.pl/prawo/konstytucja-rp/zrodla-prawa.

7. A. Fijalkowski, *From Old Times to New Europe: The Polish Struggle for Democracy and Constitutionalism* (London: Routledge, 2010); M. Roclawska and A. Bulat, "Towards and American Model of Criminal Process: The Reform of the Polish Criminal Procedure," *Baltic Journal of*

Law and Politics 7, no. 1 (2014): 1–11; Z. Kinowska-Mazaraki, "The Polish Paradox: From a Fight for Democracy to the Political Radicalization and Social Exclusion," *Social Sciences* 10, no. 3 (2021): 112.

8. M. Pluciennik and M. Heldak, "Outdoor Advertising in Public Spaces and Its Legal System in Poland over the Centuries," *IOP Conference Series: Materials Science and Engineering* 471, no. 11 (2019), doi:10.1088/1757-899X/471/11/112046; B. Nowak, "Implementation of Directives into Domestic Legal System: The Case of Poland," *Journal of Interdisciplinary Economics* 17, no. 3 (2006): 289–312, https://doi.org/10.1177/02601079X06001700303.

9. M. Brzezinski, *The Struggle for Constitutionalism in Poland* (London: Palgrave Macmillan, 1998), https://link.springer.com/book/10.1057/9780230508620#about.

10. D. Albertazzi and S. Mueller, "Populism and Liberal Democracy: Populists in Government in Austria, Italy, Poland and Switzerland," *Government and Opposition* 48, no. 3 (2013): 343–71.

11. A. Gajdos, L. Arendt, A. P. Balcerzak, and M. B. Pietrzak. "Future Trends of Labour Market Polarisation in Poland: The Perspective of 2025," *Transformations in Business and Economics* 19, no. 3 (2020): 114–35.

12. M. Baylis, "The Police and Policing in Poland," in *Global Perspectives in Policing and Law Enforcement*, ed. J. Mbuba (Lanham, MD: Lexington Books, 2021).

13. W. Klaus, "Criminalisation of Beggars: The Causes and Consequences of the Phenomenon," *Contemporary Central & East European Law* 1, no. 133 (2019): 132–41; K. Krajewski, "Prosecution and Prosecutors in Poland: In Quest of Independence," *Crime and Justice: A Review of Research* 41, no. 20 (2012): 75–115.

14. P. Hillyard and S. Tombs, "Beyond Criminology?," in *The Palgrave Handbook of Social Harm*, ed. P. Davies, P. Leighton, and T. Wyatt (Cham: Palgrave Macmillan, 2021), 11–36, https://doi.org/10.1007/978-3-030-72408-5_2.; J. Frauley, "On Imaginative Criminology and Its Significance," *Societies* 5, no. 3 (2015): 618–30, https://www.mdpi.com/2075-4698/5/3/618; I. S. Yazhborovskaya, "Poland 2015–2016: Chronicle of Neoauthoritarian Revanche, Polis," *Political Studies* 5 (2016): 49–65, https://www .politstudies .ru/en/article/5173; F. Pakes, "Comparative Criminology," in *Comparative Law and Society*, ed. D. S. Clark, (Cheltenham: Edward Elgar, 2012), 61–76.

15. A. Dziuban, F. Faust, T. Sekuler, J. Struzik, L. Bonde, and E. J. Nicholls, "HIV/AIDS and Its Monsters: Negotiating Criminalisation along the Monster–Human Continuum," *European Journal of Cultural Studies* 25, no. 4 (2021), https://doi .org/10.1177/13675494211017911; Klaus, Witold, "Criminalisation of Beggars: The Causes and Consequences of the Phenomenon," *Contemporary Central & East European Law* 1, no. 133 (2019): 132–41.

16. See Kinowska-Mazaraki, "Polish Paradox"; A. Fijalkowski, "Transitional Criminal Justice: The Polish Way," in *Transitional Criminal Justice in Post-Dictatorial and Post-Conflict Societies*, ed. A. Fijalkowski and R. Grosescu, 101–122 (Intersentia, 2015), 101–22, https://doi.org/10.1017/9781780685687.005; M. Raclawska and A. Bulat, "Towards an American Model of Criminal Process: The Reform of the Polish Criminal Procedure," *Baltic Journal of Law and Politics* 7, no. 1 (2014): 1–11; Brzezinski, *Struggle*.

17. Raclawska and Bulat, "Towards an American Model of Criminal Process."

18. K. Buczkowski, B. Czarnecka-Dzialuk, W. Klaus, A. Kossowska, I. Rzeplińska, D. Woźniakowska-Fajst, and D. Wójcik, *Criminality and Criminal Justice in Contemporary Poland: Sociopolitical Perspectives* (London: Routledge, 2016); Krajewski, "Prosecution."

19. M. Cieślak, *Dzieła wybrane. Tom II. Polska procedura karna. Podstawowe założenia teoretyczne* [Selected Works. Volume II. Polish Criminal Procedure. The Basic Theoretical Assumptions] (Krakow: Jagiellonian University Press, 2011), cited in Raclawska and Bulat, "Towards an American Model of Criminal Process."

20. Baylis, "Police and Policing"; J. Modrzejewski and A. Potasz, "Enforcement of Judgements and Arbitral Awards in Poland: Overview," Thomson Reuters Practical Law, October 1, 2020, https://uk.practicallaw.thomsonreuters.com/0-619-3441?transitionType=Defaultandcon textData=(sc.Default)andfirstPage=true; Fijalkowski, *From Old Times*.

21. The Polish CJS consists of many various actors representing various public and private organizations (i.e., the courts, the tribunals, the Prosecution Office, the police, and the Prison and Probation Service).

22. Baylis, "Police and Policing"; Fijalkowski,*From Old Times*.

23. Biuletyn Informacji Publicznej, Sad okregowy w Warszawie, Struktura organizacyjna [General Information, the Regional Court in Warsaw, the Organizational Structure], accessed May 14, 2022, https://bip.warszawa.so.gov.pl/artykuly/1937/struktura-organizacyjna.

24. K. Dunaj, "Sady Wojskowe jako organy wymiaru sprawiedliwosci" [The military courts as part of criminal justice system], *Studia Iuridica Lublinensia* 24, no. 4 (2015): 9–20.

25. Rozdzial VIII Sady I Trybunaly [Chapter VIII The Courts and Tribunals], accessed May 14, 2022, https://www.sejm.gov.pl/prawo/konst/polski/8.htm.

26. M. Lasek-Markey, "Poland's Constitutional Tribunal on the Status of EU Law: The Polish Government Got All the Answers It Needed from a Court It Controls," *European Law Blog*, October 7, 2021, https://europeanlawblog.eu/2021/10/21/polands-constitutional-tribunal-on-the-status-of-eu-law-the-polish-government-got-all-the-answers-it-needed-from-a-court-it-controls.

27. Marshal of the Sejm, "Announcement of the Marshal of Sejm of the Republic of Poland from October 14, 2019, in Terms of Announcing the Unitary Approach towards the Content of the Act of the Tribunal of State," *Journal of Laws 2019*, item 2122 (October 14, 2019), accessed March 8, 2022, http://isap.sejm.gov.pl/isap.nsf/DocDetails.xsp?id=WDU20190002122.

28. O Sadzie Najwyzszym, *Status Prawny* [About the Highest Court, the Legal Status], accessed May 14 2022, https://www.sn.pl/osadzienajwyzszym/SitePages/Status_prawny.aspx.

29. O Sadzie Najwyzszym, *Status Prawny*.

30. S. G. Grimmelikhuijsen and A. J. Meijer, "Does Twitter Increase Perceived Police Legitimacy?," *Public Administration Review* 75, no. 4 (2015): 598–607.

31. Baylis, "Police and Policing."

32. Ł. Starzewski, "SN: Sady Zle Zastosowaly Przepisy o Recydywie; Skuteczna Kasacja Rzecznika" [Supreme Court: The courts have incorrectly applied the procedures of recidivism; the effective application of the spokesman], *Biuletyn Informacji Publicznej RPO* [Public Information Bulletin of the Ombudsman], June 18, 2019, accessed March 1, 2022, https://bip.brpo.gov.pl/pl/content/sady-zle-zastosowaly-przepisy-o-recydywie-skuteczna-kasacja-rpo; R. Huff and M. Killias, "Wrongful Convictions, Miscarriages of Justice, and Political Repression: Challenges for Transitional Justice," in *Wrongful Convictions and Miscarriages of Justice: Causes and Remedies in North American and European Criminal Justice Systems*, ed. C. R. Huff and M. Killias (London: Routledge, 2008), 287–301.

33. "Sadownictwo, Niewinny spedzil 18 lat w wiezieniu: Sad przyznal Tomaszowi Komendzie 12 mln zl zadoscuczynienia," Polskie Radio 24, last updated February 8, 2021, accessed March 8, 2022, https://www.polskieradio24.pl/5/1222/Artykul/2675432,Niewinny-spedzil-18-lat-w-wiezieniu-Sad-przyznal-Tomaszowi-Komendzie-12-mln-zl-zadoscuczynienia.

34. "Sadownictwo."

35. K. Kafka, "Urban Planners in Poland: Practicing the Urban Planning Profession in Poland and Other European Countries," *Sciendo* 115, no. 5 (2018): 39–51, https://sciendo.com/pdf/10.4467/2353737XCT.18.071.8553; J. L. Schulenberg, A. Chenier, S. Buffone, and C. Wojciechowski, "An Application of Procedural Justice to Stakeholder Perspectives: Examining Police Legitimacy and Public Trust in Police Complaints Systems," *Policing and Society* 27, no. 7 (2017): 779–96.

36. A. Goldsmith, "Police Reform and the Problem of Trust," *Theoretical Criminology* 9, no. 4 (2005): 443–70, http://www.slcdocs.com/ODHR/Website/Right%20to%20Safety/Literature/PoliceReformAndTheProblemOfTrust.pdf.

37. P. Szkudlarek and M. Zakrzewska, "Trust as a Component of Social Capital: Comparative Analysis of Students from Poland, Lithuania and Slovakia," *Human Resources Management and Ergonomics* 11, no. 2 (2017), http://frcatel.fri.uniza.sk/hrme/files/2017/2017_2_07.pdf.

38. W. Walczak, "Korupcja naruszeniem konstytucyjnych wartości i praw obywateli," *Studia Prawa Publicznego* 4, no. 32 (2020): 109–50.

39. Ambiguity is among the complicating factors of this complexity. See B. Nowak, "Implementation of Directives into Domestic Legal System: The Case of Poland," *Journal of Interdisciplinary Economics* 17, no. 3 (2006): 289–312.

40. Modrzejewski and Potasz, "Enforcement."

41. Modrzejewski and Potasz, "Enforcement."

42. The Polish government is represented by the lower house of Parliament (Sejm) and the upper house of Parliament (Senat). "Rozdzial IV Sejm I Senat" [Chapter IV: Sejm and Senate], Prezydent.pl, accessed March 1, 2022, https://www.prezydent.pl/prawo/konstytucja-rp/iv-sejm-i-senat.

43. Fijalkowski, *From Old Times.*

44. R. Markowski, "Transformation Experiences in Central and Eastern Europe," 2017, accessed May 14 2022, https://library.fes.de/pdf-files/id-moe/13169.pdf ; Fijalkowski, *From Old Times.*

45. Fijalkowski, *From Old Times.*

46. Fijalkowski, *From Old Times.*

47. Fijalkowski, *From Old Times.*

48. Fijalkowski, *From Old Times.*

49. Fijalkowski, *From Old Times.*

50. Fijalkowski, *From Old Times.*

51. Krajewski, "Prosecution."

52. Krajewski, "Prosecution."

53. Krajewski, "Prosecution."

54. Ministerstwo Sprawiedliwosci [Ministry of Justice], accessed March 8, 2022, https://www.gov.pl/web/sprawiedliwosc.

55. Institute of National Remembrance, accessed May 14 2022, https://ipn.gov.pl/en.

56. "Informacje" [Information], Ministerstwo Sprawiedliwosci [Ministry of Justice], accessed May 14 2022, https://www.arch.ms.gov.pl.

57. B. Zemla, "Rezonans Medialny Nowelizacji Ustawy O Instytucie Pamieci Narodowej W wybranych tygodnikach opinii" [Media reaction to the amendments to the Act on the Institute of National Remembrance in selected opinion weeklies], *Polityka i spoleczenstwo* [Politics and Society] 16, no. 3 (2018): 48–66, https://www.ceeol.com/search/article-detail?id=740675.

58. Baylis, "Police and Policing."

59. A. Wentkowska, "Dzialania Rzecznika Praw Obywatelskich w zakresie problematyki osob zaginionych" [The course of action of the ombudsman in missing-persons cases], *Nowa Kodyfikacja Prawa Karnego* 56 (2020): 207–23, https://wuwr.pl/nkp/article/view/11566.

60. A. Misiuk, *Historia policji w Polsce: Od X wieku do wspolczesnosci* (Akademickie i Profesjonalne, 2008), cited in Baylis, "Police and Policing."

61. Baylis, "Police and Policing."

62. Baylis, "Police and Policing."

63. Misiuk, *Historia policji w Polsce,* cited in Baylis, "Police and Policing."

64. Baylis, "Police and Policing."

65. Baylis, "Police and Policing."
66. Baylis, "Police and Policing."
67. Baylis, "Police and Policing."
68. Baylis, "Police and Policing."
69. Baylis, "Police and Policing"; F. Skiba, *Policja w Polsce: Dzialalnosc Formacji na obszarze aglomeracji miejskiej* (Szczytno: Wyzsza Szkola Policji w Szczytnie, 2015).
70. *Pomagamy I Chronimy* [We Help and Protect] (podcast), Policja.pl, December 23, 2021, accessed March 8, 2022, https://policja.pl/pol/podcasty/17109,Pomagamy-i-chronimy.html.
71. https://info.policja.pl, cited in Baylis, "Police and Policing."
72. "Stan kadrowy Policji na dzien 1 marca 2021 roku" [The staff numbers of police for March 1, 2021], Zarządu Głównego NSZZ Policjantów, last updated March 18, 2021, accessed March 2022, https://nszzp.pl/aktualnosci/stan-kadrowy-policji-na-dzien-1-marca-2021-roku.
73. M. Rakusa-Suszczewski, "Polityka krzywdy PiS," *Przeglad Socjiologiczny* 67, no. 2 (2018): 119–38, cited in Baylis, "Police and Policing."
74. D. Stola, *Kampania Antysyjonistyczna w Polsce 1967–1968* [The Anti-Zionist Campaign in Poland 1967–1968] (Warsaw: PAN, 2018); P. Jakubowski, "Strategie triki i bledy partii politycznych w kampanii parlamentarnej 2007," cited in Baylis, "Police and Policing."
75. Baylis, "Police and Policing."
76. "Letni Bartosz z Lublina zmarl po policyjnej interwencji: Prokuratura szuka kobiety z nagrania" [Thirty-four-year-old Bartosz from Lublin died after the police intervention: The prosecutor's office is looking for the woman from the recording], TVN24, February 2, 2022, accessed March 8, 2022, https://tvn24.pl/lodz/lubin-smierc-34-letniego-bartosza-po-policyjnej-interwencji -prokuratura -szuka -kobiety -z-monitoringu -jej -zeznania -moga -miec -istotne -znaczenie-w-sprawie-5583073; "Protest przed komenda policji w Lubinie po smierci zatrzymanego" [Protest after the death of a detainee in front of police commander unit in Lubin], *Rzeczpospolita*, last updated August 8, 2021, accessed March 8, 2022, https://www.rp.pl/spoleczenstwo/art18470901-protest-przed-komenda-policji-w-lubinie-po-smierci-zatrzymanego.
77. M. Baylis and A. Matczak, "Tracking the Evolution of Police Training and Education in Poland: Linear Developments and Exciting Prospects," *Police Practice and Research* 20, no. 3 (2019): 273–87, https://www.tandfonline.com/doi/full/10.1080/15614263.2019.1598072?journalCode=gppr20.
78. Baylis, "Police and Policing."
79. M. Baylis, "Police Reforms and Community Policing in Poland 2017–2020," in *British Society of Criminology*, October, 25, 2017, accessed March 1, 2022, https://bscpostgrads.wordpress.com/2017/10/25/police-reforms-and-community-policing-in-poland-2017-2020-by-monika-baylis.
80. Starzewski, "SN."
81. Starzewski, "SN."
82. "Informacja dotyczaca sposobu zlozenia skargi/wniosku w Komendzie Glownej Policji" [Information regarding making an official complaint at the main headquarters of police], Policja.pl, accessed March 8, 2022, https://policja.pl/pol/kontakt/skargi-i-wnioski/895,Informacja-dotyczaca-sposobu-zlozenia-skargiwniosku-w-Komendzie-Glownej-Policji.html.
83. Baylis, "Police and Policing"; R. Czerniawski, "Police Prevention Units in Poland from 1918 to Modern Times," *Scientific Journal* 22, no. 3 (2018): 21–25, https://www.ceeol.com/search/article-detail?id=740370.
84. J. Czapska and M. Szafranska, "Analiza spolecznych konsekwencji policyjengo programu w zakresie community policing (Analysis of the social consequences of a community policing program)," in M. Bryla, *Bezpieczne dzielnice w Kaliszu: program zarzadzania bezpieczenstwem dzielnic* (Safe zones in Kalisz: programme management of safe zones) (Kalisz: Media Rynek, 2013), 75–149.

85. Baylis, "Police and Policing"; T. Safijanski and A. James, "Europol's Crime Analysis System-Practical Determinants of Its Success," *Policing: A Journal of Policy and Practice* 14, no. 2 (2020): 469–78, https://academic.oup.com/policing/article/14/2/469/4967846?login=true.

86. Baylis, "Police and Policing."

87. A. Polak-Kruszyk, "Probation, Parole and Penitentiary Law, Class 3: Probation and Parole Practices according to the Polish Penal System" (presentation), Uniwersytet Wroclawski, Katedra Prawa Karnego Wykonawczego, last updated June 2021, accessed March 1, 2022, https://globcci.org/wp-content/uploads/2021/06/Probation-Parole-and-Penitentiary-Law-in-Poland-2020_21.pdf.

88. Polak-Kruszyk, "Probation."

89. Polak-Kruszyk, "Probation."

90. Polak-Kruszyk, "Probation."

91. Polak-Kruszyk, "Probation."

92. Polak-Kruszyk, "Probation."

93. Articles 70–71 of the Executive Penal Code.

94. Articles 90–72 of the Executive Penal Code; Polak-Kruszyk, "Probation."

95. Article 81 of the Executive Penal Code; Polak-Kruszyk, "Probation."

96. Polak-Kruszyk, "Probation."

97. Polak-Kruszyk, "Probation."

98. Polak-Kruszyk, "Probation."

99. Polak-Kruszyk, "Probation."

100. Polak-Kruszyk, "Probation."

101. Article 90 of the Executive Penal Code; Polak-Kruszyk, "Probation."

102. Article 105(4) of the Executive Penal Code; Polak-Kruszyk, "Probation."

103. Article 106a(3) of the Executive Penal Code.

104. Polak-Kruszyk, "Probation."

105. Polak-Kruszyk, "Probation."

106. Polak-Kruszyk, "Probation."

107. Polak-Kruszyk, "Probation."

108. Polak-Kruszyk, "Probation."

109. B. Stando-Kawecka and J. Grzywa-Holten, "Offender Electronic Monitoring in Poland: Expectations and Results," *Neue Kriminalpolitik* 27, no. 2 (2015): 158–70, accessed March 1, 2022, https://www.jstor.org/stable/26315683?seq=1#metadata_info_tab_contents.

110. B. Stando-Kawecka, "Continuity in the Welfare Approach: Juvenile Justice in Poland," in *International Handbook of Juvenile Justice* (New York: Springer, 2006), 351–76.

111. Polak-Kruszyk, "Probation."

112. Polak-Kruszyk, "Probation."

113. Baylis, "Police and Policing."

114. Polak-Kruszyk, "Probation."

115. "Summary Information on Probation in Poland," Confederation of European Probation, accessed March 1, 2022, https://www.cep-probation.org/wp-content/uploads/2018/10/Summary2008-information-on-Poland.pdf.

116. Polak-Kruszyk, "Probation."

117. Polak-Kruszyk, "Probation."

118. Polak-Kruszyk, "Probation."

119. Article 3 of the Polish Criminal Code; Article 4(1) of the Polish Executive Penal Code; Polak-Kruszyk, "Probation."

120. Polak-Kruszyk, "Probation."

121. Polish Penal Code; Polak-Kruszyk, "Probation."

122. Polak-Kruszyk, "Probation."

123. D. Solodov and E. Zebek, "Environmental Criminal Enforcement in Poland and Russia: Meeting Current Challenges," *Utrecht Law Review* 16, no. 1 (2020): 140–50, https://www .utrechtlawreview .org/article/10.36633/ulr.532/?utm_source=researcher_appandutm_medium=referralandutm_campaign=RESR_MRKT_Researcher_inbound; K. Krajewski, "Sentencing in Poland: Failed Attempts to Reduce Punitiveness," *Crime and Justice* 45, no. 1 (2016): 175–219; C. Weber, S. Schumann, and R. Soyer, "Treatment and Punishment of Drug-Addicted Offenders: Insights from a Quantitative Empirical Survey," in *Treatment versus Punishment for Drug Addiction: Lessons from Austria, Poland, and Spain*, ed. R. Soyer and S. Schumann (Cham: Springer, 2015), 39–65; K. Krajewski, "Punitive Attitudes in Poland: The Development in the Last Years," *European Journal on Criminal Policy and Research* 15, no. 1 (2009): 103–20.

124. K. Laszczynowska, "The Concept of Penalty Clause in Polish and Spanish Law: A Comparison," *Comparative Law Review* 24, no. 1 (2018): 191–205, https://www.ceeol.com/search/article-detail?id=803023.

125. K. Mamak, J. Dudek, and M. Koniewski, "A Failed Attempt to Radically Reduce Inter-Court Sentencing Disparities by Legislation: Empirical Evidence from Poland," *European Journal of Criminology*, August 2020, https://doi .org/10.1177/1477370820952729; Stando-Kawecka and Grzywa-Holten, "Offender Electronic Monitoring."

126. S. Mocek, "A Map of Political Discourse regarding Polish Public Service Media," in *Public Service Broadcasting and Media Systems in Troubled European Democracies*, ed. E. Połońska and C. Beckett (Cham: Palgrave Macmillan), 195–226, https://link.springer.com/chapter/10.1007/978 -3-030 -02710 -0_10; M. Krzyzanowski, "Discursive Shifts in Ethno-Nationalist Politics: On Politicization and Mediatization of the 'Refugee Crisis' in Poland," *Journal of Immigrant and Refugee Studies* 16, no. 1–2 (2018): 76–96, https://www.tandfonline .com/doi/full/10.1080/15562948.2017.1317897; M. Gora and N. Styczynska, "The EU Enlargement Policy in the Polish Political Discourse after 2004," in *Central and Eastern European Online Library* (Sofia University, 2015), 183–93, https://www.ceeol.com/search/chapter -detail?id=952694.

127. See M. A. Abubakar, H. Elrehail, M. A. Alatailat, and A. Elci, "Knowledge Management, Decision-Making Style and Organizational Performance," *Journal of Innovation and Knowledge* 4, no. 2 (2019): 104–14, https://www .sciencedirect .com/science/article/pii/S2444569X17300562; K. Hawkins, "Order, Rationality and Silence: Some Reflections on Criminal Justice Decision-Making," in *Exercising Discretion, Decision-Making in the Criminal Justice System and Beyond*, ed. L. Gelsthorpe and N. Padfield (Portland, OR: Willan, 2012), 186–219; and A. Laupacis, "On Bias and Transparency in the Development of Influential Recommendations," *Canadian Medical Association Journal* 174, no. 3 (2006): 335–36, https://www.cmaj.ca/content/174/3/335.short.

128. See J. Dyck and E. L. Lascher, "Direct Democracy and Political Efficacy Reconsidered," *Political Behavior* 31 (2009): 401–27, https://link.springer.com/article/10.1007/s11109 -008 -9081-x, and S. Karstedt and G. LaFree, "Democracy, Crime and Justice," *Annals of the American Academy of Political and Social Science* 605, no. 1 (2006): 6–23, https://journals.sagepub .com/doi/abs/10.1177/0002716206288230.

129. C. Lyall, A. Bruce, W. Marsden, and L. Meagher, "The Role of Funding Agencies in Creating Interdisciplinary Knowledge," *Science and Public Policy* 40, no. 1 (2013): 62–71, https://academic.oup.com/spp/article/40/1/62/1649389?login=true.

130. Baylis, "Police and Policing."

CHAPTER 10

Ministry of Justice and Law Enforcement in the Republic of Serbia

Dalibor Kekić, Miloš Milenković, and Filip Kukić

In the spirit of human and minority rights, the Constitution of the Republic of Serbia proclaims that all people are entitled to court protection if their human or minority rights as guaranteed by the Constitution have been violated or denied; it also proclaims the right to the elimination of the consequences of said violations. In addition, it proclaims that all people have the right to an appeal or to another legal remedy against any decision taken regarding their rights, duties, or interests based on the law. Therefore, the Constitution guarantees some minimum protection of human rights, in accordance with the requirements of international regulations; does not deal specifically with the jurisdiction and composition of the courts; and allows for the establishment, organization, jurisdiction, organization, and composition of the courts to be regulated by law.

Serbia's judicial system is generally weaker than those of EU member states. In terms of efficiency, the system struggles with the legacy of bureaucracy. Poor draft laws, inconsistent case law, and high appeal rates affect the quality of judicial services. Outdated tools for standardizing quality in service delivery, such as forms and checklists for routine procedures, do not exist. Access to basic legal information, such as consolidated laws and layman-adapted basic law formats, is insufficient. The prospect of alternative dispute resolution is promising but seems unattainable because of a series of failed reforms.

Progress has been made in some areas of court management, such as information, communication, and technology improvements and procedural reforms. However, these results are fragile and have yet to bring about changes in behavior among judges, prosecutors, lawyers, and court staff.[1]

Policing and Law Enforcement

BRIEF HISTORY

The history of Serbian police activity dates back to the time of the Nemanjić dynasty, from the twelfth through the fourteenth centuries. During that time, the *kefalija*, the mayor or parish manager, was in charge of public safety, especially road safety. He had at his disposal "special people, dressed in black suits, [who] guarded the roads and protected the passengers from robbers."[2]

The roots of public security in the renewed Serbia appear during the First and Second Serbian Uprisings in the first half of the nineteenth century. Police power in the administrative areas was entrusted to the dukes and stable princes and, in the principalities, to the local dukes. The executive officers of the stable princes were represented by so-called naked or beggar officers. Later, the role of the executive bodies of the newly established courts—the magistrates—was taken over by the police.

During the nineteenth century (and later in the Kingdom of Serbia), the organization of police forces in the principality changed. After World War I, on December 7, 1918, the Ministry of the Interior was established as the supreme administrative and supervisory authority over all administrative and police bodies in the newly formed Kingdom of Serbs, Croats, and Slovenes. With the Decree on the Formation, Equipment, Competences, Duties, and Teaching of the Gendarmerie (February 26, 1919), the gendarmerie became an integral part of the army, a permanent cadre tasked with overseeing public order and security, maintaining order and peace, and enforcing the law.

In order to educate the gendarmerie staff, on February 1, 1920, the Gendarmerie NCO School was formed in Sremska Kamenica. The first Police School, organized by Archibald Rice, opened in Belgrade on February 8, 1921. On March 7, 1945, the Commission of the Interior grew into the Ministry of the Interior. The following year, the Law on the People's Militia and the Rule on the Clothes of the People's Militia were adopted. On July 18, 1956, the Law on Internal Affairs was adopted. The Serbian police continued to reorganize in the postsocialist period, harmonizing its structure with the requirements of the country's foreign policy.[3]

ORGANIZATION

Based on the existing division, the Serbian police force is one of the only centralized police systems. There is a single police force in the entire country, headed by the Ministry of Internal Affairs as an administrative body. Police affairs are organized within the General Police Directorate at the national level while Regional Police Directorates and police stations are organized at the regional and local levels. This practice is common in countries of similar size and with similar security challenges, risks, and threats.[4]

The Police Directorate was formed to oversee police and other internal affairs. It consists of organizational units at the level of its headquarters—directorates, centers, units, and, notably, Special Police Units. Outside the headquarters, the Police

Directorate includes the Police Directorate for the City of Belgrade, Regional Police Directorates, and police stations. The Special Police Unit is the Special Antiterrorist Unit. Notably, the police units at the headquarters of the General Police Directorate are the gendarmerie, Helicopter Unit, Protection Unit, and Security Unit for certain persons and facilities, and the Police Directorate for the City of Belgrade contains the Police Brigade and Intervention Unit 92.

Regional Police Directorates are organizational units of the General Police Directorate that are outside the seat in Belgrade, and there are twenty-seven territorially differentiated organizational units. These Regional Police Directorates are divided according to geographical categories. In terms of territorial differentiation, each Regional Police Directorate consists of two or more police stations distributed throughout the territory. The main task of the organizational units of the General Directorate outside headquarters is to perform all tasks within its competence in the territory for which they were formed.

OPERATIONS

To implement and support the community law standards of the European administrative space, in recent years, the Ministry of Interior has significantly improved its strategic management. Strengthening the capacity for strategic management and leadership has enabled a clear division of coordination and the coordination of reform activities in all organizational units. The starting point for a new approach to management at the strategic level is the attitude that the police are in the service of the citizens and that police officers are citizens in uniform.

In recent years, practical cooperation has been established with individual EU member states, and as a result, a number of police operations have been conducted in cooperation with the authorities in EU member states, the authorities of other countries in the region, Interpol, and Europol. In addition to harmonizing laws through the process of Serbia's integration into the European Union, specialized training, better coordination, and adequate budgetary resources in each segment are needed among institutions.

A strategic approach to the development of the ministry is recognized as one of the key priorities in the overall reform of public administration and as one of the key elements of the European integration of the Republic of Serbia because, as a candidate for EU membership, Serbia is expected to meet the conditions for membership through an adequate adjustment of administrative procedures. Seeing the situation this way, the past ten years or so ensured the development of the ministry as an institution that has become flexible and innovative, whose approach to maintaining security is integral and citizen oriented. It contributed to the strengthening of capabilities in the fight against crime, a more efficient use of information technologies, and the development of new knowledge and skills among employees.

In order to intensify this cooperation, as one of the most important preconditions for the realization of all reform processes and the development of the police of the Republic of Serbia, a large number of laws about the ratification of agreements and protocols was passed, numerous multilateral and bilateral agreements were signed with neighboring and other countries, and forms of crime that can cause more serious consequences, such as illegal migration, human trafficking, and drug trafficking, were defined.

In the future, the Ministry of Interior should have two main priorities. The first priority is to continue reforms that lead to strengthening the strategic management of the ministry. The second is the continuation of the process of the total depoliticization of the Police Directorate with the basic goal of bringing the directorate closer to the rest of the state administration. Both of these priorities will directly contribute to Serbia's EU integration process.

Judiciary

ORGANIZATION

The Constitution of the Republic of Serbia does not have a specifically determined jurisdiction and composition of courts. The Constitution allows the formation, jurisdiction, organization, and composition of courts to be regulated by law.

The jurisdiction of the Serbian courts is related mostly to the subject matter and is regulated primarily by the Law on Organization of Courts; subject matter and territorial jurisdiction are regulated in procedural laws. Regarding subject matter jurisdiction, there is a distinction among the Courts of General Jurisdiction: there are basic, higher, and appellate courts and the Supreme Court of Cassation. Among the Courts of Special Jurisdiction, there are Commercial Courts, the Commercial Appellate Court, Misdemeanor Courts, the Misdemeanor Appellate Court, and the Administrative Court. The Law on Organization of Courts provides that only certain courts can act in certain legal matters. The Law on Seats and Territories of the Courts and Public Prosecutors Offices specifies which courts can act in certain types of legal matters in which no other court with subject matter jurisdiction can act. The composition of the court when acting in civil proceedings is governed by the Civil Procedure Code and, in nonlitigious proceedings, by the Law on Nonlitigious Proceedings. As regards acting in criminal matters, the composition of the courts is regulated by the Criminal Procedure Code. In administrative matters, the composition of the courts is determined by the Law on Administrative Disputes.

FUNCTIONS

In civil proceedings, if a panel adjudicates in the first instance, it is composed of one presiding judge and two lay judges. In cases judged by individual judges, the judge has the powers of the presiding judge, that is, the panel, as provided by the Law on Administrative Disputes. In the first instance, a single judge acts in special employment proceedings and in commercial disputes.

In nonlitigious proceedings, a single judge usually acts in the first instance, except in housing matters involving occupancy rights or certain powers that are the essence of the occupancy rights. In these cases, the first-instance court decides in a panel consisting of one judge and two lay judges. Unlike nonlitigious trial courts, criminal trial courts, per the Criminal Procedure Code, are overseen in the first instance by a single judge, who acts in criminal offenses for which a fine or imprisonment of up to eight years is prescribed. In administrative matters, administrative disputes are resolved by the Administrative Court.

Correctional System

BRIEF HISTORY

The first prison in Serbia is in Čačak, which dates from the first half of the nineteenth century. However, the history of punishment in Serbia dates back to medieval times. Courts were established during the Nemanjić dynasty. Legal sources from this period, which are rare, contain the grounds for punishment. Some legal sources were preserved in treaties with other states, and other sources have been found in monasteries. Dušan's Code, passed in 1349, envisages the death penalty, exile for heretics and half-believers, corporal punishment, fines, confiscation, imprisonment, and the loss of honorary rights. Corporal punishment was executed cruelly, and the orders had to be approved by the ultimate authority.

Dušan's Code included several types of dungeons: patrimonial, church, at the patriarchal court, and state dungeons, including the dungeon at the royal court. The code prescribes a dungeon for an indefinite period of time in two cases: against monks who throw off their monk's habit and against drunkards. Deprivation of liberty is envisaged as a measure to protect the accused and to protect those wrongfully accused of debt.

Karadjordje's Criminal Code of 1807 includes detention as a punishment. This punishment was most often imposed on perpetrators of minor crimes. Sometimes this form of punishment was included with corporal punishment, and sometimes detainees were at risk of being detained after being beaten until they compensated damages to their victims. The first District Court of 1840 prescribes lag (life or temporary with or without light or heavy labor), detention (perpetual or temporary), and imprisonment (light, public, or domestic).

Male convicts served their sentences in Topčider, near Belgrade, and Ćuprija, as of 1865. Convicts have been serving their sentences in Ćuprija since 1866. Adult male convicts were transferred in 1865 from Ćuprija to Požarevac, and the following year, juveniles joined them. In the 1860s, about 300 convicts were used to work in Kragujevac's Topolivnica, about 200 at Belgrade's Fortress, about 100 in Ljubičevo at the state stud farm, and forty in the Belgrade city administration. Conditional release was first introduced in Serbia in 1869.

ORGANIZATION

The Directorate for the Execution of Criminal Sanctions is part of the Ministry of Justice. It is in charge of the correctional system in Serbia. The directorate has the following duties:

- Organize, implement, and supervise the execution of imprisonment, juvenile imprisonment, security measures during mandatory psychiatric treatment, custody in health institutions, and so on
- Perform activities related to the preparation of proposals for pardon, amnesty, and conditional release
- Monitor the execution of institutional sanctions and regulations

The current system of penitentiary institutions consists of district prisons, penitentiary prisons, special prison hospitals, correctional facilities for minors, penitentiaries for women, and penitentiaries for juveniles.[5]

District Prison in Belgrade is a semi-open prison with a department for the accommodation of convicted persons, a closed department, and a special closed department for the accommodation of detained persons. Special detention units have been established in the District Prison in Belgrade, namely, the Special Detention Unit for Execution of Detention Measures Determined in Criminal Proceedings for Organized Crime and the Special Detention Unit for Execution of Detention Measures Determined in Criminal Proceedings for War Crimes.

The District Prison in Čačak is categorized as a semi-open institution for the execution of prison sentences of up to three months and the execution of detention measures. The current prison building was built around 1875, and the last reconstruction was done in 1995. However, the construction of the prison was planned as early as May 16, 1838. The District Prison in Kragujevac was established by the Municipal Assembly of Kragujevac on December 24, 1971, and opened on January 1, 1972. The capacity of the institution is designed to accommodate 120 convicts and fifty detainees. The average number is sixty convicts, thirty-five detainees, and ten people who have been convicted in misdemeanor proceedings.

The Kraljevo District Prison is categorized as a semi-open institution for the execution of prison sentences of up to three months and the execution of detention measures. The prison was established in 1968. The capacity is designed to accommodate eighty-eight persons who have been deprived of their liberty, and the average number is eighteen convicts, twenty detainees, and five who have been convicted in misdemeanor proceedings. The district prison in Kruševac is intended for serving prison sentences of up to three months, execution of detention measures, and execution of prison sentences imposed in misdemeanor procedures. It is categorized as a semi-open institution for convicted and detained persons.

The District Prison in Leskovac is a semi-open institution for the execution of prison sentences and the execution of detention measures. After World War II, the Leskovac prison changed its location. It had been located in one place and consisted of lagoons and obscure rooms of large houses in the center of Leskovac. Since 1945, a prison has been in Leskovac at the county level within the municipal police station, located in the extension of the building of what was then the Municipal Court.

The Negotin District Prison is a semi-open prison for serving prison sentences and executing detention measures. This prison existed before World War II. The other district prison, which is located in Novi Pazar, has existed since the middle of the nineteenth century and was located in the Novi Pazar fortress. The district prison in Novi Sad was founded at the beginning of the twentieth century. Although it is categorized as a semi-open district prison, in an architectural sense, it is a closed type of institution, as it is fenced in by high concrete walls with watchtowers and an integrated video surveillance system.

The District Prison in Pančevo is a semi-open prison for serving prison sentences of up to one year primarily for convicted persons, predicate felons up to three months, persons punished in misdemeanor procedures, and execution of detention measures. The prison building, which also houses the prison's headquarters, was built in the first quarter of the nineteenth century during the reign of Maria Theresa (1800–1825) as a "royal court."

The District Prison in Prokuplje is a semi-open institution that has a closed ward, an open ward, and a ward for the execution of detention measures. The District Prison in Smederevo is of the semi-open type for serving sentences of up to three months. It has a closed ward for the execution of detention measures. There are records of the existence of a prison in the Smederevo fortress during Turkish rule. In later times, people were imprisoned in the fortress. There are also several other district prisons in Subotica, Užice, Vranje, Zaječar, and Zrenjanin.

The Penitentiary in Ćuprija was founded during the rule of Miloš Obrenović, when convicted persons were sent to work on the Dobričevo agricultural estate. The building, which can accommodate about eighty people, was built in 1852. In 1998, the penitentiaries in Padinska Skela, Šabac, and Sombor became open penitentiaries. The penitentiaries in Zabela and Sremska Mitrovica are of a strictly closed type, built on the model of the Pennsylvania concept of the cell system, that is, the Irish cell system.

OPERATIONS

The system of execution of criminal sanctions in the Republic of Serbia is based on the empirical and theoretical foundations of the Irish progressive system, which, in various modifications, is the dominant concept of execution of sanctions in countries with a long democratic tradition and developed penitentiaries. This system in the Republic of Serbia is a complete unit that includes general and specialized institutions for different categories of perpetrators of crimes.

The system of execution of criminal sanctions in the Republic of Serbia employs more than 3,500 people who work with different categories of convicted and detained persons. This ratio between persons deprived of liberty and employees, which is approximately two to one, ranks the penitentiary system of the Republic of Serbia among the most progressive systems. In this system, special attention is paid to the legal, professional, and humane treatment of persons deprived of liberty.[6]

The percentage of recidivism in the Serbian system is approximately 65 percent, which is unfavorable from the point of view of resocialization.[7] Despite the high percentage of recidivism in the Serbian system, the emphasis is on serving sentences in semi-open and open conditions and institutions. In terms of the number of convicted persons in relation to the total population, the Serbian system fits the average of developed European countries. Since the concept of resocialization is the dominant orientation in the Serbian penitentiary system, special attention is paid to the treatment of convicts on legal, professional, scientific, and humane bases and to the realization and protection of the rights of persons deprived of their liberty, so in that context, there is an effort to harmonize this area with European legislation.

Juvenile Justice

STRUCTURE

Juvenile criminal law provides for three basic types of criminal sanctions that may be imposed by a court on juvenile offenders following the procedures and under the conditions provided by law: educational measures, juvenile imprisonment, and security measures. These are measures of social reaction toward juvenile perpetrators of crimes that they commit against statutory bodies.

Corrective measures are the basic type of juvenile criminal sanctions, that is, basic measures of social reaction to juvenile delinquency. They are pronounced regularly, as a rule, and are customary in court proceedings as provided by law. They may be imposed on both younger and older juvenile offenders and, under certain conditions, also toward younger adults. These special measures are a way to provide juveniles with specialized education or, more precisely, reeducation or socialization with as few elements of coercion as possible.[8]

The purpose of criminal sanctions against juveniles is to supervise and provide them with protection and assistance as well as to provide general and vocational training that affects minors' development and strengthens their personal responsibility. It is also intended to help develop their personality in order to ensure the reintegration of minors into society.[9]

Serbian regulations relating to minors must comply with the UN Convention on the Rights of the Child, specifically its Havana Rules, which, in relation to juvenile offenders, require the exclusion or reduction to a minimum of any form of deprivation of liberty. That is, parties to the convention are required to provide, whenever possible and desirable, measures to treat children and minors who have broken the law without resorting to court proceedings. This means that instead of criminal sanctions, various measures of an alternative nature are applied, such as corrective orders, instructions, prohibitions, or recommendations aimed at avoiding or delaying criminal proceedings to a juvenile offender.[10] In addition to corrective orders, which are not criminal sanctions, are newly introduced criminal sanctions and special obligations that also reduce the institutional nature of a social response to minors.

According to Serbian regulations, there are three types of corrective measures: warning and guidance measures, enhanced surveillance measures, and institutional measures. The following types of criminal sanctions may be imposed on juveniles for committed criminal offenses: corrective measures, juvenile imprisonment, and security measures provided for in Article 79 of the Criminal Code, except for the prohibition of execution vocations, activities, or duties. Only corrective measures can be imposed on younger minors. Older minors' corrective measures may be imposed, and, exceptionally, a sentence of juvenile imprisonment may be imposed. Under the conditions provided by this law, measures may be imposed on minors' security.

FUNCTIONS

The development and improvement of the juvenile justice system in Serbia includes changes at the value-conceptual level, which, although not fully articulated, strongly determine the general policy of social care for children and minors at risk and in conflict with the law.[11] The need for a special system of juvenile justice, such as a special law, is based on knowledge about the characteristics of children and minors in relation to adults. Children and minors are different from adults in that their emotional reactions are different, they think and make decisions differently, and they behave differently than adults do. Consequently, different policies, laws, and measures are needed for children than are used for adults. Essentially, a feature of this approach is the effort to ensure a high degree of individualization to take procedures and measures in line with minors' development needs and opportunities.

A person who has not reached the age of fourteen at the time of committing an illegal act cannot be declared criminally liable under the law. Sanctions and other measures provided by the Criminal Code cannot be applied against such persons. A minor is a person who at the time of committing criminal acts has turned fourteen years old but has not turned eighteen. In practice, there are problems with the application of the educational measure of referral to a special institution for treatment and training given that such institutions do not exist in the Republic of Serbia. The tendency of legislators is instead to rely on security measures, such as mandatory psychiatric treatment and health care institutions, when the conditions for that are met and certain categories of minors warrant such measures.

Conclusions

Regarding the Serbian Ministry of the Interior, priorities and goals are grouped within three strategic areas: security, development of institutional capacities and cooperation, and citizen service. It was identified that strengthening public security requires continuous development of organizational structure, development of intersectoral coordination and functional integration, exchange of information and cooperation at all levels (including strengthening regional and international cooperation), development of material-technical-technological capacities, and provision of necessary funds. Harmonization of the normative framework of the Republic of Serbia with the *acquis communautaire*, implementation of the ministry's policies in accordance with the common policies of the European Union, and organizational adjustment for the implementation of those policies and the normative framework are preconditions for improving interinstitutional cooperation and efficient performance.

The correctional system in the Republic of Serbia is a complete unit that includes general and specialized institutions for different categories of perpetrators of criminal acts of the system. The number of prisoners in the Republic of Serbia is around 11,000. The basic function of the prison is to ensure the fulfillment of the basic purpose of sentencing convicts to imprisonment, which is based on ensuring the resocialization and rehabilitation of convicts, that is, training convicts to respect constitutional, legal, and other social norms or to enable most convicts not to commit criminal and other sanctioned acts again.

The progress and maturing of the juvenile justice system in Serbia are particularly significant changes at the value-conceptual level, which, although not yet fully operationalized, strongly determine the general policy of social protection of children and juveniles in danger and conflict with the law. The jurisdiction of the courts in Serbia, mainly in the territorial sense, is regulated primarily by the Law on the Organization of Courts, while the subject and local jurisdiction are procedural laws.

Notes

1. Multi-Donor Trust Fund for Justice Sector Support in Serbia, *Funkcionalna analiza pravosuđa u Srbiji* [Functional Analysis of the Judiciary in Serbia], Report 94014-YF, October 2014, https://www .mdtfjss .org .rs/data/pub/sjfr/sr/Funkcionalna-analiza -pravosudja -u-Srbiji .pdf, 3.
2. Aleksandar Stojanović, "Policija Srbije: Funkcija, istorija i organizacija" [Serbian police: Function, history, and organization], *Nova naša reč* [Our New Word], April 19, 2021, https://novanasarec.org.rs/policija-srbije-funkcija-istorija-i-organizacija.
3. Stojanović, "Policija."
4. Stojanović, "Policija."
5. Ministarstvo Pravde [Ministry of Justice], Uprava za izvršenje krivičnih sankcija [Directorate for Execution of Criminal Sanctions], http://www.uiks.mpravde.gov.rs, accessed June 2, 2022.
6. Ministarstvo Pravde, Uprava.
7. Ministarstvo Pravde, Uprava.
8. Dragan Jovašević, "Kažnjavanje maloletnika u krivičnom pravu: Maloletničko pravosuđe u Republici Srbiji, Beograd" [Punishing juveniles in criminal law: Juvenile justice in the Republic of Serbia, Belgrade], in *Zbornik radova: Maloletničko pravosuđe* [Proceedings: Juvenile Justice], ed. I. Stevanović (Belgrade: Center for the Rights of the Child, 2012), 265.
9. Tatjana Skakavac, "Krivične sankcije prema maloljetnicima—Stanje i promjena" [Criminal sanctions against minors—Condition and application], *Maloletničko pravosuđe u Republici Srbiji* [Juvenile Justice in the Republic of Serbia] (Belgrade: Center for the Rights of the Child, 2012), 283.

10. Skakavac, "Krivične," 284.

11. Đurađ Stakić, "Unapređenje kvaliteta donošenja odluka u sistemu maloletničkog pravosuđa" [Improving the quality of decision making in the juvenile justice system], in Stevanović, *Zbornik radova*, 69.

CHAPTER 11

The Criminal Justice System in Germany

Raluca Enescu, Aneta Leszczynska, and Carsten Momsen

Policing and Law Enforcement

BRIEF HISTORY

Although the term "policy" appeared in an administrative text in the fifteenth century, a police force in today's sense—as domestic law enforcement and as permanent administrative staff—developed first in the nineteenth century. Until then, the military remained the representative and even more real power factor of the state's monopoly of force.[1]

Today, the police are a part of the executive power in Germany.[2] In a modern, functioning state, legitimacy for police action is provided by laws that are passed by Parliament. A corresponding understanding of the police as a state executive body that ensures public security and order and is allowed to exercise direct coercion and direct violence within the legal framework created by the respective parliaments is also reflected in current German police laws.[3]

The history of the German policing reflects the history of Germany itself, especially the times of the constitutional monarchy,[4] the Weimar Republic,[5] the (so-called) Third Reich,[6] and the division (East and West Germany[7]) and reunification of Germany.[8] During these periods, various legal acts were in force and various police formations established.[9]

ORGANIZATION

Law enforcement in Germany is divided into federal, state, and municipal law enforcement agencies. It is partially an outcome of the federal structure of the Federal Republic of Germany.

In the area of police matters, the legislative and administrative powers lie largely—except for special federal powers that have been detached from the federal states (Art. 30 GC)—with the federal states. For example, the GC grants the federal government legislative and administrative powers for border protection (Art. 73 [1] No. 5, 87 I 2 GC) and for the performance of central tasks in the field of criminal prosecution by the Federal Criminal Police Office (Art. 73 [1] No. 10, 87 [1] 2 GC).[10] Thus, the general competence to avert danger and its implementation are a matter belonging to the federal states (Art. 70 GC).

Federal Level

The principal federal law enforcement agency is the Federal Police (FP; Bundespolizei). At the federal level also operates the Federal Criminal Police Office (FCPO; Bundeskriminalamt). Additionally, there is the Federal Intelligence Service (FIS; Bundesnachrichtendienst)[11] and the Federal Office for the Protection of the Constitution (FOPC; Bundesamt für Verfassungsschutz).[12]

FEDERAL POLICE

The legal status and the jurisdiction of the FP[13] is regulated in the GC[14] (Art. 70, 73, 87 GC) and mostly in the Federal Police Act (FPA; Gesetz über die Bundespolizei) as well as in numerous other legal provisions in, for example, the Residence Act (Aufenthaltsgesetz), the Asylum Act (Asylgesetz), and the Aviation Security Act (Luftsicherheitsgesetz).

The FP is a specialized task force responsible for border protection (§ 2 FPA), including railway policing (§ 3 FPA) and aviation security (§ 4–4a FPA).[15] The responsibilities of the FP also include the protection of federal bodies (§ 5 FPA), protection tasks at sea (§ 6 FPA), and employment abroad and in emergencies as well as in case of defense of the country (§§ 7–8 FPA). The FP is also designed to support other federal agencies (§§ 9–11 FPA) and to reinforce the state police if requested to do so by a state government (§ 11 FPA).[16] In addition, the ability of the FP to conduct its own criminal investigations is limited (§ 12, § 13 FPA).

The Federal Police Headquarters (FPH; Bundespolizeipräsidium) in Potsdam is directly subordinate to the Ministry of the Interior and Homeland (MIH; Bundesministerium des Innern und Heimat).[17] The FPH also contains the GSG 9—a special task force of the FP that focuses on counterterrorism. The GSG 9 is also directly subordinate to the Ministry of the Interior.[18] Under the special task forces for counterterrorism of the FP is also the Evidence Preservation and Arrest Unit, known as the BEF+ (Beweissicherungs- und Festnahmeeinheit).

Furthermore, the FPH supervises nine federal police departments (Bundespolizeidirektionen) that are distributed across the country, each of which is responsible for one federal state (i.e., Bayern, Baden-Württemberg, or Nordrhein-Westfallen) or several federal states (these are known as area directorates). They are seated in Bad Bramstedt, Hannover, Sankt Augustin, Koblenz, Stuttgart, München, Pirna, Berlin, and the Frankfurt Airport. The federal police departments are subdivided into a total of seventy-seven federal police inspectorates (Bundespolizeiinspektionen).[19]

FEDERAL CRIMINAL POLICE OFFICE

The FCPO is the second major federal police institution in Germany.[20] The legal status and the jurisdiction of the FCPO is regulated first in the GC (Art. 73 I No. 10, Art. 87 I 2 GC)[21] and second in the Federal Criminal Police Office Act (FCPOA; Bundeskriminalgesetz). However, the German FP does not have a function and competence comparable to the American FBI.

The FCPO has a specific dual function: on the one hand, it serves as a central office in the field of so-called criminal police and as a police information and intelligence institution (§ 2 FCPOA); on the other hand, it serves as a criminal prosecution authority.[22] Thus, the FCPO also serves as the central office for cooperation between the federation (Bund) and the federal states in all criminal police matters (§ 1 and § 3 FCPOA).[23] But it is authorized in matters of combating international crime and counterterrorism (Art. 73 I No. 10 and 9a GC, §§ 4a, 20a et seqq. FCPOA), so it can be described as the "federal criminal police."[24]

The FCPO is divided into nine departments—including International Coordination (in Berlin), Serious and Organized Crime (in Wiesbaden), Central Criminal Police Services (in Wiesbaden), and the Forensic Science Institute (in Wiesbaden)—and it is also directly subordinate to the MIH.[25] Additionally, the FCPO constitutes the National Central Office for Interpol (in Wiesbaden) and for Europol.[26]

State Level

Generally, in Germany, the police are responsible for danger prevention (security), tasks in the area of administration (e.g., road traffic police), and criminal prosecution.[27] However, there are fundamental differences between those federal states that follow a unit system and those that differentiate between the police and the regulatory (municipal) authorities (Polizei- und Ordnungsbehörden)—so-called separate systems.[28] Thus, there can be only a unit state police (e.g., Baden-Württemberg, Bremen, and Saarland)[29] formation or both a state police and municipal law enforcement, which specializes in detecting misdemeanors or petty offenses. This separate system of state police operating alongside municipal law enforcement is the system used in cities such as Bremen, Berlin, and Hamburg.[30]

STATE POLICE AND MUNICIPAL LAW ENFORCEMENT

The state police (SP; Landespolizei) operate exclusively in their dedicated state. Because of the federal structure of Germany, there are sixteen federal states (Länder) and, thus, sixteen SP law enforcement agencies.[31] Those sixteen federal state authorities maintain their own police forces within their territory. Each federal state is enabled to pass its own police legislation and to exercise police authority.[32]

The legal status of the SP and municipal agencies is regulated separately for each federal state in state acts. For example, in the unit system that is used in Bremen, there is a Bremen Police Act (Bremisches Polizeigesetz). But in separate systems, such as in Bayern, there are different regulations, one for the SP, a Police Duties Act (Polizeiaufgabengesetz), and a second one for municipal law enforcement, a State Criminal and Ordinance Act (Landesstraf- und Verordnungsgesetz).

An essential common feature of the distribution of competencies between municipal authorities and the SP in those federal states with a separate system is that the tasks of the SP are basically determined according to the enumeration principle. According to this principle, within the framework of averting danger, they have to fight criminal offenses in particular.[33] Consequently, the municipal agencies are responsible for detecting petty offenses, such as illegal parking, and for prosecuting perpetrators. And for most cases, there will be administrative penalties imposed (e.g., warnings or fines). But the "principle of separation" in those systems does not block cooperation between the SP and the municipal agencies. In truth, this kind of support, especially as "informational" cooperation, is needed.[34]

However, only the SP can be involved in the criminal proceedings. The so-called criminal police is the branch of the police that is concerned with the investigation of criminal offenses. It therefore acts only in a repressive capacity. The authorities of the criminal investigation department in the federal states are criminal investigation departments, district criminal investigation departments, and the State Criminal Investigation Office, or equivalent departments. The criminal investigation department acts as an investigative body of the public prosecutor's office.[35] Furthermore, the SP laws regulate which ranks of the SP may be deployed in some specific areas of the criminal prosecution. Additionally, the Code of Criminal Procedure (CCP; Strafprozessordnung), which regulates criminal proceedings for the whole territory of Germany, grants police officers of specific ranks with special competencies, such as investigators of the public prosecutor's office (IPPO; Ermittlungsperson der Staatsanwaltschaft). In Berlin, according to the Ordinance on the Investigators of the Public Prosecutor's Office (Verordnung über die Ermittlungspersonen der Staatsanwaltschaft, § 1 3 No. 1) the IPPO are those police officers who have attained the rank of detective. According to Article 163 (3) CCP, witnesses are obliged to appear before investigators of the public prosecutor's office and to testify on matters when their summons is based on an order from the public prosecutor's office. Only IPPO are authorized to confiscate movable property in the "event of imminent danger" (Art. § 111j CCP).[36] Thus, only when carried out by these police officers are investigative measures such as searches legitimized and the evidence obtained usable.

Only prosecutors can charge a person with a criminal offense (Art. 152 [1] CCP; Anklagebehörde), so there is no authority for the police officers to release an indictment.

The Judiciary System in Criminal Matters in Germany

ORGANIZATION AND FUNCTIONS

Article 92 of the GC stipulates only that "judicial power is vested in the judges. It is exercised by the Federal Constitutional Court, the federal courts provided for in the Basic Law, and the courts of the federal states (regional administrations)."

The court system is characterized according to specialization and to region, though ultimately the system is hierarchically integrated at a federal level. In terms of specializations, there are five basic systems of courts: ordinary (civil and criminal) courts, administrative courts, tax courts, labor courts, and social courts. Each of these systems has its own first-instance and appeal courts at the state level, with the Federal Supreme Court (FSC; Bundesgerichtshof) as the superior court.[37] Hence, the FSC has jurisdiction in criminal matters; however, it is not a first-instance court.

Criminal justice is therefore a branch of the ordinary jurisdiction that is responsible for criminal proceedings, and there is a strict separation between criminal and civil courts. The jurisdiction of the courts in criminal matters is regulated in the Jurisdiction Act (JA; Gerichtsverfassungsgesetz) and in the CCP. Criminal cases are decided in the first instance by (1) the district courts (Amtsgericht) and heard by criminal judges as single judges or the (simple or extended) court of lay assessors (§§ 24, 24, and 29 JA); (2) the regional courts (Landgericht) and heard by the (large) criminal chamber, which can also operate as a jury court, state protection chamber, or economic criminal chamber (§§ 74 et seqq. JA); or, finally, (3) the higher regional courts (Oberlandesgericht) and heard by the criminal senate (§§ 120 et seqq. JA).[38]

The classification of cases heard by each of these courts in the first instance is based on the gravity of a given crime. Furthermore, there is no jury in German criminal courts as there is in the common law system. The jurors operate as the lay judges (Schöffen or Laienrichter) who participate alongside professional judges in some criminal cases. Additionally, the lay judges serve only at district courts or regional courts. They have the same powers as far as verdicts and sentencing are concerned that professional judges have. In the court of lay assessors at the district court, the number of lay assessors (two) outweighs the number of professional judges (one). The importance of the lay judges is therefore considerably lower in Germany than in the United States. The conduct of proceedings is in the hands of the professional judges, that is, presiding judges.

CRIMINAL PROCEDURE

The law of criminal procedure includes all legal norms regulating the proceedings that are set up to enforce substantive criminal law and thus to achieve the various purposes of punishment, namely, compensation for guilt and individual and general prevention of crime. The basic source of rules of criminal procedure is the CCP of February 1,

1877.[39] Further provisions are contained in particular in the JA, GC, and the European Convention on Human Rights, which contains central procedural guarantees for the accused. Additionally, there is also the Juvenile Courts Act (Jugendgerichtsgesetz),[40] the Fiscal Code (Steuergesetz), the Administrative Offenses Act (Ordnungswidrigkeitengesetz), and the Act on International Mutual Assistance in Criminal Matters (Gesetz über die Internationale Rechtshilfe in Strafsachen).

The modern German criminal procedure can be described as quasi-inquisitorial. On the one hand, during a trial, presiding judges are given a leading role, and the parties only supplement the judge's actions by, for example, submitting evidence. Thus, the burden of proof is mostly in the hands of the court, which is obliged to stay objective during the trial. On the other hand, because of several legal transplants, this traditional structure is partly shifting to a more adversarial one, thanks in part to the increased use of plea bargaining over the past fifteen years.

Criminal proceedings are usually divided into several sections, the first of which are the preliminary proceedings (Ermittlungsverfahren; §§ 158 et seqq. CCP).[41] Second are the intermediate proceedings (Zwischenverfahren), in which a decision is made on the opening of the main proceedings (§§ 199 et seqq. CCP); however, in Germany, this decision belongs not to a grand jury but to the trial court, which also later tries the case itself.[42] Third are the court main proceedings (Hauptverfahren), including proceedings on appeal until the decision becomes final (§§ 213 et seqq. CCP).[43] Execution proceedings are fourth (§§ 449 et seqq. CCP).[44]

Preliminary proceedings are conducted by the prosecutor. In Germany, the role of the public prosecutor's office in the preliminary proceedings is commonly described as "die Staatsanwaltschaft als Herrin des Ermittlungsverfahren," which can be translated as "the public prosecutor's office as a master of the preliminary proceedings." However, in practice, it is the police who undertake most of the proceedings on their own initiative or under supervision by the prosecutor.[45] In preliminary proceedings, the circumstances of the case are to be clarified to such an extent that the prosecutor can finally decide whether there is sufficient reason to bring charges against a person and to file an indictment[46] or to dismiss the case. The role of the court during this stage of proceedings is limited to deciding on specific matters as required by law, such as pretrial detention (§§ 112 et seqq. CCP).

In the intermediate proceedings, the court examines whether the indictment contains all necessary formal requirements and especially whether there is sufficient suspicion as claimed by the prosecutor in the indictment; if so, the court admits the indictment to the main proceedings.[47] Regarding judgment biases, it must be said that at this point, the same judges decide which judges will adjudicate the case in the main proceeding. By reviewing the indictment without proof of evidence, they decide whether it is likely that they will convict the defendant in the main trial, as the indictment proposes. Thus, an independent body for the intermediate proceeding is missing in German criminal procedure—that is, there is no grand jury trial. Once the case passes the intermediate trial, the conviction quota is around 85 to 95 percent.

The court proceedings, as a rule, are conducted in open court. Trials start with a determination of the presence of the parties: the presiding judge determines whether the accused, defense counsel, and any other parties involved in the proceedings have appeared. Then the witnesses must leave the courtroom, and the chairperson questions the accused about his or her personal circumstances. The accused must provide this information, such as name, surname, and occupation. Furthermore, the accused has the right to remain silent during the trial. Whether defendants testify and lie in their depositions, however, is not a matter of punishment because in principle it can be part of the defendants' defense strategy and their right to defense. Then the witnesses are questioned, experts are heard, documents are read out, and evidence is examined.[48] But there is no established right for defendants to confront witnesses and no right to cross-examine witnesses who are called by the other party, as happens in the common law system. After this, the prosecutor and the defense can make their closing arguments; the accused has the last word. After deliberation, the trial court announces its verdict.[49]

This is the decision model designed for the usual case. In practice, however, it is an exception. Only a few cases are brought to court, and most of them are not conducted in the ordinary proceedings but are mostly settled in "penalty order proceedings" (Strafbefehlverfahren, §§ 407 et seqq. CCP)[50] or by making a plea agreement (e.g., § 257c CCP).

Generally, a nonfinal judgment given in the first instance by the district court can be challenged by way of appeal to a higher court (§§ 312, 313 CCP). For district courts, the higher court is the regional court. Appeals constitute a retrial and encompass a factual and legal review of the case.[51] Moreover, appeals have a "suspensive" effect: appeals that are admissible and that are filed appropriately and timely suspend the formal legal effect—that is, the judgment may not be enforced. They also have a "devolutive" effect: the proceedings now take place in the superior court, and the appealed judgment must not be enforced.[52]

In German criminal proceedings, however, a ruling given in the first instance by the regional and the higher regional court may be subject only to a revision (§ 135 I JA; revision) heard by the FSC. The revision involves a purely legal review of the first-instance judgments of the regional courts and of the first-instance judgments of the higher regional courts (in political criminal cases). Revision also involves a legal review of the appeal ruling of the second-instance court and, thus, of the regional court's appeal rulings. To be more accurate, instead of filing an appeal against a judgment of the district court and then pursuing a revision, defendants can file a "leap-revision" directly to the higher regional court (§ 335 CCP).[53] This means that at the district court level, there are two appellate measures: an appeal and then a revision, or a leap-revision. However, against the judgments of regional and higher regional courts, there is only one appellate measure: revision.[54]

Final judgments can be changed solely through extraordinary measures of appeal, such as the reopening of proceedings (Wiederaufnahmeverfahren; §§ 359–373a CCP). This extremely formalized procedure is the only way to have a wrongful conviction overturned.[55]

The Correctional System

BRIEF HISTORY

Depriving individuals of their liberty took place until 1970 in institutions with different forms of confinement; in descending order of severity, incarceration took place in a Zuchthaus, Gefängnis, Einschliessung, or Festungshaft. Each institution had different regimes and was reserved for a category of individuals or for a category of crimes. The most difficult conditions were found in the Zuchthaus type of prison; inmates who were not condemned to death were forced to perform physically hard labor in these prisons, such as breaking rocks until exhaustion or collapse. Prisons today derive from Gefängnis institutions, while on the other side of the spectrum, individuals of a higher status were granted better conditions in Einschliessung and Festungshaft forms of confinement.[56] An important reform of the criminal justice system started in the 1960s, and finally, on March 31, 1970, the reform of the penal code abolished these institutions. Since then, a prison is called a Justizvollzugsanstalt (justice enforcement facility).[57]

The enforcement of prison sentences is a duty of each of the sixteen German states, or Länder, and prisons are governed by the state via public servants in accordance with the GC (Art. 33 par. 4). Until the 1950s, there was no strong incentive to build new prisons since many monasteries and castles could serve as incarceration places.[58] After extensive legal preparation in the early 1990s to allow for a public–private partnership, specific areas of imprisonment have been put in private hands. For example, some prisons have a privatized house management department, which provides such services as kitchen maintenance, cleaning, surveillance of the building, and daily checks of security devices, health services, socio-pedagogical services, oversight of work areas, sport and leisure activities, and leisure activities such as music and library services. Such services can be given by contract to private companies or persons. The departments of the prison dealing with inmates (e.g., organization, surveillance, transfers, disciplinary measures, contact with visitors, and trips out of prison) remain public.[59] The first semiprivate prison opened in 2005 in the state of Hessen, followed by two prisons in 2009: one in Baden-Wüttemberg and one in Sachsen-Anhalt.[60] In a political stunt, the minister of justice of Hessen slept as a guest in the prison the day before its opening to demonstrate the quality of the premises.[61]

ORGANIZATION

The first Prison Act (Strafvollzugsgesetz) was passed by federal legislation and entered into force on January 1, 1977. Almost three decades later, in 2006, the German Parliament decided to reorganize relations between the federal government and the states in a so-called reform of federalism. In a decisive turn, prison legislation was assigned to the states, and between 2008 and 2016, new prison codes came into effect in all sixteen states to transfer the duties from the federal to the state level.[62] The Federal Prison Act remains in use for issues uncovered by the state laws, such as organizational and technical issues of the judiciary. Since then, prisons in Germany have fallen under the responsibility of the Ministry of Justice in each state via its respective prison service department. In countries where risk management is dominant, the consequence of this reform is that the conditions of incarceration became more restrictive and differ widely from state to state[63]: southern states like Bavaria and Baden-Wüttemberg emphasize security measures and the protection of society (restriction of visits and a ban on internet), while northern states focus on the resocialization of prisoners.[64]

The prison service department controls the organization of prisons, human resources, staff training, budgets, construction, employment, training, and the education of prisoners. It also reviews petitions and complaints, and the department's representatives visit and inspect the prisons regularly. Direct contact between the Ministry of Justice and the prisons ensures fair knowledge of the prisons in the state.[65] A board of advisers is attached to each prison, whose function is to represent the public interest and to supervise and advise the directors of the prison. In parallel to the advisory group, citizens offer voluntary work in cultural and social activities with the inmates, which are subject to the instructions and rules of the institution.[66]

OPERATIONS

The German criminal justice system relies heavily on noncustodial sanctions and diversion away from prosecution in order to reduce the burden on courts and to regulate the prison population.[67] These joined efforts result in only 5 percent of convicted offenders serving a prison sentence, 12 percent receiving a suspended prison term, and 83 percent being fined.[68] The incarceration rate in Germany is seventy-six per 100,000 residents compared to 693 per 100,000 residents for the United States.[69]

In Germany, two-thirds of convictions in criminal cases result from penal orders. In the southwest state of Baden-Württemberg, they amount to 79 percent of all convictions.[70] Penal orders are entirely written procedures that are reserved for cases presenting clear and simple evidence. In theory, there is no doubt about an offender's culpability. In practice, wrongful convictions happen at a higher rate than they do in an ordinary procedure.[71] This procedure is limited to minor offenses called Vergehen, but some felonies in the United States, such as burglary and aggravated assault, also belong to this category.[72] After receiving the prosecutor's file containing a sentence, judges routinely issue penal orders consisting of a fine and sometimes an additional measure, such as community service, driving restrictions, or mediation.[73] Penal orders can also impose suspended prison terms of a maximum of one year. Fines are imposed in daily units representing a number of imprisonment days complemented by the value of a day based on the offender's personal income.[74] A day fine should have the same detrimental effect on individuals who have committed equally serious crimes but live under different financial circumstances. The total fine derives from the number of days, reflecting their degree of guilt, and the monetary value of a day, reflecting their ability to pay.[75] If the fine cannot be paid, the sentence changes in nature, and the number of imprisonment days has to be carried out. Thus, a fine that is not paid transforms into an incarceration. Among prisoners, 10 percent are incarcerated because they have defaulted on paying a fine.[76]

The sentencing system in Germany limits the longest prison sentence to fifteen years, which can be extended only if the dangerousness of a prisoner is confirmed.[77] The correctional system is organized around the objectives of resocialization and rehabilitation rather than incapacitation and retribution.[78] Prison time aims at preparing inmates to be socially responsible and to live a life free of crime on release while at the same time protecting society from further crimes after their release. The Constitutional Court stated that the protection of the public is not an objective of the confinement but rather a "self-evident" task of any confinement measure. This task is successfully completed if an offender reintegrates into society without reoffending.[79] Punishment consists of the deprivation of liberty and the separation from society, which are imposed by the custodial sentence. In order to prepare individuals for their life after prison, the conditions of confinement should not be punitive and should avoid any other detrimental effect. This preparation requires that prison life resemble as much as possible community life; this approach follows what is known as the principle of normalization. Prisoners are treated as citizens behind bars rather than pariahs. During their prison terms, they learn basic skills in order to lead more fruitful lives in society. They are encouraged to have a fair amount of control over their daily schedule, and their privacy is respected as a matter of basic human rights. They wear their own clothes, sometimes prepare their meals, can smoke, and use their own phones. Moreover, both work and education are required and remunerated in order to build a sense of self-worth. Their dignity is also supported by their right to vote, which they maintain as prisoners. These measures underline the idea that the sole aspect taken away from them while they are incarcerated is their liberty.[80]

Although compulsory work in prison has been allowed by both the Constitutional Court and the European Court of Human Rights, the practice sheds light on a problematic approach. Prison work is considered a form of treatment that aims to resocialize offenders. The remuneration per hour ranges from one to three euros, out of which no contribution is paid to social insurance for unemployment or retirement benefits that might be needed after the prison term. Companies might pay ten euros per hour to the prison; the difference is then transferred to the prison service department of the state.[81] Prisoners receive de facto an additional punishment beyond the deprivation of liberty despite the fact that, apart from their confinement, their living conditions should remain similar to living conditions in society.

Correctional staff are professionals who undergo extensive training for two years, with one year of theoretical education followed by one year of practical training. Courses include constitutional law, criminal law, educational theory, psychology, social education, stress and conflict management, communicating with prisoners, and self-defense. Their interactions with prisoners emphasize positive reinforcement, for which they use incentives and rewards, and disciplinary measures, such as solitary confinement, are applied moderately.[82]

A brief history of penal policies over the past century shows that Germany has massively improved the conditions granted to inmates. They are rightfully considered citizens behind bars, deserving of respect and entitled to exercise their citizenship rights as much as possible during incarceration.[83] This evolution comes in response to the inegalitarian society of earlier centuries and contrasts with the leveling down of the treatment of prisoners in the United States.[84] A similar difference between countries can be found in the social welfare system. The welfare state, known as Sozialstaat, is rooted in the GC[85] and has served as a clear support for a penal policy, promoting the idea that offenders are individuals to be helped while in prison.[86]

Juvenile Criminal Law in Germany

The German Juvenile Criminal Law is regulated in the Juvenile Court Act (JCA; Jugendgerichtsgesetz [JGG]) of August 4, 1953, in the version published on December 11, 1974 (BGBL. 1974 I 3427), which was last amended by Article 21 of the Act of June 25, 2021 (BGBL. I S. 2099).[87] The Guidelines for the Juvenile Courts Act in the version from August 1, 1994 (Richtlinien zum Jugendgerichtsgesetz), has supplementary force.

The basic idea for juvenile criminal law is that just as a criminal behavior per se is not innate, neither is the ability to respect rules set by society. Rather, people go through a socialization process in which they learn general social behavior and internalize compliance with legal requirements. According to Article 6 (2) of the GC, in this socialization process, parents have the right and the duty to shape freely the learning process that is referred to as "education" in principle and to do so before other so-called educational institutions do.[88] Accordingly, only in cases of a breach of the law by a young person is the state authorized to step in. However, according to the German criminal law system, the sanctioning of a criminal offense requires culpable conduct. Offenders must be able to be accused of being capable of recognizing the injustice of their actions when breaking a norm and of acting on the basis of this insight, that is, of deciding freely in favor of right or wrong. Thus, since young persons are supposed to acquire this ability only in the process of socialization, this must be taken into account in the state's response to norm breaking by offenders who are still developing.[89] Because of this idea of having more education and less punishment, it is possible to set a longer sentence if it seems to be useful for education purposes—for example, to complete an apprenticeship during the time served.

Hence, the general criminal and criminal procedural law applies to a juvenile or to an adolescent only insofar as the JCA does not contain special provisions (§ 2 [2] JCA). In principle, more of the general law (adult law) applies for adolescents than for juveniles. To be more accurate, pursuant to § 1 (2) of the JCA, the general criminal and criminal procedural law applies to juveniles—defined as individuals who are fourteen but not yet eighteen at the time of an offense—as well as to adolescents—individuals who are eighteen but not yet twenty-one at the time of an offense. Children—those who are not yet fourteen years old at the time of an offense—are not criminally responsible at all (§ 19 of the Criminal Code; Strafgesetzbuch).[90]

Furthermore, the application of juvenile criminal law is intended primarily to prevent juveniles from committing new crimes (§ 2 [1] JCA).[91] Subsequently, pursuant to §§ 1 and 3 JCA, juveniles are only conditionally responsible—namely, to the extent that they possess the necessary capability for insight and will formation according to their development.[92] Adolescents, however, are fully responsible, so that their maturity does not have to and may in fact be specially determined.[93] In addition, pursuant to § 105 (1) of the JCA, substantive juvenile criminal law may be applied to adolescents under two conditions: (1) an overall assessment of the offender's personality shows that at the time of the offense, the adolescent was still equivalent to a juvenile in terms of moral and mental development, or (2) the nature, circumstances, or motives of the offense are such that it is a case of juvenile misdemeanor. In any other cases, the adolescent is to be punished like an adult would be according to general criminal law.[94]

Pursuant to § 33 (2) of the JCA, the German juvenile courts can operate in the following forms: as a criminal judge (juvenile judge), as a court of lay assessors (juvenile court), or as part of the criminal division (juvenile division).[95] As a rule, the juvenile courts decide cases in the first instance (§ 40 JCA) and adjudicate in a panel composed of one professional juvenile judge and two juvenile lay judges (§ 33a JCA). The public prosecutor, however, may bring a charge before a juvenile judge as a criminal judge only if educational measures or disciplinary measures are to be expected (§ 39 JCA). Furthermore, among its other duties, the juvenile division—rather than the juvenile court (§§ 33b, 41 JCA)—decides (§ 41 JCA) in cases of, for example, high treason and treason against the state (§ 102 JCA).

Special public prosecutors are appointed in juvenile proceedings as juvenile public prosecutors who, like juvenile judges and juvenile lay judges, should be educationally qualified and experienced in youth education (§§ 35 et seqq. JCA).[96] Juvenile criminal proceedings (§§ 43–81 JCA) differ considerably from general criminal proceedings.[97] In juvenile criminal proceedings, the possibilities of discontinuation are to be examined first (§§ 45, 47 JCA).[98] This is because the formal criminal proceedings often seem superfluous and inappropriate in light of the normality and pettiness of the majority of juvenile delinquency.[99]

The preliminary investigation extends from the first activity of the police or the prosecutor, from the time when they have learned that a criminal offense by a juvenile or an adolescent may have been committed to the time when the prosecutor files charges or the proceedings terminate. The aim of the preliminary proceedings is to investigate the facts of the committed offense.[100] Additionally, a psychosocial diagnosis of a juvenile or an adolescent is required. The legal framework indicates "the living and family circumstances, the background, the previous behavior of the accused and all other circumstances that can be used to assess his or her psychological, mental and character traits" (§§ 43 [1] and 109 JCA).[101] If a juvenile punishment (imprisonment, § 17 JCA) is to be expected, the prosecutor or the presiding judge of the juvenile court is obliged to interview the accused before an indictment is filed (§ 44 JCA). In juvenile proceedings, there is also a requirement, as far as possible, that young people be spared the particular stresses of pretrial detention. In accordance with the principle of subsidiarity, therefore, alternative forms of detention must be examined first (§ 72 [1] JCA).

The charges against a juvenile or an adolescent can be brought in formal juvenile proceedings or in simplified juvenile proceedings (§ 76 et seqq. JCA). In principle, the course of the main hearing is governed by the same provisions of §§ 226–75 of the CCP as those against an adult.[102] However, the court must endeavor to conduct its proceedings in such a way that no disadvantages could arise for young defendants with regard to their further personality development. In any case, the main hearing shall not be public (§ 48 JCA), and it may even be held without the defendant if this would be permissible in the general proceedings, according to the CCP, and if there are special reasons for this and if the prosecutor agrees (§ 50 [1] JCA). Legal representatives and legal guardians have the right to be heard. Furthermore, the juvenile court assistance shall participate in order to bring educational, social, and caring aspects to bear (§ 50 JCA). The appeal procedure, according to § 55 JCA, is immensely limited (e.g., it is available only when certain, less severe legal consequences are ordered).[103] This is intended to promote the speedy closure of the proceedings. In this respect, the legislators of the former "JGG 1953" (JCA from 1953) were concerned that juveniles might be resentful of any delay in their prosecution, especially as they grow older and may begin to think differently about the offense that is being belatedly punished or may not recognize the punishment as a reaction to their offenses anymore.[104]

Additionally, only juvenile sentences are recorded in the Criminal Register; educational measures and disciplinary measures are entered in the Educational Register, according to the Act on the Central Register and the Education Register (Gesetz über das Zentralregister und das Erziehungsregister).[105]

The law provides for three categories of sanctions as the original consequences of criminal misconduct by juveniles. These categories include educational measures, such as issuing educational instructions or ordering institutions to provide help with education by, for example, providing an appointed educational supervisor (§ 5 [1], 9 et seq. of the JCA). Another category is disciplinary measures, such as issuing warnings and conditions and ordering juvenile detention (§§ 5 [2], 13 et seq. of the JCA). The third category is juvenile punishment (§§ 5 [2], 17 et seq. of the JCA), that is, imprisonment in a juvenile facility (six months to five years).[106]

A juvenile offense (§ 1 JCA) is to be punished primarily by educational measures. If educational measures are not sufficient, disciplinary measures may be applied. These also include juvenile detention. Juvenile punishment, however, is imposed only if other disciplinary measures are insufficient because the offense has revealed the juvenile's harmful tendencies or because of the juvenile's particularly serious culpability (§§ 5, 9 et seqq. of the JCA).

Notes

1. Falco Werkentin, "Geschichte der Polizei," *Politische Vierteljahresschrift* 33, no. 2 (1992): 293. See also Antonio Vera, *Von der "Polizei der Demokratie" zum "Glied und Werkzeug der nationalsozialistischen Gemeinschaft": Die Polizei als Instrument staatlicher Herrschaft im Deutschland der Zwischenkriegszeit (1918–1939)* (Baden-Baden: Nomos, 2019), 41–49, 78 ff., https://doi.org/10.5771/9783845297972; Markus Thiel, *Polizei- und Ordnungsrecht* (Baden-Baden: Nomos, 2020), 33; Wolf-Rüdiger Schenke, *Polizei- und Ordnungsrecht* (Heidelberg: C. F. Müller, 2021), 1–8; and Thorsten Kingreen, Ralf Poscher, Bodo Pieroth, Bernhard Schlink, and Michael Kniesel, *Polizei- und Ordnungsrecht: Mit Versammlungsrecht* (Munich: C. H. Beck, 2020), 1–4.
2. Art. 20 of the German Constitution [GC] or the Basic Law; Grundgesetz.
3. Vera, *Von der "Polizei der Demokratie,"* 47.

4. Robert Harnischmacher and Arved Semerak, *Deutsche Polizeigeschichte eine allgemeine Einführung in die Grundlagen* (Stuttgart: W. Kohlhammer, 1986), 56–71. See also Matthias Bäcker, Erhard Denninger, and Kurt Graulich, eds., *Handbuch des Polizeirechts: Gefahrenabwehr—Strafverfolgung—Rechtsschutz* (Munich: C. H. Beck Nördlingen, 2021), 12–26.

5. Harnischmacher and Semerak, *Deutsche Polizeigeschichte*, 72–91. See also Bäcker et al., *Handbuch des Polizeirechts*, 26–31.

6. Harnischmacher and Semerak, *Deutsche Polizeigeschichte*, 92–109.

7. Daniell Bastian, *Westdeutsches Polizeirecht unter alliierter Besatzung (1945–55)* (Tübingen: Mohr Siebeck, 2010), 7–77, 137–86. See also Bäcker et al., *Handbuch des Polizeirechts*, 32–48, 49 ff.

8. Harnischmacher and Semerak, *Deutsche Polizeigeschichte*, 110 et seqq. See also Hendrik Burke, *Die Polizeiverordnung* (Berlin: Duncker and Humblot, 2019).

9. See more about the German police enforcement history in Vera, *Von der "Polizei der Demokratie,"* 89 ff., and Harnischmacher and Semerak, *Deutsche Polizeigeschichte*.

10. Gunther Dietrich Gade and Marita Kieler, *Polizei und Föderalismus: Aufgabenfelder der Bundes—Und Landespolizeien im verfassungsrechtlichen Gefüge der Bundesrepublik Deutschland* (Stuttgart: Kohlhammer, 2008), 7.

11. See more about the FIS in Schenke, *Polizei*, 291–92, and Thiel, *Polizei*, 39.

12. See more about the FOPC in Schenke, *Polizei*, 289–91, and Thiel, *Polizei*, 39.

13. See more about German FP in Gade and Kieler, *Polizei*, 105 ff.

14. Gade and Kieler, *Polizei*, 25–27.

15. Gade and Kieler, *Polizei*, 49–105.

16. See more in Gade and Kieler, *Polizei*, 126–209.

17. Bäcker et al., *Handbuch des Polizeirechts*, 195.

18. Bäcker et al., *Handbuch des Polizeirechts*, 195.

19. Bäcker et al., *Handbuch des Polizeirechts*, 197.

20. See more about the history of FCPO in Harnischmacher and Semerak, *Deutsche Polizeigeschichte*, 193 ff.

21. Gade and Kieler, *Polizei*, 212; Schenke, *Polizei*, 286.

22. Gade and Kieler, *Polizei*, 212, 103; Schenke, *Polizei*, 287.

23. Kingreen et al., *Polizei*, 63.

24. Bäcker et al., *Handbuch des Polizeirechts*, 198; Kingreen et al., *Polizei*, 64.

25. Bäcker et al., *Handbuch des Polizeirechts*, 198.

26. Thiel, *Polizei*, 38; Schenke, *Polizei*, 300–302.

27. Werner Beulke and Sabine Swoboda, *Strafprozessrecht* (Heidelberg: C. F. Müller, 2020), 79.

28. Schenke, *Polizei*, 293; Thiel, *Polizei*, 40–41. See also Horst Wüstenbecker, *Polizei–und Ordnungsrecht* (Münster: Alpmann and Schmidt, 2019), 2.

29. Schenke, *Polizei*, 293.

30. Schenke, *Polizei*, 294.

31. For more about the history of the state police organizations, see Harnischmacher and Semerak, *Deutsche Polizeigeschichte*, 135–97.

32. See Wüstenbecker, *Polizei*, 3–4.

33. Schenke, *Polizei*, 295.

34. Thiel, *Polizei*, 45.

35. Beulke and Swoboda, *Strafprozessrecht*, 77–78, 81–82.

36. See Beulke and Swoboda, *Strafprozessrecht*, 83.

37. See John Bell, *Judiciaries within Europe: A Comparative Review* (Cambridge: Cambridge University Press, 2009), 110.

38. Beulke and Swoboda, *Strafprozessrecht*, 44–48. See also Armin Engländer and Klaus Volk, *Grundkurs StPO* (München: C. H. Beck, 2021), 8 ff.

39. In the version published on April 7, 1987, Federal Law Gazette Part I, pp. 1074, 1319, which was last amended by Article 2 of the Act of March 25, 2022, Federal Law Gazette Part I, p. 571.

40. Beulke and Swoboda, *Strafprozessrecht*, 1–2.

41. Beulke and Swoboda, *Strafprozessrecht*, 29–35.

42. Beulke and Swoboda, *Strafprozessrecht*, 156–61.

43. Beulke and Swoboda, *Strafprozessrecht*, 162–69, 184 ff.

44. See an overview in Engländer and Volk, *Grundkurs StPO*, 6–7.

45. See more in Shawn Marie Boyne, *The German Prosecution Service Guardians of the Law?* (Berlin: Springer, 2014).

46. Engländer and Volk, *Grundkurs StPO*, 6–7. See also Beulke and Swoboda, *Strafprozessrecht*, 241 ff.

47. Engländer and Volk, *Grundkurs StPO*, 7, 156 ff. See also Beulke and Swoboda, *Strafprozessrecht*, 272 ff.

48. Engländer and Volk, *Grundkurs StPO*, 7, 162 ff.

49. Engländer and Volk, *Grundkurs StPO*, 7, 162 ff. See also Beulke and Swoboda, *Strafprozessrecht*, 279 ff.

50. Engländer and Volk, *Grundkurs StPO*, 7.

51. Beulke and Swoboda, *Strafprozessrecht*, 421 ff. See also Engländer and Volk, *Grundkurs StPO*, 302 ff.

52. Beulke and Swoboda, *Strafprozessrecht*, 415.

53. Beulke and Swoboda, *Strafprozessrecht*, 427.

54. Beulke and Swoboda, *Strafprozessrecht*, 49–52, 414–38. See also Engländer and Volk, *Grundkurs StPO*, 315 ff.

55. Beulke and Swoboda, *Strafprozessrecht*, 443–47. See also Engländer and Volk, *Grundkurs StPO*, 333–38.

56. Peter Rellensmann, "Die Entwicklung des deutschen Strafgesetzbuches," *Jura Individuell*, October 25, 2020, https://www.juraindividuell.de/artikel/die-entwicklung-des-deutschen-strafgesetzbuches.

57. Hans-Dieter Schwind, Alexander Böhm, Jörg-Martin Jehle, and Klaus Laubenthal, eds., *Strafvollzugsgesetz: Bund und Länder* (Berlin: De Gruyter, 2013).

58. Hans von Hentig and Joseph Willen, "Germany's Prison System," *Annals of the American Academy of Political and Social Science* 157 (1931): 174–79.

59. Susann Barisch, *Die Privatisierung im deutschen Strafvollzug: Unter Einbeziehung des Jugendstrafvollzuges und unter Berücksichtigung entsprechender Entwicklungen in Großbritannien, Frankreich und den USA* (Münster: Waxmann, 2010).

60. Torsten Kunze, "Privatisierung im Strafvollzug: Das hessische Modellprojekt einer teilprivatisierten Justizvollzugsanstalt," in *Rechnungswesen und Controlling in der öffentlichen Verwaltung: Konzepte, Erfahrungsberichte und praktische Lösungen*, ed. Erik Meurer and Günter Stephan (Freiburg: Haufe, 2003), 695–715.

61. *Justizminister: Privatisierung im Strafvollzug erweist sich als großer Erfolg* (Hessen: Ministry of Justice, 2004).

62. Hans-Dieter Schwind, Alexander Böhm, Jörg-Martin Jehle, and Klaus Laubenthal, eds., *Strafvollzugsgesetz* (Berlin: De Gruyter, 2019).

63. Myles Frederick McLellan, "Wrongful Convictions and the State Risk Harm Paradigm," *International Journal of Law and Public Administration* 2, no. 1 (2019): 23–39, https://doi.org/10.11114/ijlpa.v2i1.4117.

64. Heribert Prantl, "Haftbedingungen in Deutschland: Haft ist nicht gleich Haft," *Süddeutsche Zeitung*, August 14, 2016.

65. Jens Puschke, ed., *Strafvollzug in Deutschland: Strukturelle Defizite, Reformbedarf und Alternativen* (Berlin: De Gruyter, 2011).

66. Ulrich Kamann, *Handbuch für die Strafvollstreckung und den Strafvollzug* (Bonn: ZAP, 2008).

67. Thomas Weigend, "Sentencing and Punishment in Germany," in *Sentencing and Sanctions in Western Countries*, ed. Michael H. Tonry and Richard S. Frase (New York: Oxford University Press, 2001).

68. Thomas Weigend, "No News Is Good News: Criminal Sentencing in Germany since 2000," *Crime and Justice* 45, no. 1 (2016): 83–106.

69. Ram Subramanian and Alison Shames, "Sentencing and Prison Practices in Germany and the Netherlands: Implications for the United States," *Vera*, October 2013, https://www.vera.org/publications/sentencing-and-prison-practices-in-germany-and-the-netherlands-implications-for-the-united-states.

70. Wolfgang Heinz, "Der Strafbefehl in der Rechtswirklichkeit in Grundfragen staatlichen Strafens," in Guido Britz and Heinz Müller-Dietz, *Grundfragen staatlichen Strafens: Festschrift für Heinz Müller-Dietz zum 70. Geburtstag*, (Munich: Beck, 2001), 272–313.

71. Raluca Enescu, "Penal Orders and the Risk of Wrongful Convictions," *Bergen Journal of Criminal Law and Criminal Justice* 7, no. 2 (2019): 3–20; Barbara Dunkel, *Fehlentscheidungen in der Justiz: Systematische Analyse von Wiederaufnahmeverfahren in Strafverfahren im Hinblick auf Häufigkeit und Risikofaktoren* (Baden-Baden: Nomos, 2018).

72. R. Enescu, A. L. Niang, and C. Momsen, "Verteidigung in Strafbefehlsverfahren in Deutschland, Frankreich und der Schweiz," *Kriminalpolitische Zeitung* 7, no. 1 (2022): 20–35.

73. S. M. Boyle, "Procedural Economy in Pre-Trial Procedure: Developments in Germany and the United States," in *Comparative Criminal Procedure*, ed. J. E. Ross and S. Thaman (Cheltenham: Elgar, 2018), 219–57.

74. N. Bögelein and M. Nagrecha, "Money as Punishment: A Review of 'Day Fines in Europe,'" *Kriminologie* [Criminology] 4 (2021): 428–34.

75. Jorg-Martin Jehle, *Criminal Justice in Germany* (Berlin: Federal Ministry of Justice, 2009).

76. N. Bögelein, "Und plötzlich ging alles ganz einfach: Die Ersatzfreiheitsstrafe in Zeiten von Corona," *Informationsdienst Straffälligenhilfe* 29, no. 1 (2021): 19–25.

77. Axel Dessecker and Elena Rausch, *Die Vollstreckung lebenslanger Freiheitsstrafen: Dauer und Gründe der Beendigung im Jahr 2019* (Wiesbaden: Eigenverlag Kriminologische Zentralstelle, 2021).

78. Prison Act of March 16, 1976 (Federal Law Gazette Part I, pp. 581, 2088), last amended by Article 1 of the Act of June 19, 2019 (Federal Law Gazette Part I, p. 840).

79. Frieder Dünkel, "German Prison Law and Human Rights" (lecture, European-American Prison Project Conference, Waldeck Prison, Dummerstorf, Mecklenburg-Western Pomerania, Germany, 2013).

80. M. Tonry, "Why Aren't German Penal Policies Harsher and Imprisonment Rates Higher?," *German Law Journal* 5, no. 10 (2004): 1187–206, doi:10.1017/S207183220001316X.

81. Timo Stukenberg and Olaya Argüeso, "'Made in Germany'—Wer von der Arbeit in Gefängnissen profitiert," *Correctiv*, July 21, 2021, https://correctiv.org/aktuelles/justiz-polizei/leben-im-gefaengnis/2021/07/21/made-in-germany-wer-von-der-arbeit-in-gefaengnissen-profitiert.

82. Subramanian and Shames, "Sentencing and Prison Practices."

83. Herbert Reinke, "Crime and Criminal Justice History in Germany: A Report on Recent Trends," *Crime, Histoire et Sociétés* 13, no. 1 (2009): 117–37.

84. James Q. Whitman, *Harsh Justice: Criminal Punishment and the Widening Divide between America and Europe* (New York: Oxford University Press, 2003).

85. J.-P. Tabin and R. Enescu, "The Normative Impact of Unemployment Insurance: A European Perspective," *Journal of Comparative Social Work* 2 (2012): 1–11.

86. Michael Tonry, "Equality and Human Dignity: The Missing Ingredients in American Sentencing," in "Sentencing Policies and Practices in Western Countries: Comparative and Cross-National Perspectives," ed. M. Tonry, special issue, *Crime and Justice* 45 (2016): 459–96.

87. Learn more about the history of the German juvenile criminal law in Klaus Laubenthal, Helmut Baier, and Nina Nestler, *Jugendstrafrecht* (Berlin: Springer-Lehrbuch, 2015), 11–30, https://doi.org/10.1007/978-3-662-45027-7, and Heribert Ostendorf, *Jugendstrafrecht* (Baden-Baden: Nomos, 2020), 33–41.

88. Laubenthal et al., *Jugendstrafrecht*, 1.

89. Laubenthal et al., *Jugendstrafrecht*, 1. See also Ostendorf, *Jugendstrafrecht*, 42 ff.

90. Laubenthal et al., *Jugendstrafrecht*, 32–34.

91. Laubenthal et al., *Jugendstrafrecht*, 3.

92. See more in Laubenthal et al., *Jugendstrafrecht*, 35–45.

93. Laubenthal et al., *Jugendstrafrecht*, 46.

94. Laubenthal et al., *Jugendstrafrecht*, 45–60. See also Ostendorf, *Jugendstrafrecht*, 46ff.

95. See more in Ostendorf, *Jugendstrafrecht*, 73 ff.

96. Ostendorf, *Jugendstrafrecht*, 73.

97. Ostendorf, *Jugendstrafrecht*, 95–139.

98. Ostendorf, *Jugendstrafrecht*, 95.

99. Ostendorf, *Jugendstrafrecht*, 95 (see also 96 ff.).

100. Laubenthal et al., *Jugendstrafrecht*, 120.

101. Laubenthal et al., *Jugendstrafrecht*, 153 ff. See also Ostendorf, *Jugendstrafrecht*, 62–64.

102. Ostendorf, *Jugendstrafrecht*, 127 ff.

103. Ostendorf, *Jugendstrafrecht*, 129 ff.

104. Laubenthal et al., *Jugendstrafrecht*, 174.

105. See Laubenthal et al., *Jugendstrafrecht*, 461 ff., and Ostendorf, *Jugendstrafrecht*, 158.

106. Ostendorf, *Jugendstrafrecht*, 140 ff.

Part 4

MIDDLE EAST AND SOUTH ASIA

CHAPTER 12

The Egyptian Criminal Justice System

STEPS FORWARD, STEPS BACKWARD

Ahmed F. Khalifa and Ibrahim Sabra

Egypt is one of the oldest political entities in the world. Its recorded history as a unified state dates back to earlier than 3000 BC. This continual existence of Egypt as a centralized state has resulted in a long history of legal regimes through different eras.

The modern legal system in Egypt dates back to 1883, when a system of national courts was introduced along with several codes that were modeled along Napoleonic lines.[1] It is not disputed that the modern legal system in Egypt, including the criminal justice system, is fundamentally influenced by the French system despite the fact that Egypt was under British occupation for more than seventy years when Egypt's modern penal law was first formed.[2] The French influence was the result of the French invasion of Egypt in 1798, which lasted for only three years yet greatly affected the formation of the modern Egyptian state in general.

The Egyptian legal system is considered a civil law system, which depends mainly on codified laws, as opposed to common law systems, which are based on judicial precedents. Similarly, the criminal justice system in Egypt has features that are based on an inquisitorial model, which is more prevalent in civil law countries and in which judges play a proactive role in the criminal procedure in their quest for the correct attribution for responsibility, as opposed to an accusatory model, which is adopted more often in common law countries and in which judges are more neutral arbitrators between the prosecution and the defense.

The Egyptian criminal justice system may be examined by looking into each of its four main phases: the pre-instruction, or policing, phase; the instruction, or prosecutorial, phase, comprising investigation and charging procedures; the trial, or judicial, phase; and the correctional system. The main laws that regulate the criminal justice system in Egypt are the Egyptian Penal Code (EPC) of 1937 until its last amendments in 2021,[3] the Egyptian Criminal Procedure Code (ECPC) of 1950 with all its amendments until 2021, the Child Law of 1996 as amended in 2008, the Prison Law of 1956 as amended in 2018, and the Police Authority Law of 1971 as amended in 2020.

The Pre-Instruction Phase: Policing in Egypt

HISTORICAL BACKGROUND

When the concept of policing came to light around 3000 BC in ancient Egypt, for each administrative jurisdiction of the empire, an official was appointed to ensure justice and security, and this official was assisted by a chief of police who carried the *sab heri seker* title, which means "chief of the hitters."[4] Yet policing in its modern form began in Egypt under the reign of Muhammad Ali, the Ottoman governor. Influenced by the Turkish criminal justice system, Muhammad Ali established the first formal Ministry of Interior, naming it the "Governor's Office," with the aim of maintaining security in Cairo.[5]

By the end of the nineteenth century, Egyptian police started replicating the British system, and in 1883, the National Police Force (NPF) was established. The training and staffing of the NPF were supervised mainly by the British until 1922, when the country gained its sovereignty back after Britain reluctantly issued the Declaration of Egyptian Independence, which officially ended the British protectorate over Egypt.[6]

On January 25, 1952, intense clashes took place in the city of Ismailia between the British forces and Egyptian police after the latter refused to give up the city's police station and hand over their weapons. This incident left around fifty Egyptian officers dead and eighty wounded, and the event is commemorated annually as National Police Day. During the eras of Gamal Abdel Nasser and Anwar Al-Sadat, policing witnessed a series of reforms that culminated with the issuance of the Police Authority Law No. 109 in 1971.

ORGANIZATIONAL STRUCTURE

According to Article 206 of the Egyptian Constitution, the police force is deemed a statutory, civil body committed to serving the people, and its sole loyalty is to the people. Its main duties derive from the Constitution and the law; these duties revolve around ensuring the safety and security of citizens, maintaining public order and morality, and respecting human rights and fundamental freedoms. Article 3 of the Police Authority Law stipulates further functions of the police, such as protection of lives, honor, and money; prevention of crime; and enforcement of laws and regulations.

Egypt's policing system is headed by the minister of interior, who has the authority to issue all decisions that regulate its affairs and the organization of the work. A Supreme Police Council is established under the Ministry of Interior in order to assist the minister of interior in formulating the public policy of the ministry, setting up its strategic plan, developing its sectors, and enhancing its work strategy in a manner that reinforces performance of the ministry's duties to the fullest. The council is headed by the most senior first assistant to the minister of interior; its membership includes (1) first assistants to the minister of interior, (2) assistants to the minister of interior,

(3) a state adviser to the Ministry of Interior, and (4) a director of the General Administration of Officers' Affairs.

The Egyptian police force is divided into sectors by subject matter and territory; however, policing remains centralized, with the chain of command emanating from the minister of interior, who holds the authority of designating a chief of police for each sector to coordinate the operational command and to maintain public order. The appointed chief should carry the title of either a first assistant or an assistant minister and assumes the leadership of the police, each within the limits of the competence entrusted to him. The chief may have one or more deputies whose duties are determined by the minister of interior.

Police Sectors and Departments

In response to myriad law enforcement issues arising across Egypt and to address these policing needs effectively and efficiently, the Ministry of Interior has created several police sectors, each with different departments that carry names clearly depicting their focus area and work objective.[7]

The Public Security Sector, which is responsible for law enforcement across the country, consists of the Criminal Investigation Department and the Criminal Evidence Verification Department. It undertakes the tasks of (1) developing a policy to monitor and follow up on the rate of criminal offenses and to develop plans to combat all criminal offenses; (2) identifying and adopting the technical measures necessary to detect and investigate crime in order to apprehend perpetrators; (3) collecting information, conducting investigations, and verifying legal evidence; (4) examining cases involving fugitives and disseminating lists of these cases to all police departments; and (5) monitoring the implementation of the law that regulates the carrying and possession of firearms, ammunition, and explosives.

The Central Security Forces Sector is a paramilitary body responsible for dealing with dangerous criminal outposts, countering terrorism, and crowd and riot control in addition to providing security for key domestic and foreign officials and guarding infrastructure, vital facilities, and strategic sites, such as Parliament, embassies, and airports. The Central Security Forces' strength includes "conscript soldiers who may do some of their military service with the force."[8]

The Homeland Security Sector, originally called the National Security Sector, holds the key role of preserving national security by investigating and fighting terrorism-related crimes, organized and transnational crimes, and internal security threats. It also specializes in both monitoring issues facing the state and measuring public reaction in this regard as well as submitting reports on these matters to the authorities concerned in order to take the necessary measures toward solving these issues and containing their effect. Additionally, this sector collects information about state safety and security, reports it to the minister of interior, and submits any studies requested in relation to these matters.

The Planning and Follow-up Sector under the Anti-Cybercrime Department was established as a reaction to the widespread use of the internet and the consequential emergence of cybercrimes. Although the Anti-Cybercrime Department was launched in 2002, it has become much more active since the adoption of the Anti-Cybercrime Law No. 175 of 2018. The department is responsible for receiving complaints in relation to any criminal activities conducted over the internet, investigating these cybercrimes, identifying suspects, and collecting relevant evidence.

The Social Security Sector includes the Counter-Narcotics Police Department, which is the oldest counter-narcotics department in the Middle East/North Africa region and which has jurisdiction over all criminal matters pertaining to narcotics and is tasked with combating and controlling the illegal smuggling, import, export, cultivation, production, possession, acquisition, exchange, and trade of narcotic substances. This sector also includes the Morality Police Department, which undertakes the tasks of monitoring criminal phenomena in the field of public morals and of coordinating efforts in fighting them. It also cooperates with international actors in combating public morals–related crimes of an international character that take place inside Egypt or that involve Egyptians abroad. Moreover, it supervises the implementation of Egypt's obligations arising from international treaties related to the trafficking of women.

The Specialized Police Sector includes (1) the General Traffic Department, which undertakes the task of regulating traffic on highways between governorates and roads within governorate borders by checking the validity of both car and driving licenses, inspecting the load and passenger capacity of vehicles, and overseeing speed limits, and (2) the Civil Defense Department, which carries out the task of extinguishing fires, overseeing disaster management and rescue operations, and ensuring compliance with industrial and civil security specifications in industrial, commercial, and residential establishments.

The Prison Service Sector—recently renamed the Community Protection Sector—undertakes the mission of policing prisons and is entrusted with the execution of sentences issued by the judiciary. It is also concerned with the implementation of the rules and instructions embodied in Prisons Organization Law No. 396 of 1956, such as the admission of prisoners, the treatment of prisoners, prisoners' education, prisoners' health care, disciplinary measures, and visits and communications.

The Ports Security Sector is responsible for securing air, sea, and land ports across the country and for the prevention of travel-related crimes. Under this sector comes the Passports, Immigration and Nationality Department, which oversees all visa, immigration, and nationality matters.

The Economic Security Sector includes the Public Funds Crime Investigation Department, Transport Police Department, Electricity Police Department, Environment and Water Police Department, Tax Evasion Police Department, Public Funds Crime Investigation Department, Supply and Internal Trade Police, and Artistic Works and Publications Crime Investigation Department.

The Security and Protection Sector includes the Tourism and Antiquities Police Department and a number of bodyguard departments, such as the VIP Protection Department and the Presidency Police Department.

Recruitment and Ranks

Under the Egyptian policing system, officers are not recruited, but a Police Academy has been established as the primary channel for receiving applications from those who are keen on becoming police officers after finishing secondary school.[9] In order to join the Police Academy, education, physical, and medical requirements must be met; however, education weighs the least. In addition to these requirements, the admission prerequisites stipulate that applicants must (1) be Egyptian, (2) enjoy a good reputation, (3) meet the age requirement, (4) not plan to get married while they are enrolled in the academy, (5) not have been fired from any other governmental job as a result of a disciplinary decision, and (6) not have been criminally sanctioned. Study in the academy lasts for four years and is conducted in Arabic, English, or French. On graduation, officers are awarded a dual bachelor's degree in law and police science. They then become officially appointed under probation for one year as officers holding the rank of lieutenant. Climbing up the career ladder, police ranks progress from lieutenant to first lieutenant, captain, major, lieutenant colonel, colonel, brigadier, and major general.

An additional admission track also opens annually for other university graduates through which they can apply to become what is called "specialist police officers." They also have to fulfill certain educational, physical, and medical requirements, and if chosen, they spend six months training at the academy, after which they begin their work with the rank of first lieutenant, from which they can move forward to the top command. More recently, a new entry program has been established exclusively for law graduates. In this program, those admitted spend two years of study at the academy and are eventually appointed as first lieutenant officers.

Another essential category in the chain of command—police secretaries—are graduates of the Institute of Police Secretaries, where they spend one year. They have to meet the previously mentioned requirements that police officers have to meet except that they can apply directly after finishing either middle school or technical school. Police secretaries have an opportunity to be promoted as police officers at the rank of lieutenant if they earn a degree in law provided that they have served less than eight years as police secretaries or thirteen years in the police authority in general.

LAW ENFORCEMENT

Police in Egypt play two crucial roles in law enforcement: crime prevention and crime detection. To prevent crime, police officers are authorized to take all precautionary measures necessary, such as investigating suspects, surveilling those who pose security risks, and carrying out patrols. Crime detection involves conducting initial inquiries for the purpose of collecting all available information about a crime and potential offenders.[10] The police may not intervene by taking any action against the liberties of individuals unless they are in an in flagrante delicto situation; otherwise, the police officer has to receive a judicial authorization from a judge or the Public Prosecutor's Office. No arrests or seizure could be made as such without a judicial order.

The Instruction Phase: The Public Prosecutor's Office in Egypt

The public prosecution in Egypt is organized based on a hierarchical, pyramidal model. The attorney general of Egypt is appointed by the president of the republic and is represented in each district by a Public Prosecutor's Office that has a sufficient number of assistants to the attorney general. The Public Prosecutor's Office members are magistrates who enjoy all the guarantees of sitting judges and are appointed, disciplined, and promoted as per the Law Regulating the Judicial Authority in Egypt of 1972. A normal appointee in the Egyptian judiciary first has to work for few years in the Public Prosecutor's Office before becoming a sitting judge. Some continue their path to higher grades of the prosecutorial hierarchy, and some work for a number of years as judges and return to serve as prosecutors.

The Public Prosecutor's Office has two main roles in the Egyptian criminal justice system: one at the trial stage and the other at the pretrial stage. First, the original role of the prosecutor is at the trial stage, and that role is to represent society in proving the responsibility of the accused before the criminal court in what may be called handling the "criminal lawsuit." Article 1 of the ECPC of 1950 states that "the public prosecution shall, except in the cases provided for by the law, solely have the jurisdiction of initiating and exercising criminal proceedings." Article 2 of the same law stipulates that "the attorney general is assigned to handle the criminal proceedings by himself or by a member of the Public Prosecutor's Office." The role of exercising the prosecutorial function before a court in criminal proceedings is the standard role of any prosecution office in any criminal legal system.

The second role is peculiar to the Egyptian criminal justice system. In this second role, the Public Prosecutor's Office functions as an investigative judge at the pretrial stage. This phase includes two roles for the Public Prosecutor's Office: gathering and documenting evidence that is and is not in favor of the criminal and then drafting and submitting the charges in the official indictment. This important role has been conferred on the Public Prosecutor's Office by Article 199 of the ECPC, which stipulates that "except where the case is investigated by the investigating judge, the public prosecution shall conduct the investigation in misdemeanors and felonies as per the applicable rules to the investigative judge."

The wide authorities that are granted to the prosecutor in conducting the role of the investigative judge include gathering and documenting officially relevant evidence, receiving testimonials of witnesses, interrogating suspects, confronting suspects with relevant evidence, ordering the arrest of suspects (arrests are executed by the police), issuing search warrant orders to seize objects, and issuing orders of surveillance in certain cases. Additionally, one of the authorities of investigative judges that is delegated only partially to the public prosecutor is the authority to detain the accused on a provisional basis before trial.

The public prosecution is authorized to issue a provisional detention order for a maximum of four days following the day of arrest. If the investigation is not concluded yet, the public prosecution has to submit relevant documents to the magistrate judge requesting an extension of the provisional detention period. The magistrate judge shall issue a ruling in this respect after holding a hearing session for both the public prosecution and the accused. In all cases, each extension shall not exceed fifteen days, and the whole provisional detention period shall not exceed forty-five days. Should the investigation remain ongoing by the end of the provisional detention period and the public prosecution deems it necessary to extend it, the prosecution has to submit the issue to the misdemeanor Court of Appeal, which is authorized to extend the temporary detention for consecutive periods, each of which shall not exceed forty-five days. In this case, the total period of provisional detention shall not exceed six months in misdemeanors, eighteen months in felonies, and two years in felonies that are punishable by life imprisonment or the death penalty (ECPC Article 143). At the end of the investigative phase, it is the public prosecutor's decision to issue a formal indictment, which initiates the trial, or in case of insufficient evidence the prosecutor may issue an *ordre de non-lieu* indicating that the case should not go to trial.

The Trial Phase: The Criminal Court System in Egypt

The Egyptian criminal justice system has several types and levels of criminal courts and a detailed organization of procedure before each stage. The main criminal court system is designed to deal with ordinary crimes, yet some specific crimes or some categories of criminals require special treatment. Before examining the court structure, we will shed light on some guarantees of the criminal justice system.

GUARANTEES DURING CRIMINAL TRIALS: DEFENSE RIGHTS AND PUBLIC HEARINGS

All criminal courts procedures guarantee defense rights for the accused. A major principle in the Egyptian procedural system is that no conviction may be enforced without hearing the defense of the accused. Article 54 of the Egyptian Constitution of 2014 guarantees that for all crimes that may be punished by any deprivation of liberty, accused persons have to be represented by a lawyer, and if accused persons do not have the resources to obtain their own lawyers, then it is the duty of the court to appoint a lawyer for the accused. Even before this constitutional provision, the ECPC of 1950 provided for the right to a defense lawyer in felonies only, not only during trial but even in the pretrial phase of interrogation. The ECPC stipulates in Article 124 that it is prohibited to interrogate accused persons or to cross-examine them in the absence of a lawyer except in cases in which accused persons are caught in flagrante delicto or in which there is a fear that evidence may be lost. The prosecutor must appoint a lawyer for accused persons in case they are not able to afford one. The law imposes the obligation on lawyers, whether court appointed or selected by the accused, to represent defendants with due diligence, and lawyers are not allowed to decline to represent someone unless permitted to do so by the court and not before another lawyer is chosen to continue representing the accused. It is clear that defense rights have been part of a theoretical improvement in the criminal justice system in Egypt.

Another guarantee that is provided for in criminal trials in Egypt is the requirement of public hearings, which is usually referred to as the publicity of trials. The principle is provided for in ECPC Article 268, which stipulates that "the court hearing must be public, however the court may, in consideration of public order and observation of morals, order the case to be heard in a secret hearing, wholly or partially, or to prevent specific groups from attending the hearing." This principle, which was always interpreted as including the ability of media to publish and inform the public opinion about trial proceedings, is considered by scholars of criminal law in Egypt as one of the main pillars of public trust in the fairness of the judiciary and also as a popular tool of supervision for the acts of the judiciary.[11] It may be argued that this principle is compromised by a new amendment of the EPC, by Law No. 71 of 2021, which added Article 186 *bis*, which criminalizes, among other things, taking notes, publishing, broadcasting, or publicizing by any other means the proceedings of a criminal trial without the prior authorization of the court and following consultation with the public prosecution. Such crime is penalized by a heavy fine and the confiscation of all the tools that were used in commission of the crime. This wide incrimination may be looked at as turning upside down the principle of publicity in trials, as it disallows publishing or even registering what is taking place in courtrooms unless the Public Prosecutor's Office and the judges allow for it, something that may be difficult to achieve. The new incrimination also does not include any precise criteria for the prosecution and the judiciary by which they may decide to accept or to refuse such authorization, which allows for wide discretionary power without clear limits.

THE CRIMINAL COURT STRUCTURE IN THE EGYPTIAN SYSTEM

Three categories of crimes exist in the Egyptian legal system: felonies, misdemeanors, and contraventions. Felonies are crimes that are punishable by the death penalty, life sentence, aggravated prison from three to fifteen years, and prison from three to fifteen years.[12] Misdemeanors are crimes that are punishable by imprisonment from one day to three years and by fines that exceed 100 Egyptian pounds.[13] Contraventions are crimes that are punishable by fines that do not exceed 100 Egyptian pounds.[14]

The main body of the criminal court system in Egypt is distinguished along two paths according to the gravity of the crime. The first addresses felonies, and the second focuses on misdemeanors and contraventions. On the one hand, each governorate of the twenty-seven governorates making up Egypt has one or more Court of Felonies, in which panels are composed of three senior judges (ECPC Article 366). The judgments of these courts can be challenged only before the Court of Cassation. The highest court in the ordinary judiciary in the Egyptian legal systems, it is only one court based in Cairo, the capital, and it accepts cases only for legal reasons or mistakes made by a lower court in applying the law. The new Egyptian Constitution of 2014 required the establishment of a Court of Appeal for felonies, but this is still not implemented.

On the other hand, misdemeanors and contraventions have another court structure. Cases are tried in first-instance courts by a single judge bench. Decisions emanating from this primary court, or court of first instance, can be appealed before the Court of Appeal for misdemeanors. Then the case may find its way to the highest court, the Court of Cassation, if there is a mistake in applying the law. This ordinary regime of courts for normal crimes does not exclude that there are special courts for certain types of crimes that have different procedural rules. For example, state security crimes have a special regime of criminal courts, and Economic Courts have criminal jurisdiction for some of the crimes that are regulated in its establishing law. Juvenile justice also has its own regime of courts and different sanctions to impose.

CHILDREN'S COURTS AND JUVENILE JUSTICE

Laws about children and the executive regulation of these laws were promulgated in 1996 and modified in 2008. The law considers any person under eighteen to be a child. The law also provides for the establishment of a Juvenile Court in each governorate that enjoys exclusive jurisdiction over children accused of committing crimes or delinquency. The Juvenile Court is composed of "three judges, assisted by two social specialists, at least one of whom is a woman, whose attendance at the court proceedings is obligatory. The two experts must submit their report to the court after examining the child's circumstances in all respects, before the court issues its ruling."[15]

The treatment of juvenile delinquents differs depending on their age. Children who are fifteen years old or younger cannot receive any criminal punishment. Article 101 of the Child Law stipulates that "the verdict for a child who has not reached fifteen years of age, in case he commits a crime, shall include one of the following interventions: (1) reproach/censure; (2) delivery to parents, guardians, or custodians; (3) training and rehabilitation; (4) committing to certain obligations; (5) judicial probation; (6) community service activities not harmful to the child's health or mental state. The by-laws shall determine the nature of this work and restrictions thereof; (7) placement in one of the specialized hospitals; (8) placement in one of the social care institutions."

Children from fifteen to eighteen years old may receive criminal punishments that are less severe than the criminal punishments that adults who are eighteen years old and older receive. Article 111 of the Child Law stipulates that no child accused shall be sentenced to death, life imprisonment, or aggravated prison if, at the time of committing the crime, he did not reach the age of eighteen years. Without prejudice to the provision of Article 17 of the EPC, if the child who has reached the age of fifteen years commits a crime punishable by a death sentence, life imprisonment, or aggravated prison, he shall be sentenced to imprisonment. Furthermore, if the crime committed is punishable by imprisonment, he shall be placed in custody for a period not less than three months. The court, instead of placing the child in custody, may sentence him with the measure stated in Article 101, Item 8, of this law. However, if the child who has reached fifteen years of age commits a misdemeanor punishable by placing him in custody, the court may, instead of sentencing the child to the penalty decreed for it, sentence the child to one of the measures set forth in Article 101, Items 5, 6, and 8, of this law.

Custodial sentences for minors or young adults are carried out in special penitentiary institutions called "rehabilitation centers." The latter focus more on socio-educational activities and vocational training for juvenile prisoners. Egyptian criminal law allows for the sentencing of imprisonment to minors from the age of fifteen.

In addition to strengthening the right of access to education and school monitoring (Article 232 R. explanatory to Law No. 12–1996), the juvenile penitentiary system is characterized by two main rules. The first concerns the disciplinary repression of minors; it prohibits the use of solitary confinement in individual cells (Article 239 R. explanatory to Law No. 12–1996). The second is the submission of the execution of the sentence to a judge of the Juvenile Court. The administration must draw up a file for juvenile prisoners, which includes any document relating to their case and the social and medical monitoring reports of their condition. This file must be made available to the juvenile judge before taking any decision concerning the execution of their sentence.

The Correctional System

The Egyptian criminal code enumerates a variety of punishments that apply to all crimes, including capital punishment and the deprivation of liberty, fines, and confiscation. Other punishments are provided for only as a subsidiary to an original punishment or as a main punishment for specific types of crimes, such as work for the public interest and the deprivation of certain civil and political rights, including the right to be a candidate for public posts or the right to vote, and the deprivation of certain professional rights, such as the suspension or cancellation of the license to practice certain professions, such as medicine or architecture. In general, the system of punishments in the Egyptian criminal justice system depends extensively on custodial sentences, yet some alternatives to detention are also provided for.

CUSTODIAL SENTENCES AND RIGHTS OF DETAINEES

In the Egyptian criminal justice system, there are four types of deprivation of liberty as a punishment, namely, aggravated prison, prison, imprisonment with work duties, and imprisonment without work duties. The differences among these types lie in the type of treatment that prisoners get and the place of their detention (EPC Articles 14–19).

The penitentiary system in Egypt is generally provided for by the law on the Organization of Prisons (Law No. 396–1956)—which is also called the Prison Code and which has been amended several times—in addition to some provisions of the EPC and the ECPC. The Prison Code contains the provisions determining the categories of penitentiary establishment and the general regulation of the life of prisoners within the institutions. Thus, it is considered the main source of Egyptian prison law. However, a large part of the body of Egyptian prison law depends on texts of a regulatory nature. In that regard, two regulations are of great importance: the internal regulations of prisons, which was promulgated in 1961 by Decision No. 79 of the minister of interior (Regulation No. 79–1961), and the Internal Regulations of Central Prisons, which was promulgated in 1971 (Regulation No. 1654–1971).

The general regulations of the prison administration grant several rights to prisoners. Article 38 of the Prison Code provides that "every convicted person has the right to correspondence." Detainees have the right to receive visits from their families and their lawyers. For personal visits, the number of visits to which detainees are entitled depends on the nature of their detention (Article 38 C. Prisons). For lawyers' visits, there is only one constraint: to obtain a prior written approval from the Public Prosecutor's Office. Otherwise, visits from detainees' lawyers are permitted at any time at the request of the lawyer or the detainee and subject to no quantitative restrictions and are not controlled in the same way that personal visits are (Article 39 C. Prisons). The right to receive proper health treatment is also granted in Article 33. Prisoners may be assigned to work under the condition that the prisoner shall be remunerated for such work (Article 22).

ALTERNATIVES TO CUSTODIAL SENTENCES

Several forms of adjustment to a custodial sentence exist in Egyptian law. On the one hand, there are forms that completely replace the execution of the sentence pronounced. On the other hand, there are forms that partially replace the full execution of the sentence. Egyptian law recognizes two forms of sentence adjustment that are considered to be substitutes for custodial sentences: suspended sentences and work for the public interest, or community service.

Egyptian law allows for the suspension of sentences for all crimes if the sentence does not exceed one year (EPC Articles 55–59). The suspension is at the discretion of the judge, who makes case-by-case decisions on the basis of an individual assessment. The judge must give reasons for the decision only if the judge decides to implement a suspension, but no obligation exists to justify the fact that the suspension is not granted. The suspension lasts for three years, at the end of which the judgment of conviction ipso facto loses all legal effect, and thus the sentence pronounced can no longer be executed, nor does it appear on the person's criminal record. However, the stay is revoked in two cases: first, if the person is sentenced during the suspended sentence to a period of imprisonment of at least one month for an act committed either before or after the agreement of the suspended sentence and, second, if it appears that the person was sentenced to a term of at least one month before the grant of the stay without the court's knowledge. In both cases, the suspension is revoked by a decision of the judge, and consequently the convicted person begins to serve the suspended sentence.

Unlike the suspension of custodial sentences, community service depends not on judges' decisions but on convicted persons themselves. ECPC Article 18 gives persons who are sentenced to imprisonment without work the right to request that their sentence be replaced by community service that is carried out outside the penitentiary establishment. Two conditions concerning the sentence must be met. First, the sentence must be imprisonment without work, so people who are sentenced to imprisonment with work do not have this option. Second, the length of the sentence imposed must not exceed six months.

After the beginning of the execution of a custodial sentence, two forms of early release are provided for in Egyptian criminal law: conditional release and medical release. Prison Code Article 52 deals in detail with the rules applicable to the conditional release of prisoners. The latter consists of releasing convicted persons before the end of the execution of their sentence on condition that certain limits be respected. Four conditions are required in order to grant a conditional release. The first depends on a temporal criterion. Detainees must have served half of the sentence imposed on them, with a minimum detention time of nine months regardless of the sentence. For those sentenced to life imprisonment, a period of at least twenty years must elapse. The second condition is related to inmate behavior during incarceration. Detainees' good behavior is essential. They must show signs of rehabilitation. This is decided on a case-by-case basis by the administration directory of the Ministry of Interior, which is responsible for the administration of prisons. The third condition is based on an assessment in abstracto of whether prisoners will be dangerous in the future. Detainees must not pose a threat to public safety. Once again, the discretion of the administration is wide. However, with regard to this condition, the prison administration is obliged to consider the opinion of the authorities who are responsible for public security before granting conditional release. The final condition concerns the financial obligations arising from the predicate offense. Prisoners may not be released if they have not paid the financial penalties imposed on them because of the offense for which they are detained. However, detainees may be exempted from this condition if they prove that they are unable to pay these fines.

Conditional release is granted by the director general of the Prison Department. The decision shall include the obligations that prisoners must assume after their release. It is often a question of respecting a social follow-up, of going regularly to checkpoints, or of avoiding frequenting certain places. Released persons remain under these obligations for the period that is left of their initial sentence. At the end of this period, the conditional release becomes final, and the person is considered free of any obligation. Release may be revoked when released persons do not comply with the obligations imposed on them before the release becomes final. In such cases, released persons return to serve the remainder of their sentence in the state where they were at the time of their release. The revocation of conditional release is done by the same granting authority, but it can be requested by the Public Prosecutor's Office.

Article 36 of the Prison Code allows for the release of convicted persons at any time because of the deterioration of their state of health. This measure applies when detainees suffer from a disease that threatens their life or that makes their state of health permanently incompatible with detention. In this case, two medical experts, the head of the medical department of prison management and a representative of legal medicine, must agree that the condition requires the prisoner's release. The decision is taken by the head of the Directorate of Prisons with the agreement of the Public Prosecutor's Office. Such release does not put an end to the relationship between convicted persons and the prison administration. A doctor from the administration must examine such inmates every six months to determine whether they can return to the institution to serve the remainder of their sentence.

Notes

1. Sadiz Reza, "Egypt," in *The Handbook of Comparative Criminal Law*, ed. Kevin Jon Heller and Markus D. Dubber (Stanford, CA: Stanford Law, 2011), 179.

2. Frederic M. Goadby, preface to *Commentary on Egyptian Criminal Law and Related Criminal Law of Palestine, Cyprus, and Iraq* (Cairo: Government Press, 1924).

3. The EPC has an unofficial translation in English as of 1999. See "Law No. 58 01: The Year 1937 Promulgating the Penal Code," International Labour Organization, accessed March 23, 2022, https://www .ilo .org/dyn/natlex/docs/ELECTRONIC/57560/111585/F1337119832/EGY57560.pdf.

4. George L. Kelling, William Francis Walsh, and Jean-Paul Brodeur, "The History of Policing in the West," *Britannica*, accessed March 23, 2022, https://www.britannica.com/topic/police/The-history-of-policing-in-the-West.

5. Egyptian Ministry of Interior, "About Ministry: The Establishment of the Ministerial System in Egypt," accessed March 23, 2022, https://moi.gov.eg/home/about.

6. Larry E. Sullivan and Maria R. Haberfeld, eds., *Encyclopedia of Law Enforcement*, vol. 3, *International Law Enforcement* (Thousand Oaks, CA: Sage, 2005).

7. Law No. 175 of 2020 amending the Police Authority Law; United Kingdom Home Office, *Country Information and Guidance—Egypt: Background Information, Including Actors of Protection and Internal Relocation*, May 2015, accessed March 23, 2022, https://www.refworld .org/docid/5564668d4.html; Mohamed Mahfouz, "On the Security Sector in Arab Countries in Transition: Toward Change; Case Study of the Security Sector in Egypt," Carnegie Endowment for International Peace, 2012, accessed March 23, 2022, https://carnegieendowment.org/files/Security_Sector_in_Egypt.pdf (in Arabic); Egypt's Interior Minister Decree No. 13507 of 2002 on the establishment of the Anti-Cybercrime Department; U.S. Department of State, "Narcotics Control Strategy Report," accessed March 23, 2022, https://2001-2009.state.gov/p/nea/ci/eg/74841.htm#:~:text=The%20ANGA%20is%20the%20oldest,cities%20and%20ports%20of%20entry; Helen Chapin Metz, ed., *Egypt: A Country Study* (Washington, DC: Library of Congress Federal Research Division, 1991), accessed March 23, 2022, https://tile .loc .gov/storage-services/master/frd/frdcstdy/eg/egyptcountrystud00metz/egyptcountrystud00metz.pdf.

8. United Kingdom Home Office, *Country Information and Guidance*.

9. Police Authority Law No. 109 of 1971; Police Academy Law No. 91 of 1975.

10. Gamel Abdelbaki Alsagheir, *Explaining the Criminal Procedure Code* (Dar El-Nahda El-Arabyia, 2015), 256 (in Arabic).

11. Ahmed Fathy Sorour, *Al Wasit in Criminal Procedure Law* (Dar El-Nahda El-Arabyia, 2016), 1319 (in Arabic).

12. EPC Article 10.

13. EPC Article 11.

14. EPC Article 12.

15. Article 121, Egyptian Child Law No. 12 of 1996.

CHAPTER 13

The Criminal Justice System of Iran

Sanaz Alasti

Iran was ruled by monastic dynasties for more than 2,500 years. Shiism became the official state religion under Safavid rule (1501–1722) and has been particularly influenced by the opinions of the sixth imam, Abu Abdullah Jafar bin Mohammad Sadegh. Iran's legal school of thought is known as Jafari jurisprudence. According to the Jafari school, sources of Islamic law are the Holy Quran, tradition (*hadith*), the consensus of the jurist (*ijma*), and reason (*'aql*). The increasing influence of foreign powers in the region under the Qajars (1795–1925) began with a series of capitulations to Europeans, beginning with the Russians, in the nineteenth century.[1] In 1906, the first Iranian Constitution was written. A series of laws was subsequently enacted relating to criminal, civil, commercial, and family law. The first Penal Code of Iran was ratified in 1926.[2]

Iran's secular criminal justice system was formed under the Pahlavi dynasty (1925–1979) and its two monarchs, Reza Shah (1925–1941) and Mohammad Reza Shah (Aryamehr; 1941–1979). Its modern criminal law is based on modern capitalist notions of crime and punishment. By 1936, Iranian legislation made secular education a requisite for serving judges.[3] The 1979 Islamic Revolution brought an end to Pahlavi dynasty. The Iranian Supreme Judicial Council issued a proclamation directing all courts that all non-Islamic legislation be suspended. The council revised all laws so that they would conform to an Islamic legal system, with Ayatollah Rohollah Mosavi Khomeini's *fatawa* serving as transitional laws. The punishment system in Iran is now based on the Twelve Imami Shii version of sharia law, which was formed in the early 1980s during the tenure of the Ayatollah Khomeini.[4] In Iran after the Islamic Revolution, the state's concept of justice derived from the religious principles of Islam, in which sharia—the general and particular rules of Islamic corpus juris—is not just a code of law but a code of conduct of behavior and ethics, an inseparable combination of law and morality.

Evidence of the relationship of the state to an Islamic concept of justice can be seen in the Penal Code of Iran. In 1983, the Statute of Retaliation and Prescribed Punishments was ratified. This statute allows capital punishment for crimes outlined in the Holy Quran and tradition. For other crimes, jurists still refer to the modern Penal Code of Iran. In 1984, the Discretionary Punishment Statute was ratified. Chapters 2 and 3 of the Islamic Penal Code, which were ratified in 1992, concern retaliation and prescribed punishments. Chapter 5 of the Islamic Penal Code was ratified in 1997.[5] The Islamic Penal Code provides the death penalty for more than fifteen crimes. Furthermore, Article 729 of the Islamic Penal Code abolishes all contrary statutes, including the modern Penal Code of Iran. Finally, in 2013, Iran ratified a new Islamic Penal Code with series of changes. The recent Islamic Penal Code of Iran has expanded the use of alternatives to imprisonment.

Policing and Law Enforcement in Iran

HISTORY OF THE IRANIAN POLICE

Iran's national police force was created in 1877. Its responsibilities include law enforcement, criminal investigations, border control, cooperation with international police, emergency services, maintaining law and order, and traffic control. The Iranian police developed into a modern force during the Pahlavi era. Iranian law enforcement consisted of two main forces: the urban police (*shahrbani*) and rural police (*gendarmerie*).[6] Mohammad Reza Shah Pahlavi (Aryamehr) was intensely concerned with matters of internal security, and in the post-1953 environment, he authorized the development of one of the most extensive systems of law enforcement agencies in the developing world.[7]

After the 1979 Iranian Revolution, the Islamic Republic began to implement Islamization as its main policy with respect to controlling society, which changed the nature of modern law enforcement of Iran. In 1990, Iran's Parliament passed legislation requiring the government to combine four Iranian law enforcement forces: the Islamic Revolutionary Committees, the urban police, the rural police, and the judicial police. Together, these forces formed a centralized police force in Iran, which became operational in April 1991. The new force—commonly referred to as Iran's national police, the Law Enforcement Force of the Islamic Republic of Iran, or the Disciplinary Force of the Islamic Republic of Iran (*niru-ye entezâmī-ye jomhūrī -ye eslâmī-ye īrân*) and abbreviated as NAJA—is the uniformed police force in Iran.[8]

LAW ENFORCEMENT TODAY

Per a decree issued by the commander in chief of the armed forces, the structure of law enforcement was promoted to that of a General Command in December 2021 and given a new name: the General Command of the Law Enforcement of Islamic Republic of Iran.[9] The contemporary police force of Iran is the General Command of the Law Enforcement of the Islamic Republic of Iran (*farmândehī-ye kol-e entezâmī-ye jomhūrī-ye eslâmī-ye īrân*).

One important aspect of modern police work is the multilayering of law enforcement. Like other military and security organizations, NAJA has different main agencies, each with specialized duties, as outlined in table 13.1.

Table 13.1. Iran's law enforcement agencies

Name of agency	*Name in Persian*	*Year established*	*Duties*
Prevention Police of NAJA	Polic-e Pishgiriyeh NAJA	2005	Crime prevention
Traffic Police of NAJA (RAHVAR)	Polis-e Rahezmaii-ye vâ Ranundgi-ye NAJA	1991	Oversee Traffic Guard and Highway Patrol
Cyber Police of NAJA (FATA)	Polis-e Fezai-ye Tulid-e vâ Tebadâl-e Atlâ'at-e Iran	2011	Stop and investigate cybercrimes
Anti-Narcotics Police of NAJA	Polis-e Mebarzh-e Ba Mivâd-e Mixedâr	1988	Combat drug smuggling and the illegal drug trade in Iran
Immigration and Passport Police of NAJA	Polic-e Mohajerat and Gozarnameh		Oversee immigration issues and issue passports for Iranian citizens
Diplomatic Police of NAJA	Polic-e Diplomatic	2000	Protect diplomatic missions in Iran
Criminal Investigation Police of NAJA	Police Āgāhi	1991	Criminal investigation
Border Guard Command of NAJA	Marzbani Iran	2000	Border control
Anti-Terror Special Unit (NOPO)	Farmandehi Yeganhaye Vijeh	1993	Suppress riots, provide urban defense, rescue hostages, and provide other antiterror services

Source: Website of the Iranian police (http://www.police.ir).

Each province has one police provincial command (*farmândehī-e nahieh-e entezâmī-e ostan*), which is under the control of the national police. The police provincial command controls all the police stations in that province. At a lower level, each city has one disciplinary district (*farmândehī-e nahieh-e entezam-e shahrestan*). At the lowest level, *kalantari* are police stations usually located in urban areas, and *pasgah* are police stations in rural areas.[10] Although the agencies of the NAJA have different duties, the police have four basic responsibilities, namely, to enforce laws, to provide services, to prevent crime, and to preserve the peace.

Iran's law enforcement is governed by its own regulations and is subject to the Law on the Use of Weapons by Armed Forces Officers in Necessary Cases. According to Article 157 of the Islamic Penal Code of Iran, "Resistance against police forces and other law enforcement officials whilst performing their duties shall not be considered a defense unless these forces exceed the scope of their duties and there is a legitimate fear that their actions may cause death or injury or violation of bodily integrity."

Although Iran's national police recruited Iranian women before the Islamic Revolution, in 1999, NAJA began to recruit Iranian women into the police forces for the first time since the revolution after Iran's Parliament approved an amendment of NAJA's charter in order to give NAJA permission to recruit and train Iranian women police. In 2003, some 400 women—the first since the revolution—became members of the police force,[11] and the number has been increased in recent years.

The Iranian Judicial System

The judiciary is an independent power from the executive and legislative branches in Iran. Articles 156 to 174 of the Constitution regulate the judiciary. The head of the judiciary is appointed by the Supreme Leader. He appoints the head of the Iranian court system, which consists of general- or specific-jurisdiction courts. The functions of the judiciary are to be performed by courts of justice, which are to be formed in accordance with the criteria of Islam and are vested with the authority to examine and settle lawsuits, protect the rights of the public, dispense and enact justice, and implement the Divine limits of Islamic law within the scope of Iran's Constitution.[12]

According to Article 156 of the Constitution, the judiciary has five groups of duties. The first group includes investigating and passing judgment on grievances, violations of rights, and complaints; resolving litigations; settling disputes; and addressing probate matters. The second group involves restoring public rights and promoting justice and legitimate freedoms. Third, the duty of the judiciary is to supervise the proper enforcement of laws. The fourth group of duties is to uncover crimes; to prosecute, punish, and chastise criminals; and to enact the penalties and provisions of the Islamic Penal Code. Finally, the fifth group of duties entails taking suitable measures to prevent the occurrence of crime and to reform criminals.

The Iranian courts are based on an inquisitorial system rather than an adversarial system. Common law countries such as the United States use an adversarial system in order to determine facts in the adjudication process. The prosecution and defense compete against each other, and the judge serves as a referee to ensure fairness to the accused. The inquisitorial system is associated with civil law legal systems, as in France. It has extensive pretrial investigations in order to avoid bringing an innocent person to trial. The inquisitorial process grants more power to the judge, whereas the judge in the adversarial system serves more as an arbiter.[13]

COURTS OF GENERAL AND SPECIFIC JURISDICTION

Before any court can hear a case, it must have jurisdiction over the persons involved in the case or its subject matter. General courts have the jurisdiction to hear all cases except those within the jurisdiction of a specific court. The general courts consist of Trial Courts and Courts of Appeal, which are themselves divided into civil and criminal courts. Almost every case begins in a Trial Court. Special courts deal with specific types of crimes, victims, and perpetrators. For example, the Revolutionary Courts deal with special types of crime, and the Clergy Court is for specific perpetrators and victims.

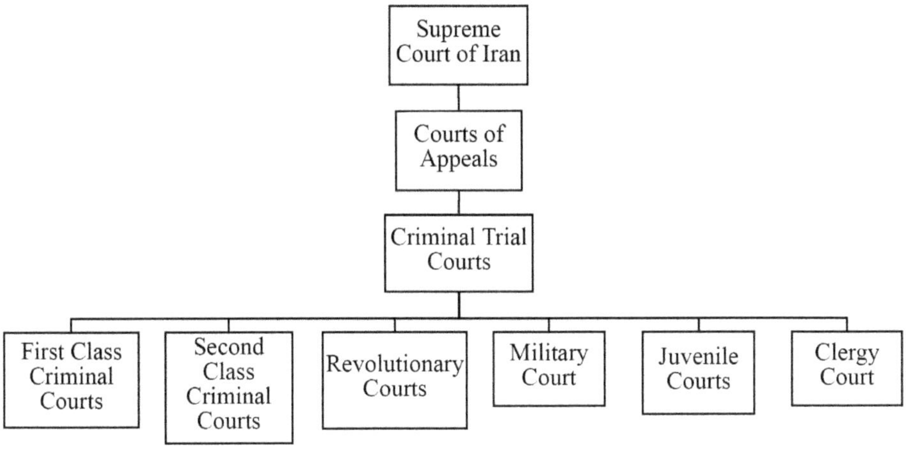

Figure 13.1. Organization of Iranian Court System. *Source:* Sanaz Alasti

TRIAL AND APPELLATE IRANIAN COURTS

Iran has a three-tiered court system. The Supreme Court is the highest judicial authority. The Courts of Appeal are the second-instance courts, and these courts review cases decided by public (civil or criminal) and Revolutionary Courts. The general courts have jurisdiction to be first-instance tribunals. Figure 13.1 summarizes the structure of the court system.

CRIMINAL TRIAL COURTS

The new Criminal Procedure Code, passed in 2014, reflects the most recent changes in the Iranian criminal court system. Criminal courts have jurisdiction over criminal cases. These courts consist of First Class Criminal Courts, Second Class Criminal Courts, Revolutionary Courts, Juvenile Courts, Military Courts, and Clergy Courts.[14]

First Class Criminal Courts

First Class Criminal Courts have jurisdiction to hear capital cases, life imprisonment, amputation of body parts, body injuries when more than at least half of *diya* (blood money)[15] is required, imprisonment of more than ten years, fines of more than 360 million rials, armed rebellion (*baghi*),[16] and press crimes.[17] Three judges sit in First Class Criminal Courts, whose geographic jurisdiction is provincial.

Second Class Criminal Courts

Second Class Criminal Courts have general jurisdiction to hear all cases except cases within jurisdiction of special courts and First Class Criminal Courts. Only one judge sits in Second Class Criminal Courts, which are based in counties.[18]

Revolutionary Courts (Dadgah Enghilab)

Revolutionary Courts have jurisdiction to hear all cases related to crimes against national and international security, armed robbery (*moharebeh*),[19] armed rebellion against the Islamic Republic of Iran (*baghi*), corruption on Earth crimes (*ifsad-i fi-l-arz*),[20] conspiracy against the Islamic Republic of Iran, and other activities against the Islamic Republic of Iran. Their jurisdiction also includes the crime of insulting Ayatollah Rohollah Khomeini and the Supreme Leader. Additionally, the Revolutionary Courts handle all smuggling and drug-related crimes as well as other cases that special legislation designates it to be the court with jurisdiction. The Revolutionary Courts have three judges for capital cases, life imprisonment, the amputation of body parts, and bodily injuries when more than at least half of *diya* (blood money) is required. In other cases, the court has only one judge.[21]

Juvenile Courts

Juvenile Courts have jurisdiction over cases against those who have not attained their eighteenth birthday. If a defendant turns eighteen years old during trial, then the Juvenile Court continues the trial. However, if the defendant turns eighteen years old before the trial starts, then the case is referred to a criminal court within the jurisdiction. In this case, the defendant still benefits from the privileges of a trial in Juvenile Courts.[22] According to Article 298 of the 2014 Criminal Procedure Act, Juvenile Courts have a judge and two social workers. Juvenile Courts are based in counties, and the number of branches in each county varies.

Military Courts

Military Courts hear cases against military and police forces if the crime is related to their duties or happened when they were on duty.[23]

Clergy Courts

The Clergy Courts (Dadgah-ha-yi Viji-yi Ruhaniat) hear all criminal cases against members of the clergy (Islamic jurists).[24] The Trial Courts' decisions—as opposed to the Supreme Court's and Administrative Court's authoritative decisions as for future cases—do not have any precedential value and are not usually codified or documented for future reference by other courts.

IRANIAN COURTS OF APPEAL

According to Article 426 of the 2014 Criminal Procedure Act, the Courts of Appeal are located in each province. A party aggrieved by the decision of a civil or criminal Trial Court has the right to appeal the decision to a Court of Appeal. The primary function of a Court of Appeal is to review the decision of a Trial Court.

SUPREME COURT OF IRAN

The Supreme Court, which is located in Tehran, is the highest Court of Appeal of both civil and criminal cases.[25] Each branch has three judges. The judges must have at least ten years of experience as a judge or lawyer, or they must be an Islamic scholar or have studied Islamic jurisprudence in a seminary for ten years. The Supreme Court has the jurisdiction to grant a motion to reopen closed criminal cases.[26] As a Courts of Appeal, the Supreme Court does not issue substantive decisions. It only reviews cases with regard to the application and interpretation of law. It then sends appeal cases to a lower court to review the facts and the laws in order for the lower court to issue a new decision. If the lower court issues the same decision and the defendant appeals again, the case would be referred to the Supreme Court General Council, which hears cases regarding the conflict of interpretation of civil or criminal laws by lower courts. The interpretation of the Supreme Court General Council has precedential value and can be overruled only by another decision by the Supreme Court General Council or subsequent statutory law.[27]

Crime and Punishment in Iran

CATEGORIES OF CRIME IN THE ISLAMIC CRIMINAL JUSTICE SYSTEM OF IRAN

The contemporary Islamic criminal justice system of Iran categorizes crimes and punishments according to the provenance of the authority to punish the offense. The Islamic Penal Code of Iran recognizes four systems or categories for crimes and punishments: prescribed punishments (*hadd* or *hodoud*), retaliation (*qisas*), blood money (*diyat*), and discretionary punishments (*taazir*).

Prescribed Punishments (Hadd or Hodoud)

Under *hadd* or *hodoud*, important crimes deemed to threaten the existence of Islam are punishable by penalties set by the Holy Quran and by the Sunna or Sunnah (the tradition of the Prophet Mohammad). Islamic jurists consider these sanctions to be immutable, and therefore judges have no discretion in their rulings on them.

High standards of proof required for conviction indicate that the application of the *hodoud* penalties can be curtailed in practice. Although confessions are generally binding proof of guilt, a confession involving a *hadd* offense may be withdrawn. It is incumbent on the judge to recommend this option to the confessor. Increasing procedural safeguards is another way to limit the imposition of these punishments when there is a fixed penalty for conviction. To be admitted into evidence, witnesses must meet strict requirements. Witnesses must possess the characteristics required for full legal capacity: they must be sane, be of legal age, and be fully responsible for themselves. According to the Penal Code of Iran, witnesses must also be of "good character" (*adl*); that is, they must not have committed "grave sins and must not persevere in small ones."[28] Limitations on the admissibility of witnesses may serve to increase the difficulty of obtaining a conviction leading to capital crimes in Iran.

Similar restrictions apply to the admissibility of confessions. For example, punishment for armed robbery (*moharebeh*) finds authority in the Holy Quran: "Punishment of those who wage war against God and His Messenger, and strive with might and main for mischief through the land is: execution, crucifixion, cutting off of the offender's hand and foot from opposite sides, or exile: These punishments represent disgrace in the world, and a heavy punishment; except for offenders who repent disgrace is: in the cases where offenders repent Allah is Oft-Forgiving, Most Merciful" (Holy Quran 5:33–34). Because the crime of armed robbery is serious, an array of punishments is authorized by God, sometimes in an indifferent manner. The values of Islamic law support the imposition of punishment that is proportionate to the harm caused. When the armed robbery does not cause the death of the victim, a strong Islamic legal tradition prohibits execution. In contrast, in cases of *moharebeh*, in which the victim's death results, with or without the successful dispossession of property, the penalty is generally death.[29]

Furthering the tradition of juristic reluctance to facilitate the imposition of *hodoud* penalties, some contemporary Iranian jurists argue that *hodoud* punishments may not be inflicted absent the establishment of a "true" Islamic society. Basic human needs must first be met, including the provision of adequate food, shelter, medical care, and employment.[30] Careful parsing of offenses is proof of the desire to make the punishment proportionate to the crime and has the effect of limiting the use of harsh punishments despite the apparent discretion given by the text.[31]

Retaliation (Qisas)

Retaliation is prescribed for offenses that are proscribed by the Holy Quran and Sunnah of the Prophet, but they are subject of private right, not public right. Retaliation applies to crimes against persons, such as murder, and crimes against the body (i.e., injury), and prescriptions related to retaliation distinguish between degrees of intent. The fundamental premise is lex talionis—the tenet of "eye for eye, tooth for tooth," which first appeared in the Code of Hammurabi. It was a progressive penal reform, at that time aimed at enhancing the principle of proportionality. It is now seen as a basis for retribution. Lex talionis is set out in the Holy Quran 5:32 and is further developed in 17:33. According to the Holy Quran, victims or their heirs are to inflict the punishment under the supervision of public authorities.

In cases of intentional murder, Iran permits the death penalty as a right of the individual (i.e., the victim's family), not of the state. Concepts of forgiveness and brotherly love in reaction to the harm caused are the preferable recourses. Judges in these cases are reminded to fulfill the letter, spirit, and values that God's law has revealed. The Quranic verses do not seem to require a nuanced inquiry into the circumstances of the murder before permitting the imposition of *qisas*. The Iranian criminal justice system requires proof of the specific intent of the murderer. It also grants certain family members the right to override *qisas* by accepting *diyat* or other compensation in lieu of the murderer's death. Additionally, the status of the victim and the murderer must also be considered.[32]

Restraints on the imposition of *qisas* are still relevant to contemporary society.[33] In examining the status of the murderer and the victim, for example, the Iranian criminal justice system considers both gender and religion.[34] Twelver Shiism contends that since the *diya* for a woman is only half that of a man's, in order for a woman victim's family to pursue *qisas* against her male assassin, the victim's family must make up the difference in the blood price.[35]

Blood Money (Diyat) and Prescribed Punishments (Taazir)

Diyat consist of prescribed restitution or compensation for victims, while *taazir* means that public authorities set their own punishment, for which the judge has wide discretion. For example, under the *taazir*, public authorities may provide for capital punishment, but no religious text requires them to do so.

CATEGORIES OF PUNISHMENT IN THE ISLAMIC CRIMINAL JUSTICE SYSTEM OF IRAN

Death Penalty

Based on Iran's Penal Code before the Islamic Revolution, in addition to murder, the death penalty was used to punish drug trafficking and offenses against public securities. In the former Penal Code of Iran, the death penalty was applied for specific crimes. After the Islamic Revolution, the application of the death penalty was expanded. The death penalty in Iran is applicable to an overly broad range of crimes in addition to murder, including incest, rape, sex between a non-Muslim and a Muslim female, adultery, sodomy, other homosexual acts after a fourth conviction, drinking liquor after three convictions, drawing arms to create fear, defamation to what is holy, drug trafficking in special amounts, corruption on Earth, fornication on a fourth conviction, false accusation of unlawful intercourse on a fourth conviction, and *hadd* theft.[36]

Under the Iranian criminal justice system, execution may be conducted in public to enhance its alleged effect of general deterrence. There is no open indication regarding public execution in the penal system of Iran. Public hangings are normally carried out sparingly in Iran and reserved for cases that have provoked public outrage, such as serial murders or child killings. Based on the regulation regarding the execution methods of retaliation sentences, "if the presence of viewers or other people during the execution is not advisable, with district attorney instruction, police may prevent the public from the execution scene."[37]

Corporal Punishments

Corporal punishment is the punishment of body. It is defined as physical punishment as distinguished from pecuniary punishment or a fine or any kind of punishment of or inflicted on the body.[38] Following the reign of the Pahlavi monarchs, flogging was

Table 13.2. Flogging in the Islamic Penal Code of Iran

Sexual offenses	*Personal offenses*	*Property offenses*	*Offenses against public morals*	*Offenses against society*
Fornication	Libel	Theft	Marrying a married woman	Escaping from prison
Sodomy with an underage person	Defamation	Forgery	Selling alcoholic beverages	Publishing false statements
Lesbianism	Stabbing	Usury	Gambling	Evidence tampering
Pederasty	Malicious harassment	Destroying government property	Drinking wine	Endangering public safety
Public display of affection	Harassing women	Bribery		
Conducting immoral business		Coercion		
Making false accusations of unlawful intercourse		Unlawfully possessing government property		

Source: Sanaz Alasti.

imposed for three crimes. Based on modern Iran's Penal Code, the only applicable corporal punishment was flogging for knife stabbing,[39] vagrancy,[40] and gaining ownership of another person's property.[41] In 1966, Iran's Parliament ratified the Abolition of Flogging Statute, and flogging was abolished in Iran in 1966.[42] However, with Islamic government approval, flogging is now permitted in Iran for various crimes, as indicated in table 13.2.

Criminalization of Status Crimes

Offenses have traditionally defined in terms of acts or failure to act.[43] Despite the general rule that in order to be considered a crime an act must be one that is prohibited or recognized as a failure to act, certain atypical offenses are defined in terms of personal status or condition of being rather than in terms of the acts committed—for example, being a vagrant, prostitute, drunkard, gambler, beggar, narcotics addict, or homosexual. The more recent tendency in the law is to hold people criminally culpable only for specific acts.[44] For example, in Iran, drug addiction as a status has been considered a crime. In Iran, first-time offenses for drug addicts carry a sentence from 500,000 rials to 1 million rials and four to twelve months of imprisonment. A second offense is punishable with a cash fine of 1 million rials to 4 million rials and one to three years of imprisonment. For government employees, the sentences are harsher: in addition to the cash fine and imprisonment, they shall be permanently dismissed from government office. The sentence is multiplied for the third and any other subsequent offense: it increases the second offense by two- to fourfold plus fifty lashes. The same punishments apply to offenders who are offered treatment in rehabilitation centers.[45]

Also, unlike in the United States, vagrancy is punishable in Iran. There is no implicit definition for what constitutes vagrancy in Iran. In the United States, some jurisdictions have repealed such traditional statutes in favor of laws prohibiting specific conduct and making no use of the term "vagrancy" or "vagrant." However, the mere fact that a statute prohibits specific conduct and eschews the terms "vagrancy" and "vagrant" does not make it proof against a challenge on vagueness grounds. In addition to the death penalty and corporal punishments such as flogging and body mutilation, the contemporary Iranian criminal justice system also provides for imprisonment, fines, *diya* (blood money restitution to victims), probation and parole, and community service.

Corrections in Iran

EARLY IRANIAN PRISONS

The first administrative code regarding prisons was approved in 1919. This code was drafted by Swedish advisers who were invited to Iran in 1912 to organize Iran's police force and to modernize prisons after the Constitutional Revolution in Iran. After 1926, prison conditions improved, and facilities were modernized. Ghasr Prison, the first large, centralized penitentiary in Iran, was erected in Tehran in 1929 as part of a much larger effort to modernize and centralize imprisonment in Iran.[46]

During the reign of Mohammad Reza Shah Pahlavi (Aryamehr) in the 1960s and 1970s, attempts were made to further modernize and reform the prison system in Iran. For the first time, a rehabilitation approach was adopted that allowed prisoners to learn different skills and attend educational training. During this era, a number of minimum-security, or "open," prisons were established that allowed prisoners the liberty to work outside the prisons contingent on their return to confinement at night. In these prisons, inmates were not supervised systematically and were not obliged to wear prison uniforms.[47] For example, Qezel Hesar Prison, which housed more than 1,000 inmates outside Tehran, was considered the model for this rehabilitative approach.

In 1975, the administrative code governing prisons was promulgated. In the modern Iranian correction system, recidivists were kept apart from other offenders, juveniles between the ages of fifteen and eighteen were segregated from adults, and prisoners younger than thirty years old were required to participate in educational and vocational training offered in prison. During this era, the focus was placed on preparing prisoners for release through a variety of training programs that ranged from teaching handicrafts and mechanical skills to training in art and sculpture.[48]

POSTREVOLUTIONARY ERA

Although imprisonment existed in sharia law in the second, sixth, and eighteenth centuries, the main use of imprisonment was for pretrial detention and administrative detention, especially imprisonment for debt. Thus, punitive detention did not have the same status in premodern sharia law that it does in modern law.[49]

In the 1980s, prison conditions rapidly deteriorated. According to human rights reports, facilities were overcrowded with political prisoners. After the 1980s, the rehabilitative approach of the secular government was replaced with a punitive system. In 1982, a new administrative code was adopted that made changes to the administration of prisons in Iran and put prisons under the control of the Prisons and Security and Corrective Measures Managerial Council. The daily schedule of prisoners remained almost the same as under the previous code, but more emphasis was placed on religious activities. In early 1986, the Iranian Parliament passed a law that replaced the Prisons and Security and Corrective Measures Managerial Council with the State Prisons and Security and Corrective Measures Organization.

THE CONTEMPORARY ERA

Iran's prisons organization operate under the judiciary. The latest administrative code governing prisons was adopted in 2005. This regulatory code has six classifications for places in which prisoners are to be held: detention centers, admission centers, closed prisons, semi-closed prisons, open prisons, affiliated industrial and agricultural institutions, and juvenile correctional facilities. As of December 2021, Iranian prisons contained 189,000 prisoners, a ratio of 228 per 100,000 Iranian people. Although the prison population rate was substantially low until 1980, it increased in the 1990s and in 2011 reached its highest rate of 331 per 100,000 Iranians. Iran has the tenth-highest incarceration rate of all countries. Pretrial detainees are 25.1 percent of the prison population in Iran, and prison facilities are still overcrowded, with an official capacity of 150,000 as of December 2018. The high percentage of male prisoners, who make up more than 95 percent of prisoners, represents to some extent the higher percentage of the adult male population.[50]

According to Iran's Prisons Organizations website, the State Prisons and Security and Corrective Measures Organization includes 253 establishments throughout the country. In recent years, the Iranian criminal justice system has used a number of different approaches to reform the system. These include adopting new criminal policies and revising both prison and penal codes, limiting the use of pretrial detention, creating more alternatives to imprisonment, and adding more rehabilitation programs. Prison conditions have improved but are still poor, and the majority of inmates are imprisoned because of drug-related offenses.[51]

The most infamous of Iran's institutions is Evin Prison. Located northwest of Tehran, the prison was ordered to be built by Mohammad Reza Shah Pahlavi (Aryamehr), and it was completed in 1972. According to historian Ervand Abrahamian, no prisoner has ever successfully escaped from Evin. Most cells have only one tiny window above the eye level of most inmates. Evin has several wards, including a quarantine ward and separate wards for women and for clergy. Solitary confinement cells lack natural light, and artificial light is on twenty-four hours a day, exacerbating the psychological pressure of solitary confinement. Several prisoners described the small, solitary cells as resembling coffins.[52] Rajaei-Shahr Prison, also referred to Gohardasht, is located in Aseman Town, north of Karaj. Construction of the new Gohardasht Prison started before the Islamic Revolution. It has hundreds of solitary confinement cells and large wards housing more than 8,000 inmates. The prison contains eight wards in each of its three halls. Mentally ill inmates are held in a separate ward. Hall 10 of Ward 4 holds prisoners who are alleged to have links to Sunni extremist terrorist groups, including al-Qaeda. In Ward 8, prisoners are kept in solitary confinement, and the most dangerous inmates are kept in the quarantine ward. Qezel Hesar Prison in Karaj has the highest number of prisoners in Iran, and the number of prisoners held there is reportedly three times its capacity. Most inmates are held for drug-related charges.[53]

PRISON SECURITY LEVELS

Three types of prisons are found in the Iranian corrections system. Based on Article 6 of Iran's Administrative Code on Prisons and Security and Corrective Measures, maximum-security, or closed, prison facilities provide the highest level of prison security. Prisoners spend the night in individual or group cells and work together during the day. These units hold those considered to be the most dangerous inmates, including serial killers and inmates who have committed assaults, murders, or other serious violations while incarcerated within less secure facilities. Medium-security, or half-open, facilities are less restrictive: prisoners spend more time together, and the guards do not carry weapons in these prisons. Minimum-security, or open, prisons generally have no fences and are not patrolled by armed guards. Prisoners here may often work on community projects. Based on Article 10 of Iran's Administrative Code on Prisons and Security and Corrective Measures, prisoners in minimum-security facilities are considered to pose little physical risk to the public and are nonviolent. Minimum-security prisoners live in less secure dormitories that are regularly patrolled by correctional officers.

DETENTION CONDITIONS AND TREATMENT OF PRISONERS

Prison conditions in Iran have not changed much. Article 32 of Iran's Constitution states that

> no person may be arrested except according to and in the manner laid down in the law. If someone is detained, the subject matter of the charge, with reasons (for bringing it), must immediately be communicated and explained in writing to the accused. Within at most 24 hours, the file on the case and any preliminary documentation must be referred to the competent legal authority. Legal procedures must be initiated as early as possible.

Article 32 goes on to say that any violation of this principle will be punished in accordance with the law, but pretrial detention can last for months. According to the Institute for Criminal Policy Research, pretrial detainees made up 25.1 percent of the prison population in December 2014.[54]

Those imprisoned often lack access to legal counsel before the trial and are held for weeks without being charged with any crime. Iran, as a party to the Universal Declaration of Human Rights and a signatory of the International Covenant on Civil and Political Rights, is committed to respecting international instruments regarding prisoners' rights. The use of solitary confinement and physical and psychological torture violates international law, and the prohibition of torture is a part of customary international law.

PRISON OVERCROWDING

One of the most difficult challenges faced by the Iranian prison system is overcrowding, which is caused mainly by the large number of prisoners who have been apprehended for drug-related offenses. In 1978, when Iran's total population was less than half of what it is today, there were only 11,000 prisoners in the entire country. In 1979, the national prison population rate was forty-eight incarcerated out of 100,000 individuals, compared to the most recent estimate of 228 out of 100,000. In Rajaei-Shahr Prison, overcrowding presents several major problems for prisoners. In 2010, it was reported that between ninety and 180 prisoners slept in hallways because of overcrowding. Overcrowding leads to housing political prisoners in cells with violent criminals, including those convicted of theft, drug trafficking, and murder. Moreover, overcrowding meant that prisoners were granted limited access to overburdened medical facilities.[55]

DAILY ROUTINES

Although the daily routine may vary from one institution to another, prisoners are generally entitled to have breakfast, lunch, and dinner every day. Based on Iran's Administrative Code on Prisons and Security and Corrective Measures, prisoners are also entitled to have access to potable water. The minimum diet for inmates includes tea for breakfast, lunch, and dinner as well as bread, cheese, fresh or dried vegetables, rice, potatoes, onions, legumes, dairy products, eggs, and seasonal fruit. In addition, prisoners are entitled to three meals containing meat every week. Prisoners may purchase additional items from the prison shop. Every convict is entitled to a bed, a mattress, a pillow, two blankets, and sheets. Although these routines have been promised in Iran's Administrative Code on Prisons and Security and Corrective Measures, these regulations are routinely violated in prisons across Iran.

Article 102 of Iran's Administrative Code on Prisons and Security and Corrective Measures requires prison infirmaries to conduct checkups on each prisoner at least once a month. The 2005 Prisons Regulations require the Categorization Council to evaluate prisoners and to make recommendations regarding their training. Illiterate inmates under the age of sixty are required to attend educational classes. The Prisons Organization is also required to provide prisoners with the opportunity to continue their education at primary, secondary, and university levels.

Article 181 of the 2005 Administrative Code on Prisons and Security and Corrective Measures states that a prisoner's spouse, parents, siblings, children, and parents-in-law have the right to visit the prisoner once a week. A visit should last a minimum of twenty minutes. The visits usually take place at booths, and the visitor and the prisoner speak through a phone while sitting on different sides of a glass partition. Prisoners who show good behavior may be eligible for in-person visits from family members.

Prisoners may also be granted a furlough for family or medical emergencies if the individual suffers from a serious illness. Some prisoners, including those convicted of national security crimes, are not eligible for furlough, and only the prosecutor or the chief judge of the judicial district may grant a furlough to these classes of prisoners. Before 2010, furlough was effectively treated as a right for most prisoners, but the new amendments redefined furlough as a privilege that is available to them through a point system. Prisoners who accumulate at least 200 points are eligible for furlough. This system encourages and rewards rehabilitation, shortens sentences, and discourages rule breaking in prisons.

ALTERNATIVES TO IMPRISONMENT

The use of alternatives to incarceration or noncustodial measures is a major part of the United Nations Office on Drugs and Crime's integrated and multidisciplinary approach to prison reform, which takes full account of the need to relate prison reform to broader criminal justice reform. It is also an area that witnessed significant developments at the national level with the entry of the new Iranian Penal Code, which includes a chapter on alternatives to imprisonment (Chapter 9) in April 2013 and the issuance of important instructions by the head of the judiciary for "criminal depopulation of prisons" in May 2013.[56]

The recent Islamic Penal Code of Iran has expanded the use of alternatives to imprisonment. According to Article 66 of the new Iranian Penal Code, if the prisoner has been sentenced to ninety-one days to six months of imprisonment, the alternative to imprisonment will be imposed. Although traditional noncustodial punishments such as parole, fines, and probation have been a part of the Iranian criminal justice system for a long time, the use of these alternatives has been expanded, and nontraditional alternatives, such as daily fines, supervised probation, home confinement, and community service, have been added to the Iranian corrections system.

Juvenile Justice

The age of criminal responsibility was eighteen under the former Penal Code of Iran. The establishment of the Iranian juvenile court goes back to 1959. The Iranian Civil

Code, following the Shiite school, states that "in Iranian law, childhood is attributed to a person who has not reached puberty age." Under Article 1210–1, "a girl achieves puberty after nine lunar years and a boy after completing fifteen lunar years." For example, under the Iranian criminal justice system, if a ten-year-old girl murders someone, then she will be tried and punished in the same way a forty-year-old woman is tried and penalized. Thus, under the Islamic Penal Code of Iran, it is permissible to issue a death sentence for a female juvenile who has reached nine years old.

Under Iranian law, there are three stages for childhood in Iran: birth to six years old, six years old to puberty, and from puberty on. In the first stage, children are not to be punished on criminal grounds or subjected to disciplinary or reformatory measures. Offenders in the second stage are subject to disciplinary actions. Those who are in the third stage are subject to the full extent of criminal law and punishment.[57] Based on the Shiite school, the criminal responsibility age starts at puberty. As the sign of puberty is nocturnal emissions, an adolescent boy's coming of age is signified by potency to impregnate. Similarly, a girl's puberty is signified by menstruation, nocturnal pollution, and pregnancy. Since signs of puberty vary and may appear in advance or be delayed, it has been deemed necessary to fix the age limits.

There is no special age for puberty based on the Holy Quran, and there are different views about puberty age in tradition. Islamic jurists are not united in their opinion. The majority of Shiite jurists believe that the age of puberty is nine years for girls and fifteen years for boys. Some jurists argue that puberty age is for praying obligations, not for penal obligations. Therefore, Iran needs puberty age plus maturity age for purposes of criminal responsibility. Maturity can be set at different ages according to conditions of the time. It is based on criminal perception. Some jurists build on Imam Jafar, saying that childhood can be divided into three seven-year periods, and conclude that childhood ends at the age of twenty-one.[58]

There are several instances in which the end of childhood is not puberty in Iranian law. For example, in Iran, marriage age is equivalent to puberty, and jurisdictional age under juvenile court is eighteen, but it is not mandatory to establish Juvenile Court in each jurisdiction, and judges can apply mitigation factors for *taazir* punishments. A court must determine whether a girl over nine or a boy over fifteen has achieved the age of maturity. Islamic law does not prohibit the increasing of lawful maturity age.[59]

In election law, sixteen is the age of responsibility, whereas for labor law, the age is fifteen, and for financial transactions, the age is eighteen. However, a person who has not reached the age of eighteen can perform financial transactions after receiving a verdict from the court.

Although in practice no child under the age of thirteen has been executed, the law allowing for such executions remains and can be imposed. The Islamic Penal Code outlaws the execution of certain offenders under the age of eighteen, but it does not apply in the case of murder (*qisas*) and prescribed punishments (*hodoud*). Article 91 of the new Islamic Penal Code of Iran clearly states that juveniles may be sentenced to death if they "understood" the crime that they committed. However, the wording is vague and calls for a suspension of the death penalty for cases in which the court proves the rationale and where adolescence is ascertained.

According to the directive issued by Ayatollah Mahmoud Hashemi-Shahrudi, head of Iran's judiciary, judges cannot issue death sentences for juveniles. If a Trial Court judge imposes a death sentence on a juvenile, it will be reversed in the Supreme Court. All death sentences must be upheld by the Iranian Supreme Court before they can be implemented.

Notes

1. Hassan Amin, *The History of Law in Iran* (Tehran: Encyclopedia of Iran, 2004), 12.
2. Sanaz Alasti and Eric Bronson, "Crime and Punishment in Iran (Islamic Republic of)," in *The Encyclopedia of Crime and Punishment* (New York: Wiley-Blackwell, 2015), 1–5.
3. Sanaz Alasti, *Cruel and Unusual Punishment: Comparative Perspective in International Conventions, the United States and Iran* (Heathrow, FL: Vandeplas, 2008), 57.
4. Alasti, *Cruel*, 58.
5. It was developed to deal with discretionary and preventive punishments. Iraj Goldouzian, *Special Criminal Law* (Tehran: Mizan, 1999), 17 (in Farsi).
6. Saeid Golkar, "The Evolution of Iran's Police Forces and Social Control in the Islamic Republic," *Middle East Brief* 120, no. 3 (2018): 1–9.
7. Iranian Law Enforcement, https://www.globalsecurity.org/intell/world/iran/naja.htm. This law enforcement agency was one of the largest and oldest police forces in the Middle East. Its central aims were to provide protection to Iranian citizens, to enforce the law, to investigate suspicious activities, to maintain law and order, and to arrest suspects accused of committing a crime.
8. Iranian Law Enforcement, https://www.globalsecurity.org/intell/world/iran/naja.htm.
9. Decree of General Command of the Law Enforcement of Islamic Republic of Iran, https://www .tasnimnews .com/fa/news/1400/09/17/2622437/رونمایی-از-طرح-سازمان-فرماندهی-انتظامی-جمهوری-اسلامی-ایران.
10. Amir Nouri, Abdallah Pymani Asel, and Saeid Kashfai, "The Ideal Structure of Police Stations for Dealing with Juvenile Delinquency," *Quarterly Crime Prevention Studies* 6, no. 19 (Summer 2011): 96 (in Farsi).
11. "Women Police in Iran," http://isfahan.irib.ir/-/پلیس-زن-در-ایران; "Country Profile: Iran," https://www.refworld.org/publisher,USLC,,IRN,4950afce2,0.html, May 2008, accessed October 22, 2014.
12. Constitution of Iran, Art. 61 (1979) (in Farsi).
13. Harry R. Dammer and Jay S. Albanese, *Comparative Criminal Justice Systems* (Boston: Cengage Learning, 2013).
14. Criminal Procedure Act of Iran, Art. 294 (2014) (in Farsi).
15. The head of the judiciary has set the amount of full *diya* at 4.8 trillion rials for the Iranian year 1400 (March 21, 2021, to March 20, 2022). Under the Islamic rules, *diya* (also spelled as *diyah*, *diyeh*, and *deyeh* and as *diyat* in the plural form) is the financial compensation paid to the victim or the heir(s) in cases of bodily harm or death.
16. *Baghi* is a political and security crime and is of particular importance in that it is against the security of the state.
17. Criminal Procedure Act of Iran, Art. 302.
18. Criminal Procedure Act of Iran, Arts. 295, 296, 201, 302.
19. *Moharebeh* (resorting to arms to frighten people) is defined as an act of robbery by a group of armed men within the territory of the Islamic state that creates anarchy and violates

the property, privacy, safety, dignity, and religious values of the people. The crime is regarded as a war against God and his messenger.

20. Under the Islamic Penal Code of Iran, the definition of corruption on Earth crimes is vague. Corruption on Earth crimes are not a crime per se. They can be attributed to crimes that include waging war against the Prophet and God, setting a mosque ablaze, destruction of state property during an internal rebellion, and any criticism of the state (i.e., crimes against public order).

21. Criminal Procedure Act of Iran, Arts. 303, 297.

22. Criminal Procedure Act of Iran, Art. 304. The offenders under eighteen may be subject only to resocialization measures. Other benefits include the selection of professionally competent judges, the mandatory participation of juvenile experts, and lighter sentences.

23. Criminal Procedure Act of Iran, Art. 307.

24. See Act Establishing Clergies Courts (*Qānūn-i tashkīl-i dādsarāhā wa dādgāh-hāi wīji ruhānīat*) (1990).

25. Criminal Procedure Act; see Arts. 462–473.

26. Criminal Procedure Act; see Arts. 462–473.

27. Criminal Procedure Act; see Arts. 462–473.

28. Joseph Schacht, *An Introduction to Islamic Law* (Westport, CT: Greenwood, 1964), 124–25.

29. Alasti, *Cruel*, 69–70.

30. Safia Safwat, "Offences and Penalties in Islamic Law," *Islamic Quarterly* 26 (1982): 149–54.

31. Alasti, *Cruel*, 156.

32. Alasti, *Cruel*, 156–57.

33. J. N. D. Anderson, "Homicide in Iran," *Bulletin of the School of Oriental and African Studies* 13 no. 4 (1951): 811, 815.

34. Ahmed I. Ali, "Compensation in Intentional Homicide in Islamic Law," *Journal of Islamic and Comparative Law* 9 (1980): 39, 45.

35. Anderson, "Homicide," 811, 815.

36. Islamic Penal Code of Iran (2013).

37. Alasti and Bronson, "Crime," 1–5.

38. Steven Hatfield, "Criminal Punishment in America: From the Colonial to the Modern Era," *USAFA Journal of Legal Studies* 1 (1990): 139.

39. General Penal Code of Iran, Art. 173 (1923) (in Farsi).

40. General Penal Code of Iran, Art. 273.

41. Statute Regarding the Transferring of Property, Art. 3 (1923) (in Farsi).

42. Abolition of Flogging Statute, Single Clause (1966) (in Farsi).

43. Forrest Lacey, "Vagrancy and Other Crimes of Personal Condition," *Harvard Law Review* 66, no. 7 (1953): 1203–1226.

44. *American Jurisprudence*, 2nd ed., vol. 21, *Criminal Laws* (Toronto: Thomson West, 2005), 31.

45. Anti Narcotic Drugs Statute, Arts. 16 and 17 (1989).

46. Mitchel Roth, *Prisons and Prison Systems: A Global Encyclopedia* (Westport, CT: Greenwood, 2005), 136–37.

47. Roth, *Prisons*.

48. Sanaz Alasti and Eric Bronson, "Corrections in Iran," in *The Encyclopedia of Corrections*, ed. Kent R. Kerley (New York: Wiley, 2017), 1–5.

49. Irene Schneider, "Imprisonment in Pre-Classical and Classical Islamic Law," *Islamic Law and Society* 2, no. 2 (1995): 157–73.

50. "World Prison Brief Data: Iran," https://www.prisonstudies.org/country/iran.

51. Alasti and Bronson, "Corrections."

52. Ervand Abrahamian, *Tortured Confessions: Prisons and Public Recantations in Modern Iran* (Berkeley: University of California Press, 1999), 17.

53. Alasti and Bronson, "Corrections."

54. Institute for Criminal Policy Research, "Iran," World Prison Brief, accessed October 20, 2016, http://www.prisonstudies.org/country/iran.

55. Iran Human Rights Documentation Center, "Rights Disregarded: Prisons in the Islamic Republic of Iran," accessed October 20, 2016, https://iranhrdc.org/rights-disregarded-prisons-in-the-islamic-republic-of-iran.

56. Alasti and Bronson, "Corrections."

57. Goldouzian, *General Criminal Law*, 273–74.

58. Abdoreza Asghari, "Age of Criminal Responsibility in Islam," *Razavi University Law Review* (2000): 80 (in Farsi); "Children's Rights Convention and Child Rights in Iran," http://www.netiran.com.

59. Alasti, *Cruel*, 188.

CHAPTER 14

Afghanistan's Criminal Justice System

Mehdi J. Hakimi and Kobra Moradi

Afghanistan has undergone profound transformation over the past two decades. The Taliban's ouster in 2001 and the ensuing state-building efforts in the country have altered its social, political, and legal landscape. These developments, while not devoid of challenges, have inevitably affected the criminal justice system. Notwithstanding, the Taliban's recent military takeover of Afghanistan has heightened concerns about backsliding on the progress of the past twenty years. This chapter examines key issues regarding crime and criminal justice in Afghanistan. The first section contextualizes the discussion by explaining the country's pluralistic legal system and core concepts that are germane to the notion of crime under Afghan law. The second section surveys policing and law enforcement. The third section explores the role of judicial institutions in adjudicating criminal cases. The fourth section analyzes the topic of penal sanctions. Finally, the fifth section discusses the implications of the Taliban's resurgence for the criminal justice system.

Crime and Legal Pluralism

Afghanistan has a pluralistic legal system.[1] Legal pluralism may be defined as the presence and interaction of different legal traditions and institutions within a single political framework. The Afghan legal landscape is shaped by constant interaction—and, at times, contestation—among civil law, sharia jurisprudence, and customary practices.[2] As such, while legal codes and statutes are often the primary source of law (like other civil law jurisdictions), Islamic principles and custom also play important roles in Afghan society. Indeed, informal dispute resolution processes, which rely heavily on religious and traditional norms, have long been a key feature of the broader justice system. The importance of Islam is underscored in the Afghan Constitution. Article 3 of the Constitution, for example, stipulates that no law may contravene the tenets and provisions of Islam.[3] Moreover, Articles 130 and 131 of the Constitution mandate that, in the absence of statutory provisions about a case, courts shall apply sharia jurisprudence.[4]

Under Islamic law, there are four categories of crimes: *hudud*, *qisas*, *diya*, and *ta'zir*. The Afghan Penal Code, promulgated in 2017, deals with *ta'zir* crimes.[5] Perpetrators of *hudud*, *qisas*, and *diya* are punished in accordance with the provisions of the Hanafi jurisprudence of Islamic law.[6] The Penal Code defines "crime" as an act or omission that is expressly prohibited by the Penal Code, and the law has prescribed punishment or preventive measures for it.[7] It is important to underscore that inaction or omission, when there is a positive legal duty to act, may also result in criminal liability.

Afghan law generally requires three elements in order to prove the commission of a crime: (1) the legal element, (2) the material element, and (3) the moral element. All three elements must be established by the prosecutor before an individual may be found guilty. The legal element of a crime is based on the principle of legality, or *nullum crimen sine lege* ("no crime without law"). The principle of legality, which is emphasized in the Constitution and the Penal Code, states that no act or omission can be considered a crime unless the law specifically prohibits that act or omission *before* its commission.[8] This principle requires the police, prosecutors, and judges to resolve disputes by applying legal rules declared beforehand. Hence, in order to satisfy the legal element of a crime, the defendant's conduct *and* the penalty for that conduct must be expressly stipulated by the Penal Code prior to the illicit act or omission.[9]

The material element of a crime is an act or omission that is contrary to the law that results in a crime, and a causal relationship is established between the act and the result.[10] The material element thus requires the existence of three factors: (1) act or omission, (2) effect, and (3) causation. Criminal liability is imposed only if there is a causal nexus between the act or omission and the resulting effect. In other words, a person shall not be held responsible for a crime that is not the result of his or her action or inaction.[11]

The moral element of a crime relates to the actor's state of mind and is generally defined as the criminal intention, knowledge, and awareness about the crime and its result.[12] Crime is considered to be intentional in various circumstances, including when the perpetrator is aware of the consequences of the act or omission and nevertheless commits the illegal act or omission.[13] It is important to note that motive is not relevant to establishing the moral element of the crime.[14] Rather, motive is pertinent only to determining the level of punishment.[15]

Afghanistan's criminal justice system operates within the pluralistic legal environment described in this section. The remainder of this chapter explores the primary components of Afghan criminal justice—the police, the judiciary, and the penal regime—along with the implications of the Taliban's reemergence on the justice system.

Policing and Law Enforcement

The police are the gatekeepers of the criminal justice system and a vital pillar of a rule-of-law society. This section surveys some of the main issues concerning the Afghan police, including the applicable legal framework; the structure, duties, and powers of law enforcement authorities; and the core challenges on the ground.

Because of decades of conflict and frequent regime changes, Afghanistan has lacked a uniform and enduring police and law enforcement system. Afghan law enforcement institutions have been influenced in large part by foreign interventions. In the 1960s and 1970s, for example, German authorities provided police development assistance to Afghanistan.[16] During the 1979–1989 Soviet invasion, the Afghan police was largely militarized and influenced by a two-track system, with one track for career officers and another for short-term conscripts.[17] In the 1990s, during the Afghan Civil War and Taliban rule, there was no civilian police force in the country.[18] Following the Taliban's fall in 2001, the intervention—led by the United States and NATO—supported efforts to reestablish state institutions, including the new Afghan National Police (ANP).

Pursuant to Afghanistan's 2004 Constitution, maintaining law and order is one of the fundamental responsibilities of the government.[19] The Constitution empowers the executive branch of the state to appoint and dismiss police officers[20] and prohibits police personnel from joining political parties.[21] The Constitution further stipulates that "discovery of crimes shall be the duty of police."[22]

The 2009 Police Law governs the obligations and powers of the police. The primary institution responsible for policing and law enforcement is the Ministry of Interior.[23] The police perform their duties under the leadership of the minister of interior in the capital, Kabul, and under the guidance of the governors and district chiefs in the provinces and districts, respectively.[24] In terms of structure, the ANP is composed of multiple pillars, including the Afghan Uniform Police (AUP), Public Security Police, Afghan Border Police, General Directorate for Intelligence and Counter Crime, Afghan Public Protection Force, and Counternarcotics Police.[25] The AUP is the largest law enforcement agency in the country and the main police force that ordinary Afghans interact with.[26]

The duties of the police include ensuring and maintaining public order and security; ensuring the security, rights, and freedoms of individuals and the broader society; adopting measures to prevent crimes; discovering crimes and arresting suspects and perpetrators in a timely manner in accordance with the law; and preserving and keeping evidence of crimes.[27] Moreover, the police must cooperate with other government institutions, such as prosecutors and other judicial entities, in investigating crimes based on the Criminal Procedure Code and other laws.[28] By the same token, other agencies and public officials must collaborate with the police in helping maintain law and order.[29] Coordination with relevant foreign and international law enforcement bodies, such as Interpol, is also an important duty of the police.[30]

In order to fulfill the previously mentioned objectives, the law empowers the police to take various measures. These include issuing notice and warnings; stopping persons to determine their identities; ordering people to leave an area; arresting and summoning individuals; levying fines; detaining individuals; searching persons, items, and premises; and preserving property.[31] These actions may be undertaken only in accordance with relevant legal grounds.

Additionally, the Police Law imposes limitations on the use of force. The police are instructed, inter alia, to use the lowest degree of force when possible.[32] Deploying firearms against children is prohibited.[33] To be deemed "legitimate," police conduct must be (1) legal, (2) proportionate to the danger, and (3) necessary.[34] All three conditions must be satisfied in order to legitimize police action.

The Police Law is supplemented by a Code of Conduct for police officers.[35] This code outlines additional standards that guide the behavior of law enforcement authorities.[36] Violation of these standards carries disciplinary consequences with the right to appeal.[37] The UN Development Program has collaborated with the Ministry of Interior in training the police to promote the adoption of the Code of Conduct.[38] In sum, although the police hold broad discretion in performing their duties, various restrictions are imposed to prevent abuse of power.

In practice, however, the Afghan police have been grappling with major challenges. These hurdles include corruption, high attrition rates, lack of support, and divided loyalties to warlords, drug traffickers, and power brokers. The police have also suffered from poor personnel management[39] and low literacy.[40] These obstacles have seriously undermined law enforcement efforts in the country. Corruption has been an endemic problem across government institutions, including the police force. A combination of factors such as "local loyalties, links to criminal networks, low or no pay, and a residual culture of impunity" have contributed to institutional graft in the law enforcement agency.[41] The police have been reportedly complicit in organized crime, particularly along key smuggling routes.[42] The culture of corruption and impunity has substantially eroded public trust in law enforcement and damaged the government's legitimacy.[43]

Another key challenge concerns high attrition rates. For various reasons—including frequent and lengthy deployments to remote regions, lack of support and equipment, difficult living conditions, and regular exposure to attacks—many police officers have left their jobs.[44] The pressing need to fight alongside the broader security forces against the insurgency has exacerbated the attrition problem. The police were under-equipped to combat the Taliban, and the focus on counterinsurgency military operations "hindered the development of anticrime and community policing capabilities."[45]

The foregoing challenges have contributed to poor implementation of the law. For example, adherence to due process during and after arrest is weak.[46] Despite the proscription against arbitrary arrest and detention, law enforcement authorities detain many citizens in violation of these legal safeguards.[47] Police officers often do not inform detainees of the charges against them.[48] In many cases, individuals have been arrested on charges that lack any basis in criminal law.[49] Furthermore, the police frequently fail to take suspects to official law enforcement facilities immediately following arrest.[50] Mistreatment after arrest and during interrogation is common and takes various forms, including physical beating and sleep deprivation.[51]

Moreover, Afghan authorities generally disregard suspects' other legal rights, such as access to counsel, objection to detention, and receiving a judicial hearing.[52] A related systemic problem, due to illiteracy and inadequate training, has been police officers' unawareness of their responsibilities under the law.[53] The lack of robust and independent judicial oversight of law enforcement has also contributed to the weak implementation of the law.[54] In light of the foregoing issues, the public's perception of the police is far from ideal, especially in terms of accountability and respect for citizens' legal rights.[55]

The Judiciary

The courts serve a critical function in the criminal justice system by adjudicating legal disputes. While the police are responsible for investigating crimes and enforcing the law, it is the judges who wield the ultimate authority in interpreting and applying the law. This section explores the core aspects of Afghanistan's judicial institutions, including its governing legal framework; the organization, responsibilities, and powers of courts; the roles of the prosecution and defense; the informal justice sector; and challenges in practice.

The judiciary is an independent organ of the state and thus, unlike the police, does not fall under the executive branch.[56] Indeed, judicial independence is vital for ensuring a robust criminal justice system and a rule-of-law society. No law or entity, under any circumstances, may exclude any case from the jurisdiction of the judiciary and submit it to another authority.[57] Therefore, under Afghan law, the accused can be found guilty of a crime and, thus, punished only pursuant to the decision of an authoritative court.

The organization and powers of Afghan courts are governed by the Law on Organization and Jurisdiction of the Judiciary.[58] The judiciary comprises three levels: the Supreme Court, Appeals Courts, and Primary Courts.[59] The Supreme Court, as the ultimate adjudicative body, is based in Kabul.[60] Courts of Appeals are based in provincial capitals, and Primary Courts are located in cities and districts.[61]

In terms of the appeals process, lower-court decisions are generally reviewable by upper courts under certain circumstances. Litigation proceedings, including criminal matters, typically commence at the Primary Court level. After a Primary Court renders a decision, that decision can be appealed to a Court of Appeals. An appellate court's decision may also be reviewed by the Supreme Court. The decisions of upper courts are binding on lower courts and must be enforced.[62] Every case begins in Primary Courts, which are organized as follows: (1) Municipal Primary Courts, (2) Commercial Primary Courts, (3) Personal Status Primary Courts (family cases), (4) Juveniles Primary Courts, and (5) District Primary Courts.[63] Municipal Primary Courts in provincial capitals are further divided into multiple *dewans* (divisions): (1) General Criminal Dewan, (2) Civil Dewan, (3) Public Rights Dewan, (4) Public Security Dewan, and (5) Traffic Crimes Dewan.[64]

The decisions of Primary Courts may be appealed to Courts of Appeals.[65] Courts of Appeals have the following *dewans*: (1) General Criminal Dewan, (2) Public Security Dewan, (3) Civil and Personal Status Dewan, (4) Public Rights Dewan, and (5) Commercial Dewan.[66] Decisions of appellate courts may be reviewed by the Supreme Court under certain circumstances. The Supreme Court comprises nine members[67] and functions as the highest judicial organ of Afghanistan.[68] The top court has five *dewans*: (1) General Criminal Dewan, (2) Public Security Dewan, (3) Civil and Public Rights Dewan, (4) Commercial Dewan, and (5) Military and National Security Dewan.[69]

Afghan law requires that court trials be held openly, and as a result, most people have the right to attend judicial hearings,[70] although there are exceptions in which certain cases are closed.[71] Regardless of whether the trial was open or closed, court judgments must be pronounced publicly in all cases.[72] Moreover, when issuing decisions, judges are obligated to state the reasons for their verdict.[73] All final court decisions must be enforced.[74] In the case of capital punishment, however, presidential approval is required for the enforcement of the death penalty.[75]

Two other related judicial institutions play crucial roles in the Afghan criminal justice system. These are the prosecution and the bar association (defense lawyers). The mandate of the prosecution, which works closely with the police, is to investigate and file cases against the accused in the court.[76] Unlike courts, which form a separate branch of the state, the Attorney General's Office (AGO) is part of the executive organ.[77] Nevertheless, as with the bench, the AGO is required to perform its prosecutorial functions independently.[78] Prosecutorial independence is essential to a fair and impartial criminal justice system. As in virtually all other jurisdictions, the presumption of innocence is a central concept in Afghan criminal law.[79] The prosecutor thus has the burden of proving the accused's guilt by establishing the three elements of the crime charged (i.e., the legal, material, and moral elements, as discussed in the first section of this chapter).

Whereas the prosecutor represents the state, the defense lawyer acts for the accused. The Afghan Constitution stipulates that every individual has the right to appoint a defense lawyer.[80] In the case of indigent or destitute persons charged with a crime, the government is obliged to provide a defense lawyer.[81] The accused also has the right to be informed of the nature of the accusation and to appear before the court within a reasonable period.[82] Moreover, any testimony or confession obtained by compulsion is invalid.[83] In addition, the law protects the confidentiality of communications between the accused and the defense attorney.[84] The rights and duties of lawyers, including criminal defense attorneys, are governed by the Advocates' Law, which is administered primarily by the Afghanistan Independent Bar Association.

Afghanistan has made important progress over the past twenty years in strengthening the courts, the prosecution, and the bar association. Consequently, due process during formal criminal trials has improved over time.[85] Nevertheless, these institutions have also been plagued by various deficiencies that have adversely affected the criminal justice system and the rule of law more broadly.[86] The judiciary has been buffeted by an array of challenges, including a flawed system of separation of powers and a disdain for judicial independence in practice.[87] Moreover, Afghan courts have been afflicted, inter alia, by widespread graft,[88] interference with judicial proceedings and sanctions, selective enforcement of court decisions, poor security protections for judicial personnel,[89] resource constraints, and underutilization of evidence during criminal trials.[90] In addition, despite enacting legislative reforms to protect women's rights, the judicial system has failed to address systematic gender-based violence in Afghanistan.[91] The public's perception of criminal courts is thus negative, particularly with respect to issues such as trial fairness, transparency, and judicial independence.[92]

The prosecution and the bar association have been similarly beset by various challenges, such as a deficient legal-training system,[93] an insufficient number of lawyers and prosecutors, a precarious security environment for legal professionals, the politicization of the AGO, and a lack of public legal literacy, among other obstacles. Additionally, while legal representation in criminal proceedings has become more common, access to defense lawyers during interrogation remains low.[94] Indeed, most attorneys meet the defendant for the first time at the beginning of the trial phase.[95]

The myriad problems in the formal justice sector have contributed to the prevalence of informal justice mechanisms, such as *shuras* and *jirgas*. Such customary practices also reflect Afghanistan's pluralistic legal system and have long been a core feature of Afghan society. While traditional dispute resolution processes may be less expensive and speedier than formal litigation proceedings, they are nonetheless fraught with their own drawbacks—particularly when it comes to criminal matters as opposed to civil disputes. For example, informal justice forums may breach the Constitution and other codified laws; contravene Islamic principles;[96] result in egregious human rights violations, especially in relation to vulnerable groups such as women and children;[97] and be susceptible to graft.[98] Additionally, the outcomes tend to be substantially influenced by local power dynamics rather than by principles of equity and justice.[99]

Punishment and the Law

This section provides an overview of how Afghanistan's justice system addresses the issue of penal sanctions. In particular, it analyzes the objectives of criminal penalties and the classification of crimes and punishment. It also addresses the principles of legality and proportionality that govern criminal sentencing, the criteria that judges must consider in determining the appropriate penalty, the correctional system, and associated challenges.

If an Afghan court convicts an accused person, then punishment ensues. Afghan criminal law outlines various objectives for punishment, including observing the law and ensuring justice, condemning unlawful behavior (denunciation), preventing the convict from endangering others (incapacitation), deterring the perpetrator and others from committing crimes in the future (deterrence), rehabilitating criminals and promoting a sense of social responsibility (rehabilitation), compensation of damages to victims (restitution), and guaranteeing the rights of citizens and the broader society.[100]

In terms of severity of punishment, crimes are classified as petty offenses, misdemeanors, or felonies.[101] Petty offenses are the least serious category of crime and are generally penalized through cash fines.[102] Misdemeanors are the intermediate category of offenses. Felonies are the most serious crimes and thus mandate the most severe sanctions, including long imprisonment and capital punishment (i.e., the death penalty).[103]

Criminal penalties are generally divided into three broad categories: principal penalties, consequential penalties, and complementary penalties.[104] Principal penalties consist of cash fines, imprisonment, and capital punishment.[105] Depending on the circumstances, the law also provides for alternatives to incarceration, such as probation, performance of community service, deprivation from social rights, and home imprisonment.[106] The death penalty is reserved for the most serious offenses, such as intentional homicide and atrocity crimes,[107] and requires both a court order and the approval of the president.[108]

Two overarching doctrines governing criminal sentencing include the principles of legality and proportionality. The principle of legality, as introduced in the first section of this chapter, mandates that no punishment be imposed unless it is stipulated beforehand in the law.[109] In other words, no person shall be sanctioned except by the verdict of a competent court in accordance with legal provisions that are enacted prior to the commission of the act.[110] The principle of proportionality requires that the punishment be proportionate to the crime committed.[111] Put differently, the sentence must reflect the offender's degree of moral culpability. The severity of a sanction should thus be commensurate with the seriousness and gravity of the offense.

While keeping the fundamental principles of legality and proportionality in mind, Afghan courts must also consider various criteria in determining the appropriate punishment for the offense committed. These factors include the motive and nature of the crime, the danger and loss to society or to an individual as a result of the crime, and the perpetrator's personality, circumstances, and background.[112]

In addition, the judge must also take into account in criminal sentencing any relevant aggravating and mitigating factors. Aggravating factors are circumstances and conditions that warrant punishment that is more severe.[113] Aggravating factors include the presence of a corrupt or malicious motive; whether the victim's physical, mental, or financial vulnerability was taken advantage of; breach of fiduciary duty; abuse of official duty, position, or influence; whether the crime was committed in an especially brutal or violent manner; whether drugs or other intoxicants were consumed for the purpose of committing the crime; and whether the offense was perpetrated on the basis of race, ethnicity, religion, gender, social status, political ideology, or other prohibited grounds.[114] Mitigating factors are circumstances and conditions that may result in the reduction of the sentence.[115] Such factors include the existence of noble motives, an immediate reaction to substantial provocation, acting in self-defense that exceeds the legitimate limits, responding to threat or duress, making efforts to mitigate deleterious consequences of the crime, voluntary compensation for any loss incurred, being a first-time offender, confessing and expressing genuine remorse, being a pregnant or breastfeeding woman when committing the crime, being forgiven by the victim, and old age.[116]

Afghanistan's corrections system is administered by various government agencies. The Ministry of Interior's General Directorate of Prisons and Detention Centers oversees all civilian-run prisons and detention centers.[117] Juvenile rehabilitation centers are run by the Ministry of Justice's Juvenile Rehabilitation Directorate.[118] The National Directorate of Security also operates short-term detention facilities.[119] The Ministry of Defense is responsible for the Afghan National Detention Facilities in Parwan province.[120] Furthermore, members of the Afghan National Defense and Security Forces as well as the Taliban have reportedly maintained illegal detention facilities across the country.[121]

Despite progress in recent years, such as establishing human rights departments at correctional facilities, prisons and detention centers remain plagued by various shortcomings.[122] These include overcrowding, lack of sanitation, limited access to medical services, and budgetary constraints.[123] In addition, detainees generally have inadequate access to food, potable water, heating, ventilation, and lighting.[124] There are also reports of widespread abuses, corruption, and inattention to detainees' sentences.[125] Moreover, despite the fact that imprisoned convicts have the legal right to leave prison for family visits, most prisons do not enforce this statutory provision.[126] Additionally, most correctional facilities ban family visits to the prison.[127] The government also lacks sufficient facilities to separate pretrial and convicted prisoners.[128] There are also inadequate facilities for female detainees.[129] These problems have forced inmates to protest their conditions, including through hunger strikes.[130] Independent monitoring of prisons and detention centers—for example, by the United Nations and the Afghanistan Independent Human Rights Commission—has been difficult because of security constraints and obstruction by Afghan authorities.[131]

Juveniles face these and other difficult conditions in the corrections system as well. For example, the authorities lack facilities to separate juveniles based on the seriousness of the charges against them.[132] Additionally, in many cases, the lack of youth support services has resulted in keeping children below age fifteen in prison with their mothers.[133] Inadequate educational and medical facilities also pose hurdles for minors.[134] Furthermore, underage inmates have at times been victims of sexual abuse in prisons.[135]

The Taliban's Takeover of Afghanistan

The Taliban seized Kabul militarily on August 15, 2021, and currently maintain de facto control of the country.[136] The Taliban's reemergence has perturbing implications for Afghanistan, including for its criminal justice system. This section discusses some salient developments since the militant Islamist movement's takeover, including its newly installed administration; the ambiguity surrounding the regime's interpretation of Afghan laws and sharia principles; concerns regarding the fate of law enforcement, judicial, and correctional institutions; and the group's flawed amnesty policy.

The Taliban's recently announced interim government is filled with hardliners, including individuals alleged to be behind numerous deadly attacks.[137] Their cabinet is led by Prime Minister Mullah Mohammad Hassan Akhund, who is a cofounder of the movement and one of several cabinet members on a UN sanctions list.[138] Several senior members of the new administration were also detained at Guantánamo Bay.[139]

The Taliban's ascendancy has created significant uncertainty concerning various key issues. There is ambiguity, for example, as to which entity—the Taliban, the deposed government, or some other authority—constitutes the official state authorities of Afghanistan. No country has recognized the Taliban regime so far. Further compounding this uncertainty has been the Taliban's stance on establishing an "Islamic" or sharia system without explaining precisely what their interpretation of Islam entails.[140] Although the centrality of Islam has already been emphasized in the 2004 Constitution and other laws, including the Penal Code, the Taliban seem determined to impose their parochial and harsh interpretation of Islamic law, which afflicted the entire population in the late 1990s.[141] During their last stint in power, the Taliban meted out extreme public punishments, such as amputation for theft, flogging for alcohol consumption, and stoning to death for adultery.[142] Public executions were common as well.[143]

In addition, there are concerns regarding the fate of other core institutions that existed under the prior administration, such as Parliament and the judicial system.[144] The Taliban have already effectively undermined the independence of the bar association by bringing it under the control of the Ministry of Justice.[145] The absence of an independent bar will adversely affect defense attorneys and their clients, including individuals charged with crimes. This is likely a portent of significant regression of the rule of law more broadly.

The responsibility for policing and law enforcement has fallen primarily to the Taliban's interior minister, Sirajuddin Haqqani, who is the head of the notorious Haqqani Network.[146] The Haqqani Network, which maintains close ties to al-Qaeda, is designated a foreign terrorist organization by the United States.[147] The FBI has offered $10 million for information leading to Haqqani's arrest.[148]

The Taliban have also resurrected their so-called religious police, which is overseen by their Ministry for the Propagation of Virtue and the Prevention of Vice.[149] The regime's religious police have issued increasingly repressive edicts, particularly targeting women and girls. In addition to curbing fundamental rights such as education and employment, the Taliban—following their extremist interpretation of sharia—have ordered women to "cover up" in public.[150] Women have also been forbidden from traveling alone on long trips.[151]

The correctional system has already been significantly affected by the Taliban's return to power. The Taliban have systematically released thousands of dangerous prisoners throughout the country, including many senior al-Qaeda operatives.[152] The freed inmates also include thousands of Daesh/ISIS-K militants.[153] Many of the released detainees are considered to be "the Taliban's most hardened fighters" and could pose threats to Afghan civilians and the international community.[154]

Moreover, despite their central role in causing thousands of civilian casualties, the Taliban have declared a general amnesty that curtails prospects for accountability and justice.[155] Notwithstanding their pledge of clemency, however, there is mounting evidence that the Taliban are seeking retribution against perceived enemies. The group has been hunting former Afghan security officials and people who may have worked with international forces.[156] Multiple sources have also confirmed that the Taliban have begun executing security officials who were associated with the former government.[157]

The Taliban's violation of their own so-called amnesty policy is not a new phenomenon. The insurgent group declared a similar clemency pledge when they first captured Kabul in 1996.[158] That promise, however, did not stop the group from committing grave atrocities, including the massacre of historically persecuted Hazara civilians in Mazar-i-Sharif in 1998.[159] Following their recent takeover, in 2021, the Taliban swiftly commenced their persecution and killing sprees of Hazaras.[160] The extent of the Taliban's atrocities is likely more widespread than current reports suggest, considering their policy of cutting off power and telecommunication services to conceal evidence of crimes in various areas under their control.[161]

The Taliban's takeover of the country, including their full control of the law enforcement and judicial apparatus, has already led to considerable backsliding on human rights and the rule of law. The extremist group's grip on power substantially jeopardizes the progress made with respect to the criminal justice system over the past two decades. The deteriorating situation in Afghanistan should prompt the global community, including institutions such as the International Criminal Court (ICC), to take urgent action to end violations and impunity.[162]

Conclusion

This chapter has explored core issues concerning Afghanistan's criminal justice system. Afghanistan has made important strides in revamping the criminal justice sector since 2001. A plethora of legal and institutional reforms have helped build a solid foundation. As with other jurisdictions, the Afghan system has its own idiosyncrasies. The country's pluralistic legal system and informal justice sector, for example, present intriguing dynamics and layers of complexity.

Despite the progress achieved thus far, formidable challenges remain.[163] Key shortcomings include the inaccessibility of the system, poor investigation methods, corruption, lack of judicial and prosecutorial independence, concerns about trial fairness, and inadequate protections.[164] Moreover, security constraints, limited resources, and weak implementation of the law across policing, judicial, and correctional institutions bedevil the criminal justice system. Most consequentially, however, the Taliban's resurgence to power has raised the specter of a significant regression of the gains made since 2001.

Notes

1. For an in-depth discussion of Afghanistan's pluralistic legal system, see Kristina Alekseyeva et al., *An Introduction to the Laws of Afghanistan*, 4th ed. (Stanford, CA: Afghanistan Legal Education Project, Stanford Law School, 2017).
2. For a discussion of the interplay between various sources of law in Afghanistan, see Alekseyeva et al., *An Introduction to the Laws of Afghanistan*, 43–55.
3. *Qanoon Asasi Jomhori Islami Afghanistan* (Constitution of the Islamic Republic of Afghanistan), January 4, 2004, art. 3 (hereinafter "Constitution").
4. Constitution, arts. 130, 131.
5. Penal Code, Official Gazette No. 1260, art. 2(1) (2017) (Afg.) (hereinafter "Penal Code").
6. Penal Code, art. 2(2).
7. Penal Code, art. 27.
8. Constitution, art. 27; Penal Code, art. 7(1).
9. Penal Code, art. 32(1).
10. Penal Code, art. 33.
11. Penal Code, art. 37(1).
12. Penal Code, art. 38.

13. Penal Code, art. 44 (2).
14. Penal Code, art. 46.
15. Penal Code, art 46.
16. Robert M. Perito, *Afghanistan's Police: The Weak Link in Security Sector Reform* (Washington, DC: United States Institute of Peace, 2009), 3.
17. Perito, *Afghanistan's Police.*
18. Perito, *Afghanistan's Police.*
19. Constitution, art. 75(3).
20. Constitution, art. 64 (13).
21. Constitution, art. 153.
22. Constitution, art. 134.
23. Police Law, Official Gazette No. 994, art. 3 (2009) (Afg.) (hereinafter "Police Law").
24. Police Law, art. 4(1).
25. U.S. Department of Defense, "Enhancing Security and Stability in Afghanistan," 2020, 58, https://media .defense .gov/2020/Jul/01/2002348001/-1/-1/1/ENHANCING_SECURITY_AND_STABILITY_IN_AFGHANISTAN.PDF.
26. U.S. Department of Defense, "Enhancing Security and Stability in Afghanistan," 58.
27. Police Law, art. 5.
28. Police Law, art. 5(18).
29. Police Law, art. 5(25).
30. Police Law, art. 5(20).
31. Police Law, art. 9.
32. Police Law, art. 20(2).
33. Police Law, art. 23.
34. Police Law, art. 2.
35. United Nations Development Program, "Afghan National Police Code of Conduct," 2014, https://www .af .undp .org/content/afghanistan/en/home/library/crisis_prevention_and_recovery/LOTFA-Police-CoC.html.
36. United Nations Development Program, "Afghan Police Officers Receive for the First Time an Illustrated Code of Conduct," 2014, https://www.af.undp.org/content/afghanistan/en/home/presscenter/pressreleases/2014/02/25/joint -efforts -to -instill -afghan -national -police -code-of-conduct.html.
37. United Nations Development Program, "Afghan Police Officers Receive for the First Time an Illustrated Code of Conduct."
38. United Nations Development Program, "Afghan Police Officers Receive for the First Time an Illustrated Code of Conduct."
39. U.S. Department of Defense, "Enhancing Security and Stability in Afghanistan," 55.
40. U.S. Department of Defense, "Enhancing Security and Stability in Afghanistan," 55.
41. Perito, *Afghanistan's Police*, 7.
42. Freedom House, "Freedom in the World 2020: Afghanistan," 2020, https://freedomhouse.org/country/afghanistan/freedom-world/2020.
43. Perito, *Afghanistan's Police*, 7.
44. U.S. Department of Defense, "Enhancing Security and Stability in Afghanistan," 57.
45. U.S. Department of Defense, "Enhancing Security and Stability in Afghanistan," 57.
46. World Justice Project, "The Rule of Law in Afghanistan: Key Findings from 2019," 2020, 7–8, https://worldjusticeproject .org/sites/default/files/documents/Final -Afghanistan -Report-2019.pdf.

47. U.S. Department of State, "Afghanistan 2020 Human Rights Report," 2021, 7–8, https://www .state .gov/wp -content/uploads/2021/10/AFGHANISTAN -2020 -HUMAN -RIGHTS-REPORT.pdf.

48. U.S. Department of State, "Afghanistan 2020 Human Rights Report," 8.

49. U.S. Department of State, "Afghanistan 2020 Human Rights Report," at 7. For example, in some cases, women were charged with "immorality" or "running away from home," neither of which constitutes a crime under Afghan law. U.S. Department of State, "Afghanistan 2020 Human Rights Report," 10.

50. World Justice Project, "The Rule of Law in Afghanistan," 8.

51. World Justice Project, "The Rule of Law in Afghanistan," 8.

52. U.S. Department of State, "Afghanistan 2020 Human Rights Report," 8.

53. U.S. Department of State, "Afghanistan 2020 Human Rights Report," 8.

54. U.S. Department of State, "Afghanistan 2020 Human Rights Report," 8.

55. World Justice Project, "The Rule of Law in Afghanistan," 7.

56. Constitution, art. 116.

57. Constitution, art. 122.

58. The Law on Organization and Jurisdiction of the Judiciary, Official Gazette No. 1109 (2013) (Afg.) (hereinafter "Judiciary Law").

59. Constitution, art. 116.

60. Judiciary Law, art. 5(2).

61. Judiciary Law, art. 5(2).

62. Judiciary Law, art. 49.

63. Judiciary Law, art. 61.

64. Judiciary Law, art. 62.

65. Judiciary Law, art. 54.

66. Judiciary Law, art. 53.

67. Constitution, art. 117.

68. Constitution, art. 116.

69. Judiciary Law, art. 42.

70. Constitution, art. 128. See also Judiciary Law, art. 11.

71. Constitution, art. 128. See also Judiciary Law, art. 11.

72. Constitution, art. 128. See also Judiciary Law, art. 11.

73. Constitution, art. 129. See also Judiciary Law, art. 12.

74. Constitution, art. 129. See also Judiciary Law, art. 14.

75. Constitution, art. 129. See also Judiciary Law, art. 14.

76. Constitution, art. 134.

77. Constitution, art. 134.

78. Constitution, art. 134.

79. Constitution, art. 25.

80. Constitution, art. 31. See also Judiciary Law, art. 16.

81. Constitution, art. 31. See also Judiciary Law, art. 16.

82. Constitution, art. 31.

83. Constitution, art. 30.

84. Constitution, art. 31.

85. World Justice Project, "The Rule of Law in Afghanistan," 8.

86. For an analysis of the state of the rule of law in Afghanistan, see generally World Justice Project, "The Rule of Law in Afghanistan." See also Mehdi J. Hakimi, "The Rule of Law Crisis in Afghanistan," *Georgetown Journal of International Law*, September 7, 2020.

87. See Mehdi J. Hakimi, "The Judiciary and the Rule of Law in Afghanistan," *Judicature International* 105, no. 3 (2021–2022), https://judicature.duke.edu/articles/the-judiciary-and-the-rule-of-law-in-afghanistan.

88. Ordinary Afghans viewed the courts as among the most corrupt institutions in the country. See, for example, The Asia Foundation, *A Survey of the Afghan People: Afghanistan in 2018*, ed. Tabasum Akseer and John Rieger (San Francisco: The Asia Foundation, 2018), 119, https://asiafoundation.org/publication/afghanistan-in-2018-a-survey-of-the-afghan-people; see also World Justice Project, "The Rule of Law in Afghanistan: Key Findings from the 2018 Extended General Population Poll," 2018, 10, https://worldjusticeproject.org/sites/default/files/documents/WJP_Afghanistan_Report_Reduced%20%281%29.pdf (Afghans viewed judges and magistrates as the most corrupt authorities).

89. For example, in 2019, targeted attacks killed thirteen judges and nineteen prosecutors. United Nations Assistance Mission in Afghanistan, "Afghanistan's Fight against Corruption: Crucial for Peace and Prosperity," June 2020, 40, https://unama.unmissions.org/sites/default/files/afghanistans_fight_against_corruption_crucial_for_peace_and_prosperity_june_2020-english.pdf.

90. World Justice Project, "The Rule of Law in Afghanistan," 8.

91. See Mehdi J. Hakimi, "Elusive Justice: Reflections on the Tenth Anniversary of Afghanistan's Law on Elimination of Violence against Women," *Northwestern Journal of Human Rights* 18, issue 1 (2020): 52–72.

92. World Justice Project, "The Rule of Law in Afghanistan," 7.

93. For a discussion of the Afghan legal education system, see Mehdi J. Hakimi, "Rule of Law from the Ground Up: Legal Curriculum Reform in Afghanistan," *California Law Review* 11 (2020): 249–81; see also Mehdi J. Hakimi and Erik G. Jensen, "Rethinking Legal Education in Afghanistan: The Law Program at the American University of Afghanistan," *Stanford Journal of International Law* 55, no. 2 (2019): 83–115.

94. World Justice Project, "The Rule of Law in Afghanistan," 8.

95. World Justice Project, "The Rule of Law in Afghanistan," 8.

96. Various rampant customary practices—such as denying women's inheritance, marriage, and education rights—violate sharia rules. See, for example, Office of the United Nations High Commissioner for Human Rights, "Harmful Traditional Practices and Implementation of the Law on Elimination of Violence against Women in Afghanistan," December 2010, 6, 11, 32, https://unama.unmissions.org/sites/default/files/harmful_traditional_practices_english.pdf.

97. Examples of these harmful traditional practices include *baad* (giving away girls to settle disputes), child and forced marriages, *badal* (exchange marriages), and "honor" killings.

98. For example, traditional justice forums are controlled by corrupt local strongmen in some areas. Moreover, some village elders exploit their connections to elicit bribes. Disputants also engage in significant forum shopping based on kinship and personal ties. See, for example, Noah Coburn and John Dempsey, *Informal Dispute Resolution in Afghanistan* (Washington, DC: United States Institute of Peace, 2010), 10–11.

99. Powerful actors—typically the wealthy, well connected, and better armed—often get their way. The poor and vulnerable serve, in many cases, as collateral damage for the "good" of the community. See, for example, Thomas Barfield et al., *The Clash of Two Goods: State and Non-State Dispute Resolution in Afghanistan* (Washington, DC: United States Institute of Peace, 2006), 3 (noting that "imbalanced power relations between landowners, landless farmers, and gun-holders tend to subvert the principles of equity"), https://www.usip.org/sites/default/files/file/clash_two_goods.pdf.

100. Penal Code, art. 134.

101. Penal Code, art. 28.

102. Penal Code, art. 29.
103. Penal Code, art. 31.
104. Penal Code, art. 136.
105. Penal Code, art. 138.
106. Penal Code, art. 150.
107. Penal Code, art. 170.
108. Penal Code, art. 169.
109. Penal Code, art. 7(2).
110. Penal Code, art. 7(3).
111. Penal Code, art. 7(4).
112. Penal Code, art. 208.
113. Penal Code, art. 217.
114. Penal Code, art. 218.
115. Penal Code, art. 213(1).
116. Penal Code, art. 213(2).
117. U.S. Department of State, "Afghanistan 2020 Human Rights Report," 5.
118. U.S. Department of State, "Afghanistan 2020 Human Rights Report," 5.
119. U.S. Department of State, "Afghanistan 2020 Human Rights Report," 5.
120. U.S. Department of State, "Afghanistan 2020 Human Rights Report," 5.
121. U.S. Department of State, "Afghanistan 2020 Human Rights Report," 5.
122. U.S. Department of State, "Afghanistan 2020 Human Rights Report," 7.
123. U.S. Department of State, "Afghanistan 2020 Human Rights Report," 5.
124. U.S. Department of State, "Afghanistan 2020 Human Rights Report," 6.
125. U.S. Department of State, "Afghanistan 2020 Human Rights Report," 6. The release of many prisoners required payment of bribes to judicial personnel—despite the completion of sentences (9).
126. U.S. Department of State, "Afghanistan 2020 Human Rights Report," 7.
127. U.S. Department of State, "Afghanistan 2020 Human Rights Report," 7.
128. U.S. Department of State, "Afghanistan 2020 Human Rights Report," 6.
129. U.S. Department of State, "Afghanistan 2020 Human Rights Report," 6.
130. U.S. Department of State, "Afghanistan 2020 Human Rights Report," 6.
131. U.S. Department of State, "Afghanistan 2020 Human Rights Report," 7.
132. U.S. Department of State, "Afghanistan 2020 Human Rights Report," 6.
133. U.S. Department of State, "Afghanistan 2020 Human Rights Report," 6.
134. U.S. Department of State, "Afghanistan 2020 Human Rights Report," 6.
135. U.S. Department of State, "Afghanistan 2020 Human Rights Report," 6.
136. Scott Neuman, "Afghanistan Falls to the Taliban Again as the US-Backed Government Collapses," National Public Radio, August 15, 2021, https://www .npr .org/ 2021/ 08/15/1027860324/the -taliban -win -control -of -afghanistan -as -the -u-s -backed -govern ment -collapses.
137. Rachel Pannett, "Who Leads Afghanistan's New Government? Here's What We Know about the Taliban's Top Officials," *Washington Post*, September 8, 2021, https://www.washingtonpost.com/world/2021/09/08/taliban-leaders-afghanistan-government-women.
138. Pannett, "Who Leads Afghanistan's New Government?"
139. Pannett, "Who Leads Afghanistan's New Government?"
140. See, for example, Arwa Ibrahim, "Explainer: The Taliban and Islamic Law in Afghanistan," *Al Jazeera*, August 23, 2021, https://www .aljazeera .com/news/2021/8/23/hold -the -taliban-and-sharia-law-in-afghanistan (noting that "Taliban officials remain vague on rules and

restrictions, and how Islamic law will be implemented. It is, therefore, unclear what life will be like in the 'Islamic Emirate of Afghanistan'—the name the Taliban refers to the country by.").

141. Ron Synovitz, "Judge, Jury, and Executioner: Taliban Brings Afghanistan's Justice System under Its Thumb," Radio Free Europe/Radio Liberty, December 1, 2021, https://gandhara.rferl.org/a/taliban-afghanistan-justice-system/31588972.html.

142. Synovitz, "Judge, Jury, and Executioner."

143. Synovitz, "Judge, Jury, and Executioner."

144. Synovitz, "Judge, Jury, and Executioner."

145. Synovitz, "Judge, Jury, and Executioner."

146. Pannett, "Who Leads Afghanistan's New Government?"

147. Pannett, "Who Leads Afghanistan's New Government?"

148. Pannett, "Who Leads Afghanistan's New Government?"

149. France 24, "Taliban Religious Police Issue Posters Ordering Women to Cover Up," January 7, 2022, https://www.france24.com/en/live-news/20220107-taliban-religious-police-issue-posters-ordering-women-to-cover-up.

150. France 24, "Taliban Religious Police Issue Posters Ordering Women to Cover Up."

151. France 24, "Taliban Religious Police Issue Posters Ordering Women to Cover Up."

152. See, for example, Ivana Saric, "Thousands of Prisoners Freed by Taliban Could Pose Threat to U.S.," Axios, August 15, 2021, https://www.axios.com/taliban-bagram-prisoners-release-87ec6885-6930-46d6-9e96-473a252dcf7d.html.

153. See, for example, Eric Garcia, "Pentagon Admits 'Thousands' of Isis-K Militants Released from US Prisons by Taliban," *The Independent*, August 27, 2021, https://www.independent.co.uk/news/world/americas/us-politics/isis-k-us-prisons-taliban-b1910021.html.

154. Saric, "Thousands of Prisoners Freed by Taliban Could Pose Threat to U.S."

155. Yogita Limaye, "Amid Violent Reprisals, Afghans Fear the Taliban's 'Amnesty' Was Empty," BBC News, August 31, 2021, https://www.bbc.com/news/world-asia-58395954.

156. Erin Cunningham and Claire Parker, "Taliban Hunting for 'Collaborators' in Major Cities, Threat Assessment Prepared for United Nations Warns," *Washington Post*, August 20, 2021, https://www.washingtonpost.com/world/2021/08/20/taliban-hunt-collaborators-united-nations.

157. Limaye, "Amid Violent Reprisals, Afghans Fear the Taliban's 'Amnesty' Was Empty." For example, the Taliban recently executed Haji Mullah Achakzai, the security director of Badghis province, and Ghulam Sakhi Akbari, security director of Farah province. The Taliban are also executing former members of the special forces.

158. Kathy Gannon, "Taliban Rebels Take Hold as Streets of Kabul Revive," *Washington Post*, September 28, 1996, https://www.washingtonpost.com/archive/politics/1996/09/28/taliban-rebels-take-hold-as-streets-of-kabul-revive/63dba67d-cdbf-452e-9821-7d2913e3f09f ("A Taliban commander named Musa said an amnesty had been declared for all government soldiers and officers who surrendered.").

159. Human Rights Watch, "Afghanistan: The Massacre in Mazar-i Sharif," November 1998, https://www.hrw.org/legacy/reports98/afghan/Afrepor0.htm.

160. Amnesty International, "Afghanistan: Taliban Responsible for Brutal Massacre of Hazara Men—New Investigation," August 19, 2021, https://www.amnesty.org/en/latest/news/2021/08/afghanistan-taliban-responsible-for-brutal-massacre-of-hazara-men-new-investigation.

161. Amnesty International, "Afghanistan" ("The brutal killings likely represent a tiny fraction of the total death toll inflicted by the Taliban to date, as the group have cut mobile phone service in many of the areas they have recently captured, controlling which photographs and videos are then shared from these regions."); see also Ben Doherty, "Civilians in Afghanistan's

Panjshir Valley Face Humanitarian Crisis as Taliban Attack," *The Guardian*, September 7, 2021, https://www.theguardian.com/world/2021/sep/08/civilians-in-afghanistans-panjshir-valley-face-humanitarian-crisis-as-taliban-attack (noting that the Taliban have cut internet and phone connections as well as setting up road checkpoints in Panjshir).

162. The ICC must commence its long-overdue investigation into war crimes and crimes against humanity in Afghanistan. For an analysis of the ICC's Afghanistan case, see Mehdi J. Hakimi, "The International Criminal Court's Afghan Dilemma: Complementarity and the Quest for Justice in Afghanistan," *Columbia Journal of Transnational Law* 60, no. 2 (2022), https://papers.ssrn.com/sol3/papers.cfm?abstract_id=3819180.

163. Public confidence in the criminal justice system remains unsurprisingly low. World Justice Project, "The Rule of Law in Afghanistan," 6.

164. World Justice Project, "The Rule of Law in Afghanistan," 6.

CHAPTER 15

The Criminal Justice System in Saudi Arabia

Hasan T. Arslan and Mohsen Alizadeh

Brief History of Saudi Arabia

The Kingdom of Saudi Arabia has strategic importance and geolocation for the Muslim and non-Muslim worlds. Having the two critical holy sites of Muslims, the cities of Makkah and Madinah, the birthplace of the last monotheist religion—Islam—the kingdom, an ally of the West, primarily the United States, carries strategic weight in the Middle East. The country is located on the largest peninsula in the world, the Arabian Peninsula. The kingdom is the largest country on the peninsula, sharing borders with Yemen, Oman, Qatar, Bahrain, the United Arab Emirates, and Kuwait. Additionally, "with approximately 30 million inhabitants, the kingdom has 13 regions, all united by the Arabic language, but each with a unique dialect, traditions, heritage, and culinary identity."[1]

The kingdom was established in 1924 after a long struggle for independence dating back to the late eighteenth century. In fact, the first, short-lived Saudi state occurred during this time. According to Bernard Lewis,

> Only one Arabian movement challenged the legitimacy of the Ottoman state, and that was Wahhabism. Its founder, a theologian in Najd called Muhammad ibn 'Abd al Wahhab (1703–87), called for a return to the pure, authentic Islam of the Prophet and the rejection of the accretions that had corrupted and distorted it—superstitions, false beliefs, evil practices, and the regimes that upheld and encouraged them. Among his converts was Muhammad ibn Sa'ud (correctly, ibn al-Su'ud), the emir of Dar'iyya in Najd.[2]

According to Bin Abdul Wahhab, known simply as the Shaikh, "The medieval law of the *ulama* (religious scholars) as fallible and, at times, unwarranted innovations (*bida*) or heresy and he called for a fresh interpretation of Islam."[3] Bin Abdul Wahhab and his student Muhammad Ibn Saud ruled most of the Arabian Peninsula, including Makkah and Madinah, until the Ottoman military ceased the rebellion and ended it in 1818. A second Saudi state was born a few years later but lasted until only 1865.

World War I resulted in the loss of control of the Arabian Peninsula by the Ottoman state in 1918. As a result, finally, in 1924, under the leadership of Abdul-Aziz al Saud, the Arabian tribes were united. In 1932, the country was named the Kingdom of Saudi Arabia, an Islamic state with Arabic as its national language and the Holy Quran as its constitution.[4]

When the modern Saudi state was established officially in 1932, it was designated as an absolute monarchy with religious Wahhabi doctrines. Despite owning 15 percent of the world's proven oil reserves and being the largest exporter of crude oil in the world,[5] the kingdom made more investment in commerce and trade than in areas during the kingdom's formative years that were more important for the welfare of its citizens and the protection of individual rights. The kingdom used this more as an economic venture than social progress. Therefore, the institutional reforms did not happen fast, and significant reforms, such as abolishing slavery and the establishment of the Ministry of Education, took place in the mid-1950s. The Ministry of Justice, the Supreme Judicial Council, and the General Presidency of Youth Welfare were established during the 1970s.

The population of the kingdom is estimated at 35.8 million, making it the second-largest Arab state after Algeria. Between 85 and 90 percent of Saudi citizens are Sunni Muslims, and Shia constitutes 10 to 12 percent of the population.[6] The criminal justice system in Saudi Arabia presents a unique and distinguished structure, unlike many world legal systems. However, there are few sources written about its criminal justice system in English. This chapter examines the criminal justice system in Saudi Arabia and compares it with other forms of Islamic government structures, with states heavily populated with Muslims, and with the United States.

Policing and Law Enforcement

BRIEF HISTORY

Three years after its foundation in 1927, Saudi Arabia consolidated its first police force. However, the modern police force, the Department of Public Safety, was established by royal decree in 1950 by King Abdul Aziz. The department is affiliated with the Ministry of Interior, which manages the administration of law enforcement functions in the country. A director in the ministry represents the Department of Public Safety, which is responsible for the appointment of managers and patrol officers in localities of provinces. The police force is centralized in the country.

Since the mid-1960s, significant effort has been made to modernize the police force. By the 1970s, the local police departments received new police vehicles, helicopters, and radio communications equipment, and uniforms were designed with the intent to reflect the culture and geography of the landscape: they featured khaki colors, olive drab, and a distinctive red beret.[7] Today, the kingdom has made significant investments and improvements in its police force by sending the police abroad for training, including to the United States and the United Kingdom. Saudi Arabia also established collaborations with criminal justice programs in U.S. universities. In addition, student exchange programs enable its young cadets to be trained and gain broad knowledge while observing the most advanced techniques and technologies in policing. For example, in 2016, the University of New Haven's Henry C. Lee College of Criminal Justice and Forensic Sciences signed an agreement in Riyadh to develop a four-year bachelor's degree program curriculum with specializations in criminal justice, homeland security, and intelligence studies at King Fahd Security College.[8] However, the university was severely criticized after the murder of Saudi writer Jamal Khashoggi in 2018. Salah Muhammed al-Tubaigy, a board member of the Society of Forensic Medicine at King Fahd Security College, was believed to be the person who dismembered Khashoggi's body in the Saudi consulate in Istanbul. A New Haven–area group of liberal academics and activists protested, asking the university to cut its ties with the Saudi College.[9]

According to BBC News, the College of Policing in the United Kingdom provided training for 270 Saudi officers between December 2012 and October 2015. Twenty Saudi officers attended the college's International Leadership Program, and eleven participated in the International Strategic Leadership Program during this time.[10] This collaboration also came under scrutiny by the International Human Rights Watch groups and the United Kingdom's Home Affairs Committee. In its report, the committee criticized the British government, saying that current safeguards against the risks of human rights abuses following training courses provided by the College of Policing may not be "fit for purpose."[11]

Many police departments have computer databases holding criminal records, information on fugitives, and auto theft incidents. Officers can share information with other districts and track potential suspects via compiled data terminals.[12] Since 9/11, the Saudi regime has also been tracking the Jihadi and Salafist movements within the kingdom. The Saudi police force is a critical part of the intelligence community in the United States and Interpol's National Central Bureau in Riyadh.

ORGANIZATION

King Fahd Security College is the primary educational institution for police and security officers. It was established by royal decree in 1935 in Makkah under the Saudi Ministry of Interior to provide training and education to law enforcement and military personnel. As recently as 1987, most police officers spent three years in training at King Fahd Security College following their graduation from high school. In addition, there is a time-in-rank for officers to go through the nine ranks for promotion during service.[13] The college moved its current building in Riyadh and now offers a four-year bachelor's of science degree in security to Ministry of Interior employees and government sectors. Additionally, "Saudi police make a substantial distinction between commissioned officers and rank-and-file police. The commissioned officers receive three years of training at King Fahd Security College and are promoted from the second lieutenant to the general."[14]

The Saudi police force is divided into three police organizations: the regular police, the *mubahith*, and the *mutawaa*. The regular police, also known as the Public

Security Police, is the most significant law enforcement force and maintains public security and safety tasks nationwide. The police force also provides security to the Saudi embassies abroad and is responsible for protecting holy sites and the lives of citizens and residents. It recruits from all country areas and holds police directorates at provincial and local levels. If necessary, the Public Security Police also receives emergency support from the national guard and military forces.

The *mubahith* is the special investigative police of the General Directorate of Investigation, which conducts criminal investigations and performs the domestic security and counterintelligence functions of the Ministry of Interior. The Directorate of Intelligence, which reports directly to the king, is responsible for intelligence collection and analysis and coordinates intelligence tasks and reporting by all intelligence agencies.

Unlike in the policing structures in the West, Saudi Arabia has religious police, called the Committee for the Promotion of Virtue and the Prevention of Vice (CPVPV), also known as *hai'a* (committee). It was established in 1940, and its enforcers, *mutawaa* or *mutaween*, were tasked to serve as society's spiritual guide. It operates under the Department of Public Safety. According to a document from the U.S. State Department, CPVPV officers often act as public morality enforcers and report only to the king and the Ministry of Interior: "Their job [is] to make sure that Saudi nationals [are] punctual in their prayers, [abide] by all the social norms, [dress] appropriately—and more."[15] The agency has more than 5,000 staff members, including 3,583 CPVPV field offices throughout thirteen provinces and 1,600 administrative support personnel.[16]

However, after the 1979 raid with explosives and guns of the Grand Mosque in Makkah by Juhayman Al-Otaibi and his followers, CPVPV was empowered with more hard-core authority. Fueled by an extreme ideology and with powers unchecked, the religious police increased the friction among the members of Saudi society. At the height of its power, the *mutaween* destroyed musical instruments, raided beauty salons, shaved heads, whipped people, and burned books.[17] More notoriously, in 2002, agents were accused of blocking the doors at a burning school, as the schoolgirls were not wearing proper attire.[18] Finally, in 2019, under Vision 2030 reforms, Crown Prince Mohammed bin Salman stripped the religious police of its unchecked power. The royal decree banned its members from pursuing, questioning, asking for identification from, arresting, and detaining anyone suspected of a crime. They are now obliged to report back to the police and security forces if need be.[19]

In 2017, a new security unit called the Presidency of State Security was established and given the specific purpose of countering terrorism and national security threats against the kingdom. It serves as a domestic intelligence unit rather than a law enforcement agency. It directly reports to the king. Like the Office of the Director of National Intelligence in the United States, the Presidency of State Security serves as an umbrella organization gathering various domestic and military units specifically combating terrorism and threats against the Saudi regime:

> The General Directorate of Investigation, the Special Security Forces, the Special Emergency Forces, General Security Aviation Command, the

> General Directorate of Technical Affairs, the National Information Center and all matters related to combatting terrorism and financial investigations will be separated from the Interior Ministry and placed under the new Presidency of State Security.[20]

POLICE INVESTIGATION AND SEARCH AND SEIZURE

Article 34 of Royal Decree (M/39), which was ratified on October 16, 2001, seems vague and does not clarify any required criterion about how accused people fail to establish their innocence during a police interview. The language of the law gives more discretionary power to the arresting officer:

> The criminal investigation officer shall immediately hear the statement by the accused. If the accused fails to establish his innocence, the officer shall, within twenty-four hours, refer him, along with the record of the Investigator who shall within twenty-four hours, interrogate the accused under arrest and shall order either that the accused be detained or released.[21]

POLICE USE OF FORCE

Under Article 41 of the Royal Decree 2001, "If the owner or occupant of a dwelling refuses to allow a criminal investigation officer free access, or resists such entry, he may use all lawful means, as may be required in the circumstances, to enter that dwelling." Clearly, the law does not regulate the use of force in affecting an arrest or preventing the escape of a suspect or prisoner. Moreover, there is no independent police oversight body in Saudi Arabia.[22]

Judiciary

ISLAMIC LAW (SHARIA): HISTORICAL EVOLUTION

Islamic legal tradition is a unique system of justice that differs from Western legal traditions. Sharia law is one of the most misunderstood and abused legal systems by both its practitioners and its opponents. While their ultrafundamentalist interpreters have politicized it on many occasions, the opponents—some of whom are Orientalists—depict it as a brutal legal system.

In Islam, rule and sovereignty belong to God. The Quran emphasizes this point in several verses. First, it declares that ruling and command belong to God: "Female and male believers, when God and His Messenger made a decision, they have no other choice anymore" (33:36). This implies that the rule belongs not only to holy and infallible spiritual leaders, as in theocracies, nor to any religious institutions under their supervision, nor to any other religious institution organized in any other way. The Quran does not allow any privilege according to family, class, race, color, wealth, or power. Thus, there is not an absolute monarchy, nor a classical democracy as known in the West, nor a dictatorship, nor totalitarianism. Second, the law orders there to be a mutual contract between the ruler and the subject. Thus, the law is superior over the ruler and the subject; it belongs only to God.[23] Islamic law serves as a blueprint for an ideal Muslim society. In the words of the famous twelfth-century Muslim jurist al-Ghazali, Islamic laws should indeed "seek the beneficial and avoid what is bad." Furthermore, another fourteenth-century Islamic jurist agreed with this sentiment: "Every situation in which justice succumbs to tyranny, mercy to cruelty, goodness to corruption, wisdom to foolishness, has nothing in common with the Shariah."[24] According to Fethullah Gulen, a prominent Sunni-Turkish Islamic scholar, the word "sharia" is, in a certain way, a synonym of religion (*deen* or *din*); it indicates a religious life supported by God's commands, the Prophet's sayings and practices, and the consensus of the Muslim community.[25]

The word "sharia," according to David Warren, an academic at the University of Edinburgh and educator about sharia law,

> would be used in different ways, at different times, to evoke different things. Sometimes it was used to refer to religion in its totality. Other times, it was used more specifically with a legalistic meaning, in reference to communal religious laws about dietary practices or marriage. At its most basic level, the word Sharia meant "path" or a "path to water" and carried the meaning that there existed a path of right conduct that was pleasing to God.[26]

The precise nature of this path was fully known only to God. Therefore, the purpose of Islamic law has two dimensions: (1) to regulate the interactions between human beings and God and (2) to serve as guidelines for the social interactions between believers.

For Islam, no aspect of life is outside the realm of religion. Sherman A. Jackson, King Faisal Chair in Islamic Thought and Culture, defines sharia "at the most basic level [as] the Muslim universe of ideals."[27] Thus, the Quran is an essential source for criminal and civil matters, including marriage, divorce, inheritance, and penalties for unlawful behaviors. The equivalent to the Quran is the Hadith, which comprises the acts and words of the Prophet Muhammad (peace be upon him), demonstrating his dealings in personal relations in the public, social, and political spheres. It serves as excellent examples for one's real life. However, there is a robust authentication method in Islam whereby early recorders of the Hadith followed a chain of transmitters by triangulating the time, occasion, and credibility of the narrator. Weakness in any of these areas placed the Hadith as a weak source; thus, Muslim jurists avoided it for legal and civil matters.

After the death of the Prophet and the end of the four Rashidun caliphs in the seventh century, the early Muslims needed jurists in specific socioeconomic matters. Thus, within the next two centuries, four legal schools of Islam—Hanafi, Maliki, Shafi'i, and Hanbali—emerged, reflecting the diverse geographic, social, historical, and cultural context in which the jurists were writing:

> During the Umayyad Empire (661–750), rulers set up a rudimentary legal system based upon the Qur'an, the Sunnah, and local customs and

> traditions. The earliest scholars of Islamic law were neither lawyers nor judges nor students of a specific university. They were men who combined professions such as trade with the study of Islamic texts. These loosely connected scholars tended to gather or associate with major personalities. Their schools of thought came to be referred to as law schools.[28]

The judiciary system of Saudi Arabia is based on Islamic law (sharia). The legal system is based on the government's application in 1926 of the Hanbali school of Sunni Islamic jurisprudence. The Hanbali system of jurisprudence rejects analogy as a source of law and gives prominence to the traditions and sayings of the Prophet Muhammad. However, the kingdom is also heavily imbued with the principles of Wahhabism, which demands the strictest form of the two primary sources of Islam: the Quran and the Hadith. In fact, the kingdom and the Islamic Republic of Iran are the only two Islamic countries that fully implement sharia in modern times.[29] The Saudi judges follow "one of the strictest interpretations" of Islamic law; "most outside observers agree that the strict use of Islamic law and a lack of checks and balances negatively affect human rights in Saudi Arabia."[30] Sunni Muslims in Saudi Arabia recognize four official sources: the Quran, Sunnah (Hadith), Ijma (consensus of Muslim scholars/jurists), and Qiyas (analogical reasoning). They are also known as the primary sources of sharia law (*adiila asliye*). The Quran is the holy text of the religion; it is believed to be the word of God transmitted through the Prophet (PBUH). Out of 6,236 verses (*ayats*) within 114 chapters (*surahs*), approximately 500 to 600 verses are considered to be "legal codes" that specifically deal with law matters such as penalty, marriage, divorce, obligations omittance, and inheritance. They are also called *ayat-ul ahkam*: "The most crucial external aid used in interpreting the meanings of the Qur'an is the Hadith—the collection of Islamic traditions from which the details of early Islamic history are derived."[31] These four sources are used as significant sources of law in Saudi Arabia.[32] In practice, when the two primary sources are silent on issues that need a legal ruling, the secondary sources become the essential rule of law.

Quranic texts provide moral directives, setting out what Muslims should aspire to as individuals and achieve as a community. The Sunnah of Muhammad (recorded in hundreds of traditions describing the Prophet's private and public life and his individual and commercial activities) illustrates Islamic faith in practice and supplements and explains Quranic principles. *Qiyas* is used to provide parallels between similar situations or principles when no clear text is found in the Quran or Sunnah. For example, a broad prohibition of alcohol is deduced from a specific prohibition of wine based on the altered mental state that both substances cause. The fourth source of law, consensus (*ijma*), originated from Muhamad's reportedly saying, "My community will never agree on an error." This came to mean that a consensus among religious scholars could determine permissibility of an action.[33]

A small percentage of the Quran includes legal issues, which leaves many legal matters that are not specified in the Quran to be determined by the traditions, statements, and actions of the Prophet, which is called Sunnah.[34] These sources of the law have been recognized by Article I of the Basic Ordinance of the Kingdom of the Saudi Arabia.[35] Many schools of thought interpret these sources of sharia under Islamic law. Among them, the Hanbali school is accepted in Saudi Arabia. This particular school has majority and minority views of different issues of Islamic jurisprudence. Furthermore, there have been instances in which courts have applied other schools of thought to apply the principle of fairness.[36] Because the sources mentioned above are not codified, trained judges interpret the sources of law in their justice administration.[37]

ORGANIZATION

The Ministry of Justice, established by King Faisal in 1970, supervises the courts and notaries and provides a legal environment derived from Islamic law to regulate and improve judicial and documentary services. The minister of justice serves as the first officer of the Supreme Judicial Council, which explicitly appoints the judges, considers their affairs, and issues regulations and rules. In 1992, the first article of the Basic Ordinance provided that the Holy Quran and the Sunnah are the constitutions of Saudi Arabia and the legal system.[38]

The new judiciary regulation was approved on October 1, 2007, and the judiciary has three layers of justice organizations.[39] The different courts are (1) the courts of the first instance (Summary and General Courts), (2) the Court of Cassation, and (3) the Supreme Judicial Council. The Board of Grievances mostly hears the cases against the government. The Supreme Court serves as the sole top appellate court of the kingdom.

At the top of the legal system is the king, who acts as the final court of appeal and a pardon source. The Supreme Council of Magistracy of Saudi Arabia, established in 1971, serves as a king's advisory body. All its members were appointed by a royal decree, and its body supervises the lower courts of Saudi Arabia. The new judiciary regulation in 2007 set a new type of court system. The change created separate court systems for civil and criminal, commercial, and labor cases. This is simply an indication that sharia courts do not have jurisdiction over criminal and civil matters.[40]

The Summary Courts (Musta' Galah Courts) use the bench trial system and have jurisdiction over misdemeanors, small domestic issues, and minor civil cases.[41] However, the bench trial (single judge) in Summary Courts does not give the judge the jurisdiction when the punishment is death, amputation, or stoning or when the blood money punishment exceeds a specified amount. Therefore, the General Courts have jurisdiction to try these cases.[42]

The General Courts (Kubra) also use the bench trial system presided by a single judge; however, a three-judge panel decides for more serious crimes. Moreover, these courts have general jurisdiction over all cases (civil and criminal) that are not under the jurisdiction of the Summary Courts. Indeed, the General Courts have jurisdiction over serious crimes, including those for which the punishments are amputation, capital punishment, or monetary compensations for crimes that are more than one-third of the blood money value.[43] The Law of the Judiciary in 2007 changed the process such that all cases in the General Courts should be presided over by a three-judge panel.[44]

The Courts of Cassation act as appellate courts for the lower courts. These courts have different divisions for administrative, civil, and criminal cases. There are three judges for the decision-making process. If the lower courts' decision is related to the death penalty, amputation, and severe flogging, the Cassation Court automatically reviews the case for accuracy.

The Supreme Judicial Council, or Supreme Court, is the highest appellate court to review other lower courts' decisions. Still, it enacts administrative rules and policies for the judiciary (hiring, promoting, transferring judges, and so on). Accordingly, the verdicts of this council are subject to the king's approval.[45] The Supreme Court consists of a president and a sufficient number of judges with the rank of appellate court president. The assembly determines general judicial principles and considers matters as indicated by law. Members are appointed and terminated by royal decree. The court's authority is determined by the Law of Civil Procedures and the Law of Criminal Procedures; however, the Judicial Council primarily monitors the application of Islamic sharia and sharia-compliant laws issued by the authorities on matters outside the jurisdiction of the general judiciary.[46] However, the king is still the head of the judicial system.

Each region in Saudi Arabia must have one or more appellate courts, represented by three-judge panels, except for the criminal panel.[47] Indeed, Article 10 of Royal Decree (M/39) confirms that "criminal panels of the Appellate Court shall consist of five judges to review sentences of death, stoning, amputation, or *qisas* (retaliatory punishment) in cases other than death. For other cases, they shall consist of three judges."

CRIMINAL PROCEDURE AND CRIMINAL LAW

The Law of Criminal Procedure that was ratified by Royal Decree (M/39) stresses this in the first article: "Courts shall apply Sharia principles to cases brought before them, as derived from the Qur'an and Sunnah as well as laws promulgated by the State that are not in conflict with the Qur'an and Sunnah and shall adhere to procedures stipulated in this Law." Saudi Arabia has no written penal code or criminal procedural law. The strict interpretation of the Quran and the Sunnah forms those sources for the judges. However, there are two principles regarding criminal intent (mens rea) that are also part of judges' interpretation: (1) *general criminal intent* indicates when someone voluntarily participates in criminal conduct, but this is not sufficient for criminal responsibility, and 2) *specific intent* implies that the person intended to commit the particular act under question without justification and cause.[48]

The related criminal procedure rules—Protection of Human Rights in Criminal Procedure and in the Organization of the Judicial System—were approved in 2001 for overseeing the criminal proceeding, including defendants' rights. The offenders' rights, the steps that should be taken from the investigation process to the trial, and how to treat a guilty person are mentioned in this document.[49] Additionally, "the Saudi Law of Criminal Procedure contains several provisions that have been borrowed from Egyptian and French law."[50]

However, today, the substantive criminal law remains uncodified and is subject to the Hanbali interpretation of sharia by the judges.[51] The highlighted points of the Saudi criminal procedure rules are as follows:

- Prohibiting torture
- Being against moral harm
- Prohibiting the degrading treatment of offenders
- Promptly notifying detainees about the reason why they have been arrested
- Notifying defendants about the exact charges and evidence against them so that they have an opportunity to defend themselves
- Giving defendants the right to an attorney[52]

When it comes to crime and punishment, sharia and Islamic scholars have not provided the general definition of crimes. However, each act of omission or omission punishable by sharia is defined separately for each crime. Therefore, most textbooks on this topic by Islamic scholars have a specific chapter devoted to explaining each crime, its particular procedure, the law of evidence, and the punishment for such crime.[53] In Saudi Arabia, the criminal procedure is informal, but the defendant is still considered innocent until proven guilty. In most cases, the proof of a crime should be verified by witness testimony. Confession can also be used as proof; however, the defendant cannot be forced to confess.[54] Sharia law classifies crimes into four categories: *hudud*, *qisas*, *diyat*, and *ta'azirat*.

1. *Hudud* (pl. *hadds*) is a specific punishment for a particular crime, defined by sharia. In most cases, *hudud* is a severe crime.[55] Therefore, *hadd* is a fixed Quranic punishment for specific crimes, and the law of evidence for each *hadd* can be found in the Quran or Sunnah.[56] Although crimes and punishments are not codified in Saudi Arabia, the Quran and Sunnah define specific penalties for them. For example, drinking wine, highway robbery, theft, apostasy, blasphemy, rebellion, defamation, adultery, fornication, and sodomy are considered to be crimes of *hudud*.[57]
2. *Qisas*, the ideas of "an eye for an eye" and "a life for life," was first mentioned in the Code of Hammurabi. The same idea, lex talionis (the law of retaliation), was in Roman law. This biblical expression, "A life for a life, an eye for an eye," is also a part of Islamic law. Sharia provided retributive justice for two different types of crimes: homicide and intentional inflicting of body injury on others. However, victims and their families have a right to forgo the punishment and set the offender free.[58] This is also supported in many of the Quranic verses.
3. *Diyat* (pl. *diyas*) is defined as an amount of money, also known as blood money, that offenders should pay to victims or their families. The closest comparison of *diya* in Western criminal justice systems is restitution.[59] In most cases, the blood money is the compensation to victims when *qisas* is not applicable or victims or their families simply do not wish to exercise their rights (applying the same type of harm to offenders or asking for retributive justice). As a result, the law of retaliation is not applicable.[60]
4. *Ta'zirat* (pl. *ta'azirs*) applies when crimes and punishment are not stated in the Quran or Sunnah. These cases qualify the judges to use discretion to find suitable penalties for offenders.[61] However, the most current crimes related to *ta'zirat* in Saudi Arabia are defined by national regulations (*nizams*). Some of these crimes

are bribery, drug abuse, and drug trafficking. Punishments for such crimes can vary, from lashes to fines or capital punishment.[62]

ADJUDICATION

Court proceedings are held primarily in public, reserving the right to keep closed hearings in some instances for security, the maintenance of public morality, or the necessity to seek the truth.[63] Article 4 of Royal Decree 2001 guarantees attorney representations to both parties during the investigation and the trial in the court. The trial begins with opening remarks, including the charges and the presentation of the evidence by the prosecutor. According to Article 174, each party is entitled to comment on the other party's account, and the accused is the last to address the court. However, during the criminal trial, the judge is the sole authority of the adjudication process. The judge holds control over the number of witnesses to call and the types of testimony needed for conviction. He seeks all the evidence during the oral proceeding, as the Quran and Sunnah dictate.[64]

The court's decision will be reversed if it contradicts the text of the Quran or Sunnah or the consensus of Islamic jurists (Article 201). Parties can seek an appeal within thirty days from the date of receipt of a copy of the judgment (Article 194).

One interesting fact about the Saudi judiciary is that, as of January 2022, women are not allowed to serve as judges. Yet, despite many Saudi women serving as members of the Shūra Council, lawyers, ambassadors, arbitrators, and recently as prosecutors, there is still a backlash against their serving as judges.[65]

There is a harsh criticism that sharia law stipulates that a woman's testimony is worth half that of a man's during a trial. First, Muslim countries that adopted sharia law do not agree on this, but the Saudi court system interprets this strictly. Verses 282 to 283 of Surah Al-Baqarah state, "Believers! Whenever you contract a debt from one another for a known term, commit it to writing . . . and call two witnesses from among your men; and if two men are not available, then a man and two women of such as you approve as witnesses, so that if one of the two women should forget, then one may remind the other." These verses have also been quoted to compound the idea that women are treated as second-class citizens in Islam. Sadly, these claims are inaccurate and in no way reflect the ideals of Islam. Second, "nowhere in the Qur'an does it say that all men are superior to, preferred over, or better than all women."[66] Third, the magic number here is the requirement of two witnesses as a safety mechanism. Therefore, contemporary scholars argue that the need for two female witnesses was based on the concern that male family members might pressure a woman to testify in their favor. Finally, witnessing is relevant in written transactions, contracts, or court cases. At the time of the revelation of this verse, literacy among women was very low, and women were not actively involved in affairs outside their homes, including business, trade, and law.[67] Regardless of the circumstances, however, the Saudi judiciary implements the most rigid interpretation and represents an injustice to all women in Saudi Arabia. Today, a single, literate female in a good mental state should have equal rights before the court. Hopefully, this will be part of the Saudi Vision 2030 reforms.

Correctional System

BRIEF HISTORY

Whereas according to sharia law sentencing guidelines are shaped primarily by the four different types of crimes—*hudud*, *diyat*, *qisas*, and *ta'zirat*—punishments under Islamic law are classified mostly under retributive justice.[68] Hence, corporal punishments are prescribed in most cases. For example, in *hudud*, sharia makes provisions for corporal punishments in different cases; these punishments can vary from flogging to capital punishment.[69] Under the strict interpretation of Islamic law, both blasphemy and apostasy can be punished by death. Yet again, by law, the punishment in Saudi Arabia for sodomy could be stoning to death. The kingdom makes use of corporal punishment, including amputation of limbs, although floggings are the most commonly used form of corporal punishment. Executions are also widespread, and officials carry out the sentences publicly.

ORGANIZATION

According to the world population overview, Saudi Arabia's total population in 2021 was 35,340,683. The crime index in the same year was 25.23. The calculation is based on the crime index, ranging from ten (lowest crime rate) to ninety (highest crime rate). Assuming that the reported or collected data are correct, the crime rate in Saudi Arabia is relatively low. It should be noted the data are almost ten years old and come only from official Saudi government sources. Table 15.1 shows trends in the kingdom's prison system operations.

The kingdom has 104 adult correctional facilities and seventeen special juvenile correctional facilities. Concerns have been raised about the poor treatment of inmates and the related issues of prison conditions. The largest correctional facility is Al-Ha'ir Prison, which is close to Riyadh. Constructing new prison facilities is part of Saudi Arabia's plan to improve the condition of its correctional facilities.[70] While most corporal and death penalty punishments are categorized under *hudud* and *qisas*, the *ta'azirat* and national regulations (*nizams*) cover different types of crime and punishment, such as drug abuse, counterfeiting, bribery, and related offenses that government officials

Table 15.1. Number of inmates in Saudi Arabia from the World Prison Brief

Year	*Number of prisoners*	*Rate per 100,000 citizens*
1998	23,088	120
2000	23,720	116
2002	28,612	131
2009	44,600	165
2011	49,000	176
2013	47,000	161

Source: "Saudi Arabia," World Prison Brief, https://www.prisonstudies.org/country/saudi-arabia, accessed May 15 2022.

commit.[71] Some examples of alternatives to the listed punishments in sharia that were provisioned in *ta'azirat* are prison, probation, fines, public humiliation, flogging, and even the death penalty in some instances.[72]

The kingdom is part of those countries that accept and practice capital punishment because sharia also accepts it in serious offenses, such as adultery, sodomy, and armed robbery. The death penalty is usually carried out either by beheading or by stoning. Although data from 2007 show that 158 people were executed, accurate capital punishment statistics are not available. Finally, although Saudi Arabia joined the UN Convention on the Rights of the Child, there are some reports that some juvenile offenders have been sentenced to death.[73]

REHABILITATION PROGRAMS

According to the General Directorate of Prisons of Saudi Arabia, prisoners are provided with social-psychological care and various health care services to encourage them to become good members of society. Saudi officials initiated counterterrorism and safety programs to reduce the violence of extremists and conservative ideologists. For example, they developed a rehabilitation and reeducation program for violent militants.[74]

Conclusion

The Kingdom of Saudi Arabia is a peculiar case to be studied for the following reasons: it has been at the center of Islamic history, has a monarchy governed by sharia law, is competing against Iran and Turkey for leadership of the Muslim world, and is a crucial ally and trade partner for the United States in the Middle East. One might even argue that the kingdom does not get along with many of its neighbors on the Arabian Peninsula. There is no separation between state and religion; thus, freedom of religion is limited and not protected under the law. The kingdom has been the face of Islam in the mind of many westerners, and so it has been constantly subjected to heavy criticism. Approximately 85 to 90 percent of its citizens are Sunni Muslims, whereas the remaining 10 to 15 percent are Shiite Muslims. According to Human Rights Watch, minority groups, primarily the Shiites, LGBT persons, and other non-Arab ethnicities, face constant discrimination, neglect, and harassment.[75] The kingdom has been criticized for its human rights violations, including how Saudi officials handled the murder of Khashoggi at the Saudi consulate in Istanbul in 2018. After several days of denials, the Saudi government accepted that Khashoggi was strangled inside the consulate during a fistfight. However, the Saudi regime failed to hold high-level officials accountable for suspected involvement in his murder. Instead, a Saudi court sentenced five of the eight lower-level operatives to death in December 2019, but the trials lacked transparency, and penalties were later reduced.[76]

The Saudi royal family has endured many harsh criticisms and domestic political plots. The kingdom's primarily male-dominated culture and religious conservatism still influence the laws and their enforcement today. However, the family's prospective leadership is aiming to change via new plans and progressive reforms. Moreover, Saudi Arabia has implemented a series of reforms under its Vision 2030 initiative and has been doing so: "Vision 2030 seeks to build not just a thriving economy, but also a more vibrant Saudi society and a higher-performing, modernized government."[77]

Since 2017, under the leadership of Crown Prince Mohammed bin Salman, the kingdom has been initiating new reforms to modernize the country and gain prestige and more respect from the world. The crown prince achieved unprecedented reforms in the public sector's operating model, economy, and society. One of the several objectives is to increase the government's response and citizens' quality of life.[78] Following are some of the reforms initiated within the past five years:

- Religious police have been stripped of their arrest powers.
- Women have the right to obtain passports to travel abroad and live independently without permission from a male guardian, or *wali*.
- The dress code for women is somewhat relaxed, and women do not have to wear an *abaya* in public. However, women must still dress modestly, which means that tight-fitting clothing and see-through materials are prohibited.
- Restaurants have ceased to enforce gender segregation.[79]

Vision 2030 promises good things for the kingdom and poses several challenges for its absolute monarchy, which has had less transparency in the criminal justice system. As stated in a report by the Washington Institute, "The biggest challenge remains the softening of ultraconservative social norms without alienating conservative citizens."[80]

Notes

1. Saudi Vision 2030, "The Process and Achievements of Saudi Arabia," accessed January 31, 2022, https://www.vision2030.gov.sa/v2030/overview.
2. B. Lewis, *The Middle East: A Brief History of the Last 2,000 Years* (New York: Touchstone, 1995), 333.
3. J. L. Esposito, *What Everyone Needs to Know about Islam*, 2nd ed. (New York: Oxford University Press, 2011).
4. Embassy of the Kingdom of Saudi Arabia, Washington, D.C., "About Saudi Arabia," accessed January 31, 2022, https://www.saudiembassy.net/history.
5. U.S. State Department, "Saudi Arabia," accessed January December 1, 2022, https://2009-2017.state.gov/documents/organization/171744.pdf.
6. "Saudi Arabia Population 2022 (Live)," World Population Review, accessed May 31, 2022, https://worldpopulationreview.com/countries/saudi-arabia-population.
7. Country-data .com, "Saudi Arabia—Law Enforcement," accessed February 1, 2022, http://www.country-data.com/cgi-bin/query/r-11681.html.
8. M. Melia, "Saudis Team with US University on Security Degree Program," Associated Press, June 3, 2016, accessed January 31, 2022, https://apnews.com/article/5b6d7ac830014369b7847474d93f4dd5.

9. J. Stein, "Jamal Khashoggi's Death Highlights Ties between a Connecticut College and Saudi Security," *Newsweek*, October 20, 2018, accessed January 31, 2022, https://www.newsweek.com/saudi-police-ties-connecticut-college-1179960?amp=1.

10. C. Vallance and K. Langton, "UK College of Policing Trains Hundreds of Saudi Police," BBC News, January 8, 2016, accessed January 31, 2022, https://www.bbc.com/news/uk-35261385.amp.

11. K. El-Bar, "UK Police Criticized for 'Secretive' Saudi Arabia Training Deals," Middle East Eye, July 9, 2016, accessed January 31, 2022, https://www.middleeasteye.net/fr/news/uk-police-overseas-training-courses-criticised-parliament-rights-groups-560177684.

12. Police of Riyadh Province, "Background: Ministry of Interior of Saudi Arabia," accessed February 1, 2022, https://www.moi.gov.sa/wps/portal/Home/sectors/publicsecurity/police/policeriyadh/contents/!ut/p/z0/fYyxDoIwFEV_hYX5VSjuJBhFBsMGb2kepWKFtFBbI38v0cHN6eacnFxAaAANPfVAXltD08Yt7gUrOT_teFIdizpjeV0dLmWRJixL4Qz4P9ge9H1ZMAeU1nj18tDMdtJSxey7kdMr9beYUWeDj8IjZh3JcXA2mP4TuVX8jOjVlcLkhTIwj9i-ASsg--Q!.

13. A. Alobied, "Police Functions and Organization in Saudi Arabia," *Police Studies* 10, no. 2 (1987): 80–84.

14. H. R. Dammer, "Policing in Selected Countries: Organization and Structure," in *Comparative and International Policing, Justice, and Transnational Crime*, ed. Sesha Kethieneni (Durham, NC: Carolina Academic Press, 2010).

15. "Everything You Need to Know as an Expat Woman in Saudi Arabia," Expat.com, updated March 3, 2022, https://www.expat.com/en/guide/middle-east/saudi-arabia/34696-everything-you-need-to-know-as-an-expat-woman-in-saudi-arabia.html.

16. U.S. State Department, "Saudi Arabia."

17. A. Bashraheel, "Rise and Fall of the Saudi Religious Police," *Arab News*, September 22, 2019, accessed January 31, 2022, https://www.arabnews.com/node/1558176/saudi-arabia.

18. A. Taylor, "The Facts—and a Few Myths—about Saudi Arabia and Human Rights," *Washington Post*, February 9, 2015, accessed October 1, 2021, https://www.washingtonpost.com/news/worldviews/wp/2015/02/09/the-facts-and-a-few-myths-about-saudi-arabia-and-human-rights.

19. Bashraheel, "Rise and Fall of the Saudi Religious Police,"

20. *Arab News*, "Saudi Arabia Forms New Apparatus of State Security, July 21, 2017, accessed February 1, 2022, https://www.arabnews.com/node/1132466/saudi-arabia.

21. Royal Decree (M/39), "Law of Criminal Procedure (Saudi Arabia)," published in Umm al-Qura Gazette No. (3867), November 3, 2001, accessed January 31, 2022, https://cyrilla.org/es/entity/74uh146jtdd9y0w302lklkrzfr?file=1589447364978r6zfeynnpd9.pdf&page=1.

22. Policinglaw.info, "The Law on Police Use of Force Worldwide," accessed January 31, 2022, https://www.policinglaw.info/country/saudi-arabia.

23. F. Gulen, "An Interview with Fethullah Gulen," *Muslim World Journal* 95, no. 3 (Summer–Fall 2005): 449–51, http://webmedia.jcu.edu/nursichair/files/2013/01/interview.x.pdf.

24. Maslaha.org, "Islamic Law: Introduction," accessed January 31, 2022, https://www.maslaha.org/UntoldIslam/In-depth/SCHOOLS-OF-ISLAMIC-LAW.

25. Gulen, "An Interview with Fethullah Gulen."

26. D. Warren, "What Did the Word 'Sharia' Mean in Seventh Century of Arabia?," April 23, 2019, accessed January 31, 2022, https://www.futurelearn.com/info/blog/what-did-the-word-sharia-mean-in-seventh-century-arabia.

27. S. A. Jackson, "What Is Shariah and Why Does It Matter?," *Huffington Post*, September 11, 2010, accessed January 31, 2022, https://www.huffpost.com/entry/what-is-Shariah-and-why-d_b_710976.

28. Esposito, *What Everyone Needs to Know about Islam.*

29. P. L. Reichel, "Justice Systems in Selected Countries," in Kethieneni, *Comparative and International Policing, Justice, and Transnational Crime.*

30. Taylor, "The Facts."

31. "The Four Main Sources of Islamic Law: Religion Essay," UKEssays, November 2018, https://www.ukessays.com/essays/religion/the-four-main-sources-of-islamic-law-religion-essay.php?vref=1.

32. H. Sebar and S. M. Ismail, "The Use of Flogging as a Punishment in Saudi Arabia from the Perspective of International Human Rights Law," *IIUM Law Journal* 29, no. 1 (2021): 77–102, https://doi.org/10.31436/iiumlj.v29i1.609

33. Esposito, *What Everyone Needs to Know about Islam.*

34. H. R. Dammer, "Saudi Arabia," in M. Nalla and G. Newman, *Crime and Punishment around the World* (Santa Barbara, CA: ABC-CLIO, 2010).

35. E. Van Eijk, "Sharia and National Law in Saudi Arabia," in *Sharia Incorporated: A Comparative Overview of the Legal Systems of Twelve Muslim Countries in Past and Present*, ed. J. M. Otto (Leiden: Leiden University Press, 2010).

36. A. Al-Ajlan and Partners in Association with Baker & McKenzie. *Introduction to the Saudi Legal & Court Systems* (Zürich: Baker & McKenzie International, 2014).

37. Van Eijk, "Sharia and National Law in Saudi Arabia."

38. Van Eijk, "Sharia and National Law in Saudi Arabia."

39. Dammer, "Saudi Arabia"; Van Eijk, "Sharia and National Law in Saudi Arabia."

40. Van Eijk, "Sharia and National Law in Saudi Arabia."

41. Dammer, "Saudi Arabia."

42. Van Eijk, "Sharia and National Law in Saudi Arabia."

43. Dammer, "Saudi Arabia."

44. Van Eijk, "Sharia and National Law in Saudi Arabia."

45. Dammer, "Saudi Arabia."

46. Ministry of Justice of Saudi Arabia, "The Supreme Court," accessed January 31, 2022, https://www.moj.gov.sa/English/Ministry/Courts/Pages/SupremeCourt.aspx.

47. Ministry of Justice of Saudi Arabia, "The Supreme Court."

48. Reichel, "Justice Systems in Selected Countries," 98.

49. Dammer, "Saudi Arabia."

50. Abdullah F. Ansary, "A Brief Overview of the Saudi Arabian Legal System," *GlobaLex*, Hauser Global Law School Program, July 2008, https://www.nyulawglobal.org/globalex/Saudi_Arabia.html.

51. Van Eijk, "Sharia and National Law in Saudi Arabia."

52. Dammer, "Saudi Arabia."

53. M. Alizadeh, "Iran," in Nalla and Newman, *Crime and Punishment around the World.*

54. R. H. Moor, "Courts, Law, Justice, and Criminal Trials in Saudi Arabia," *International Journal of Comparative Criminal Justice* 11, no. 1 (1987): 61–67.

55. Alizadeh, "Iran."

56. Van Eijk, "Sharia and National Law in Saudi Arabia."

57. Moor, "Courts, Law, Justice, and Criminal Trials in Saudi Arabia"; Dammer, "Saudi Arabia."

58. Alizadeh, "Iran."

59. Alizadeh, "Iran."

60. Alizadeh, "Iran."

61. Alizadeh, "Iran."

62. F. E. Vogel, *Islamic Law and Legal System: Studies of Saudi Arabia* (Leiden: Brill, 2000).

63. Article 155 of the royal decree, 2001.
64. Reichel, "Justice Systems in Selected Countries," 98.
65. S. Al-Agha, "Female Judges in Saudi Arabia: Hope versus Reality," *Arab Law Quarterly*, https://doi.org/10.1163/15730255-BJA10084.
66. Esposito, *What Everyone Needs to Know about Islam.*
67. Esposito, *What Everyone Needs to Know about Islam.*
68. Sebar and Ismail, "The Use of Flogging."
69. Alizadeh, "Iran."
70. Dammer, "Saudi Arabia."
71. Vogel, *Islamic Law and Legal System.*
72. Vogel, *Islamic Law and Legal System.*
73. Dammer, "Saudi Arabia."
74. T. Bjorgo and J. G. Horgan, eds., *Leaving Terrorism Behind: Individual and Collective Disengagement* (New York: Routledge, 2008), https://doi.org/10.4324/9780203884751.
75. Taylor, "The Facts."
76. Human Rights Watch, "Saudi Arabia: Events of 2021," 2021, accessed January 31, 2022, https://www.hrw.org/world-report/2021/country-chapters/saudi-arabia.
77. S. Grand and K. Wolff, "Saudi Vision 2030: A 2020 Review," Rafik Hariri Center for the Middle East, Atlantic Council, June 2020.
78. Grand and Wolff, "Saudi Vision 2030."
79. "What Women Can and Can't Do in Saudi Arabia," *The Week*, August 25, 2021, accessed September 30, 2021, https://www.theweek.co.uk/60339/things-women-cant-do-in-saudi-arabia.
80. F. G. Schneider, "The Stalling Visions of the Gulf: The Case of Saudi Arabia's Vision 2030," Washington Institute, May 14, 2021, accessed February 1, 2022, https://www.washingtoninstitute.org/policy-analysis/stalling-visions-gulf-case-saudi-arabias-vision-2030.

Part 5

WESTERN HEMISPHERE

CHAPTER 16

An Overview of the Criminal Justice System in the United States of America

Joselyne L. Chenane

The U.S. criminal justice system comprises three main components: police, courts, and corrections. Each component serves a unique purpose, but the components are also interdependent. Thus, it is important to understand how the system operates and what role each component, independently and collectively, plays in the United States. This chapter provides an overview of each component of the U.S. criminal justice system, focusing on the role that each plays in U.S. society and government and their historical development as well as on contemporary issues and how they affect the day-to-day operation of the U.S. criminal justice system. Furthermore, the chapter addresses the interconnectedness of the components of the criminal justice system, emphasizing the criminal justice process and exploring pertinent issues that occur at different stages of the process, including conflict between crime control and due process as well as issues of race and justice.

Overview of the U.S. Criminal Justice System

The U.S. criminal justice system has its cradle in the English common law tradition. One of the hallmarks of the U.S. criminal justice system is an emphasis on two competing and equally important ideologies: U.S. citizens demand both security and freedom from governmental abuse of power, commonly referred to as individual rights or civil liberties.[1] The criminal justice system may be defined as a collection of rules and people working together to protect the public from harm. At the core of the criminal justice system are the principles of individual rights and public order, which shape Americans' views about the concept of justice—that is, fairness. Proponents of individual rights favor the protection of individual freedoms and rights, as outlined in the U.S. Constitution, within the criminal justice process.[2] The emphasis on individual rights gained prominence in the 1960s and 1970s, when the United States faced issues with civil rights for its citizens, which became glaringly obvious in the criminal justice system. The focus during this time period was on making sure that all criminal defendants had access to their rights, such as due process in court and protection from unlawful searches and seizures of property.[3]

Conversely, public order advocates posit "that under certain circumstances involving a criminal threat to public safety, the interests of society should take precedence over individual rights."[4] In other words, proponents of public order favor social order over prioritizing individual rights as a way of controlling crime in the United States. For example, after 9/11, the U.S. Congress passed the Patriot Act, allowing for diminished individual privacy and for law enforcement to have greater power and access to individual information. Prior to 9/11, people going through airports in the United States did not have to be scrutinized by Transportation Security Administration agents or pass through metal detectors or X-ray machines, as doing so would have been seen as not protective of their individual rights and freedoms. However, public order advocates believe this is necessary and a reasonably inconvenient circumstance to ensure that no one commits a terrorist attack while on an airplane.[5]

Scholars have identified three types of justice: social, civil, and criminal. Social justice entails all aspects of civilized life linked to fundamental notions of fairness and to cultural beliefs about right and wrong.[6] Civil justice derives from civil law, the law of civil procedure, and the array of procedures and activities having to do with private rights and remedies sought by civil action.[7] Criminal justice deals with the criminal (penal) law, the law of criminal procedure, and the array of procedures and activities having to do with enforcement of this body of law.[8]

The criminal justice system is divided into three broad components—police, courts, and corrections—or the three Cs—cops, courts, and corrections.[9] Although each of these components plays an important and unique role, the policing aspect of the criminal justice system is the most visible, with police often referred to as the gatekeeper of the U.S. criminal justice system. Police make initial contact, investigate crimes, apprehend offenders and potential offenders (arrest), and then book them in the local jail; however, in the United States, police officers do not determine guilt or innocence, hand down punishments, or implement punishments.[10] Police are often the first and sometimes only agents of the criminal justice system that the public encounters. As such, public perceptions of the police are always more pronounced compared to perceptions of other actors in the criminal justice system. Conversely, the primary role of the courts is to determine whether an offender should be charged with a crime and to determine the type of charge and sanction to be given for breaking a law. Each component of the criminal justice system is independent and serves its own unique function, yet these components are interconnected and interdependent. For example, police officers are often called to provide security during court sessions, and judges work closely with probation and parole officers.

The three components have the same basic function, which is to respond to crime. However, "saying that the criminal justice system has the purpose of 'responding to crime' results in a dramatically oversimplified view of how the system works. Every agency within the criminal justice system will agree that it responds to crime, but we find profoundly different mission statements, goals, objectives, and methods among these myriad agencies. A major reason for these differences is that the public has several conflicting definitions of the concept of justice."[11] Challenges notwithstanding, these components are held together by the rule of law, which is the idea that no one is above the law. Lawmakers and enforcers are just as accountable to the law as those who break the law. The U.S. criminal justice system operates as a funnel, with more cases at the initial stage of the process and fewer cases as one progresses through the system. As an illustration, the police make many arrests; however, few cases result in a trial, and an even smaller percentage of cases lead to a conviction.

This chapter focuses on the three components of the criminal justice system, starting with the police. The chapter details the role of each of the constituents of the criminal justice system and then outlines their interconnectedness. We then briefly discuss the challenges that the criminal justice system continues to face and note some of the solutions to existing challenges.

The Police

HISTORY OF U.S. POLICING

Policing in the United States has its roots in both the English model and slavery. Sir Robert Peel, considered the father of policing, founded the London Metropolitan Police, and years later, the U.S. police was influenced heavily by this model. Peel was instrumental in helping pass the Metropolitan Police Act of 1829, which facilitated the creation of the London Metropolitan Police—the first full-time police organization as we think of policing today. He was also responsible for the design and structure of the London Metropolitan Police.[12] Prior to the London Metropolitan Police, watchmen were responsible for maintaining order and catching criminals. Peel introduced the concept of crime prevention.[13] The bobbies, as they were commonly referred to, were assigned to patrol areas of the city, referred to as the "beats," in order to know the people in their neighborhoods and prevent crime and disorder.[14] These ideas became influential in U.S. policing in the early days. Pioneer English colonists in the United States created their own law enforcement agency that borrowed from their English heritage.[15] The influence of the English model in the early forms of U.S. policing was seen in the tradition of limited local police authority and decentralized and fragmented police systems.[16]

Three institutions that were adopted from the English model for U.S. colonies were the sheriff, constables, and the watch. County sheriffs, appointed by the governor, became the most important law enforcement agents in the United States.[17] They had broad roles, including law enforcement, collecting taxes, supervising elections, maintaining bridges and roads, serving subpoenas, and other miscellaneous duties.[18] Constables also had the responsibility of enforcing the law and carrying out certain legal duties. Initially, constables were elected; however, the position gradually evolved into a semiprofessional appointed office. In larger cities such as Boston and New York, the office of the constable became a desirable and often lucrative office.[19] Night watches (or the watch) closely resembled the modern police in their roles. The watchmen patrolled cities to report fires, crime, and disorder. They also raised a hue and cry, maintained street lamps, and arrested or detained suspicious individuals.[20] Initially, there were only night watches; however, as towns grew larger, day watches were added. Boston created its first watch in 1636, New York in 1658, and Philadelphia in 1700.[21] Given that the watch system was mostly reactive in nature, they were not a particularly effective crime control device.[22] The watch evolved into a paid professional position.[23]

Conversely, policing in the United States was also influenced by slavery and other factors that are unique to the U.S. context. The first formal slave patrol was created in the Carolina colonies in 1704.[24] Slave patrols were prominent in the southern states, where slavery existed. Their role was to guard against slave revolts and capture runaway slaves, among other duties.[25] These vigilante-style organizations evolved to serve primarily as a means of controlling freed slaves who were laborers working on farms and to enforce the "Jim Crow" segregation laws.[26] The Charleston, South Carolina, slave patrol had about 100 officers in 1837, larger than any city police force at the time.[27] When slavery ended, several groups merged with former slave patrols to maintain control over African Americans. As time went by, these groups began to operate in a similar fashion to the newly established police departments in the United States.[28]

As time went by, many police departments became expanded versions of existing night watch systems (e.g., the Boston police department) or slave patrols in southern states. These departments contained vestiges of the English model as well as local influences. Policing scholars have noted that the development of local, centralized bureaucratic police forces throughout the United States was a result of necessity. Similar to England, the rapid urbanization of many U.S. cities along with industrialization and immigration put pressure on the old and informal systems of law enforcement.[29] Crime and disorder went up as the population grew, particularly in the newly established urban areas, which meant that the watch and constables were no longer an adequate form of social control.[30] Some scholars have noted that with urbanization, there was an increase in mob violence, particularly violence directed at immigrants and African Americans by White youths. There was also an increase in public disorder, mostly public drunkenness and sometimes prostitution, which was at that time more visible and less easy to control in growing urban centers than it had been in rural villages.[31] Policing scholars have generally classified three eras of policing—political, professional/reform, and community. Each of these eras had its own unique features and challenges. The political era was rife with political interference with no personnel standards for police officers. During the reform/professional era, the focus was on making the police a professional body and eliminating politics from policing. The community era, however, emphasized fostering better police–citizen relations.

STRUCTURE AND FUNCTIONS OF THE U.S. POLICE

The U.S. police force has a quasi-military structure, which in many regards resembles that of the military. For example, the police wear uniforms, use military-style rank designations (e.g., sergeant and captain), and have a hierarchical command structure similar to that of the military.[32] Another unique characteristic of the U.S. police is that it is highly fragmented; there is no formal, centralized system for coordinating or regulating all the law enforcement agencies in the country.[33] There are approximately

18,000 local, state, and federal police agencies across the United States. Out of the 18,000 agencies, 12,500 are local police departments, about 3,000 are sheriff's departments, fifty are state police departments, about 1,700 are special police agencies, and seventy-three are federal agencies.[34] Each of these agencies is tasked with different roles and responsibilities, and their organization structures may differ. Under local police agencies, there are municipal police, county police, and county sheriffs. State police agencies are made up of state police and bureaus of criminal investigation, while at the federal level, there are federal law enforcement agencies and military law enforcement agencies. There are also special district police, such as public school officers (commonly referred to as school resource officers), transit police, and college and university police. Other law enforcement agencies include Native American tribal police and private security firms and security personnel.

Most law enforcement personnel are employed by local and state police departments. Specifically, approximately 785,000 sworn police officers are employed by local and state agencies. In fact, the number of local and state police officers has increased significantly, with about 35 percent more full-time police officers now compared to 1987.[35] In 2016, local police departments employed about 468,000 full-time sworn officers.[36] More than two-thirds (71 percent) of local police departments serve populations of fewer than 10,000 residents, about one in eight local police officers and about one in ten first-line supervisors were female, and about one in four local police officers and about one in five first-line supervisors were Black or Hispanic. The majority of departments serving 100,000 or more residents had specialized units with personnel assigned full-time to address child abuse, drug enforcement, and gangs. And an estimated 2.5 percent (11,870) of full-time local police officers served as school resource officers.[37]

Municipal or city police departments make up more than 70 percent of law enforcement agencies and employ more than 60 percent of the officer workforce.[38] Because police are the most visible branch of the U.S. criminal justice system, police and police departments are heavily influenced by their environments (e.g., by location and the demographic composition of the population). The external environment has a more significant effect on municipal police departments. For example, police departments within large and diverse cities handle a higher number of serious crimes than smaller/rural police departments. Moreover, urban police departments are expected to deal with a wide range of emergencies and additional duties, such as order maintenance.[39] The largest police departments in the United States are located in New York (New York City Police Department), Illinois (Chicago Police Department), California (Los Angeles Police Department and Los Angeles County Sheriff's Department), Texas (Houston Police Department), and Pennsylvania (Philadelphia Police Department). While the populations of these cities represents about 7 percent of the U.S. population, these cities experience approximately 23 percent of all violent crimes in the United States and about 34 percent of all robberies.[40]

Law enforcement looks different in small and rural police departments when compared to urban police departments. An assessment of calls to the police in rural areas has shown that the bulk of calls are for traffic problems, public disturbances, family problems, and stray dogs.[41] About half (50.4 percent) of the municipal police departments employ fewer than ten sworn police officers.[42] In contrast, although the largest police departments represent a small fraction of all police departments in the United States, they employ about 13 percent of all sworn police officers.[43] The majority of police departments employ fewer than 100 full-time sworn officers, yet the New York City Police Department employs approximately 36,000 full-time police officers. This is more than three times the number employed by any other police department. The second-largest police department, Chicago, had about 11,965 sworn officers as of 2016.[44]

FUNCTION OF POLICE IN THE UNITED STATES

Police in the United States wear many hats, which is in line with their mission statement: to serve and protect. Although the functions and roles of the police are multifaceted and vary across police departments, scholars have generally classified their duties into five categories: law enforcement, peacekeeping and order maintenance, crime prevention, protecting citizens' civil rights, and service delivery.[45] The law enforcement role of the police involves the enforcement of traffic, criminal, and civil laws. Police intervene when the law has been violated, and they identify and apprehend suspects. The police cannot enforce all laws, and, as such, enforcement is at their discretion. While most people think of law enforcement as the primary role of the police, the police have other responsibilities. Only a handful of calls to the police are for law enforcement; the rest are for purposes other than law enforcement. Peacekeeping and order maintenance involves sanctioning behavior that disturbs or threatens to disturb the public peace. For example, citizens may call the police when they spot a drunk driver who is disturbing the peace of a community.

Another core function of the police is crime prevention. Police are expected to deter crime and disorder in communities. Those in support of this idea have posited that the mere presence of police officers in the community could deter would-be criminals from committing crime. Additionally, the police are responsible for protecting the civil rights of Americans. Police protect the right to free speech and assembly during peaceful protests. The service-delivery role of the police encompasses a wide variety of noncriminal activities, such as helping motorists and finding and returning stray animals. The bulk of policing activities in the United States falls under the umbrella of service delivery. Often, there is a clash between the roles of police officers. On one hand, the police are expected to enforce the law by performing duties such as arresting and apprehending criminals. On the other hand, the police perform mundane tasks, such as responding to calls to assist individuals with mental illnesses or to address complaints against noise. For example, the police are expected to protect citizens' right to free speech during peaceful protests; however, when the protests turn violent, the police shift their role to law enforcement.

ISSUES IN POLICING

The relationship between U.S. police and minority communities has historically been frayed and characterized by distrust.[46] The tension between police and the African American community as well as other minority communities can be traced back to early policing in the United States. During the era of slavery in the United States, the control of minorities was a key feature of policing. Some states had slave patrols: groups of three to six White men who enforced laws related to slavery. They were organized to prevent revolts and escapes. Congress later gave slave patrols nationwide jurisdiction to capture runaway slaves. Police drove "paddy rollers" or "paddy wagons" to transport slaves. After the Civil War and the abolition of slavery, slave patrols were converted into city and county police forces. Officers enforced the law, including Jim Crow laws.[47] Policing in the United States has come a long way, yet there is still more to be done, particularly on the topic of building trust and mending the relationship between police agencies and individuals and communities of color. Indeed, the recent fatal encounters between police and minority citizens such as George Floyd, Breonna Taylor, and Michael Brown, among others, underscore the need for reconciliation and to ensure equitable justice. Blue-ribbon commissions and collaboration among several stakeholders have been formed in an effort to mend the relationship between police and communities of color.

In sum, police play an important and central role in the U.S. criminal justice system. Although the English model had a huge influence on U.S. policing, there are key distinctions between the two systems. Unlike the English system, the U.S. police force has a decentralized structure. Decentralization means that there is no single national police force in the United States; rather, there are federal, state, and local police organizations distributed throughout the United States. Historically, the U.S. police force has had strained relationships with minority communities; however, recent events involving fatal encounters between the police and minority citizens have revealed an urgent need to address these issues.

Courts

Similar to policing, the U.S. court system also borrows heavily from the English tradition but has its own unique features as well. Although less visible, courts serve an important and unique role in the criminal justice system. The primary goal of the courts is to determine whether an offender is guilty of violating a law and to determine the type of punishment that should be given for the offense. Courts oversee a jurisdiction, which is "the territory, subject matter, or people over which a court or their justice agency may exercise lawful authority as determined by statue or constitution."[48]

THE PROCESS

Before an individual is brought before a court, there is a process that is followed to determine whether there is enough evidence to file charges against the individual. First, the police will forward information to the district attorney—also known as a prosecutor—for review, and the district attorney will determine the type of charges to be brought against an offender, also known as the defendant. If the prosecutor determines that there is enough evidence to charge an individual for committing a crime, then charges will be filed. At this stage, the defendant will be informed about rights accorded to them by the Constitution, such as the right to legal counsel. The accused will then be asked to enter a plea of guilty or not guilty, and a trial date will be set.[49] Prosecutors play an important role throughout this process, as they must evaluate the quality and type of evidence presented in order to ascertain whether a case should be taken to trial. If the evidence is not convincing, then charges can be dropped at this juncture. A majority of cases end up in a plea deal in which the accused may plead guilty, which would make it unnecessary for the case to go through full trial. Nonetheless, those who take a plea bargain must first appear before a judge and admit guilt; then they would be released or given a reduced sentence. Given the volume of cases within the U.S. criminal justice system, some have referred to plea bargaining as a "necessary evil," although others question its ethics.[50]

In summary, the pretrial process begins with the "first appearance," in which offenders' rights are read to them, and public defenders are appointed for those who cannot afford an attorney. At this stage, the judge will also determine whether bail will be granted and, if it is granted, set the amount for bail.[51] Courts do not always require money for bail; instead, defendants may be released on their own recognizance with a promise to appear in court as needed.[52] The stage at which defendants are released either on bail or on a promise to appear in court is referred to as "pretrial release." Next, defendants appear before a grand jury hearing (in some jurisdictions) or a judge for a preliminary hearing. Attorneys are not present in grand jury hearings; however, preliminary hearings are conducted in ways that are similar to trials, in which judges preside and prosecutors, defense lawyers, and defendants are present. Arraignment comes after preliminary and/ grand jury hearings. During arraignment, defendants must appear before the court for formal charging, and they must enter into a plea of guilty or not guilty.[53] In some instances, defendants can plead guilty in return for the government's agreement to drop certain charges or for a lenient sentence; this agreement is called a "plea bargain." However, before a plea bargain agreement, a judge must first determine that the defendant entered into the agreement knowingly and voluntarily.

Key personnel during a trial generally consist of judges, prosecutors, defense attorneys, and a jury. Usually, a judge oversees the court. A prosecutor is an attorney whose official duty is to conduct criminal proceedings on behalf of the state or people against those accused of having committed criminal offenses.[54] Public defenders are defense attorneys who are licensed trial lawyers and who are hired or appointed by the state to conduct the legal defense of a person accused of a crime and to represent them before a court of law.[55] Defense attorneys can be private attorneys who are licensed trial lawyers and who are hired for their services by defendants or in instances in which defendants are indigent or unable to afford an attorney during a criminal trial. In those circumstances, public defenders will be appointed on their behalf, which is a unique feature of the U.S. system. The U.S. court system uses an adversarial approach; as such, there must be two teams in any court case.[56] Prosecutors present defendants' guilt; defense attorneys present evidence in favor of the defendants' innocence. In essence, the defense attorney's goal in a trial is to infuse reasonable doubt, while the prosecutor's goal is to prove beyond a reasonable doubt that a defendant is guilty. The standard for criminal litigation in the United States is "innocent until proven guilty."

STRUCTURE AND FUNCTIONS OF U.S. COURTS

The United States has a unique three-tier court system comprising local, state, and federal courts. Each of the local, state, and federal courts has its own organizational structure and jurisdiction. The federal court system covers the whole country, and a separate and independent state and local court system covers the states and U.S. territories.[57] Essentially, what this means is that each system has its own unique jurisdiction, but all can cover the same ground in terms of criminal, civil, and administrative laws.[58] For example, there are federal and state laws against different types of crime (e.g., federal and state laws against the crime of murder), and, as such, lawsuits can be brought against the same people in both federal and state systems.[59] The running of the two parallel systems (i.e., federal and state or local courts) simultaneously on the federal and state levels is referred to as "federalism."[60] Although the courts run parallel to each other, under the Constitution's supremacy clause, federal laws are the supreme law of the land—that is, federal laws have control over contrary state laws.[61] This also means that when a ruling is issued by the U.S. Supreme Court, it must be followed by every state and every court in the country. There are some exceptions to this rule, however, in which the federal government is not authorized by the Constitution to act; when it does not act, state laws apply under the reserve clause of the Tenth Amendment to the Constitution.[62]

FEDERAL COURTS

The federal court system was established by Article III of the Constitution; however, new judges in the courts are appointed by the president and confirmed by Congress.[63] The details of the jurisdiction and functions of the federal court system were discussed in the first U.S. Congress, which passed in the Judiciary Act of 1789.[64] The act created the federal judiciary system that is still used in the United States today.[65] The original federal judiciary system comprised a Supreme Court, presided over by six justices; three appeals courts, presided over by two Supreme Court justices and a District Court judge; and thirteen trial courts, each presided over by a district judge.[66] With time, however, the number of courts and judges has changed to accommodate the changing needs of the population.

STRUCTURE OF FEDERAL COURTS

The federal court system has a three-tier system comprising District Courts at the lowest level, Courts of Appeal, and the Supreme Court at the highest level. There are ninety-four District Courts, which hear federal-level civil and criminal cases. Judges are appointed by the president and confirmed by the Senate.[67] The District Courts handle the bulk of cases within the federal system. For example, in 2016, more than 80,000 criminal cases were filed in U.S. District Courts.[68] There are twelve Courts of Appeal in the federal system. These courts do not handle as many cases, as they specialize in handling appeals from the District Courts and they are also fewer in number. Courts of Appeal are typically presided over by three-judge panels but can agree to hear a case or reconsider a decided case en banc, which means that all judges in the circuit would hear the case simultaneously and vote on the decision.[69] Cases decided by federal Courts of Appeal can only be appealed to the Supreme Court. There is only one Supreme Court, which consists of nine justices who are nominated by the president and confirmed by the Senate. Supreme Court justices enjoy life tenure unless they retire or are removed by congressional impeachment. They are responsible for the judicial review of actions and decision made by other agencies of government. The Supreme Court receives approximately 5,000 requests each year to hear cases but takes only about 200.[70] The Supreme Court is in session from October to July. When the Supreme Court takes on a case, they listen to arguments from the attorneys on both sides, have a meeting about it, vote on upholding or overturning the lower court's decision, and then write an opinion to clarify the position. These are known as concurring ("for") and dissenting ("against") opinions.[71]

THE ROLE OF THE SUPREME COURT

The Supreme Court is the highest court in the country and as such is an important organ of the judiciary. The Court's decisions on all matters involving federal or constitutional law are final. The Supreme Court has appellate jurisdiction over all U.S. courts and original (trial) jurisdiction over some cases.[72] The Constitution and the Judiciary Act of 1789 grant the Supreme Court original jurisdiction over cases between states, cases between states and foreign governments, issues involving ambassadors and foreign public officials, and other cases.[73] Most original jurisdiction Supreme Court cases involve actions between states. For example, in the 1998 case *New York v. New Jersey*, the Supreme Court held a trial and determined that most of Ellis Island belongs to New Jersey.[74]

The main function of the Supreme Court is its appellate jurisdiction. As the court of last resort, the Supreme Court can hear only appellate cases from either federal appellate courts or the highest available state courts, usually the state supreme courts. If the appeal comes from a state court, the Supreme Court may rule only on the basis of federal or constitutional law. If a case requires an interpretation of a state law, the Supreme Court can certify a question to a state supreme court, asking it to advise on relevant matters of state law.[75] The Supreme Court decides to accept or reject cases through a complex process called *certiorari*, a Latin word that means "to be informed of, or to be made certain in regard to."[76] Moreover, the Supreme Court's time is limited, and its jurisdiction is so broad that it can accept only about 2 to 3 percent of cases appealed to it.[77] As such, the Supreme Court generally accepts cases that have national significance, cases that can resolve conflicts over decisions in the Circuit Courts, and cases that address other important constitutional or legal issues.[78]

STATE COURTS

State court systems are established by state laws and the Constitution.[79] Similar to federal courts, state courts use an adversarial system whereby the state is against the defense. Federal courts are not considered "higher" than state courts except for the Supreme Court. Rather, they are parallel systems.[80] State courts are independent of federal courts, except that they must follow decisions of the Supreme Court on matters of federal law.[81] They need not follow precedent from federal appeals or trial courts. As such, state court decisions cannot be appealed to any federal court except the Supreme Court, though state court actions are sometimes reviewed by federal courts in criminal cases based on applications in federal court for writs of habeas corpus.[82] Depending on the court and the state, judges may be appointed, elected, or selected by panels or other judges.[83]

The structure of state courts varies, but generally there are trial courts and appellate courts within the state court system. Trial courts have general jurisdiction, as they hear both criminal and civil cases, and this is where the court process begins.[84] Trial courts are sometimes called Circuit Courts, District Courts, and/or superior courts (or, in New York, "supreme"). Trial courts are also called lower courts since they are the first points of contact and higher courts can make decisions about their rulings. These courts may also have divisions, including domestic relations, probate, veterans', drug, and juvenile divisions.[85] In addition, all states have intermediate appellate courts.[86] Depending on the state, these courts may go by different names. For example, appellate courts are called "Supreme Court–Appellate Division" in New York, while Maryland calls the equivalent court the "Court of Special Appeals."[87] Additionally, some states have separate "supreme" courts for civil and criminal cases.[88] As an illustration, Oklahoma and Texas have two separate supreme courts. In both states, criminal cases are heard by the Court of Criminal Appeals, and civil cases are heard by the Supreme Court.[89] Generally, there may be two tiers within appellate courts system: a Court of Appeal and a state supreme court.[90] Although state appellate courts take appeals from their states' trial courts, these courts have discretion to determine which appeals they want to hear. In this way, they are similar to the Supreme Court, which accepts cases at its discretion.[91] The highest-level court within state courts is the court of last resort, at which point the case would move to the federal process, that is, the Supreme Court.[92]

LOCAL COURTS

In state systems, there are more local courts of special and limited jurisdiction than there are on the federal level, such as family court, probate court, and traffic court.[93] In addition to trial and appellate courts, some states offer specialized courts to address focused needs of the communities they serve.[94] A specialized court is a "low-level court that focuses on relatively minor offenses and handles special populations or addresses special issues such as reentry."[95] These courts usually operate in conjunction with community corrections. Specialized courts usually focus on addressing issues such as substance abuse (drug courts) and issues related to veterans (veterans' courts), among others. These courts collaborate with service providers to address these particular needs in the context of the problems that individuals may face. Thus, they are also often called problem-solving courts because rather than focusing on punishing for the crime, they focus on the solving the problems that led to the crime.[96] Conversely, municipal courts, which are local courts that are part of their state court systems, handle traffic cases, small claims, and misdemeanors. Some localities set up special courts to handle specific matters, such as domestic violence and misdemeanor drug cases. Some cities, towns, and villages have mayor's courts, justices of the peace, and other smaller courts. These typically have limited jurisdiction.[97]

Overall, the United States has a complex, multitiered court system with parallel federal and state systems. These systems operate mostly independently of each other, but the Supreme Court is the highest court in the land. In recent years, the appointment of Supreme Court justices has been at the center of political lobbying. Police enforce the law on the street, and offenders are brought to courts to determine whether they are guilty. At the end of the trial process, guilty offenders are handed down a sentence, which may be served in a correctional institution or within community corrections.

Corrections

"Corrections" is the umbrella term used to describe many different criminal justice activities that ensue after an individual has been convicted of a crime by the court. Corrections can be divided into two main types: institutional corrections and community-based sanctions (e.g., probation and parole). Institutional corrections include jails and prisons. There are approximately 1,719 state prisons, 102 federal prisons, 1,852 juvenile correctional facilities, 3,163 local jails, and 80 Indian Country jails.[98] Jails are usually operated at the local level, most often under the leadership of a county sheriff.[99] Jails are most commonly thought of as holding individuals who have been arrested and are awaiting a first appearance in court. Legally, these individuals are presumed innocent because they have not been proven guilty or convicted of any crime. However, jails also house individuals who have been convicted of relatively minor offenses (misdemeanors) and, in most states, are serving sentences of less than one year. Although jails were designed to serve a more transient population, jails are increasingly being used to house prisoners who are awaiting trial or who have been convicted of serious offenses and are awaiting transfer to a state prison.[100] According to the Bureau of Justice Statistics, more than 20 million people enter and exit jail each year. However, people who are convicted of serious crimes can be sentenced to a prison term. In the United States, prisons are generally larger and more secure, and they provide more services than jails. The reason for these extra services is that prisons are designed for longer sentences than jails. Prisons are most often run at the state level of government, but there are also many federal prisons.

In the United States, incarceration as punishment is a relatively new idea.[101] Previously, those who violated laws were sentenced to corporal punishments, fines, and death. The first modern prisons in the United States were established in the eighteenth century, when the Quakers considered them to be an alternative to corporal and capital punishments. These reformers introduced a new way of thinking about the goals of punishment that was contrary to tradition. Their intention was to rehabilitate offenders through hard physical labor, religious study, and penitence.[102] However, the current political climate has largely replaced these altruistic ideas with the ideas of deterrence, retribution, and incapacitation, which might explain high recidivism rates. According to a Bureau of Justice Statistics report on recidivism rates for prisoners, seven in ten incarcerated people in thirty-four states in 2012 who were released were rearrested within five years.

An important feature of prisons in the United States is that they use a classification system to help achieve their goal of housing inmates and keeping both the prisoners and staff safe. Classification systems are "used by prison administrators to assign inmates to custody levels based on offense history, assessed dangerousness and other factors."[103] Inmates are classified and assigned to prisons based on security levels: supermax, maximum security, medium security, and minimum security. Supermax prisons are known to house the worst of the worst prisoners. The most prominent of these facilities is the Florence Correctional Facility in Colorado, which is operated by the Federal Bureau of Prisons.

In addition to jails and prisons operated by the state or federal government, in recent years corrections relies on private prisons to house inmates. A private prison is a correctional facility that is managed by a private firm on behalf of a local or state government.[104] Although approximately 8 percent of inmates are housed in private prisons according to the Bureau of Justice Statistics, scholars, politicians, and policymakers have questioned the ethics and efficiency of private prisons.

COMMUNITY CORRECTIONS

As an alternative to institutional corrections, offenders can receive community sanctions, or what scholars refer to as "community corrections." Indeed, current statistics reveal that a majority of people under correctional control are under community supervision.[105] Accordingly, community supervision is "the use of a variety of officially ordered program-based sanctions that permit convicted offenders to remain in the community under conditional supervision as an alternative to a prison sentence."[106] The two main types of community supervision are probation and parole. In the

United States, probation refers to a sentence of imprisonment that is suspended as long as the person meets certain conditions of behavior, whereas parole may be granted to a convicted offender who has been conditionally released from prison by a paroling authority before the expiration of a sentence and who is placed under supervision of the parole agency.[107] Simply put, probation is given in lieu of serving time in prison or jail, and parole is granted after a prisoner has served some time in prison. It is important to note that the number of people under community supervision has been on a downward trend. For example, a recent report by the Bureau of Justice Statistics shows that an estimated one in fifty-nine adults in the United States was under community supervision at the end of 2019, down from one in forty-six in 2000.[108] Crime rates in the United States have been on a downward trend in the past three decades, and this could help explain why the number of people in community supervision has been trending downward.

Scholars have attributed the origins of probation to a Massachusetts resident, John Augustus, who in the 1850s took on the supervision and responsibility of people who he felt could be reformed. However, probation as an official sentence was not formalized until 1901 in New York, and by 1925, nearly every state and the federal government had enacted probation laws.[109] Probation is the most common form of criminal sentence, comprising 58 percent of criminal cases. For example, in 2016, there were 3,763,100 people on probation in the United States.[110]

The United States has often been referred to as the incarceration capital of the world, which means that the United States has the largest prison population in the world. Needless to say, many U.S. prisons are overcrowded because of the large number of inmates who are currently behind bars. This increase in incarceration over time, often called mass incarceration, has led to overcrowding in facilities and an increasing number of people with a criminal record. Many states are realizing that this method of punishment is costly and not sustainable. One of the remedies to help reduce prison overcrowding is parole. Parole is the process by which inmates are released back into the community after spending some time in prison. The governing body that determines whether someone is released from prison early is called the parole board or "state paroling authority."[111] There are two main types of release mechanisms used by the parole board: mandatory release, which is the release of an inmate from prison as determined by statute or sentencing guidelines rather than by a parole board, and discretionary release, which is the release of an inmate from prison to supervision as decided by a parole board.[112]

Certain conditions must be met by individuals who are on probation or parole; these are known as conditions of supervision. For individuals under community supervision, general conditions are set by state statutes and include such conditions as not breaking laws, reporting to probation or parole officers, and being employed or going to school. Special conditions are set by the court or parole authority and are specific to each individual case, such as going to substance abuse treatment.[113] When probationers and parolees fail to abide by these rules, they may violate their probation or parole. If the violation is something that is not a new crime, it is called a "technical violation." When this happens, the court (for probation) or the parole board (for parole) may be notified and would then have to decide to have a hearing about the behavior. A revocation hearing is "a hearing to determine whether a parolee or probationer has violated the conditions and requirements of his or her parole or probation."[114] If the court or parole board agrees that the problem behavior occurred, it may revoke the probation or parole, and the individual may be sent to prison.[115] However, if the court or parole board does not revoke the probation or parole, the court or board can issue a continuance of the supervision, usually with additional conditions to address the problem behavior.[116] Some of the advantages of community supervision include reduced cost and support from the community.

ISSUES IN CORRECTIONS

Minorities are overrepresented in every stage of the criminal justice system, including corrections. The justice system in the United States has seen a rebirth of the caste-like system that was inherent in Jim Crow system. This has resulted in millions of African Americans being incarcerated for minor drug offenses.[117] Black Americans are incarcerated in state prisons across the country at nearly five times the rate of Whites.[118] To put things into perspective, one in eighty-one Black adults in the United States is serving time in state prison, with the state of Wisconsin leading the nation in Black imprisonment rates; one of every thirty-six Black Wisconsinites is in prison.[119] Additionally, more than half the prison population is Black in Alabama, Delaware, Georgia, Illinois, Louisiana, Maryland, Michigan, Mississippi, New Jersey, North Carolina, South Carolina, and Virginia. And the states of California, Connecticut, Iowa, Maine, Minnesota, New Jersey, and Wisconsin have a Black/White disparity larger than nine to one.[120] Scholars have identified a few explanations for racial disparities in corrections and the criminal justice system, including a legacy of racial subordination, biased policies and practices that create or exacerbate disparities, and structural disadvantages that perpetuate disparities.[121] Furthermore, people of color are sentenced more severely (e.g., they are more likely to receive capital punishment) and to be wrongfully convicted than their White counterparts. For example, a report by the American Civil Liberties Union notes that people of color have accounted for a disproportionate (43 percent) of total executions since 1976 and make up 55 percent of those currently awaiting execution.[122]

Notes

1. Adam J. McKee, *Criminal Justice: An Overview of the System* (Booklocker.com, 2016).
2. John Worrall and Frank Schmallenger, *Policing* (New York: Pearson, 2017).
3. Worrall and Schmallenger, *Policing*.
4. Worrall and Schmallenger, *Policing*, 9.
5. Worrall and Schmallenger, *Policing*.
6. Worrall and Schmallenger, *Policing*.
7. Worrall and Schmallenger, *Policing*.
8. Worrall and Schmallenger, *Policing*.
9. Worrall and Schmallenger, *Policing*.

10. Alison S. Burke, David Carter, Brian Fedorek, Tiffany Morey, Lore Rutz-Burri, and Shanell Sanchez, *Introduction to the American Criminal Justice System* (Corvallis, OR: Open Oregon Educational Resource, 2019).

11. McKee, *Criminal Justice*, 1.

12. Samuel Walker and Charles M. Katz, *The Police in America: An Introduction*, 9th ed. (New York: McGraw-Hill, 2017).

13. Walker and Katz, *The Police in America*, 9th ed.

14. Walker and Katz, *The Police in America*, 9th ed.

15. Craig D. Uchida, "The Development of the American Police: An Historical Overview," in *Critical Issues in Policing: Critical Readings*, ed. Roger G. Dunham and Geoffrey P. Alpert (Prospect Heights, IL: Waveland, 1993), 16–32; Walker and Katz, *The Police in America*, 9th ed.

16. Samuel Walker and Charles M. Katz, *The Police in America: An Introduction*, 8th ed. (New York: McGraw-Hill, 2012).

17. Uchida, "The Development of the American Police."

18. Walker and Katz, *The Police in America*, 9th ed.

19. Walker and Katz, *The Police in America*, 9th ed.

20. Uchida, "The Development of the American Police."

21. Gary Potter, *The History of Policing in the United States*, 2013, https://www.academia.edu/30504361/The_History_of_Policing_in_the_United_States.

22. Potter, *The History of Policing in the United States*; Uchida, "The Development of the American Police."

23. Walker and Katz, *The Police in America*, 9th ed.

24. Potter, *The History of Policing in the United States.*

25. Walker and Katz, *The Police in America*, 9th ed.

26. Uchida, "The Development of the American Police."

27. Walker and Katz, *The Police in America*, 9th ed.

28. Carol A. Archbold, *Policing: A Text/Reader* (Los Angeles: Sage, 2012).

29. Walker and Katz, *The Police in America*, 9th ed.

30. Uchida, "The Development of the American Police."

31. Uchida, "The Development of the American Police"; Walker and Katz, *The Police in America*, 9th ed.

32. Walker and Katz, *The Police in America*, 9th ed.

33. Walker and Katz, *The Police in America*, 8th ed.

34. Walker and Katz, *The Police in America*, 9th ed.

35. Walker and Katz, *The Police in America*, 9th ed.

36. Shelley S. Hyland and Elizabeth Davis, *Local Police Departments, 2016: Personnel*, Bureau of Justice Statistics, October 2019, https://bjs.ojp.gov/library/publications/local-police-departments-2016-personnel.

37. Hyland and Davis, *Local Police Departments, 2016.*

38. Walker and Katz, *The Police in America*, 8th ed.

39. Walker and Katz, *The Police in America*, 8th ed.

40. Walker and Katz, *The Police in America*, 8th ed.

41. Walker and Katz, *The Police in America*, 8th ed.

42. Walker and Katz, *The Police in America*, 9th ed.

43. Walker and Katz, *The Police in America*, 8th ed.

44. Hyland and Davis, *Local Police Departments, 2016.*

45. Worrall and Schmallenger, *Policing.*

46. Daniel K. Pryce and Joselyne L. Chenane, "Trust and Confidence in Police Officers and the Institution of Policing: The Views of African Americans in the American South," *Crime and Delinquency* 67, nos. 6–7 (2021): 808–38.
47. Walker and Katz, *The Police in America*, 9th ed.
48. Worrall and Schmallenger, *Policing*, 208.
49. McKee, *Criminal Justice.*
50. McKee, *Criminal Justice.*
51. McKee, *Criminal Justice.*
52. McKee, *Criminal Justice.*
53. McKee, *Criminal Justice.*
54. Worrall and Schmallenger, *Policing.*
55. Worrall and Schmallenger, *Policing.*
56. McKee, *Criminal Justice.*
57. McKee, *Criminal Justice.*
58. "The American Court System," Lawshelf.com, https://lawshelf.com/videocoursesmoduleview/the-american-court-system-module-1-of-5.
59. "The American Court System."
60. McKee, *Criminal Justice.*
61. "The American Court System."
62. "The American Court System."
63. "The American Court System."
64. "The American Court System."
65. "The American Court System."
66. "The American Court System."
67. Worrall and Schmallenger, *Policing.*
68. "The American Court System."
69. "The American Court System."
70. Worrall and Schmallenger, *Policing.*
71. Worrall and Schmallenger, *Policing.*
72. "The American Court System."
73. "The American Court System."
74. *New Jersey v. New York*, 523 U.S. 767, 1998.
75. "The American Court System."
76. "The American Court System."
77. "The American Court System."
78. "The American Court System."
79. "The American Court System."
80. "The American Court System."
81. "The American Court System."
82. "The American Court System."
83. "The American Court System."
84. Worrall and Schmallenger, *Policing.*
85. "The American Court System."
86. "The American Court System"; Worrall and Schmallenger, *Policing.*
87. "The American Court System."
88. "The American Court System."
89. "The American Court System."
90. Worrall and Schmallenger, *Policing.*
91. "The American Court System."

92. Worrall and Schmallenger, *Policing*.
93. "The American Court System."
94. Worrall and Schmallenger, *Policing*.
95. Worrall and Schmallenger, *Policing*, 285.
96. Worrall and Schmallenger, *Policing*.
97. "The American Court System."
98. Peter Wagner and Wendy Sawyer, "Mass Incarceration: The Whole Pie 2018," March 14, 2018, https://www.prisonpolicy.org/factsheets/pie2018_allimages.pdf.
99. McKee, *Criminal Justice*.
100. McKee, *Criminal Justice*.
101. McKee, *Criminal Justice*.
102. McKee, *Criminal Justice*.
103. Worrall and Schmallenger, *Policing*, 445.
104. Worrall and Schmallenger, *Policing*.
105. Worrall and Schmallenger, *Policing*.
106. Worrall and Schmallenger, *Policing*, 391.
107. Worrall and Schmallenger, *Policing*.
108. Barbara Oudekerk and Danielle Kaeble 2021. "Probation and Parole in the United States, 2019," July 2021, https://bjs.ojp.gov/library/publications/probation-and-parole-united-states-2019.
109. Worrall and Schmallenger, *Policing*.
110. Worrall and Schmallenger, *Policing*.
111. Worrall and Schmallenger, *Policing*, 394.
112. Worrall and Schmallenger, *Policing*.
113. Worrall and Schmallenger, *Policing*.
114. Worrall and Schmallenger, *Policing*, 398.
115. Worrall and Schmallenger, *Policing*.
116. Worrall and Schmallenger, *Policing*.
117. Michelle Alexander, "New Jim Crow: Mass Incarceration in the Age of Color Blindness," 2012, https://www .ojp .gov/ncjrs/virtual -library/abstracts/new -jim -crow -mass -incarceration-age-colorblindness.
118. Ashley Nellis, "The Color of Justice: Racial and Ethnic Disparity in State Prisons," October 13, 2021, https://www.sentencingproject.org/reports/the-color-of-justice-racial-and-ethnic-disparity-in-state-prisons-the-sentencing-project.
119. Nellis, "The Color of Justice.".
120. Nellis, "The Color of Justice."
121. Alexander, "New Jim Crow"; Nellis, "The Color of Justice."
122. American Civil Liberties Union, "Race and the Death Penalty," accessed May 21, 2022, https://www.aclu.org/other/race-and-death-penalty.

CHAPTER 17

The Uruguayan Criminal Justice System

Diego Sanjurjo and Joaquín Arigón

Despite the political stability and socioeconomic prosperity of recent decades, crime indicators have grown steadily in Uruguay[1] since the end of the twentieth century. As a result—and contrary to common belief—modern Uruguay does not have low but rather medium levels of crime, as it went from traditionally being one of the safest countries in the region to having the fourth-highest homicide rate in South America.[2] This juncture is also mirrored by a strong sense of fear regarding insecurity in recent decades on the part of Uruguayans.

Beyond this deterioration, Uruguay has a relatively robust criminal justice system, which stands out in the region for the legitimacy of its police forces and the certainties provided by its judiciary. The Uruguayan National Police (UNP) is the most important security actor in the country and is a unified, nationwide, civilian, and professional police force. It was founded in 1829 with the birth of the republic, but its history dates back to the eighteenth century and the colonial period. Since then, its development has been driven by political and social circumstances as well as by the need to curb rising crime and to increase its legitimacy in the eyes of the public.

These improvements, however, cannot hide the fact that the UNP faces considerable difficulties in providing its citizens with basic safety.

This chapter provides an overview of the Uruguayan criminal justice system. To this end, each of the following sections presents one of its main elements, that is, the UNP, the judiciary, the penitentiary system, and the juvenile penal system.

The UNP

The UNP[3] falls within the jurisdiction of the Ministry of Interior and constitutes a unified and nationwide security force of a civilian and professional nature. The Uruguayan armed forces are generally not involved in the prevention of, control of, investigation of, or fight against crime. Instead, they are responsible for providing security against external threats, whereas the UNP is tasked with providing internal security, surveillance, and order inside the country's borders.

Such a division is common among consolidated Western democracies and has been reinforced in many Latin American countries since the military dictatorships of the twentieth century. However, exceptions apply. The surveillance and control of coastal areas and the shores of navigable rivers and lakes is the responsibility of the National Naval Prefecture, a division of the National Navy. Likewise, the other branches of the armed forces have taken on a series of tasks to support the UNP on an exceptional basis, which include surveillance tasks in border areas, providing external perimeter security in prison facilities, and the performance of aerial police functions in cooperation with the UNP.[4]

ORGANIZATION

The structure and organization of the UNP is hierarchical in nature, and its direction falls into the hands of the national director of the UNP, who is the fourth in command at the Ministry of Interior and whose essential task is the professional operational command of the force. Several UNP directorates depend on the National Directorate of the UNP. Among the most important are the Directorate of Police Planning and Strategy, the National Directorate of Scientific Police, the General Directorate for the Repression of Illicit Drug Trafficking, the National Directorate of Traffic Police, the National Directorate of Civil Identification, the National Directorate of Migration, the General Directorate of Business Control, and the Unified Command Center.

The Departmental Headquarters also depend on the Directorate of the UNP. There are nineteen police headquarters in the county, one for each department of the republic. Since more than half of Uruguayans live in the capital and it concentrates a large share of the country's criminal activity, the Montevideo Police Headquarters (MPH) is the largest and plays a leading role. On a territorial level, the MPH is divided into four operational jurisdictions and twenty-five sectionals, but there is also a fifth operational headquarters with units and bodies common to the entire department. These include the Transit Police Corps, the Tactical Reserve Group, and the Eventual Services Coordinator, among others.

Between civilian and police personnel, the UNP hired more than 32,500 workers in 2020, 24,000 of whom were executive personnel, actively working in crime prevention, deterrence, investigation, and repression. The actual police officer rate stands at 679 per 100,000 inhabitants, the highest rate in Latin America and a rate that is considerably higher than 326, the median rate of the European Union.[5]

Police education and training takes place at the Police Education Directorate, and it differs depending on whether they are officers or subordinates. The training of officers is presented as a three-year, tertiary education option that begins on completion of high school. The subordinates constitute 90 percent of the force and receive six months of training that requires only three years of secondary education.[6]

Finally, police salaries have risen significantly in recent years and almost doubled since 2000. Thus, the monthly salary of the lowest police rank in 2019 was U.S.$865,[7] which is well ranked among Latin American police salaries. However, the average police salary that year was approximately U.S.$980, which is still six times lower than the average salary of a police officer in the United States.[8]

REFORMS AND OPERATIONS

The bulk of the Uruguayan police force follows operational practices that resemble the standard model of policing[9]—that is, a one-size-fits-all strategy based on routine preventive patrols, rapid responses to service calls, and retrospective investigations. Consequently, local police authorities usually attempt to fight rising crime by increasing the number of police officers on the streets and their public visibility as well as by enforcing saturation patrols and intensive arrests.[10] There are no alternatives to these practices in the countryside, but they also dominate urban landscapes, with perhaps the sole exceptions of Montevideo and Maldonado. However, this is still the prevailing policing model in the force even in these cities.

At times, it seems as if the UNP is transitioning between policing philosophies. The past two decades were an era of reform marked by an impulse to modernize the force and go from a public safety paradigm to a type of community safety paradigm known as a "citizen security" paradigm.[11] While the former paradigm implies concerted crime-fighting efforts by security institutions, the latter corresponds to the Spanish term *seguridad ciudadana* and places greater emphasis on community interaction and on social cohesion.[12]

These changes began in the late 1990s, driven by regional and global discussions on public security, citizen security, and human security.[13] Alongside the need to demilitarize and depoliticize police institutions, these goals have generally guided attempts to reform police institutions in Latin America.[14] In the case of the UNP, the Inter-American Development Bank led and financed a large part of these reforms through the Citizen Security Program—later the Comprehensive Citizen Security Program—of the Ministry of Interior.[15] Overall, this transition implied a moderate advance toward a police organization that prioritizes preventive and community practices.[16]

On an operational level, changes can be grouped into three phases. The first involved pilot efforts to promote crime prevention strategies (1998–2004), including traditional community policing programs, domestic violence approaches, and social crime prevention plans. The second phase included structural reforms to professionalize the force (2005–2012), such as the creation of civilian directorates, the centralization of police management, the introduction of management commitments, and the improvement of working conditions. The third phase involved a commitment to evidence-based strategies (2013–2020), which included the further development of criminal analysis and investigation, a reform of police education, and the application of preventive policing models.[17]

All these reforms were accompanied by relevant investments in police technology. These include the expansion of a closed-circuit video surveillance system that covers large parts of the country's metropolitan areas;[18] the development of the Public Security Management System, which manages and centralizes all administrative records on criminal incidents, accidents, and police events throughout the country;[19] the implementation of a terrestrial radio communications system that allows encrypted communications and GPS tracking of vehicles and agents; and the massive incorporation of police vehicles, tablets, body cameras, and electronic monitoring systems for perpetrators of domestic violence.

In relation to policing strategies and models, the High Operational Dedication Program stands out, which is an evidence-based policing strategy focused on hot spots. The program was first implemented in 2016 and gradually expanded to adjacent parts of Montevideo and the cities of Canelones and San José.[20] Its monitoring and coordination are overseen by the Criminal Analysis Directorate of the Unified Command Center, and it can be considered the result of a long process of professionalization by the UNP in resource management, data analysis, and crime mapping.[21]

Another innovation is the development of problem-oriented policing programs[22] that came to supplant traditional community policing strategies of the 1990s that never had the expected results. Although the problem-oriented policing programs had some successful projects, difficulties linked to organizational resistance, inadequate leadership, and a lack of resources prevented its consolidation and development.[23] Despite these problems, the program has recently expanded under the name "problem-oriented community policing" and is still active, but its future remains highly uncertain.

In short, preventive police efforts have gained some recognition in recent times, but they are still far from achieving the same status, support, and development within the UNP as criminal investigations and deterrence and response strategies.[24] In this regard, the Uruguayan experience is in line with those who affirm that there are still no true community policing programs in Latin America, as these have been only circumstantial and have not led to lasting changes in police institutions.[25] Consequently, it would be incorrect to state that the UNP has adopted a citizen security paradigm. So far, the change in philosophy is nothing more than an aspiration.[26]

LEGITIMACY AND POLICE ABUSE

Along with Chile and Costa Rica, Uruguay is arguably one of the few countries in Latin America with a police force that resembles or conforms to David H. Bayley's democratic policing criteria, namely, a police organization that is accountable to the law rather than to the government, that protects human rights, that is constrained in the use of force, and that has the protection of citizens as its highest priority.[27] Its exceptional situation in a region marked by the presence of corrupt and nondemocratic policing is largely the result of a successful democratic transition and its ability to maintain something close to a monopoly on violence.[28]

This reality is reflected by public opinion polls that suggest that citizens trust the UNP significantly more than in most countries of the region. Thus, according to the Latinobarómetro Corporation, whereas only 36 percent of Latin Americans trusted the police in 2020, in Uruguay, this percentage rose to 66 percent, the highest among nineteen countries.[29] Similar to what usually happens in large cities, institutional trust seems to be lower in the capital, as a survey by Corporación Andina de Fomento found that police trust fell to 34 percent among Montevideo residents.[30] Similar results were captured by Uruguay's latest crime victimization survey, which found that 60 percent of respondents had confidence in the police, whereas 51 percent were satisfied with the way in which the police handled complaints, and 71 percent were satisfied with the treatment given to complainants.[31] Finally, the anticipated emergency response time looks particularly promising, as only 3.5 percent of respondents believed that it could be three hours or longer, the same percentage as in the United States.[32]

However, abuse and the unnecessary use of force are considered common elements of police practices in the region.[33] According to opinion surveys from 2016 and 2017, only 2.9 percent of respondents in Uruguay reported that a police officer had asked them for a bribe in the past twelve months, a figure much lower than the regional average of 12 percent.[34] Similarly, in a region where, on average, 44 percent of those surveyed think it is possible to bribe police officers, in Uruguay, this percentage stands at 21 percent, the second lowest after Chile.[35] Finally, Uruguay is one of the few countries in Latin America—along with Chile and Panama—that does not show empirical evidence of systematic state violence.[36] This includes torture, extrajudicial executions, extortion, and kidnapping by government actors as well as state collusion with criminal organizations, among other forms of state violence.

STRENGTHS AND WEAKNESSES

Among the main strengths of the UNP are its capacity to maintain something close to a monopoly on violence, its adherence to the law and legal framework, its apparently low levels of institutional corruption, and its technological equipment and capabilities. However, its weaknesses are insufficient levels of education and training, low salaries that do not allow for the recruitment of suitable personnel, inadequate criminal investigation and analysis, and a general lack of cooperation with other state actors.

The Judiciary

The judiciary oversees the interpretation and application of criminal laws. Broadly speaking, its main function is to decide on the criminal legal responsibility of any individual accused of having carried out conduct that the law establishes as a crime. To reach a decision, a judicial process will take place that usually involves a judge, a prosecutor, and the defense of a defendant or defendants. Only through a resolution of the judicial system is it possible to impose a custodial measure on an individual, whether it is a penalty or only a precautionary measure.

In turn, the courts with criminal jurisdiction play a crucial oversight role, as they must guarantee respect for the fundamental rights of the defendants during the development of the criminal process. However, they also oversee and control the performance of the police during their interventions and the well-being of all those serving a precautionary measure or custodial sentence in prison.

ORGANIZATION

The Uruguayan judiciary is hierarchically structured as follows:

- Supreme Court of Justice: Superior organ of the judiciary, with competence in cassation and revision
- Courts of Criminal Appeal: Courts of second instance that hear appeals
- Courts of First Instance in Criminal Matters (Montevideo) and Courts of First Instance of the Interior (all of Uruguay except Montevideo): Courts for hearing formal and substantial questions that arise at any point from preliminary investigations to definitive sentences and interlocutory sentences that entail definitive force
- Criminal Court of First Instance Specializing in Organized Crime: Located in Montevideo but with jurisdiction throughout the country and with exclusive competence in economic, tax, organized crime, and child pornography or prostitution crimes
- Courts of First Instance for Enforcement and Surveillance: Courts that hear all formal and substantial questions that arise after a final judgment becomes final
- Courts of Misdemeanors and Departmental Peace Courts: Courts with jurisdiction in cases promoted by misconduct, the former in Montevideo and the latter in the rest of the country
- Courts of First Instance for Minors: Courts with jurisdiction in situations of the abandonment of children and in the preventive, educational, and corrective procedures that follow criminal acts committed by minors

A circumstantial but important element of the Uruguayan judiciary is that there are currently two criminal procedure codes in operation. The first is the Code of Criminal Procedure (CCP), sanctioned in 1980 by Decree Law No. 15.032. The CCP is primarily inquisitive, with a judge in charge of directing the investigation and judging and with practically mandatory pretrial detention.[37] The CCP continues to be applied in cases that were pending as of November 1, 2017, when Law No. 19.293—known as the new Code of Criminal Procedure (nCPP)—came into force. Although the nCPP has undergone multiple modifications since its sanction,[38] its adoption meant the abandonment of a mixed criminal procedural system in favor of an accusatory criminal process that is configured as contradictory, adversarial, oral, and public.[39]

Among the main changes that the implementation of the nCPP entailed, the most crucial is perhaps the new role of the intervening parties, especially that of the judge and the Public Prosecutor's Office (FGN). Whereas with the CPP it was the judge who directed the investigation, with the nCPP it is the prosecutor, who is also the sole holder of the criminal action. This change meant breaking with a sort of "contamination" of the previous inquisitorial system, in which the judge directed the investigation and also collected the evidence.[40] Another relevant change is that the nCPP recognizes the victim as having procedural rights and powers that were not available in the CPP. In so doing, the victim becomes an adjunct to the prosecutor with probative powers and can request protection measures and oppose some decisions of the prosecutor.[41]

CRIMINAL PROCEDURES

Among the most important types of criminal procedures are the ordinary structure or oral trial, the abbreviated process, the simplified process, and alternative conflict resolution mechanisms.

Ordinary Structure or Oral Trial

The oral trial is supposed to be the main procedural route of the nCPP. Mostly because of a lack of material and human resources, however, in practice less than 4 percent of all investigations take place through this mechanism.[42]

Broadly speaking, an oral trial begins with a preliminary investigation in which the facts are investigated under the direction of the prosecutor, who will determine whether to request a formalization. If affirmative, then a hearing will be convened to dictate the formalization and to impose precautionary measures if deemed necessary. Once formalized, a summary process begins that can last up to one year with the possibility of a one-year extension, after which the prosecutor must make an accusation or request a dismissal. If an accusation is made, the defense has thirty days to respond, and an accusation control hearing is summoned to oversee the evidence and issue the opening of an oral trial. A new judge takes over from this moment on to oversee the oral trial in a public hearing in the presence of the prosecutor, the accused, and the accused's defender. The oral trial must be carried out continuously and extended in successive sessions until its completion and the issuance of a sentence.

If the sentence is appealed, then the second instance proceeds before a Court of Criminal Appeals, and its resolution can, in turn, be appealed before the Supreme Court of Justice. Once the sentence is final, the file goes to a Law Enforcement and Surveillance Court.

Abbreviated Process

This is a summary process that consists of the admission by the accused of the facts and background of the investigation in exchange for a reduction in its punishment (plea bargaining). The process begins with the formalization of the investigation and lasts until the expiration of the deadline for accusing or requesting a dismissal. The accused must comply in all terms with the agreement made with the prosecutor, which is reached under the supervision of a judge who ensures that the formal requirements of the agreement are met as are the free and voluntary consent of the accused and the accused's explicit acceptance of the facts.[43] The abbreviated process is not suitable for every crime. Especially aggravated or very especially aggravated homicide cannot be processed in this way, and the same goes for cases in which the base crime is punished with a minimum penalty of more than four years in prison. Likewise, the reduction of the sentence cannot push the lower limit of that which is provided for the offense in question. Despite these limitations and because of the gains in terms of time and effort that the abbreviated process affords, currently 88 percent of all investigations culminate in this way.[44]

Simplified Process

The simplified process is a procedural route that was recently incorporated into the nCPP through the 2020 Urgent Consideration Law. If the prosecutor requests such a procedure and does not solicit the imposition of a penalty greater than three years in prison for the accused or those prosecuted, then the judge must necessarily admit the request. Once admitted, the prosecutor must make the accusation at a hearing, transferring it to the defense in the same act, which can respond in this instance or do so in writing within a ten-day period. After the defense has replied to the accusation, the accused persons are consulted about admitting their responsibility for the facts contained in the accusation. If they admit responsibility, then the sentence is passed immediately. If not, the trial proceeds, calling for a new hearing within a period of twenty to forty days, during which time the parties must present all the evidence. Their initial and final arguments are received, and a judgment is passed. The second instance transpires in the same way as that described for the oral trial.

Alternative Conflict Resolution Mechanisms

Reparatory agreements involve material or symbolic reparation and are applicable to crimes for which there is no public interest in their prosecution, which is usually determined through instructions from the FGN. These include those punishable by a fine, the crimes of personal injury or serious injury, and those of patrimonial content. Reparatory agreements do not proceed in cases of sexual crimes or domestic violence. The signing of a reparatory agreement and its strict compliance imply the issue has been settled.

Another form of alternative conflict resolution, extraprocedural mediation, requires the consent of the victim and of the alleged perpetrator and is designed for cases of apparently criminal conduct that are not considered severe. They are processed in mediation centers of the FGN, and their goal is a settlement agreement between the parties.

STRENGTHS AND WEAKNESSES

In general terms, the Uruguayan judiciary is characterized within Latin America by the integrity of its administration of justice and by the provision of broad guarantees for the upholding of the rule of law. Hence, the country is ranked second in the region on the "Criminal Justice" factor of the World Justice Project *Rule of Law Index 2022* behind only Costa Rica.[45] Likewise, 58 percent of Uruguayans trust the judiciary, the highest percentage in the region.[46] Despite this, the judiciary has some important weaknesses as well. Perhaps the most important is the historical lack of material and human resources, which hinders the swift and fluid development of criminal proceedings. Coordination with other relevant actors of the criminal justice system is also still deficient, even though the nCPP has made important improvements. These factors produce delays in the processes, excessive bureaucracy, and distrust among the population. Additionally, statistical information related to criminal proceedings needs to be improved for the sake of transparency and evaluation.

The Correctional System

As in most of Latin America,[47] the prison population has experienced constant and sustained growth in Uruguay since the last decades of the twentieth century. While the country's population increased by 34 percent between 1963 and 2020, the prison population increased by almost 900 percent. Consequently, inmates went from 4,369 in 2000 to 13,402 in the first quarter of 2021 (figure 17.1). The figures of 2021 indicate an incarceration rate of 383 inmates per 100,000 inhabitants, the highest in South America (figure 17.2).[48]

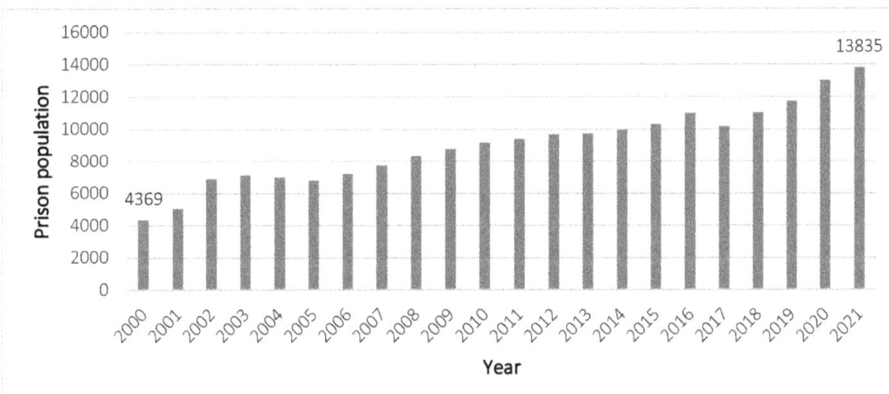

Figure 17.1 Prison population of Uruguay, 2000–2020. *Source:* Data from Uruguayan Ministry of Interior.

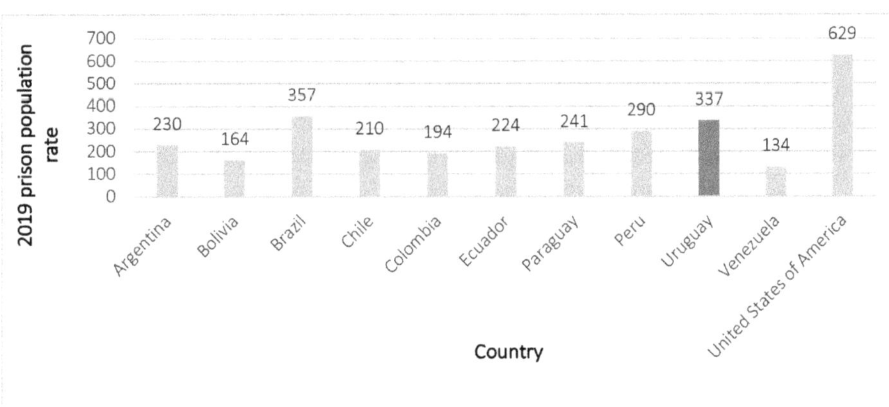

Figure 17.2 Prison population rates for South America and the United States in 2019 for every one hundred thousand inhabitants. *Source:* Data from Uruguay-CPP (2019) and World Prison Brief (2022).

The prison population is predominantly male since women represent less than 7 percent of the total. Regarding age, 70 percent of inmates are under thirty-five years of age, which contrasts with the rest of the population, in which this percentage is close to 35 percent. When it comes to their educational level, two out of ten inmates do not know how to read or do so only with great difficulty, only more than 50 percent have a complete or incomplete primary education, and only 1 percent have access to tertiary education. With regard to their professional skills, only 51 percent of inmates declare having a trade or profession, and among these, 75 percent correspond to manual trades.[49]

Another important element is that 69.3 percent of all inmates were pretrial detainees in 2017. However, the introduction of the new nCPP resulted in a significant improvement, leading to a reduction of that rate to 22.3 percent by 2020.[50] Likewise, although recidivism is not officially measured, it is roughly estimated to affect around two-thirds of those who are released. Finally, drug use and addictions are common and widespread within prisons and are considered one of the biggest obstacles to improving the system.

ORGANIZATION

The governing body of the prison system is the National Rehabilitation Institute (INR) of the Ministry of Interior. There are twenty-six penitentiary units across the national territory, operating in urban, suburban, and rural establishments. Each unit is headed by a director, in charge of an administrative subdirectorate, a technical directorate, and a security directorate. In general terms, the system is heterogeneous and presents different and even conflicting realities in both size and work methods, coexistence, and response capability.[51] The system also suffers from overcrowding, as most inmates are concentrated in a small number of macro-units in which the number of inmates generally exceeds by far the number of places available. Specifically, in 2017, 68 percent of inmates were confined in nine units of the metropolitan area.[52]

Prison units are classified according to the type of confinement regime as closed, semi-closed, or open. Closed-regime units usually have a maximum-security level and operate with strict controls over common activities and with limited relations with the outside world. In semi-closed regimes, detainees have greater freedoms, whereas units with an open regime have minimal security and living conditions that emulate the outside world. Moreover, according to Decree Law No. 14.470 of 1975, the administrative prison regime must be based on three central principles: the classification and individualization of inmates, their consequent separation by categories, and their gradual progression through seclusion and treatment regimes. In practice, these principles are implemented only in a circumscribed way. The separation of inmates by sex is enforced throughout the system, and efforts have been made to increase the separation in other categories. However, these efforts continue to be largely insufficient in larger prisons, and the same applies to progressivity, which works only partially in open units.

There is also a Diagnosis and Referral Center, which is the entry port for all male detainees from Montevideo, Canelones, and San José. At this center, detainees undergo a medical checkup and an admission protocol to assert their vulnerability and risk. Depending on the results and availability, inmates are transferred to one penitentiary unit or another.

REENTRY AND REHABILITATION

Article 26 of the Constitution of the Republic of 1967 establishes that "in no case shall prisons be allowed to serve to mortify, and only to contain the prosecuted and convicted, pursuing their reeducation, aptitude for work and prevention of crime."[53]

Unfortunately, the lack of adequate human and material resources currently prevents the Uruguayan prison system from fulfilling this function. The figures are veracious in this regard. In 2019, formal education covered only 23.5 percent of the prison population, and the educational quotas offered were far from those demanded, which constitutes the denial of a basic human right. Similarly, job opportunities are few, and that year only 36.4 percent of inmates carried out any type of work activity. Besides, most work activity—78 percent—was unpaid and did not contribute in any meaningful way to the inmates' work history or personal or professional development.[54]

Similar shortcomings can be found in other areas. In terms of health, for example, the medical services of most units are limited to treating illnesses and do not carry out primary care or preventive activities. The situation is even more complicated in macroprisons, where basic medical services cannot meet demand. Similarly, mental health resources are highly insufficient, and there are hardly any facilities to care for people with psychiatric pathologies or drug addictions.

There have been significant advances in terms of rehabilitation and reentry in recent decades, especially since 2010.[55] Nevertheless, it is undeniable that the prison system does not currently provide most inmates with the necessary skills and tools to reenter society and prevent recidivism. Consequently, and as in most Latin American countries,[56] the Uruguayan prison system has (re)designed its norms and regulations to include rehabilitation and reentry among its main goals, but these changes are no more than a symbolic first step in a long process that has barely been addressed.

STRENGTHS AND WEAKNESSES

Among the strengths of the Uruguayan correctional system are the consolidation of a national governing body (the National Rehabilitation Institute), the establishment of norms and regulations that correspond with international conventions, the use of standardized admission protocols for most inmates and the recent experimentation with reentry programs, and alternative measures to deprivation of liberty. Notwithstanding these strengths, the system stands out for its serious shortcomings and weaknesses. Among the most acute are widespread violence between inmates, growing and critical overcrowding of some units, limited and highly insufficient services and programs for rehabilitation and reentry, the prevalence of custodial prison practices, the scarce use of alternative measures to the deprivation of liberty, and the lack of institutional transparency, accountability, and communication.

The Juvenile Justice System

Unfortunately, the shortcomings and weaknesses found in the Uruguayan judiciary and correctional system apply to the juvenile justice system as well. Whereas judges and prosecutors are well trained and highly regarded by their peers, the widespread lack of human and material resources hinders the proper development of criminal proceedings, creating delays and excessive bureaucracy. Furthermore, for adolescents who are deprived of their liberty, this implies internment in juvenile detention centers that are characterized by systematic failure to fulfill custodial and reeducational functions.[57]

HISTORY

The so-called Children's Code was enacted in 1934, echoing the need for specialized justice in the matter of minors who commit crimes or are in situations of abandonment.[58] After the enactment of the UN Convention on the Rights of the Child in 1989, a process of public debate began that would culminate in the local enactment of the Code of Childhood and Adolescence (CNA; Law No. 17.823) in 2004. The CNA determines that criminally charged adolescents are the competence of the Juvenile Courts in the first instance and of the Courts of Family Appeal in the second instance. This regulation is still in force and established the paradigm of comprehensive protection for minors who are in conflict with the law.[59]

It is also from this milestone that the Uruguayan Child and Adolescent Institute (INAU) would establish itself as a public agency in charge of safeguarding the rights of children and adolescents in the country. In 1995, the Technical Institute for Youth Rehabilitation was created within the framework of the INAU as a special body in charge of managing judicial measures applied to adolescents who are in conflict with the law. This role was subsequently carried out by the System for the Execution of Measures for Juveniles in Infringement and then by the System of Adolescent Criminal Responsibility. The latter was in place until 2016, when the National Institute for Adolescent Social Inclusion (INISA) was created as a decentralized service; it is currently in charge of implementing judicially mandated measures for adolescents who commit criminal law offenses.

STRUCTURE AND PECULIARITIES

The juvenile penal system is applied to adolescents, whom the CNA defines as those between thirteen and eighteen years of age. Adolescents as such are unimpeachable and therefore incapable of crime. However, they do commit offenses to the criminal law if they commit malicious actions or make omissions that are typified in the nCPP and in the other special criminal laws and if they commit conduct—active or omissive—to which culpability can be assigned. This is the case provided that acting judges gather the sufficient elements of conviction for determining whether the minors had the cognitive ability to understand the consequences of their actions. The Uruguayan Constitution imposes the creation of this special regime in Article 43.

Another peculiarity of the juvenile justice system is that in the previously mentioned cases, adolescents will be considered offenders as long as they have acted as perpetrators or co-perpetrators, reserving the hypothesis of the punishment of complicity only for very serious offenses. It should be noted that the CNA classifies offenses as serious and very serious, the latter being specially aggravated homicide and very specially aggravated homicide, very serious injuries, rape, robbery, aggravated deprivation of liberty, kidnapping, extortion, drug trafficking, and, in general, any typical crime whose minimum penalty is greater than six years.

Finally, and as required by international regulations, there are courts with specific jurisdiction on the matter: two Adolescent Courts in the capital and sixty-eight Courts of First Instance in the rest of the country that have jurisdiction in criminal, customs, and adolescent matters.

FUNCTIONING

The criminal process for juveniles is regulated by the CNA, to which some provisions of the nCPP apply. Before the actual judicial process, the police authority must carry out all actions aimed at apprehending the adolescent in such a way that it causes the least harm, and then it must immediately inform the relevant prosecutor's office. A medical examination must be ordered to assess the physical health of the detainee, and the presence of the adolescent's parents or guardians must always be ensured.

A hearing must be convened in which a decision will be made on the formalization of the investigation against the adolescent allegedly responsible for a criminal offense, and precautionary measures may be determined. In cases of serious offenses or sexual abuse and aggravated sexual abuse, deprivation of liberty will be mandatory if the accused is fifteen years of age or older. This regulation contradicts the CAN, which states that deprivation of liberty must be applied only as a last resort and always for the shortest possible duration. Precautionary measures can also include a semi-open regime, which implies that adolescents can visit their families or carry out activities outside the detention center.

Once the investigation has been formalized, the prosecutor has thirty days to deduct the accusation or to request a dismissal, after which the defense has another thirty days to respond and provide evidence. Subsequently, within a period of no more than forty-eight hours, the court must issue the order to open an oral trial and summon a hearing, which must be held within the following thirty days. On completion of the trial hearing, a judgment must be issued prior to the filing of evidence, and the acting judge may request an exceptional extension for up to fifteen days.

The punishments imposed may be of the same nature as the precautionary measures: deprivation of liberty, placement in a semi-open detainment regime, or alternative measures. Alternative measures must always be opted for except in those cases in which the application of deprivation of liberty is mandatory. Deprivation of liberty has a maximum duration of five years except in cases of specially and very specially aggravated homicide, rape, and specially aggravated sexual abuse, for which the duration can be extended up to ten years. Deprivation of liberty is carried out in an establishment of INISA. When adolescents who are declared judicially responsible for a criminal offense reach the age of eighteen, they will be transferred to another prison establishment to finish serving their sentence, separated from other adolescents. The institute of early release does not apply to adolescents.

Conclusion

The analysis of the Uruguayan criminal justice system sheds light and casts shadows, at least with regard to its most important elements. The UNP is one of the few police organizations in Latin America that conforms to democratic policing criteria.[60] This means that it is a police organization that is accountable to the law and not to the government; it protects human rights, is restricted in the use of force, and has the protection of citizens as its highest priority.[61] Despite the shortcomings, this is quite the achievement in a region marked by the presence of largely corrupt and nondemocratic police forces. The judiciary also enjoys relatively high levels of legitimacy, even having recently moved from an inquisitorial to an accusatory model.[62] In general terms, it is characterized by the integrity of its administration of justice and by the provision of broad guarantees for the upholding of the rule of law. Unlike the UNP, however, its greatest obstacle is the lack of human resources.

The weakest link in the Uruguayan criminal justice system is undoubtedly the correctional system, which presents the same shortcomings and difficulties that characterize other correctional systems in the region. These include overpopulation, violence, corruption, and a general lack of human and material resources. Consequently, the Uruguayan correctional system does not currently have the ability to guarantee the fundamental rights of offenders or to fulfill its primary function, which is none other than their rehabilitation. Even if to a lesser degree, this is also the case of juveniles and adolescents that are deprived of their liberty through the juvenile penal system. Ultimately, it might then be fair to say that the Uruguayan criminal justice system is improving but still suffers from a general inability to fulfill its custodial and rehabilitative functions.

Notes

1. Uruguay, officially the Oriental Republic of Uruguay, is situated in the eastern part of the Southern Cone of South America. Geographically, Uruguay is the second-smallest nation in South America after Suriname and is home to an estimated 3.3 million people, the smallest population of all independent countries in the subregion. The republic is subdivided into

nineteen departments and eighty-nine municipalities, with 40 percent of its population—1.4 million—living in the metropolitan area of Montevideo, its capital and largest city.

2. United Nations Office on Drugs and Crime, "UNODC Statistics Online: Intentional Homicide Victims," 2022, https://bit.ly/3jzk22w.

3. For an in-depth analysis and review of the UNP, see Diego Sanjurjo, Nicolás Trajtenberg, and Federico del Castillo, "Policing in Uruguay: History, Modernization and Features," in *Global Perspectives of Policing and Law Enforcement*, ed. Jospeter Mbuba (Lanham, MD: Rowman & Littlefield, 2021).

4. Rodríguez Cuitiño and María Del Rosario, "La Lucha Contra El Crimen Organizado y El Terrorismo En Uruguay: Un Desafío a Enfrentar." *Revista de Estudios En Seguridad Internacional* 4, no. 1 (2018): 55–71, https://doi.org/10.18847/1.7.4.

5. Programa de las Naciones Unidas para el Desarrollo (PNUD), *Informe Regional de Desarrollo Humano 2013–2014. Seguridad Ciudadana Con Rostro Humano: Diagnóstico y Propuestas Para América Latina* (Panama City: PNUD, 2013), 113; Eurostat, "Police, Court and Prison Personnel Statistics," 2018, https://bit.ly/30AX9D0.

6. Nilia Viscardi and Ricardo Fraiman, "Educación Policial En Uruguay. Transformaciones Para La Consolidación de Un Modelo de Protección Integral," in *Conflictos Sociales, Luchas Sociales y Políticas de Seguridad Ciudadana*, ed. César Barreira, José Vicente Tavares dos Santos, Jaime Zuluaga Nieto, Roberto González Arana, and Felipe González Ortiz (Mexico City: Autonomous University of Mexico State, 2013), 281–310, https://bit .ly/2SKKNIf; Timote Correa and Guillermo Andrés, "Aspectos Normativos de La Enseñanza Policial En El Uruguay. Notas Para Pensar La Formación Policial Uruguaya," *Revista Policía Y Seguridad Pública* 7, no. 1 (2017): 401–32, https://doi.org/10.5377/rpsp.v7i1.4315.

7. Ministerio del Interior, "Remuneraciones 2019," 2019, https://bit.ly/2CxoEpe.

8. Andrew DePietro, "Here's How Much Money Police Officers Earn in Every State," *Forbes*, 2020, https://bit.ly/2EgFclT.

9. David Weisburd and John E. Eck, "What Can Police Do to Reduce Crime, Disorder, and Fear?," *Annals of the American Academy of Political and Social Science* 593 (May 2004): 42–65, https://doi.org/10.1177/0002716203262548.

10. Juan Ariel Bogliaccini, James Edward Monogan, and Juan Ignacio Pereira, "Tackling Druglords in an Incipient Market: Police Raids and Drug Crime in Uruguay," paper presented at the 115th American Political Science Association Annual Meeting and Exhibition, 2019, https://bit .ly/2UxNKJO; Alejandro Cid, "Saturation Policing and Robberies: Quasi-Experimental Evidence about the Effect of Sudden and Quick Operations," *Justice Evaluation Journal* 2, no. 2 (2019): 164–80. https://doi.org/10.1080/24751979.2019.1629827.

11. Sanjurjo et al., "Policing in Uruguay."

12. Beatriz Abizanda, Joan Serra Hoffman, Lina Marmolejo, and Suzanne Duryea, *Citizen Security: Conceptual Framework and Empirical Evidence* (Washington, DC: Inter-American Development Bank, 2012).

13. Alejandro Vila, "La Matriz Policial Uruguaya: 40 Años de Gestación," in *Uruguay: Inseguridad, Delito y Estado*, ed. Rafael Paternain and Álvaro Rico (Montevideo: CSIC—Universidad de la República), 203–29.

14. Lucía Dammert, "Challenges of Police Reform in Latin America," in *Routledge Handbook of Law and Society in Latin America*, ed. Rachel Sieder, Karina Ansolabehere, and Tatiana Alfonso (New York: Routledge, 2019), 1–26; Mark Ungar, *Policing Democracy: Overcoming Obstacles to Citizen Security in Latin America* (Baltimore: Johns Hopkins University Press, 2011), https://doi.org/10.1353/book.60322.

15. Nicolás Trajtenberg, "Políticas Públicas: El Caso Del Programa de Seguridad Ciudadana," in *Violencia, Inseguridad y Miedos En Uruguay. ¿Qué Tienen Para Decir Las Ciencias*

Sociales?, ed. Rafael Paternain and Rafael Sanseviero (Montevideo: Friedrich Ebert Stiftung, 2008), 171–76.

16. Mary Fran T. Malone and Lucía Dammert, "The Police and the Public: Policing Practices and Public Trust in Latin America," *Policing and Society* 31, no. 4 (2021): 1–16, https://doi.org/10.1080/10439463.2020.1744600.

17. Rafael Paternain, "Políticas de Policía y Gobiernos de Izquierda: El Caso de Uruguay," *Delito y Sociedad* 2, no. 44 (2017): 161–200, https://doi.org/10.14409/dys.v2i44.7627; Alejandro Vila, "La Política de Seguridad Ciudadana Del Mujiquismo: Entre Acuerdos y Disensos," in *El Decenio Progresista: Las Políticas Públicas de Vázquez a Mujica*, ed. Nicolás Bentancur and José Miguel Busquets (Montevideo: Fin de Siglo; Banco Interamericano de Desarrollo and Ministerio del Interior, 2018), 255–77; Banco Interamericano de Desarrollo and Ministerio del Interior, *¿Cómo Evitar El Delito Urbano? El Programa de Alta Dedicación Operativa En La Nueva Policía Uruguaya* (Montevideo: Banco Interamericano de Desarrollo and Ministerio del Interior de la República Oriental del Uruguay, 2018).

18. Ignacio Munyo and Martín A. Rossi, "Police-Monitored Cameras and Crime," *Scandinavian Journal of Economics* 122, no. 3 (2019):1027–44, https://doi.org/10.1111/sjoe.12375.

19. United Nations Office on Drugs and Crime–INEGI, "El Sistema de Gestión de Seguridad Pública Del Ministerio Del Interior de La República Oriental Del Uruguay," Serie de Publicaciones Sobre Buenas Prácticas Para La Calidad Estadística (Mexico City: Naciones Unidas, 2021), https://bit.ly/3uVaPXz.

20. Banco Interamericano de Desarrollo and Ministerio del Interior, *¿Cómo Evitar El Delito Urbano?*; Spencer P. Chainey, Rodrigo Serrano-Berthet, and Federico Veneri, The Impact of a Hot Spot Policing Program in Montevideo, Uruguay: An Evaluation Using a Quasi-Experimental Difference-in-Difference Negative Binomial Approach," *Police Practice and Research* 22, no. 5 (2020): 1–16, https://doi.org/10.1080/15614263.2020.1749619.

21. Federico del Castillo, "Génesis, Desarrollo y Profesionalización Del Análisis Criminal En La Policía Nacional," in Banco Interamericano de Desarrollo and Ministerio del Interior, *¿Cómo Evitar El Delito Urbano?*.

22. Herman Goldstein, "Improving Policing: A Problem-Oriented Approach," *Crime and Delinquency* 25, no. 2 (1979): 236–58.

23. Federico del Castillo, "Obstacles to Problem-Oriented Policing in Montevideo," *Policing* 42, no. 3 (2019): 334–46, https://doi.org/10.1108/PIJPSM-02-2018-0025.

24. Federico del Castillo, "¿Uruguay Tiene Una Policía Preventiva? La Situación de La Prevención Del Delito en la Reforma Policial Uruguaya," *Fronteras* 14, no. 1 (2020): 28–40.

25. Hugo Frühling, "A Realistic Look at Latin American Community Policing Programmes," *Policing and Society* 22, no. 1 (2012): 76–88, https://doi.org/10.1080/10439463.2011.636816; Annabelle Dias Felix and Tina Hilgers, "Community Oriented Policing Theory and Practice: Global Policy Diffusion or Local Appropriation?," *Policing and Society*, https://doi.org/10.1080/10439463.2020.1776280.

26. Sanjurjo et al., "Policing in Uruguay."

27. David H. Bayley, "A Foreign Policy for Democratic Policing," *Policing and Society* 5, no. 2 (1995): 79–93, https://doi.org/10.1080/10439463.1995.9964713.

28. Mariana Mota Prado, Michael Trebilcock, and Patrick Hartford, "Police Reform in Violent Democracies in Latin America," *Hague Journal on the Rule of Law* 4, https://doi.org/10.1017/S1876404512000164; José Miguel Cruz, "State and Criminal Violence in Latin America," *Crime, Law and Social Change* 66, no. 4 (2016): 375–96, https://doi.org/10.1007/s10611-016-9631-9.

29. Corporación Latinobarómetro, "Análisis Online," 2022, https://www.latinobarometro.org/latOnline.jsp.

30. Corporación Andina de Fomento, *Por Una América Latina Más Segura: Una Nueva Perspectiva Para Prevenir y Controlar El Delito* (Bogota: Panamericana Formas e Impresos S.A., 2014), 230–32.

31. Ministerio del Interior, "Encuesta Nacional de Victimización 2017," 2017, https://bit.ly/3jBXj5N.

32. Mollie J. Cohen, Noam Lupu, and Elizabeth J. Zechmeister, eds., *The Political Culture of Democracy in the Americas, 2016/17: A Comparative Study of Democracy and Governance* (Washington, DC: United States Agency for International Development, 2017).

33. Cruz, "State and Criminal Violence in Latin America"; Dammert, "Challenges in Latin America."

34. Cohen et al., *The Political Culture of Democracy in the Americas.*

35. Corporación Latinobarómetro, *Informe Latinobarómetro 2017* (Buenos Aires: Corporación Latinobarómetro, 2017).

36. Cruz, "State and Criminal Violence in Latin America."

37. Cf. Dardo Preza Restuccia, *El Proceso Penal Uruguayo* (Montevideo: Fundación de Cultura Universitaria, 2009), and Marccello Franco, *La prisión preventiva: ¿Remedio eficaz para enfrentar la amenaza a la seguridad pública o tan solo aseguramiento procesal?* (Montevideo: Editorial Carlos Álvarez, 2010).

38. Cf. Alejandro Abal, "Antecedentes del Nuevo C.P.P.: Las iniciativas de codificación procesal penal en Uruguay," in *Curso sobre el Nuevo Código del Proceso Penal* (Montevideo: Fundación de Cultura Universitaria, 2018), 17–37.

39. Eduardo Sasson and Martín Arroyo, "Indagatoria preliminar: Deberes y límites del accionar fiscal en la recolección de evidencias, derechos del imputado y herramientas de la defensa," in *IX Jornadas Nacionales de Derecho Procesal* (Lavalleja: Fundación de Cultura Universitaria, 2020), 365–78.

40. Diego Camaño, "El encarcelamiento cautelar en el modelo acusatorio de justicia penal," in *Estudios sobre el Nuevo Proceso Penal* (Montevideo: Fundación de Cultura Universitaria, 2018), 133–57.

41. Gabriel Valentin, "Las partes," in *Estudios sobre el Nuevo Proceso Penal,* 259–365.

42. Fiscalía General de la Nación, "Sistema penal uruguayo: Balance a diciembre de 2020," 2021, https://bit.ly/3Gaw9Nk.

43. Cf. Ignacio Soba, *Proceso penal uruguayo: Estructuras procesales y vías alternativas* (Montevideo: La Ley Uruguay, 2020).

44. Fiscalía General de la Nación, "Sistema penal uruguayo."

45. World Justice Project, Rule of Law Index 2022, 2022, https://bit.ly/3X07p4h.

46. Corporación Latinobarómetro, "Análisis Online."

47. Carlos Vilalta and Gustavo Fondevila, "Prison Populism in Latin America: Reviewing the Dynamics of Prison Population Growth," Strategic Note, Igarapé Institute, 2019.

48. Institute for Criminal Policy Research, "Highest to Lowest—Prison Population Total," World Prison Brief, https://bit.ly/2ZTUQMh.

49. Álvaro Garcé, Lucía Casal, Carlos Díaz, and Lucía Donnangelo, *Privación de Libertad y Reinserción Social En Uruguay* (Montevideo: CERES and CAF, 2017).

50. Institute for Criminal Policy Research, "Highest to Lowest."

51. Cf. Comisionado Parlamentario Penitenciario, *Informe Anual 2019* (Montevideo: Parlamento del Uruguay, 2019).

52. Garcé et al., *Privación de Libertad y Reinserción Social en Uruguay.*

53. "En ningún caso se permitirá que las cárceles sirvan para mortificar, y sí sólo para asegurar a los procesados y penados, persiguiendo su reeducación, la aptitud para el trabajo y la

profilaxis del delito." Uruguay-IMPO, "Constitución de la República Oriental del Uruguay," 1967, https://www.impo.com.uy/bases/constitucion/1967–1967.

54. Comisionado Parlamentario Penitenciario, *Informe Anual 2019.*

55. Víctor González, Emiliano Rojido, and Nicolás Trajtenberg, "Sistema Penitenciario de Uruguay (1985–2014): Cambios, Continuidades y Desafíos," in *Discutir La Cárcel, Pensar La Sociedad: Contra El Sentido Común Punitivo*, ed. Gianella Bardazano, Aníbal Corti, Nicolás Duffau, and Nicolás Trajtenberg, Colección Artículo 2 (Montevideo: CSIC Universidad de la República, Trilce, 2015), 127–52.

56. Lucía Dammert, "Rehabilitation in Latin America: Could Innovation Be Fostered in Precarious Conditions?," 2016, https://bit.ly/3ySuE46.

57. Luis Eduardo Morás, "Más Allá y de Las Ideologías: Sistema Penal Juvenil y Consenso Punitivo En Uruguay," *Boletín Criminológico* 3, no. 184 (2019): 1–13.

58. Claudia Romano and Eduardo Cavalli, "Particularidades del proceso penal de adolescentes," in *Estudios sobre el Nuevo Proceso Penal* (Montevideo: Fundación de Cultura Universitaria, 2018), 421–38.

59. Morás, "Más Allá y de Las Ideologías."

60. Bayley, "A Foreign Policy for Democratic Policing."

61. Sanjurjo et al., "Policing in Uruguay."

62. Corporación Latinobarómetro, "Análisis Online."

CHAPTER 18

The Brazilian Criminal Justice System

Fabio R. Bechara and Leandro Piquet Carneiro

There is an emerging consensus among political leaders and public opinion that crime and violence are serious social problems in contemporary Brazil. This complex social phenomenon undermines the country's capacity to achieve a more equitable society and a competitive economy. The role and modernization of criminal justice institutions are at the core of the debate about the public actions needed to minimize the effects of crime and violence in Brazilian society.

This chapter describes Brazil's criminal justice system and its constitutive elements. Brazil is a federation with twenty-six states and a federal district. The 1988 Constitution of the Federative Republic of Brazil (CF), which was promulgated after the military regime of 1964–1985, defined the current organization of the Brazilian criminal justice system (BCJS). The BCJS encompasses institutions at all three levels of the Brazilian federation, including the executive and the judiciary. All twenty-seven federative units are entitled to organize their own police forces, judiciaries, and prosecution under the same constitutional rules. The BCJS is organized into three main subsystems—public security, criminal justice, and criminal enforcement—that pursue the prevention of criminal offenses, the investigation of crimes, prosecution, judgment, and penal reform.

Criminal prosecution follows procedural rules that are established in the CF, and different actors share responsibility for prosecutorial operations. The duty to investigate crimes is shared by the federal police department, state-level civil police, and state prosecution offices or the federal prosecution office. However, the prosecution is the exclusive duty of the prosecution office and, notably, the victim. The trial is the exclusive purview of the judiciary. The execution of the sentence is shared among the judiciary, the executive, prosecution offices, and civil society organizations; each institution has a specific role in supervising the offenders.

The CF is a landmark for Brazilian democracy and human rights, with an undeniable influence over the criminal justice system. It defines institutional duties for the promotion and protection of rights and guarantees, and it provides for decentralized organization and shared duties. It also establishes a complex system of checks and balances. Notably, the CF banned all cruel punishments. Judicial impartiality ensures the dialectical and contradictory character of the process and the equality of access to legal assistance during the trial.

However, this was not always the case, and although this process is constantly evolving and improving, a brief historical account of its development is in order. The Portuguese criminal justice system model influenced the use of normative reference in Brazil. The main characteristics of this system of inquiry, which was used in colonial times, include the concentration of powers, judicial activism, the secrecy of court proceedings, and the reduced control by the interested parties. Over time, this model changed. For example, the Brazilian Criminal Procedure Code of 1941 was influenced by the fascist-influenced 1930 Italian Penal Code—also referred to as the Rocco Code—which is still in force. However, the Brazilian Criminal Procedure Code has since been amended numerous times to eliminate certain elements of inquiry and to adapt it better to the CF principles.

The legal framework of the BCJS comprises the CF, the Penal and Criminal Procedure Codes, the Penal Correctional Law, and special criminal legislation. The 250 articles of the CF define the infraconstitutional codes' general principles. It also establishes the normative principles that guide the legal organization of the country and its criminal justice system, including the dignity of the human person, the prohibition of cruel punishments, and the guarantee of due process of law, among other contemporary civil and political rights. The Penal Code (Código Penal [CP]) defines crimes and penalties (e.g., deprivation of liberty, fines, restriction of rights). It also establishes the respective rules of application in time and space, rules of judicial interpretation, criteria for defining sanctions, and the criteria for characterizing the infractions. The Criminal Procedure Code regulates prosecution and defense, investigation, jurisdiction, judicial decisions, and appeals. The Penal Correctional Code defines not only the procedure for the sentencing but also prison enforcement agencies, the rights and protection of inmates, infractions and disciplinary sanctions in prison facilities, and, above all, the role of the community as a determining factor so that the penalty fulfills its resocialization function. Special penal legislation is an option for Brazilian legislators in regulating specific issues individually instead of modifying the role codes, which apply in issues that have both criminal law and procedural law provisions, such as money laundering, organized crime, environmental crimes, and financial and tax crimes.

The Structure and General Functioning of the Judiciary in the Country

ORIGINS AND DEVELOPMENT OF THE BRAZILIAN CRIMINAL PROCEDURE SYSTEM

In the Americas, procedural systems evolved after the second half of the twentieth century and have been increasingly influenced by international human rights documents that emphasize ideals of the fair process model of justice, judicial impartiality, bodily and personal respect for the accused, and the inviolability of the defense regardless of the inquisitional or accusatory origin of the procedural system. Brazil's criminal procedural system, despite its inquisitional background, was deeply influenced by this international judicial reform movement and biased toward the adversarial model. Consequently, the BCSJ has been incorporating mechanisms of agreement between prosecution offices and defendants since the 1990s in order to reduce the length of time that criminal justice proceedings take. These mechanisms cover almost 90 percent of the crimes of Brazilian criminal statutes.

In this sense, it is worth highlighting the characteristics of the Brazilian criminal procedure as recognized in the CF. These include separation of the functions of accusing and judging. The role of accusation is reserved exclusively for the prosecution office and, remarkably, in cases expressly provided for by law, for the victim. Nevertheless, the function of judging is committed to the judiciary for the judgment of common crimes and to the legislative power in the case of political crimes, such as cases of impeachment. Other characteristics of the Brazilian criminal procedure include the wide publicity of procedural acts, the prohibition of illegal evidence, the presumption of innocence, the impartiality and independence of the judge, motivation for judicial decisions, contradictory and full defense, equality of defense, and the right to appeal.

Within this framework, it is worth mentioning the changes in the role of judges over time. The approval in 2019 of a federal law separates judges from investigations in trials. For a judge to exercise judicial functions and be a valid subject of proceedings, the judge must be able to act in his or her role as a judge.

STRUCTURE OF THE BRAZILIAN JUSTICE SYSTEM

The Brazilian judiciary is organized in the CF at the federal and state levels. Hierarchically, higher courts oversee decisions made by lower courts. Each body of the judiciary has the duty to determine the type of matter to be discussed at trial, the location of the offense, the actions of the author of the crime, and the victim's domicile. In the BCJS, the task of judging crimes has some unseemly peculiarities. For example, if a citizen commits a murder in Rio de Janeiro, the state justice of Rio de Janeiro will judge them. However, if the author of the same crime is the president of the republic or a minister, a supreme federal court judge, or another high-level federal public official, the federal Supreme Court has the jurisdiction to judge them regardless of where the crime was committed. The rationale for those intertwined criteria for jurisdictional allocation is adequate for maximizing the preservation of evidence at the location of the infraction, the social repercussion of the crime, the safeguard of public functions, and the specialized knowledge needed for trial-specific matters. Allegedly, from the perspective of the Brazilian legislators who built the 1988 CF, these are criteria that rationalize the distribution of justice.

At the level of the state-level judiciary, all Brazilian states have the same two-level structure of trial courts and appellate courts. A judge decides most criminal cases without a jury present. Only cases of homicide require a jury; all other criminal and noncriminal offenses are subject to a single judge's decision. Justice Courts are appellate courts composed of multimember judges who overview the procedures in matters of criminal law, public law, and civil law. Each state has appellate courts that do not retry cases or hear new evidence and do not empanel juries.

At the federal level, the federal Supreme Court (Supremo Tribunal Federal [STF]) is the highest body of the judiciary and the one that interprets the CF. The STF is the court of appeal for any constitutional matter and can serve as the first court for cases within its jurisdiction or even for common criminal offenses committed by the president of the republic and ministers of cabinet, the members of the National Congress, the STF judges, and the attorney general of the republic. Below the STF, there are three superior courts to interpret infraconstitutional legislation: the Superior Labor Court (Tribunal Superior do Trabalho [TST]), the Superior Electoral Court (Tribunal Superior Eleitoral), and the Superior Court of Justice (Superior Tribunal de Justiça [STJ]). The STJ is responsible for disciplining federal law interpretation throughout Brazil based on constitutional principles. Therefore, it is the final instance of the Brazilian Judiciary for infraconstitutional causes, the body of convergence of ordinary justice from state-level courts.

The Superior Electoral Court monitors the electoral legislation and ensures the legitimacy of the election process by organizing elections and overviewing populations' political rights in the country. Brazilian polls are organized by a professional contingent of judges who try electoral crimes (e.g., fraud, voter coercion, corruption, and illegal financing practices) and, with the help of a professional body of public officers, organize the voting process. In the current democratic period, Brazil has achieved a high level of electoral integrity thanks to the professional characteristic of its electoral justice.

The TST's constitutional mission is to standardize labor jurisprudence in the country and trial offenses against the infraconstitutional labor laws. It also has the power to judge appeals against decisions of Regional Labor Courts from the states (Tribunais Regionais do Trabalho [TRTs]). The TRTs are decentralized federal courts that function as the entry door for cases about such matters as agreements between worker's unions and employers. However, crimes against workers' rights (e.g., workplace law violations, the illegal employment of children, and attempts to submit workers to labor conditions analogous to slavery) are judged by state or federal courts, depending on whether the matter at hand is an individual or a collective concern.

The CF additionally defines the organization of military justice at the federal and state levels. If a military police officer is indicted on charges of murdering a civilian, then that officer will face a jury trial at a state court. The military courts at the federal level judge only crimes committed by members of the military. The federal Military Court, under the *ratione materiae* criterion, is tasked with trying military personnel for military crimes. When the competence of the state military justice is at stake, the criterion *ratione personae* (the quality of the agent as a military) is required in order to proceed with the trial.

The Prosecution System

The Brazilian Public Prosecutor's Office (PPO) is a permanent and essential institution of the BCJS. Defined in Article 127 of the CF, its mission is to defend the democratic regime, the legal order, and collective and individual rights. The PPO is independent of the judiciary and the executive. Therefore, prosecutors are irreplaceable and have functional independence in Brazil. The Brazilian consensual model of democracy[1] explains the logic of separation of powers—the division of government responsibilities into distinct branches—that ensures the institutional autonomy of the Brazilian PPO, which is unique in institutional design in Latin America.[2] In Mexico, for example, the Procuraduría General de la Republica's failure in its mission to reduce criminality, violence, and corruption by carrying out professional criminal investigations is regarded as a direct consequence of its ties to the executive branch.[3] The Brazilian PPO is not encumbered by such ties.

The PPO is organized into two independent levels: federal and state. The federal prosecution functions are divided between the federal public PPO, the military PPO, the labor PPO, and the PPO of the federal district and territories. The head of the PPO of the union is the republic's attorney general, appointed by the president of the republic. The state governor appoints the state attorney general after forming a triple list through election by members of the state's PPO.

A state's attorney general mediates the jurisdictional conflicts between members of the same PPO. The republic's attorney general resolves the jurisdictional conflicts between members of different branches of the PPO of the union. When the dispute implicates jurisdictional conflicts at the state level, the state PPO mediates the conflict. The STF recognized the constitutionality of the investigative power of the PPO. The civil police at the state level and the federal district are also responsible for carrying out investigations of criminal offenses.

The civil police and the PPO are entitled to conduct investigations although with distinct roles in the criminal prosecution process. The civil police service is dedicated to ordinary cases and maintaining the routine services at police precincts. In most federal states, the PPO is engaged in more complex investigations against organized crime and political corruption. The PPO has an additional and vital function: to act as an external controller of the police activity at the federal and state levels. The states' PPOs also control the military and the civil police, the federal PPO, and all the federal police forces, as discussed below.

Historically, Brazil has passed through significant regime transitions. Since its independence in 1822, Brazil has had seven constitutions (1824, 1891, 1934, 1937, 1946, 1967, and 1988), marking essential transitions in its political regime. Since the inception of the 1988 CF, the PPO as an institution is no longer controlled by the executive branch but is an independent institution that plays a decisive role in the BCJS. Therefore, the autonomy of the actual PPO is the direct result of the democratization of the Brazilian state during the past thirty-three years.

Police and Law Enforcement

Following the country's civil law, the existing police forces derive their authority from the CF through the following bodies: a federal police force, federal highway police, federal railway police, federal prison police, state civil police, state military police, and state prison police. In addition, the municipalities are responsible for creating local municipal guards, bodies with only limited police powers. Civil and military police forces are state-level institutions regulated by state laws and the CF. Since Brazil is a federal republic formed by the union of twenty-six federal states and the federal district, fifty-four state police forces are responsible for policing and performing crime control and investigation activities.

At the local level, 60 percent of the 5,000 municipalities have a municipal guard.[4] According to Brazilian federalism principles, states are not allowed to pass any penal legislation or change the organization of police forces. States have both military and civil police forces per the CF. Although recognized as part of the federation, municipal governments have not had a constitutional mandate to institute a security police organ. The Municipal Guard typically provides security services on local government facilities. Still, in recent years, the Municipal Guard has considerably expanded its role in law enforcement activities. A federal law from 2014 authorized it to carry out preventive patrolling activities, a significant change from the original intention of the 1988 CF. This change was motivated primarily by mayors and local administrations in the face of the overwhelming pressure of violence and rising crime rates in Brazil.[5] This significant institutional adaptation led to social demand for a more adequate and effective response to public security problems.

In addition to these agencies, the Office of the Public Prosecutor (OPP) also has the authority to undertake criminal investigations. The federal OPP is notably diligent in political corruption cases, and the states' OPPs are responsible for investigating organized crime cases. Both federal and state OPPs are vested in the external control of police activities. As a result, criminal offenses committed by police officers and the violation of constitutional rights of prisoners who are in direct custody of the police authorities are monitored and investigated by federal and local OPPs. There is no formal subordination of the police forces to the OPP at the national or state level. However, if a prosecutor confirms any disciplinary faults, then the prosecutor must make a report to their superiors about the offending police officer and propose appropriate legal sanctions.[6]

The Correctional System

Penal enforcement in Brazil is governed by the Penal Correctional Law (Lei de Execução Penal [LEP]). However, those principles in the CF also shape the sentencing process for criminal offenses in Brazil, such as the individualization of the sentences. Additionally, the CP defines the rules for the sentencing process, notably those related to the characteristics of prison regimes.

In conceptual terms, criminal enforcement can be defined as the procedure for the application of different types of criminal sanctions provided for in criminal law. Criminal sanctions range from penalties such as prison sentences, rights restrictions, and fines.[7]

Prison sentences in Brazil can change over the duration of the sentence. For example, a prison term could be changed into an arrangement whereby the offender stays in a penal facility at night but leaves to work during the day, or the offender could regain freedom under probation. The correctional authority offers such a progressive regime to prisoners who meet their sentences' eligibility and suitability requirements. This progressive regime is mandatory, and all sentenced inmates need to progress through all the stages in order to achieve progression to an open prison or release. The progression is subject to two basic restrictions: the length of the sentence and the behavior of the convicted.

The Brazilian correctional system is an excellent example of how criminal enforcement in the country requires the intervention of multiple public agents with different attributions and overlapping tasks. Therefore, a complex system of checks and balances is the most prominent characteristic of the Brazilian criminal enforcement system. According to the LEP, the correctional institutions in Brazil are the National Council for Criminal and Penitentiary Policy (CNPCP), the Correctional Court, the PPO, the Penitentiary Council, the Penitentiary Departments, the Patronage, the Community Council, and the Public Defender's Office.

The CNPCP is a collegiate body based in Brazil and linked to the Ministry of Justice. It comprises thirteen members, who are appointed by the Ministry of Justice; researchers, specialists, and practitioners in criminal law, criminal procedure, correction, and related sciences; and members of society and other ministries. The mission of the CNPCP is to recommend to the Ministry of Justice criminal and correctional policies regarding crime prevention, penal law, and the administration of the criminal justice system. Additionally, the CNPCP has a relevant role in evaluating criminal justice system policies, the training of correctional facilities personnel, the production of criminal statistics, and the inspection of correctional facilities nationwide. Every four years, the CNPCP presents the National Criminal and Correctional Policy Plan, a white paper that contributes to guiding the executive and the judiciary through a presidential term.[8]

The Penitentiary Departments are organized into the National Penitentiary Department (Departamento Penitenciário Nacional [DEPEN]) at the federal level and into state-level Penitentiary Departments. The DEPEN is subordinate to the Ministry of Justice and directly linked to the CNPCP, providing the CNPCP with administrative and financial support. Ultimately, the DEPEN is the executive body that implements the national correctional policies formulated and supported by the CNPCP.

The work of the DEPEN is not restricted to the federal realm. It is the executive body responsible for integrating federal and state governments, which makes its role in the BCJS significant insofar as it limits variations among federation units in correctional policies matters.[9] In this capacity, the DEPEN's functions include planning and coordinating national policy on penal services, monitoring the application of criminal enforcement rules throughout the national territory, periodically inspecting penal establishments and services, technically assisting states with implementing the principles and rules established in the LEP, and collaborating with the federation units in carrying out training courses for penitentiary personnel, convicts, and inmates. This extensive list of responsibilities and activities demonstrates that the DEPEN is a critical agent in correctional system governance.

For the most part, the DEPEN relies on relatively weak mechanisms for coordinating the national correction system since the states have sufficient autonomy to formulate and execute their correctional policies. The responsibility for decision making on correctional policies remains at the ministry level with federal institutions, but the states have a great deal of autonomy in developing and implementing local policies. However, there is a critical lack of reliable and up-to-date statistical information for planning long-term policies or determining the priorities to be addressed by national and local authorities. To overcome this information gap, the CNPCP's National Criminal and Correctional Policy Plan (2020–2023)[10] has established a goal of carrying out a census in order to collect information on prisoners and to take a snapshot of the system. Additionally, this plan entails the creation of the National Electronic Information System, which gathers data for the purpose of fostering cooperation and supporting the governance of the national penitentiary system.

Final Remarks

There are enormous challenges for how the cogs and gears of the criminal justice system fit together and respond to the country's high crime rates. Based on the World Bank's data on homicides, Brazil is the sixth most violent country globally, with 27.4 homicides per 100,000 inhabitants in 2018.[11] The ten most violent countries in the world are in the Americas region.[12] Compared with some of its South American neighbors or other countries with similar socioeconomic indicators in South America, such as Argentina, Chile, and Uruguay, Brazil has performed remarkably poorly on crime control and prevention policies.[13] What also puzzles researchers on crime and violence in Brazil is that the country became more violent during the decades of 2000s and 2010s, a span of time in which inequality and poverty fell substantially in the country.

We raise the hypothesis that the current institutional design of the BCJS and the crime control policies implemented by federal and state governments are critical variables for understanding the Brazilian failure to develop more effective policies to curb crime and violence. In our view, the criminal justice system is the locus of the present crisis, which spans decades. It is a common intellectual and political feature of Latin American countries to be particularly lenient in applying legal penalties to criminals. Considering the level of crime observed in the region, it is not surprising that indulgent laws, short minimum sentences, a low number of police officers per inhabitant, and low levels of incarceration have contributed to the fact that, in general, these countries have high levels of criminal impunity.[14]

Another primary concern among specialists is the amount of time that the criminal justice system takes in Brazil. In Rio de Janeiro, 66 percent of homicide cases remain open after three years, and among the sentenced cases, the average time elapsed until the sentence begins is two years. The state of São Paulo performs better: 59 percent of homicide cases remain open after three years, and the average time between the beginning of the procedure and the sentence is the same as in Rio de Janeiro (two years).[15] Moreover, reviews and appeals in criminal proceedings within the same courts and appeals to superior courts are ordinarily managed by defendants—usually wealthier ones—which helps them delay proceedings and evade justice.

Overall, the framework of Brazilian federalism is particularly flawed in producing coordination between federal levels thanks to overlapping jurisdictions and competencies and, consequently, inadequate allocation of resources. Additionally, the Brazilian judiciary is overspecialized, fragmented, and rigidly hierarchical. The separation among criminal, electoral, military, and civil courts, all with concurrent jurisdictions in criminal cases, illustrates the extent of the problem of specialization in the BCJS.

However, Brazil has made significant advances in international cooperation in criminal matters. The country has been an active member of multilateral cooperation institutions since World War II and has ratified all relevant conventions and protocols in the field, including the Convention for the Prevention and Punishment of the Crime of Genocide (1948); the 1951 Refugee Convention; the Protocol Relating to the Status of Refugees (1966); the International Covenant on Civil and Political Rights (1966); the International Convention on the Elimination of All Forms of Racial Discrimination (1965); the International Convention on All Forms of Discrimination against Women (1979); the Optional Protocol to the Convention on the Elimination of All Forms of Discrimination against Women (1999); the Convention against Torture and Other Cruel, Inhuman, or Degrading Treatment or Punishment (1984); the Convention on the Rights of the Child (1989); the Rome Statute of the International Criminal Court (1998); the Optional Protocol to the Convention on the Rights of the Child on the Sale of Children, Child Prostitution, and Child Pornography (2000); the Optional Protocol to the Convention on the Rights of the Child on the Involvement of Children in Armed Conflict (2000); and the United Nations Convention against Transnational Organized Crime and the Protocols Thereto (2000).[16] These conventions and protocols were converted into domestic legislation, particularly by the CF of 1988. In this sense, it is possible to affirm that the country's active participation in multilateral cooperation organizations in the post–World War II period has contributed to producing a domestic legal order that is aligned with solid liberal democratic principles. Unfortunately, however, problems of governance, institutional organization, corruption, police violence, and racism persist in the BCJS, which prevents the potential benefits of this liberal democratic order from reaching most of the population.

Notes

1. A. Lijphart, *Democracies: Patterns of Majoritarian and Consensus Government in Twenty-One Countries* (New Haven, CT: Yale University Press, 1984).

2. Centro de Estudios de Justicia de las Américas, *Desafíos del Ministerio Público Fiscal en América Latina*, 2005, accessed February 20, 2022, https://biblioteca.cejamericas.org/bitstream/handle/2015/1754/CEJA_PERS-01.pdf?sequence=1&isAllowed=y.

3. X. Suárez-Enríquez and Ú. Indacochea, *A Fiscalía That Works in México: Report from WOLA and Due Process of Law Foundation*, 2018, https://www.dplf.org/sites/default/files/eng-fiscalia-report.pdf.

4. Instituto Brasileiro de Geografia e Estatística (IBGE), "Pesquisa de informações básicas municipais," in *Instituto Brasileiro de Geografia e Estatística* (Rio de Janeiro: IBGE, 2012), accessed September 15, 2020, http://www .ibge .gov .br/home/estatistica/economia/perfilmunic/2012.

5. Instituto De Pesquisa Econômica Aplicada (IPEA), *Atlas da violência: Retratos dos municípios brasileiros* (Rio de Janeiro: IPEA, 2019).

6. For a more detailed analysis of the Brazilian polices and law enforcement institutions, see L. Piquet Carneiro, "The Organization and Functioning of Police Forces in Brazil," in *Global Perspectives in Policing and Law Enforcement*, ed. Jospeter M. Mbuba (Lanham, MD: Lexington Books, 2021).

7. A. C. de Brito, *Execução Penal* (São Paulo: Editora Saraiva, 2020).

8. In Brazil, the executive and Congress have the same four-year term.

9. Brito, *Execução Penal.*

10. Ministério da Justiça e Segurança Pública, "Plano Nacional de Política: Criminal e Penitenciária (2020–2023)," https://www.gov.br/depen/pt-br/composicao/cnpcp/plano_nacional/PNPCP-2020-2023.pdf.

11. World Bank, "Intentional Homicides (per 100,000 People)," https://data.worldbank.org/indicator/VC.IHR.PSRC.P5.

12. El Salvador, Jamaica, Honduras, Venezuela, Mexico, Brazil, Colombia, Guatemala, and St. Lucia. World Bank, "Intentional Homicides."

13. L. Piquet Carneiro and Fabio R. Bechara, "O impacto no Brasil dos mercados ilícitos globais e do crime transnacional," in *Criminalidade organizada: Investigação, direito e ciência* (São Paulo: Almedina), 69–104.

14. Rodrigo R. Soares and J. Naritomi, "Understanding High Crime Rates in Latin America: The Role of Social and Policy Factors," in *The Economics of Crime: Lessons for and from Latin America* (Cambridge, MA: National Bureau of Economic Research, 2010), 19–55.

15. L. Ribeiro, I. Machado, and K. Silva, "Tempo na ou da justiça criminal brasileira: Uma discussão metodológica," *Opinião pública* 18, no. 2 (2012,): 355–82.

16. V. de Oliveira Mazzouli, *Curso de direito internacional público*, 5th ed. (São José do Rio Preto: Revista dos Tribunais, 2011), 818.

CHAPTER 19

The Criminal Justice System in Mexico

Carlos Daniel Gutierrez-Mannix

Policing and Law Enforcement

BRIEF HISTORY

The history of policing in the territory that is now occupied by Mexico stretches back centuries. While dozens if not hundreds of nations flourished in the geographical area now known as Mexico, most of our knowledge about policing before the Spanish colonization of the area comes from what we know about the Aztec Empire. For example, it is understood that the Aztec capital was composed of *campas*, or neighborhoods. *Topillos*, or guardians, were assigned to each neighborhood, and they were in charge of maintaining peace and order. Among their tasks were mandating hygiene standards, establishing public order, and detaining and processing criminals.[1] However, it was the Cihuacoatl, or supreme judge, who dictated sentences and provided punishment.[2] In this regard, the position of guardian was one of great merit during pre-Columbian Mexico. In the Aztec Empire, guardians were chosen in a public ceremony and assigned to neighborhoods.[3] They each received a colored belt that identified them with a neighborhood, or *barrio*.

In the Spanish colony, the task of policing was modified to parallel the French model of policing. The police force was centralized, and it controlled many aspects of public life. For example, they were in charge of corrections, repairing roads and bridges, guaranteeing free trade, and transporting criminals.[4] However, the role of police forces in Mexico was not fully codified into law until after the country gained independence in 1810. For example, the 1848 Constitution created a police administration with 500 members, and by 1856, the main goal of this national police force was to prosecute criminals and provide security.[5] Another early goal of this centralized system was to selectively repress political groups and to ensure centralization of political control.[6] It is important to note that most of the policing capacity in Mexico was strongly concentrated in Mexico City. During the late nineteenth and early twentieth centuries, the growth and bureaucratization of the police force in Mexico was notable.[7] This organization encompassed a professionalizing armed force, a bureaucratic section that dealt with administration, and a fire prevention and response brigade. Notably, between 1869 and 1931, this police force quadrupled in size.

Although communal policing was common for much of Mexican history, by the early twentieth century, it had been outlawed, and the role of policing became exclusively practiced by both state and federal governments. While the Constitution of 1917 allowed for an expanded scope of action by police forces, it did not set appropriate limits to their jurisdiction. This inevitably led to a situation in which police forces around the country became increasingly influential and powerful. It also led to an increased inclusion of policing in everyday life in Mexico.[8] By 1978, a plethora of police forces existed to complete several tasks. This included police forces assigned to traffic, trade, agricultural management, sanitation, fiscal matters, communications, transport, customs and border protection, and military police, among other areas. Although many of these police forces gained considerable power at various times, it was the federal transit police force that enshrined its power at the federal level. The federal transit police had jurisdiction over all federal roads and for more than four decades was actively incorporated into the army.[9]

A consequence of the federal nature of the federal transit police force was the centralization of power in Mexico City. In turn, several reforms during the 1980s and 1990s aimed to create better coordination among the federal government and all other levels of government. These reforms also had the goal of consolidating the service part of this police force. That is, they were tasked with protecting the public and their belongings rather than with taking a repressive role.[10] For example, in 1995, the Zedillo presidency created the National Secretariat of Public Security. This institution was tasked with integrating all federal, state, and municipal institutions by sharing information that could lead to crime prevention.[11]

Additionally, in the context of the ongoing drug war, several reforms have been created in order to tackle the increasing levels of violence and criminality. For example, several federal agencies were either merged or expanded in order to prepare them for fighting organized crime.[12] Similarly, investigation and forensic analysis became the jurisdiction of state and federal agencies. This is in sharp contrast to how investigation was performed prior to these reforms, as only the federal government had jurisdiction in these matters before the reforms were instituted. In 2009, another important reformed allowed the federal police to aid and to work closely with states and municipalities in order to tackle the rise in violence associated with criminal organizations.

ORGANIZATION

The historically centralized nature of policing in Mexico led to the creation of a powerful system that had its roots in Mexico City but that also had important control over states and municipalities for more than a century. In this section, we cover the legal parameters that set the function of policing in Mexico. Policing in Mexico can be better understood under the scope of federalism. Both the state governments and the federal government have jurisdiction over a plethora of security issues. However, certain issues, such as organized violence, are regularly understood as falling under the purview of the federal government. This is not to say that state governments cannot lead or participate in action against organized criminal groups. However, the federal government does have an advantage in how it drafts policing policy. For example, Article 69 of the Mexican Constitution states that the Office of the President will draft and present before the Senate a policy report that clearly delineates the federal strategy for public safety. The Senate then ratifies or dismisses the report. If ratified, the president must then submit a yearly report on any progress made. In this regard, the federal government has the power to delineate clearly how it plans to tackle criminality, usually with Senate approval. This means that federal policing strategy and the budget needed to implement it are normally easy to achieve for the executive.[13]

While Article 69 of the Constitution creates a direct link between the federal government and its duties as a guarantor of public safety, Article 21 clearly delineates roles and responsibilities at the state and local levels. In this article, the federal government, states, and municipalities have the function of protecting individuals. All levels of government are expected to fulfill this task through the prevention, investigation, and prosecution of crimes. Moreover, Article 21 is clear that public safety should be under the jurisdiction of civilian institutions only. Although the Constitution is clear that the armed forces (e.g., the army or the navy) should not have any jurisdiction over public safety, they often work alongside police in tasks against organized crime. Another important part of Article 21 is that it places individual safety at the center of the policing debate. For example, it states that public and civil associations should be consulted when creating policy at the state and federal levels. This is because feedback and recommendations from civil organizations are seen as pivotal in the process of policy creation.

OPERATIONS

Law enforcement centralization in Mexico has often been perceived as a growing threat to efficiency and democracy. For example, an ongoing topic of discussion is the creation of the National Guard under the administration of President Andrés Manuel López Obrador. The force that was initially created from state police officers, army recruits, and the now extinct federal police was marketed as a new security apparatus that would be able to tackle growing violence and rampant corruption.[14] However, this new policing force has been hampered by allegations of internal corruption, strife, and incompetence.[15] Since its inception, the National Guard has become a contentious subject because it has been seen as potentially militarizing the country at a faster pace. This is because more than half of initial recruits have come from the army.[16]

Policing by national institutions has taken the spotlight in recent years in part as a consequence of the federal government's reduction of funding for training state and local police forces. In fact, a recent report found that spending for training state and local forces was reduced by around 76 percent.[17] This, however, is not to say that state institutions do not have an effect on policing. To the contrary, each state has jurisdiction over public safety affairs. This means that each state has its own police force. Normally, public safety at the state level is managed directly by the secretary of public safety. This office regulates the operation of the state's secretary of public safety and has direct control over how it manages personnel. This office also regulates the operations of the state police force, forensic units, and crime prevention activities.

Judiciary

As is the case with policing, the power of the judiciary can also be found rooted in the Constitution. Article 94 establishes the judicial power of the federation and centers this power in the Supreme Court of Justice, the Supreme Electoral Court, Circuit Courts, and District Courts.[18] Article 1 allows state courts to hear cases of federal jurisdiction when federal courts are not present in a given city or town. This means that, in all, the Mexican federal judiciary has around 710 courts.

Similarly to the U.S. court system, the Mexican federal judiciary is topped by the Supreme Court of Justice. However, in Mexico, eleven justices sit in the court, and they have fifteen-year term limits. The appointment process begins when the president submits a list of three candidates to the Senate. The Senate then reviews each candidate, and the candidate who reaches a two-thirds majority of Senate votes is elected to the position.[19] The president of the Supreme Court is elected by all eleven justices and can serve in this function for only a four-year term. Moreover, the court is divided by areas of expertise—composed of three or four justices—and each area has a president. Normally, when a case reaches the court, it will first be directed to an area of expertise and will then be debated by all justices.[20] The structure of the court is also interesting because it is regulated by the *General Organization Manual*, which can be reformed by Congress and which sets the parameters under which the court operates.

A component that sets the Mexican judiciary apart from many other judicial systems is the existence of the Federal Judiciary Council.[21] This council has the power to regulate how all courts below the Supreme Court and the Supreme Electoral Court operate. This means that all Circuit and District Courts are regulated by this council. The idea behind this is to ensure that tribunals are objective, professional, and honest in applying the law. It also means that this council has the power to oversee trial decisions. The council is formed by seven counselors, one of whom is the president of the Supreme Court.

Another court that is unique to the Mexican judicial system is the Supreme Electoral Court.[22] Although Mexico has had an Electoral Court since 1987, its rulings could be easily overruled by the electoral collegiate organizations that are found in Congress. This meant that the ruling, while important, was not binding. This changed with the creation of the Federal Electoral Tribunal in the early 1990s. In 1993 and 1996, the Mexican Congress overhauled the entire electoral landscape of the country by formally incorporating the Electoral Tribunal into the federal judicial branch. This provided the Electoral Court with the jurisdiction needed to settle any electoral controversy at any level of government. This means that local, state, and federal elections that are settled in court are ultimately decided by the Electoral Tribunal.[23]

Circuit Courts exist in two modalities. The first is a Unitarian Court, which has one magistrate and several staff members. The second is usually called a Collegiate

Court and is formed by three magistrates and several staff members. District Courts are considered to be at a lower level of the federal court system. They are usually formed by one federal judge and several staff members. Additionally, specialized courts for certain legal areas, such as antitrust, employment, and taxation matters, are also in operation.[24]

The Mexican federal judiciary operates within a unique belief system and under a set of quasi-legal parameters. For example, a series of interviews with employees of the Mexican federal judiciary has indicated that hierarchical structure, employee salaries, gender inequalities, influence peddling, and corruption are common features of this system.[25] It has also been found that nepotism in the Mexican judiciary is pervasive.[26]

CRIMINAL PROCEDURE

Another segment of the Mexican judicial system that was greatly reformed is that of criminal procedure. In 2008, a federal reform overhauled the entire federal criminal court system and replaced it with an oral-adversarial system. The main purpose of this overhaul was to rid the system of rampant corruption and wrongful convictions. Before this reform, the documents used throughout the trial process were often written in a way that obscured accountability and that allowed prosecutorial discretion to turn into corruption.[27] Because the new system requires that the litigants engage directly with the judge, it also allows the judge to dismiss trials that may have been erroneously processed. In criminal cases, the public prosecutor has the responsibility to gather all evidence, and the police have the responsibility to record any action related to the investigation. When in trial, the defendant has the right to review all evidence and to review how this evidence was recollected and recorded. Defendants also have the right to request from judges copies of any records related to their trial.[28] Oral examinations are exclusive to criminal cases. The four pillars of the 2008 reform are immediacy, continuity, publicity, and contradiction. Criminal proceedings are open to the public, and journalists are allowed to be present.[29]

FUNCTIONS

The functions performed by the judiciary are also divided into either civil or criminal proceedings. In civil proceedings, when judges convene the first instance, they will require that the parties provide enough information to put their claim forward. A second trial is convened if the judge believes that either side has compelling evidence. However, in the context of the ongoing war on drugs, criminal procedure is somewhat different. Once in trial, criminal procedure is normally divided into the investigation stage, the intermediate stage, and the trial stage. In criminal cases, defendants and plaintiffs provide oral evidence to judges, who have no prior information on the case. Here, judges fulfill the function of intervening between both parties and helping to consolidate all arguments and evidence. Importantly, the Mexican judiciary also follows the doctrine of the "fruit of the poisoned tree" and rejects all evidence that may have been secured by a prosecutor using unlawful means. The court must establish who has the burden of proof. Normally, in a criminal case, the prosecution has the burden of providing evidence so as to clarify the facts, whereas in a civil case, evidence must be brought forward by the party asserting the complaint.[30]

It is also the function of the court to provide a binding verdict. However, here again, the court will differ depending on whether the case is criminal or civil. In civil cases, judges must decide between a declaratory and a constitutive verdict. Declaratory verdicts are created when establishing a new legality. For example, if the judge decides that a contract is no longer binding regardless of whether it was binding in the past, then this can be understood to be declaratory. When the verdict is constitutive, the judge accepts a legal reality that affects the past. For example, invalidating a legal act has the effect of invalidating not only all future proceedings but also the effects that it had in the past. In the case of criminal trials, the judge normally convicts or acquits parties in question. A conviction will usually follow when the defense was not able to prove that the evidence brought by the prosecution was not compelling enough to prosecute.

Correctional System

OVERVIEW

The oldest records of a correctional system in Mexico can be found in the pre-Hispanic era. Prisons during this era served the function of detaining inmates who were usually sentenced to death.[31] In this sense, prisons during the pre-Columbian era strove not to reintegrate or readapt prison inmates but rather to detain inmates who could pose a flight risk. During the time when Mexico was a Spanish colony, prisons served many functions and existed in many shapes and forms. For example, homes for abandoned women were common during the colonial era and had the goal of preventing women from living in the streets.[32] However, it is also mentioned that prison existed as military forts, presidios, correction centers, and even palaces such as the National Palace, where the current federal government is housed. Importantly, during this period, prisons were often places where torture and abuse were common.[33] During this time, because of the medieval structure of government that existed during the colonial period, much of the property, services, and penalties were administered by the Catholic Church. This lasted until almost the end of the colonial period and was overhauled only by a royal decree requiring that secular judges decide sentences.[34] However, most prisoners received harsh sentences, and rehabilitation was not a goal. This started to change once Mexico became an independent country. During the presidency of Benito Juárez, several reforms were created in order to ensure that prisoners were treated humanely and that rehabilitation was an important goal. This reform was in line with the liberal nature of President Juárez and proved to be popular although not effective.[35] No other major reform was instituted for more than a century after these reforms, and this led to overcrowded conditions and severe abuse and neglect.[36] Dire conditions in Mexican prisons were well documented in 1979, when a UN report established that only one-third of Mexican inmates were held in conditions that met humanitarian standards.[37]

The 2008 reforms modified the way in which the judiciary operates, and the creation of an oral-adversarial system was implemented as a way to lower sentences and to provide alternative sentences that did not involve prison terms. This is in line with Article 22 of the Constitution, which states that prison penalties should be proportional to the damage and to the public good created by the penalty.[38] However, it has been argued that the increased influence of organized power in Mexican society, the lack of opportunities, and the existence of a punitive system have led to negative consequence for inmates.[39] Additionally, the standards of living for Mexican inmates remain low, and the infrastructure is often dilapidated.[40]

ORGANIZATION

Another consequence of the 2008 criminal justice system reforms was to ensure that the corrections system has as its main purpose the reintegration and readaptation of inmates into society.[41] In Mexico, this is especially important because many former inmates continue to suffer from the consequences of the stigma of being incarcerated. In this regard, the 2008 criminal reforms also had the goal of ensuring that once inmates have served their sentences, they are allowed to integrate properly into society with full use of their rights.[42] This is also consistent with the new focus on human rights, which should yield individualized prison sentences that are created for specific cases and that can adjust to the context of each crime.[43]

Nonetheless, an often ignored issue is that the 2008 criminal reforms contemplate that sentences should be issued regularly in order to clear the backlog of cases. This is important because many inmates are incarcerated without ever being sentenced. In fact, research conducted by the National Institute of Statistics and Geography (INEGI) found that more than one-third of all inmates have not received a sentence.[44] This is worrisome because it shows that the 2008 criminal system reforms are not producing the intended effects of clearing the backlog. It is also a sign that the Mexican system is failing to implement proper standards so as to protect basic human rights. The most obvious reason for this is that the Mexican criminal justice system also makes use of a tool known as preventive prison. This mechanism is regulated by the National Code for Criminal Procedure. It allows judges to incarcerate alleged felons or criminals for several reasons. However, usually judges must first determine that a case complies with the following three standards: (1) the crime in question requires prison as a penalty, (2) there is a flight risk or a possible risk to the supposed victim, and (3) the incarceration would protect the criminal process. However, the judge may also provide preventive prison if the public prosecutor argues that this is in the interest of safeguarding justice. For example, if there is evidence that the defendant committed a separate crime that also requires a prison term, the prosecutor may request the judge to provide preventive prison.[45] Although preventive prison is usually limited to a couple of days or a week, inmates can see their cases drag on longer. This inevitably means that many inmates are incarcerated for periods longer than allowed. For example, between 2019 and 2020, the number of incarcerated inmates without a sentence grew, while the number of inmates with a sentence declined.[46]

In criminal cases that require a prison sentence, judges must abide by the National Code for Criminal Procedure. For example, the code states that when the sentence is provided by more than one judge, the decision must be either unanimous or made by a majority of the judges. Judges must write an explanation of their decisions, but the main judge will write the main decision.[47] Although they are free to arrive to their own conclusions, judges must set the prison sentence in a manner that abides by the National Code for Criminal Procedure. This means that judges must take into consideration several factors, such as the age of the perpetrator, behavioral issues that may be relevant, the emotional stability of the defendant, the social and economic circumstance of the defendant, and any relation between the defendant and the victim. Moreover, the trial court must provide special protection to members of native cultures and to their customs. Once a sentence of guilty has been provided, the trial court will convene a separate audience in order to determine the length of the sentence. The code also regulates when sentences begin and how they must begin, although judges may exert discretion about these parameters. For example, when sentences are provided, trial judges will abide by the code in setting a prison term but can also use the code to order defendants to repair damages resulting from their actions. That is, prison sentences regularly are accompanied by a reparation clause. This means that sentenced inmates are sometimes also required to make payments to victims.

Although state and federal courts may use alternative penalties that do not involve prison terms, they rarely do so. In fact, sentences not involving a prison term are in disuse. At the state level, this has inevitably meant a rise in prison sentences, and by 2011, 6 percent of all criminal cases ended up in a prison sentence. However, the situation is even more dire at the federal level, where only 6 percent of all criminal sentences ended without a prison sentence.[48] In Mexico, at the federal level, 95 percent of crimes have a prison sentence. At the state level, this percentage is as high as 98 percent.[49] Notably, the number of inmates at the national level increased between 2004 and 2013.[50]

Research conducted in 2020 by the Decentralized Institute of Prevention and Social Readaptation found that 95 percent of all current inmates were men and that 76 percent of inmates had achieved only a basic education.[51] The same study found that most of the incarcerated population ranged between twenty-five and thirty-nine years of age.

The correction system is currently organized into 251 state penitentiaries, nineteen federal prisons, around eighty municipal prisons, and fifty-three correction centers for juveniles.[52] Mexico's state-level correctional facilities are managed by the states, and federal penitentiaries are administrated by the federal government. States with larger populations tend to have more prisons, and most of these can be found in the northern and central regions of the country.

In Mexico, inmates are housed in federal, state, or municipal facilities. However, since 2005, the number of inmates housed in federal facilities has dropped, markedly so since 2018.[53] On the contrary, the total number of inmates housed in local and state-managed penitentiary systems has increased since 1995.[54]

In 2020, 5,956 inmates were processed at federal facilities, and 104,395 were processed at state-level facilities.[55] Not all inmates processed in state or federal facilities remained incarcerated. Although thousands are released every year, many more are detained only temporarily. For example, between 2017 and 2020, local and state facilities processed around 100,000 inmates per year, while federal facilities process between 4,000 and 7,000 inmates per year.[56]

Although the number of correctional facilities and the number of inmates housed in these facilities vary depending on whether they are state or federal facilities, inmates in those facilities are housed for different types of crimes. Federal facilities house individuals who have committed a crime that is classified under federal law or federal jurisdiction, and state or local facilities house individuals who have committed a crime or felony under what could be understood to be Mexican common law (*fuero común*). For example, theft and homicide constitute more than half of all crimes for inmates in state-level facilities. In turn, crimes related to weapons, explosives, kidnapping, and narcotics constitute more than half of crimes for inmates in federal facilities.[57]

Juvenile Justice

OVERVIEW

Although international standards exist to ensure that countries treat their incarcerated underage population properly, Mexico has been a latecomer in adapting to these standards. Progress has been made, although it has been slow and uneven.[58] In Mexico, policies regarding juvenile justice have been created at both state and federal levels. Most of these policies have been influenced by direct experiences and international treaties. One of the first steps in the field of juvenile justice was made between 1920 and 1940, when the first juvenile detention centers were inaugurated.[59] The first tribunal specializing in minors began operations in 1923 and provided special focus to the juvenile condition of the defendants. These courts provided lower penalties, and the guilty were sent to the juvenile sections of prisons. In 1928, another tribunal that had as its main mission the reintegration of juvenile offenders was inaugurated. However, it was not until 1974 that a federal law created specialized juvenile detention centers.[60] Although few reforms in the matter of juvenile justice were implemented for several decades, in 1990, Mexico ratified the UN Convention on the Rights of the Child. This was followed by a series of federal reforms that overhauled the system of processing juveniles. In these reforms, state and federal juvenile systems had to consider the collective and individual rights of children and teenagers and were given a short period of time to implement these reforms in their facilities.[61] States have also drafted their own policies in regard to juvenile correctional centers. Many states have their own laws that apply to juveniles, and currently, most of these laws cover individuals between the ages of eleven and eighteen.

In 2005, Article 18 of the Constitution was amended in order to account for the protection of minors incarcerated in the juvenile correction system. This new legislation established a set of standards that both the federal government and states had to abide by. These included specific types of facilities—juvenile correction centers for minors, rehabilitation centers for juveniles below age twelve, and specialized tribunals that had to take into consideration the rights of children—as well as policy changes, including a focus on family reintegration and shorter prison terms. In fact, this legislation mandated that judges should use prison terms as the last resource available.[62]

However, much of this legislation was amended, and the current status of juvenile justice in Mexico is the result of a mix of state and federal regulations. That is, currently, there are thirty-two different items of legislation for the thirty-two different states.[63] This does not mean that courts at both federal and state levels do not have the tools to protect juveniles. This is because states are forced to adhere to the General Law on Girls, Boys, and Adolescents. This federal law mandates that judges must consider the rights of children and adolescents and must use age as a determinant of prison terms. For example, the law establishes that when children commit a crime or felony, they should be subjected to rehabilitation rather than to a prison term. Similarly, there is a focus on reintegrating minors with their families. The law also establishes that people between ages fourteen and eighteen must be considered minors regardless of the state in which they reside. Moreover, Mexican judges are also forced to adhere to national and international jurisprudence. This means that they must abide by the precedents established by the Inter-American Court of Human Rights and its body of law on children's rights. In short, the main idea of the General Law on Girls, Boys, and Adolescents is to treat minors between ages fourteen and eighteen as a separate class. The main goal of this law is to foster family and community reintegration by allowing minors to spend shorter detention sentences while also offering rehabilitation and alternative sentences. In 2017, for example, 65 percent of minors who were processed under the juvenile system did not receive a prison sentence.[64]

Because states are allowed to manage their own juvenile systems as long as they abide by the basic parameters implemented by the federal government, juvenile justice in Mexico has developed in a decentralized fashion. For example, most states have a limited number of personnel who are specialized in juvenile justice. At the state level, an average of 3.8 percent of state correction agencies specialize in juvenile justice, while only 2 percent of the overall state personnel are specialized in this area.[65] However, since many of these agencies do not keep good records on their current employees, it is hard to establish whether personnel are qualified to work in juvenile justice. Finally, current data indicate that no state has more than 6 percent of its personnel specialized to work in this area.[66]

BASIC STATISTICS

In 2017, the INEGI conducted a national survey in order to have a better understanding of the current makeup of juvenile inmates in the entire country. This survey was conducted in fifty-three juvenile correction centers in all thirty-two states. The survey shed light on who was incarcerated at the time and what the conditions were that led to their incarceration. For example, 60 percent of all inmates in juvenile centers were between ages eighteen and twenty-two. Seventy-five percent had some degree of basic education, and 95 percent were fully literate. Around 40 percent of juvenile inmates had left their homes before being incarcerated, and around 6 percent were living in a state of homelessness.[67] In this regard, allowing juveniles to rehabilitate and reintegrate with their families is understood to be an important milestone for the juvenile system in Mexico since an important objective of the General Law on Girls, Boys, and Adolescents is to ensure that juvenile offenders are reintegrated with their families.

Regarding the experience of juvenile inmates, it has been found that around 10 percent of the current juvenile population had been previously incarcerated. Moreover, more than 90 percent of all juvenile detentions are made by either state or local police forces.[68] This is an important consideration given that most detentions are for crimes that are not under the usual federal jurisdiction. However, it may also be the reason that around 70 percent of the detainees reported being verbally abused during their detention and 50 percent being physically abused. This is possibly related to the fact that local and state police agencies tend to be less professional and lacking in enough personnel who are specialized in juveniles.

However, a possible result of the current protections that are provided for minors is that most of them receive a speedy process. For example, up to 82 percent of all juveniles who were processed under the juvenile system received a sentence, and for more than 70 percent, this occurred just over forty-eight hours after being apprehended.[69] This is in clear contrast to the more than one-third of adults who are awaiting trial. Additionally, for those who received a prison sentence, only 12 percent received a sentence higher than six years. In the case of juveniles under prison sentences, the most common felonies and crimes are theft, homicide, rape, and bodily injuries.[70] Although the circumstances behind each of these crimes is very complex, research can shed light on what might be behind some of the patterns of crimes in Mexico. For example, periods of extreme economic and political hardship in Mexico have been shown to lead to increases in juvenile delinquency.[71] Specifically, the 1980s—when the Mexican population suffered a series of economic crises—saw a steady rise in juvenile violence. However, the early 2000s were years of economic and political stability and were followed by years of stable juvenile crime rates.[72]

Notes

1. EDOMEX, "Historia: Breve historia de la policía en México," 2021, https://sseguridad.edomex.gob.mx/historia.
2. Fiscalía General de Justicia, "Nuestras Raíces: La historia policial en México," September 2020, https://ifpeducacionenlinea.mx/wp-content/uploads/2020/09/CFPDI_DP_M2_Unidad-3.-Nuestras-raices-la-historia-policial-en-Mexico.pdf.
3. E. Ramirez Ramirez, *Ética en la formación de la policía manual de capacitación* (Mexico City: Porrúa, 2009).
4. A. P. Petit Gonzalez, "Policía en México: 75 años de su implementación," in *Evolución del sistema penal en México: Tres cuartos de siglo*, ed. S. García Ramírez and O. Islas de González Mariscal (Mexico City: National Institute of Criminal Sciences, 2017).
5. Petit Gonzalez, "Policía."

6. E. L. Portillo Vargas, "La policía en México: Función política y reforma," Smith Richardson Foundation, February 2000, https://pdba.georgetown.edu/Security/citizensecurity/mexico/evaluaciones/policia.pdf.

7. D. Pulido, "Gendarmes, Inspectors and Superintendents: A History of the Police System in Mexico City, 1870–1930," *Ler história* 70 (2017): 37–58, https://doi .org/10.4000/lerhistoria.2696.

8. M. Gonzalez Oropeza, *Policía y Constitución: Armario jurídico* (Mexico City: National Autonomous University of Mexico, 1986).

9. Petit Gonzalez, "Policía."

10. J. Ramirez Marin, *Seguridad publica y Constitución* (Mexico City: Porrúa, 2003).

11. Petit Gonzalez, "Policía."

12. Maureen Meyer, "La policía en México, muchas reformas, pocos avances," *WOLA: La oficia en Washington para asuntos Latinoamericanos*, May 2014, https://www .wola .org/wp -content/uploads/2014/05/La -Polici%CC%81a -en -Me%CC%81xico_Muchas -Reformas -Pocos-Avances.pdf.

13. Seguridad Pública del Gobierno, "Decreto por el que se aprueba la Estrategia Nacional de Seguridad Pública del Gobierno de la República," May 15, 2019, https://www.dof.gob.mx/nota_detalle.php?codigo=5560463&fecha=16/05/2019#gsc.tab=0.

14. Elizabeth Melimopoulos, "Mexico's National Guard: What, Who and When," *Aljazeera*, June 30, 2019, https://www.aljazeera.com/news/2019/6/30/mexicos-national-guard-what-who -and-when; Marcos Muedano, "Dan 30 mil policías mas a Durazno para la Guardia Nacional," *La silla rota*, October 6, 2019, https://lasillarota.com/nacion/dan-30-mil-policias-mas-a-durazo -para-la-guardia-nacional/289923.

15. A. Ford, "Why Mexico's National Guard Remains Vastly Unqualified," *InSight Crime*, June 9, 2021, https://insightcrime.org/news/mexico-national-guard-vastly-unqualified; Maureen Meyer, "One Year after National Guard's Creation, Mexico Is Far from Demilitarizing Public Security," WOLA, May 26, 2020, https://www .wola .org/analysis/one -year -national -guard-mexico.

16. Amnesty International, "What Is the Significance of the Creation of the National Guard for Mexico?," March 6, 2019, https://www.amnesty.org/en/latest/news/2019/03/que-significa -para-mexico-la-aprobacion-de-la-guardia-nacional.

17. "Mexico: Overhaul Police Forces; Protests Highlight Abuse, Impunity, Corruption, Lack of Training," *Human Rights Watch*, July 24, 2020, https://www .hrw .org/news/2020/07/24/mexico-overhaul-police-forces.

18. M. A. Lopez Olvera, *La responsabilidad administrativa de los Servidores Públicos en México* (Mexico City: National Autonomous University of Mexico, 2013).

19. M. Martinez Perez, "Legal Systems in Mexico: Overview; Practical Law," November 1, 2018, https://vonwobeser.com/images/PDF_news/PDF_articles/2018/Legal-systems-in -Mexico_-overview-_-Practical-Law_ManuelMartnez.pdf.

20. Supreme Court of Justice of the Nation (SCJN), "Supreme Court of Justice of the Nation: Visitor's Guide," SCJN, September 2019, https://www.scjn.gob.mx/sites/default/files/pagina/documentos/2019-10/SCJNVisitorsGuide-sept2019.pdf.

21. Lopez Olvera, *La responsabilidad administrativa.*

22. Electoral Tribunal of the Federal Judicial Branch, "The Electoral Tribunal of the Federal Judicial Branch Guarantees the Constitutionality of the Elections," June 2012, https://www.te .gob .mx/publicaciones/sites/default/files/archivos_libros/The%20Electoral%20Tribunal%20of%20the%20Federal%20Judicial%20Branch%20Guarantees%20the%20Constitutionality%20of%20the%20elections.pdf.

23. Electoral Tribunal of the Federal Judicial Branch, "Electoral Tribunal."

24. Martinez Perez, "Legal Systems."

25. G. Ferreyra, "Unpacking the Mexican Federal Judiciary: An Inner Look at the Ethos of the Judicial Branch," *Mexican Law Review* 11, no. 1 (2018), https://doi .org/10.22201/iij.24485306e.2018.1.12511.

26. P. Brassiolo, R. Estrada, G. Fajardo, and J. Martínez-Correa, "Family Rules: Nepotism in the Mexican Judiciary," 2021, CAF, http://scioteca.caf.com/handle/123456789/1798.

27. World Justice Project and Lawyers and Cameras, "Mexico's New Criminal Justice System: Substantial Progress and Persistent Challenges," World Justice Project, June 2018, https://worldjusticeproject.org/sites/default/files/documents/WJP-NewJusticeSystemMexico_.pdf.

28. Martinez Perez, "Legal Systems."

29. Martinez Perez, "Legal Systems."

30. Martinez Perez, "Legal Systems."

31. L. A. Herrera Rodriguez, "El sistema penitenciario y los derechos humanos," *EcosSociales* 7, no. 19 (2019), https://revistas.ujat.mx/index.php/ecosoc/issue/view/335.

32. E. Mendoza Bremaunts, "La Revolución Mexicana a 100 años de su inicio: Pensamiento social y jurídico," Repositorio universitario jurídicas, November 29, 2010, http://ru.juridicas .unam.mx/xmlui/handle/123456789/12929.

33. J. C. Varillas Lima, "La trasformación de las cárceles históricas mexicanas de centros penitenciarios a centros turísticos, espacios culturales y cívicos," *Revista de historia de las prisiones* 6 (January–June 2018): 124–37, https://www .revistadeprisiones .com/wp -content/uploads/2018/06/6_Varillas.pdf.

34. Mendoza Bremaunts, "La Revolución Mexicana."

35. J. Olivero, "The Crisis in Mexican Prisons: The Impact of the United States," in *Comparing Prison Systems*, ed. Robert P. Weiss and Nigel South (Hoboken, NJ: Taylor and Francis, 2014).

36. M. Sarre, "Ejecución de sanciones y medidas penales privativas de la libertad," Instituto de Investigaciones Jurídicas, 2013, https://archivos .juridicas .unam .mx/www/bjv/libros/8/3568/25.pdf.

37. Mendoza Bremaunts, "La Revolución Mexicana."

38. G. Zepeda Lecuona, *Situación y desafíos del sistema penitenciario mexicano*, México Evalúa, Centro de Análisis de Políticas Públicas, 2013, https://www.mexicoevalua.org/mexico-evalua/wp -content/uploads/2016/05/El -Sistema -Penitenciario -Mexicano -GZEPEDAL -2013.pdf.

39. A. Sanchez Galindo, "Historia del penitenciarismo en México," in Ramírez and Mariscal, *Evolución del sistema penal en México*.

40. A. Velazquez Estrada, *Nuevo sistema de justicia penal para México* (Mexico City: Autonomous University of Mexico, 2009).

41. A. Guerrero Alcantara, *La reinserción social comunitaria en México: Diagnóstico, recomendaciones y rutas de acción*, 2021, Centro de Estudios y Acción por la Justicia, https://ceajusticiasocial.org/wp-content/uploads/2021/09/CEA_REINSERCION_COMUNITARIA_FINAL_DIGITAL.pdf.

42. M. Hubert and M. Bravo, "Reinserción social y servicios postpenales: Más allá del cambio de vocabulario," *Defensor* 14, no. 12 (2018): 18–23.

43. R. Ochoa Romero, *La justificación de la pena* (Mexico City: Porrúa, 2012).

44. National Institute of Statistics and Geography (INEGI), "Censo nacional de sistema penitenciario federal y estatales 2021," INEGI, October 2021, https://www.inegi.org.mx/contenidos/programas/cnspef/2021/doc/cnsipef_2021_resultados.pdf.

45. M. Peláez Ferrusca, "La prisión en el sistema acusatorio," in Ramírez and Mariscal, *Evolución del sistema penal en México*.

46. National Institute of Statistics and Geography (INEGI), "Censo nacional de sistema."

47. Peláez Ferrusca, "La prisión."

48. Zepeda Lecuona, *Situación.*

49. Zepeda Lecuona, *Situación.*

50. Zepeda Lecuona, *Situación.*

51. Órgano Desconcentrado de Prevención y Readaptación Social, *Cuaderno mensual de información estadística penitenciaria nacional,* January 2021, https://www.gob.mx/cms/uploads/attachment/file/620658/CE_2021_01.pdf.

52. National Institute of Statistics and Geography (INEGI), "Encuesta nacional de adolescentes en el sistema de justicia penal (ENASJUP)," accessed June 13, 2022, https://www.inegi.org.mx/programas/enasjup/2017.

53. Zepeda Lecuona, *Situación.*

54. Zepeda Lecuona, *Situación.*

55. INEGI, "Censo nacional."

56. INEGI, "Censo nacional."

57. INEGI, "Censo nacional."

58. Centro de Investigación para el Desarrollo, A. C. (CIDAC), *Justicia para adolescentes en México: ¿Se garantizan los derechos de los jóvenes?,* CIDAC, 2016, http://cidac.org/wp-content/uploads/2016/02/adolescentes-web.pdf.

59. Efrén Arellano Trejo, "Sistema integral de justicia para adolescents," Centro de Estudios Sociales y de Opinión Pública, September 2006, http://www3.diputados.gob.mx/camara/content/download/40799/165045/file/Documentos%20de%20Trabajo%203.pdf.

60. R. L. Villanueva Castilleja, "Régimen de menores de edad que infringen la ley penal," in Ramírez and Mariscal, *Evolución del sistema penal en México.*

61. E. García Méndez, *Derecho de la infancia-adolescencia en América Latina: De la Situación Irregular a la Protección Integral* (Bogotá: Forum Pacis, 1994).

62. Villanueva Castilleja, "Régimen."

63. CIDAC, *Justicia.*

64. INEGI, "Encuesta nacional de adolescentes."

65. CIDAC, *Justicia.*

66. CIDAC, *Justicia.*

67. INEGI, "Encuesta nacional de adolescentes."

68. INEGI, "Encuesta nacional de adolescentes."

69. INEGI, "Encuesta nacional de adolescentes."

70. INEGI, "Encuesta nacional de adolescentes."

71. M. A. Olivares, "Neoliberalismo y autoritarismo: Unidad para la crisis; El periodo de Miguel de la Madrid," *Encuentros,* 2010, https://docplayer.es/16393336-Neoliberalismo-y-autoritarismo-unidad-para-la-crisis-el-periodo-de-miguel-de-la-madrid.html.

72. L. D. Vazquez Romero, "Acercamiento estadistico a la realidad de los menores infractores en Mexico: Legislacion y crimen organizado, nuevos desafios," *Universitas psychologica* 11, no. 4 (2012): 1105–114.

Index

About the Authors

Nenadi Adamu, PhD, is a senior lecturer in applied social studies at the University of Bedfordshire, United Kingdom. Her research focuses on young people in the informal economy and the link between crime and social structures. Her research interests include inequalities, social justice, and the role of social policy. She is the course coordinator for the BA Health and Social Care, University of Bedfordshire.

Sanaz Alasti is associate professor of criminal justice and director of the Center for Death Penalty Studies at Lamar University, Texas State University System, United States, where she teaches criminal justice and legal classes. After her professional experience as a postdoctorate at Harvard Law School, she started teaching at Lamar University. Alasti has researched, written about, and made presentations about the death penalty and Islamic criminal justice systems for the past twenty years. During her time at Lamar University, she has maintained an active research agenda in her discipline, received consistently high evaluations for her teaching, developed nine new courses, mentored multiple students in their research, received prestigious grants from SPME and ASMEA, and enthusiastically engaged in service. She has presented multiple conference papers every year, published peer-reviewed articles and book chapters, and attended numerous conferences in the United States, the Middle East, and Europe to discuss the arbitrariness of capital punishment. In 2012, she was invited to Italy as a lecturer to provide instruction to military officers, legal advisers, and political and policy advisers on sharia law and Islamic criminal justice systems at a seminar hosted by the NATO School. In the summer of 2015, she was invited to organize a conference attended by law professors from Harvard, New York University, and the University of California, Berkeley, for the Onati International Institute for the Sociology of Law in Spain. Her interviews have been featured in magazines such as *The New Yorker* and *The Examiner* and the Law Library of Congress website.

Mohsen Alizadeh holds a PhD in criminal justice from the City University of New York (Graduate Center), a master of philosophy from the City University of New York, a master's degree in criminal justice from the John Jay College of Criminal Justice, a master's degree in criminal law and criminology from Azad University of

Tehran, and a bachelor's degree in law from Azad University of Rafsanjan. He joined the Division of Justice and Law Administration of Western Connecticut University in 2016. His research focuses on theory testing in criminology, comparative criminal justice systems, and policing systems. His recent manuscript "Police Policy Shifts after 9/11—From Community Policing to Homeland Security—A New York Case" was published in *Springer Briefs in Policing*.

Joaquín Arigón studied law and social sciences at the University of the Republic and is currently pursuing a postgraduate degree in economic criminal law at the University of Montevideo, Uruguay. He is dedicated to the liberal exercise of the profession, and his main area of research is criminal law with a special emphasis on economic crimes, human rights, and the prison system.

Hasan T. Arslan is an associate professor of justice and law administration in the Ancell Business School at Western Connecticut State University. He holds a law degree from Marmara University, Istanbul, Turkey. He received his PhD from the College of Criminal Justice at Sam Houston State University of Huntsville, Texas, in 2008. Dr. Arslan worked nine years at the Institute for the Study of Violent Groups, where he contributed as a supervisor and in an analyst role to the development of a database capable of tracking more than 2,000 global and domestic extremist groups. His teaching interests include criminology, terrorism, organized crime, and research methods. His primary research interests are in the field of homeland security and police use of force. Before coming to WestConn, he taught at the University of New Haven, Western New England University, and Pace University. He is currently involved in an ongoing comprehensive database project to define and consolidate information of police shooting incidents throughout the United States. The database is called SHOT (Statistics Help Officer Training). The primary objective of the project is to establish a repository of national data that will help give law enforcement officials the ability to analyze this information and be better prepared to make the right judgments during hostile situations.

Monika Baylis is based at the University of Leicester, United Kingdom, where she is a teaching fellow in criminology. Her work and teaching focuses on global policing and police decision-making processes while addressing antisocial behavior (ASB)/youth crime among young people in Poland and England. She has received numerous awards (e.g., a winner of the Huddersfield Association of Women Graduates Outstanding Female PhD Student Prize in 2020 and the Postgraduate Research Award granted by the Institute for Research in Citizenship and Applied Human Sciences in 2016), reflecting her passion about comparative research in general. She has contributed to various national and international conferences and police officers' training within the European Union Agency for Law Enforcement Training (CEPOL) and the Police Academy in Szczytno, Poland; the Police University/College in Tampere, Finland; and the Fire Service Academy (Internal Security Institute), Poland, where she is an active fellow member. She writes on ASB, the policing of youth crime, terrorism, models of police, and the criminal justice system in Poland and England for police magazines in both countries and different academic journals. This also links to her previous professional career as a Polish/English interpreter in the United Kingdom.

Fabio R. Bechara, PhD, is a professor of criminal law at Mackenzie Presbyterian University and holds a PhD in law from São Paulo University, Brazil. He is a Woodrow Wilson International Center for Scholars Global Fellow and leader of the research group "Economic Criminal Law and International Justice" at Mackenzie Presbyterian University. He is state prosecutor of São Paulo. He is a member of the Steering Committee of the University of São Paulo's School of Multidimensional Security. He is the former head of the Anti-Organized Crime Special Unit of Prosecutors and the former head of the Intelligence Integrated Center of Public Security of São Paulo.

Mark F. Briskey, PhD, is associate professor of criminology and associate chair of the master of criminology program at Murdoch University, Australia. Prior to his academic career, he was both a state and a federal police officer, serving in Australia and holding some long-term overseas postings. The Australian and Indonesian governments decorated him for his role in counterterrorism investigations and for work in Pakistan, Afghanistan, and Sri Lanka. He is a former head of the Australian Graduate School of Policing and was involved in initial efforts to establish the Jakarta Centre for Law Enforcement Cooperation and Transnational Crime Centre in Indonesia. Mark obtained his PhD at the Australian Defense Force Academy at the University of New South Wales, Australia.

Leandro Piquet Carneiro, PhD, is a professor at the Institute of International Relations, University of São Paulo, Brazil, where he coordinates the School of Multidimensional Security. He was a visiting fellow at the Taubman Center for State and Local Government from the Kennedy School of Government, Harvard University, from 2007 to 2008. He graduated in economics at the Federal University of Rio de Janeiro and received his doctorate in political science. His major research field is crime and violence in Latin America. He is a member of the State of São Paulo Public Security Council and the Rio de Janeiro City Hall Advisory Council. He was a member of the Academic Council of the National Minister of Public Security (2018).

Joselyne L. Chenane, PhD, is an assistant professor in the School of Criminology and Justice Studies at the University of Massachusetts, Lowell. She is also an alumnus of the African Diaspora Carnegie Fellowship Program (USIU-Africa, Summer 2021). She earned her PhD in criminology and criminal justice from the University of Nebraska, Omaha, in 2018. Additionally, she holds a master's degree in criminal justice from the State University of New York, College at Buffalo, and a bachelor's degree in education arts (with a specialization in English and literature) from Egerton University, Kenya. Her research interests include immigration, police–citizen relations, police legitimacy, consequences of contact with the criminal justice system, race and justice, neighborhood contexts, and crime and comparative criminal justice. She has published work in journals such as *Criminal Justice and Behavior*, *Youth Violence and Juvenile Justice*, *Policing and Society*, the *British Journal of Criminology*, *Crime and*

Delinquency, and *Race and Justice*. She has authored and coauthored more than fifteen peer-reviewed articles and book chapters. She is an active member of the American Society of Criminology's divisions, including Policing, International Criminology (executive council member), and People of Color and Crime. She is currently serving on the editorial board of the *SN Social Sciences Journal* and the *International Journal of Criminology and Sociology*. She is a recipient of many awards and recognitions.

Mengliang Dai is an assistant professor at Macau University of Science and Technology. He earned his PhD at City University of Hong Kong. His current research focuses on police service calls, wrongful convictions, and police discretion. His recent articles have appeared in *Journal of Contemporary China*, the *British Journal of Criminology*, *Crime & Delinquency*, *Policing: A Journal of Policy and Practice*, and *Security Journal*.

Raluca Enescu earned her PhD in criminology from the School of Criminal Justice at the University of Lausanne, Switzerland, on the choice of verdict. The Swiss Science Foundation replicated her study at a national level with all adjudicating judges at criminal courts. The results led to recommendations for the reform of the unified code of criminal procedure. After moving to Berlin, she has been leading projects at the Free University Berlin, the University of Hamburg, and the Max Planck Institute for the History of Science. Since 2015, she is a senior researcher at the Centre Marc Bloch, where she investigates summary proceedings, forensic methods, and wrongful convictions. In 2016–2017, she was invited as a guest professor in forensic sciences, forensic psychiatry, and criminology at Humboldt University Berlin.

Giulia Fabini, PhD, is a research fellow in criminology at the Department of Legal Studies DSG, University of Bologna, Italy. She holds a PhD in law and society from the University of Milan and was a student researcher at the Center for the Study of Law and Society at the University of California, Berkeley. Her research focuses on border control and the interaction between migrants and the police. She is also interested in migrants' struggles and immigration courts and the prison system from a gender perspective.

Carlos Daniel Gutierrez-Mannix, PhD, was born in El Naranjo, San Luis Potosi, Mexico. He obtained his BA in sociology and MA in public policy and management at the University of Texas Rio Grande Valley (UTRGV). After completing his first graduate degree, he worked during a year as a lecturer at UTRGV. In 2017, he received a full scholarship to complete a PhD in political science at the University of Texas at Dallas. During his tenure in the doctoral program, he taught several courses, attended research conferences, and published scholarly research. He is currently a full-time lecturer of political science at the University of Texas Rio Grande Valley.

Mehdi J. Hakimi, LLM, candidate at Harvard Law School, is the executive director of the Rule of Law Program at Stanford Law School, United States. He develops and implements projects in the Middle East, South Asia, and Africa. As lecturer in law, he also teaches classes on comparative law, law and development, and legal education at Stanford. He was the former chair of the Department of Law at the American University of Afghanistan. He has worked with various institutions on international development and human rights issues, including the Asia Foundation and Yale Law School. He has served as a subject matter expert on comparative and foreign law issues in various jurisdictions, including major country guidance cases in Europe and North America. He has advised international organizations, governments, academic and research institutions, and global law firms on, inter alia, the Afghan legal system. His scholarship is published or forthcoming in the *California Law Review*, the *Yale Journal of International Law*, the *Stanford Journal of International Law*, the *Columbia Journal of Transnational Law*, the *Georgetown Journal of International Law*, and the *Northwestern Journal of Human Rights*, among others. He has authored or coauthored multiple books on the laws of Afghanistan. He has been cited and quoted in judicial decisions and litigation briefs, government reports and policy documents, academic literature, and popular media outlets. A licensed attorney, he holds a JD, an MBA, and a BA (economics and law).

Pingping Huang is a PhD student in the Faculty of Law at the Macau University of Science and Technology. Her research interests include criminal law and juvenile delinquency.

Uche K. Kalu, PhD, is a lawyer and an adjunct professor of administration of justice at Texas Southern University, United States. He earned his PhD in management from the College of Management and Technology, Walden University, United States. He holds a master of law degree from the University of Houston Law School, an MBA from Strayer University, and master of philosophy from Walden University. Prior to joining Texas Southern University in 2018, he taught at the Texas Corrections Academy. His main research interests are in the areas of law enforcement and crime control, constitutional limitations on law enforcement, criminal justice, and law enforcement in minority communities.

Anita Kalunta-Crumpton, PhD, is professor of administration of justice at Texas Southern University, United States. She received a PhD in criminal justice from Brunel University London, United Kingdom. Prior to joining Texas Southern University in 2008, she taught for several years at a few universities in England. Her main research interests are in the areas of race/ethnicity, crime, and criminal justice; drug use and drug trafficking; violence against women; and comparative criminology/criminal justice. She is the author and editor of several books. Her work has also appeared in a wide range of peer-reviewed scholarly journals.

Dalibor Kekić, PhD, is associate professor at the University of Criminal Investigation and Police Studies, Department of Police Sciences, Belgrade, Republic of Serbia. He earned his PhD in security management studies, specializing in police management and emergency management. He is interested in human resources, emergency management, police organization, and security management. He has authored or coauthored about 130 publications, including one textbook. He has participated in more than thirty national and international scientific conferences. He has also organized or participated in many seminars, workshops, and projects organized for different entities and subjects.

Ahmed F. Khalifa is an assistant professor of criminal law and international criminal law at Ain Shams University, Cairo, Egypt. Since 2014, he serves as the deputy secretary-general of the International Association of Penal Law and serves also as the Middle East regional coordinator for the University of Oxford Price Media Moot Court Competition. He is currently an expert consultant with several international organizations, including the International Committee of the Red Cross, the United Nations Office on Drugs and Crime in the MENA Region, and the United Nations Children's Fund in Egypt. Previously, he served as a full-time in-house legal consultant with the United Nations Interregional Crime and Justice Research Institute, Torino, Italy. He obtained his PhD in international criminal law from Poitiers University in France after finishing his LLM, focusing on international human rights law from Temple University, United States.

Filip Kukić is a physical fitness assessment and research expert in the Testing Section of the Police Sports Education Center, Abu Dhabi Police, United Arab Emirates. He earned his PhD in developing the screening model of physical fitness of police officers through the assessment of body composition. He is interested in integrating physical activity into the occupational health of police officers by developing policies aligned with those of the agency. He has published about sixty papers, including one textbook. He has participated in numerous scientific national and international conferences, organized or participated in many seminars and workshops, and reviewed papers for journals of international and national importance.

Aneta Leszczynska, PhD, is a senior research fellow at the Department of Comparative Criminal Law, Criminal Procedure, Economic and Environmental Criminal Law at the Free University of Berlin. From 2021 to 2022, she was also a research fellow at the Department of Criminal Procedure at the Jagiellonian University Krakow. She graduated from Jagiellonian University in 2015. Shortly after that, Leszczynska enrolled in a doctoral study at Jagiellonian University (2015) and began her attorney training at the Bar Association of Attorneys-at-Law in Katowice in 2016. In December 2021, she presented her doctoral thesis, "Presumption of Innocence and Its Consequences in Criminal Procedure," which resulted in the award of the doctoral degree in January 2022. She accomplished her attorney training in 2018 as well. She has participated in various scientific projects and published several scientific contributions.

Samuel M. Makinda, PhD, is professor of security and counterterrorism and the founding chair of security, terrorism, and counterterrorism studies at Murdoch University, Australia. He was awarded the Order of Elder of the Burning Spear by Kenyan President Mwai Kibaki in 2011. He served on the Australian foreign minister's National Consultative Committee for International Security Issues (2001–2008). In 1985–1986, he was a foreign affairs analyst in the Parliamentary Research Service of the Australian Parliament. He has been a researcher at the Brookings Institution; the International Institute for Strategic Studies; St. Antony's College, Oxford University; and the Global Security Program, Cambridge University. A former editor of the *Daily Nation* in Kenya, he has published five books and numerous chapters and journal articles.

Jospeter M. Mbuba, PhD, is the department chair and professor of criminal justice and public administration at Purdue University Fort Wayne, United States. He has published widely and delivered numerous professional and invited presentations on the topics of crime prevention and public safety. He is also a curriculum development consultant, a three-time fellow with the Carnegie African Diaspora Fellowship Program, and a one-time visiting scholar with the Council for the Development of Social Science Research in Africa. He is a member of the Academy of Criminal Justice Sciences, American Society of Criminology, and Kenya Scholars and Studies Association. He has chaired presentation panels at the annual conferences of these organizations. He is a 2014 alumnus of the FBI Citizen's Academy, Indianapolis Division, and serves as manuscript reviewer for several journals, among his many professional engagements.

Miloš Milenković is team leader at the Emergency Management Sector, Ministry of Interior, Belgrade, Republic of Serbia. He earned his MSc in organizational studies, specifically in human resources. He is interested in human resources, emergency and security management, and police organization. He is the sole author or coauthor of about thirty papers and has participated in more than ten scientific national and international conferences. He has also organized or participated in many exercises and workshops for different entities and on various subjects.

Carsten Momsen is a tenured full professor at Freie Universität Berlin, School of Law, Germany. After full professorships at the University of the Saarland and University Hanover, Momsen is the chair of the Department of Comparative Criminal Law, Criminal Procedure, Economic and Environmental Criminal Law at the Free University of Berlin since 2015. He was visiting professor at Symbiosis Law School in Pune. He has also served several times as visiting professor to the Faculty of Law, University of Toronto, Canada. Since 2020, Momsen is affiliated as an ongoing visiting professor at the Center for International Human Rights at the John Jay College of Criminal Justice at City University New York and as scholar in residence at New York Law School, New York, United States. Momsen is a standing member of the Program Committee of the "SADFE" Conference Series (Systematic Approaches for Digital Forensic Engineering) and the "Anglo-German Dialogue on Core Concepts in Criminal Law and Justice." He has been a founding member and principal investigator of the "Einstein Center Digital Future." He directs the project "FU Law Clinic—Practice of Criminal Defense" and codirects the "German Wrongful Conviction and Reconviction Project" he cofounded in 2019. Momsen works part-time as a criminal defense attorney, especially in appellate and white-collar criminal law as well as in proceedings related to the United States. He has authored/coauthored more than ten books, several law commentaries, and more than 150 contributions.

Kobra Moradi is a lawyer at the Australian Centre for International Justice. She has previously worked at the UN Assistance to the Khmer Rouge Trials, Afghanistan Human Rights and Democracy Organization, and the Clooney Foundation for Justice. Kobra is a law and international relations graduate and has completed an honors thesis examining prosecutorial impartiality and independence in situation and case selection at the International Criminal Court. She has also completed a thesis on victim-centered transitional justice and Islamic law as part of master of international law and diplomacy at the Australian National University.

Timi Osidipe, PhD, is a senior lecturer in criminology at the University of Bedfordshire, United Kingdom. His research focuses on ethnicity and the criminal justice, victimization, and the intersection of social justice and criminal justice, public policy, and criminology. He is the joint course coordinator of the bachelor's degree programs in criminology and sociology, University of Bedfordshire.

Ibrahim Sabra is an assistant lecturer of law with multifaceted experience in the field of law and technology. He received his bachelor of laws from Ain Shams University, Egypt, and obtained his master of laws in information technology and intellectual property law from the University of East Anglia, United Kingdom, as an awardee of the prestigious UK government's Chevening Scholarship. He currently teaches law at the British University in Egypt Faculty of Law, where his teaching includes tutorials on human rights law, EU law, and international law for undergraduates and involved delivering seminars for the postgraduate courses on cyberlaw and cybercrime. Ibrahim is also a researcher at Columbia University Global Freedom of Expression, where his work involves research, analysis, writing, and editing tasks regarding landmark court decisions to identify national, regional, and global trends with a focus on freedom of expression and digital rights. He previously worked with Global Freedom of Expression on different research projects pertaining to internet shutdown and Strategic Lawsuits Against Public Participation (SLAPPs). Ibrahim focuses primarily on artificial intelligence governance and internet-related issues: free speech, privacy and data protection, and other digital rights. His current research centers around exploring the interplay between information technology law, human rights, and criminal justice.

Diego Sanjurjo holds a PhD in political science from the Autonomous University of Madrid and master's degrees in public policy and international development. He specializes in security policies and teaches at the Uruguayan Catholic University and is currently the coordinator of focused police crime prevention strategies at the Comprehensive Citizen Security Program of the Uruguayan Ministry of Interior, Montevideo, Uruguay. His main areas of research include public policy theories and security and gun and drug policies.

Alvise Sbraccia, PhD, sociologist, is professor of criminology at the Department of Legal Studies DSG, University of Bologna, Italy. Through ethnography and biographical methods, his empirical research focuses on the process of migrants' criminalization in Italy, urban segregation and control, drug markets, and police strategies. His main theoretical contributions are related to prison studies, postcolonial criminology, and recidivism.

Jonathan South is a retired police officer who has worked in various roles and police departments. He has worked in education since 2010 in either teaching or training roles. He is the course coordinator for the new Degree in Professional Policing offered by the University of Bedfordshire, which is part of the Police Educational Qualification Framework designed by the College of Policing, a degree he took the lead in designing. His research interests involve the investigation and management of police misconduct and corruption and community policing.

Yik Koon TEH, PhD, received her BA in law and sociology and her MA in sociology from the University of Kent, Canterbury, and her PhD in sociology (criminology) from the London School of Economics and Political Science. She was a Fulbright Scholar at the University of California, Los Angeles (2002); a participant in the three-week Symposium of East Asia Security organized by U.S. Pacific Command and the U.S. State Department (2012); an individual expert in criminology at the 13th UN Congress on Crime Prevention and Criminal Justice in Doha, Qatar; and a visiting fellow at the Rajaratnam School of International Studies, Nanyang Technological University, Singapore (2015). She has just retired in December 2022 as a professor at the National Defense University of Malaysia. Her latest book is *From BMF to 1MDB: A Criminological and Sociological Discussion.*

Han Wang is a PhD student in the Department of Social and Behavioral Sciences at the City University of Hong Kong. Her research interests include sociological theory, criminological theory, penology, corruption, criminal networks, and quantitative analysis of crime data.

Sebastian Okello Wang'ombe earned his bachelor of arts in sociology from Egerton University, Kenya, in 2000 and a master's degree in criminology from Masinde Muliro University of Science and Technology, Kenya, in 2015. He is currently pursuing his PhD in criminal justice at the University of South Africa. He has worked as security and risk assessment project manager with Bedrock Holdings Limited, district children's officer with the Ministry of Children and Youth Affairs, and senior administrative assistant and tutorial fellow at Kibabii University. He has written one notable and widely used undergraduate and graduate book titled *Handbook of Criminal Justice System*. He has written several research papers in refereed journals. He specializes in criminal justice systems and juvenile delinquency and recidivism research. Currently, he is writing a book to be titled *Restorative Justice System: The Core.*

Yunyun Yang, PhD, is a lecturer at Guangxi Normal University, China. She earned her PhD from City University of Hong Kong. Her work has appeared in *Rural China* and *Social Science Research*. Her research interests include social control, grassroots governance, county-level governance, and policing.

www.ingramcontent.com/pod-product-compliance
Ingram Content Group UK Ltd.
Pitfield, Milton Keynes, MK11 3LW, UK
UKHW050955290926
15470UKWH00006B/1828

9 781538 173145